GEOFFREY GRIGSON'S COUNTRYSIDE

THE CLASSIC COMPANION TO RURAL BRITAIN

GEOFFREY GRIGSON'S
COUNTRYSIDE

THE CLASSIC COMPANION TO RURAL BRITAIN

EBURY PRESS
LONDON

Published by Ebury Press
National Magazine House
72 Broadwick Street
London W1V 2BP

First impression 1982

©Geoffrey Grigson 1982

The text of this book was previously published as
The Shell Country Alphabet.

ISBN 0 85223 223 3

Endpapers: Grasmere, Cumbria; previous pages:
Bembridge, Isle of Wight; opposite: Godrevy
lighthouse, Cornwall; following pages: Ullswater,
Cumbria.

Illustrated by Robert Micklewright
Filmset in Great Britain by
Advanced Filmsetters (Glasgow) Limited
Printed and bound in Italy by
Arti Grafiche Amilcare Pizzi S.p.A. Milan

Contents

Foreword

This book aims to illustrate or explain things we come across in the countryside, chiefly things due to our ancestors of the last five thousand years, the artificial objects and also (though it is not a book of natural history) some of the natural objects and phenomena which caught their fancy and still appeal to ourselves, I cannot think of a word which covers in that way, let us say, rainbows and gravestones and green men, dene-holes and mazes and mistletoe, or place-names and prehistoric remains, or sham ruins and waterfalls and zodiacal light. But I can perhaps explain by a personal experience. Making a ten-mile shopping journey every Friday, while the entries in the book were being compiled and were piling up (not a journey always to the same town or by the same way), we would test its inclusiveness by keeping an eye open for something that hadn't been explained so far. There was an avenue of horse chestnuts: could anything useful be said about *avenues*? (Look and see.) Or about *horse chestnuts*? Or about the *workhouse* beyond the trees and the avenue, now transformed with a truer modern charity into a children's convalescent home? And on the way back, what about the '*Celtic*' *fields* visible when shadowed by the descending sun, which also turned the long *barrow* into an inverted cruse of darkness? And at home again, why 'Bassett' tacked to the other half of a town name on the signpost? (Look up *Feudal place-names*.) Also how and when (if the why may be obvious) came *signposts*?

We accept familiar sights with only half the answer about them. *Stocks* are commonly encountered. We know comic drawings of vagrants or buffoons with their feet coming through. But who had the power to put someone in the stocks, and why? For what offences? And how long did offenders stay in them?

Where possible the short pieces in this book (for casual reading, as well as reference) try to connect facts or objects, not to isolate them. I think one may look twice at *mediaeval tiles* on a chancel floor, given a clue to the aura of *angels* which filled a *chancel* (see how the entries are mounting up) of a village church in 1400; and given a reminder that the rest of the church might be floored only with beaten earth and a top layer of new-cut rushes from down by the river.

Even then the mixture in this book may not be quite what you expected. It is about the visible. It is not only about man-made objects, or objects introduced by man. Also it is about some of the words he used, about natural objects, or conditions, or occurrences, that we are traditionally affected by.

This book emphasizes England, with excuse. But it forays repeatedly (and would foray more than twice as much, if it could have been twice as long) into Wales and Man and Scotland and (all of) Ireland. We are sometimes forgetting, rather meanly so, that we live in the British Isles, even if parts of them have separate governments. All these Isles have contributed to each of us.

Geoffrey Grigson

Broad Town,
Wiltshire

A Country Dictionary

Aber-

This word, found at the beginning of Welsh (and some Scottish) place-names, means the place where a stream joins a river, or where a river or stream joins the sea, a confluence, a watersmeet, and so often an estuary or river mouth. Usually it is followed by a stream or river name. Inland: Abergavenny, where the small Gavenny (Afon Gafenni) joins the larger Usk. On the coast: Aberdaron, at the end of the Lleyn peninsula, where the little Afon Darón empties into the sea. In Scotland: Aberdeen, the watersmeet of the Dee and the North Sea. Aber- is also found in Brittany – Aber-Benoît, l'Aber Wrac'h, etc.

Acre

A word containing more history than one might guess. Our remoter English ancestors would have understood by *aecer* a stretch of land surface of no special size or kind. Then it came to mean a particular piece of land cleared for ploughing and planting or grazing, then as large a strip of an open FIELD as could be ploughed by a yoke of oxen in a single day. As a measure of land Edward I at last standardized the acre as a piece 40 rods long by 4 rods wide, taking the rod (derived from the rod, the perch or pole used to drive oxen) as $5\frac{1}{2}$ yards. In German *Acker* keeps the old sense of farmer's land, with *Ackersmann* meaning a ploughman or a farm labourer, much as *aecermann*, an 'acreman' in Old English, meant a farmer. Farmer was a term which came in during the Middle Ages, the farmer paying a *firma*, a firm or fixed rent.

Agger

The raised earthen platform of a ROMAN ROAD, often visible as a grass-green ribbon across fields.

Agnus Dei (Lamb of God)

In churches from Norman to modern times on tympana, fonts, bosses, rood-screens, bench-ends, etc., the most frequently encountered emblem of Christ. The Agnus Dei derives from the many descriptions of the Lamb in power and glory in the Revelation, and from St. John the Baptist (St. John's Gospel 1. 29) saying 'Behold the Lamb of God, which taketh away the sins of the world', as Christ walks towards him where he is baptizing in Jordan. Christ having risen from the dead, the Lamb holds with one forefoot the banner of victory over death attached to a cross.

Alabaster

Alabaster is a form of gypsum (calcium sulphate) which occurs in beds in various rocks, especially in the north Midlands, and was much used in church sculpture. North Midlands sculptors in the 14th century found it more profitable to work in this soft, quickly carved material than in harder stone, and monuments and effigies from their workshops occur (now and again with traces of the original colour and gilding) in churches in many parts of England, especially in Derbyshire, Nottinghamshire, Staffordshire, Lincolnshire and Yorkshire. The effigies in Hanbury church in Staffordshire were all carved from alabaster quarried in the parish. Alabaster effigies feel soft and smooth. The original white, or white stained with red, will have gone a dirty grey, and as likely as not cheek or thigh or armour will have been scratched with a medley of names and dates.

For monuments alabaster was favoured into Jacobean times. Up to the Reformation the alabaster carvers, especially at Nottingham, also made little tablets or panels in relief showing coloured scenes from the life of Christ, the lives of the saints, etc., which were combined into retables or altarpieces. These were in demand all over Europe, and are now much commoner in continental than in English churches.

Almshouses

These often go back to the Middle Ages, in spite of being refounded and rebuilt after the Reformation, with some change of function. To begin with, they were charitable foundations which gave hospitality and care to the poor, the sick, the old or the wayfarer, especially the pilgrim. Each was a hospital or 'spital' (other names were spital house, Maison Dieu, God's House and bedehouse, literally speaking a house of prayer) organized like a small monastery under a master, warden or prior. The basic elements were an infirmary hall for lodging the sick and the poor, and a chapel, built on at one end. This is the plan of

St. Mary's Hospital at Chichester (13th century) and of the Bedehouse (15th century) in the churchyard of Higham Ferrers, in Northamptonshire. A spital devoted to lepers or lazars, a lazar house, independent or belonging to the nursing Order of St. Lazarus, might have small cottages or divided cells, instead of a large infirmary. Later in the Middle Ages the spitals, though they still gave hospitality to the poor traveller, often became prototypes of the almshouse as we know it, a permanent home for the aged poor. In 1547 most of the spitals, whatever their kind, were dissolved as places in which prayers were offered for the souls of the founders. But this left a gap in society. Wealthy and charitable Elizabethans refounded and refashioned old hospitals as almshouses, or, like others who came after them in the 17th and 18th centuries, established new almshouses in the style of the time. The poor inmates were carefully selected for their virtue. In London the great hospitals of St.

Bartholomew and St. Thomas both began as mediaeval institutions with duties of a broad hospitality.

Altars

Openly situated as they usually are today in a parish church, altars mark a principal difference between modern and mediaeval concepts of worship. In the mediaeval church, the altar, where the priest celebrated a mystery, was more or less hidden from the laity outside in the nave. The high altar was made practically invisible by the Rood screen, altars in side chapels or in Chantry chapels were shut away behind a parclose, a screen of stone or timber open-work. The reformers brought the laity into the chancel. The fixed stone altars of mediaeval custom (often with a cavity in or under the stone slab for the relics of a saint) were generally broken up and replaced with movable communion tables made of wood – the name given them at first was the

Lord's Board, or God's Board, or the Lord's Table – round which the laity could kneel to communicate as a family of men. In the 17th century (*see* COMMUNION RAILS) the altars were moved east, and railed off; and in the 19th century screens across the chancel were destroyed, opening up a long view from end to end of the church.

Amber

A fossil resin exuded from conifers, amber can be picked up in small pebbly lumps on the shingle beaches of the east coast, particularly around the bulge of East Anglia. These will be scraps rolled across the North Sea from the amber deposits of the Baltic (where amber is mined, in what was East Prussia). The scratched, dulled surface of such lumps does not, at first sight or touch, suggest the rich yellow of amber, but if a lump is rubbed, its resulting electrification will make it attract hairs, etc. It is this quality which possibly explains the old European repute of amber as a defence against evil, poison and infection, the amber drawing such influences to itself, away from the wearer.

Ammonites

Ammonites or snakestones, fossil remains (generally internal casts) of coiled shellfish which floated in seas of the Mesozoic period, are abundant in many different rocks, Jurassic and Cretaceous; but now that quarrying is restricted, they are most easily found along the beaches and cliffs of Yorkshire (especially in the Whitby area) and Dorset. Ammonites vary in diameter from a penny to a car-wheel. Larger kinds in harder limestone were often used in the 18th century as architectural ornaments, attracting the classically-minded by their resemblance to the curled horns on the head of the ram-god called Ammon by the Egyptians and Zeus Ammonis by the Greeks, who thought highly of his oracle in the Libyan desert. These *cornua Ammonis*, horns of Ammon, suggested the name ammonite. Less sophisticated people were convinced that ammonites were snakes transformed to stone. At Keynsham, near Bristol, where large ammonites occurred in the limestone beds, the petrifier of the snakes was supposed to have been the British holy woman, St. Keyne. The Yorkshire story, popularized in Scott's *Marmion*, is that snakes there were petrified by prayers of the Anglo-Saxon St. Hilda, when she was abbess of Whitby. St. Hilda would be surprised to find herself commemorated in the name *Hildoceras* (Hilda's Horn) bestowed on a

A reminder of the presence of ANGELS *in the Church of the Holy Trinity at Blythburgh, Suffolk. The 15th-century woodwork of the church's tie-beam roof has turned silvery with age.*

genus of common ammonites.

In the sand under the shale and limestone cliffs of Dorset (especially at Tidmoor Point, near Chickerell) little ammonites abound which have been transformed to bronze-like iron pyrites. But these crumble away after a time, unless given a grease coat by frequent handling or dipped once a year in glycerine to preserve them.

Amphisbaena

An allegorical beast of the dragon family derived from the mythical natural history of the ancient world, frequent in mediaeval church carvings. He has wings and a head at either end enabling him to move backwards or forwards, a symbol of the wiliness of the Devil.

Angels

Carved and pictured in churches, angels from the Anglo-Saxon angels of Winterbourne Steepleton in Dorset, Deerhurst in Gloucestershire or Bradford-on-Avon in Wiltshire, to the angels of 15th century glass or along the hammer-beams of churches in East Anglia, have a special reason for their presence. They were set up to remind worshippers of the angels believed to be present though invisible in the church itself, especially in the chancel around the high altar. It was anciently held that angels were always present at the sacrifice of the Mass, the sacrifice of the body of Christ, just as they had been present (see St. John's Gospel) at the entombment of his body; and worshippers had always to be mindful of the presence of angels from the moment they entered church. Angelic beings were divided into nine orders, made up of three hierarchies. Cherubim, Seraphim and Thrones were the superior hierarchy, attendant on God like ministers on a king; then came Dominations, Virtues and Potestates; then Principates, Angels and Archangels. The nine orders are sometimes depicted, as on the 15th century rood-screen at Barton Turf, in Norfolk. Though St. Michael among (often peacock-) feathered beings of heaven can be identified by the dragon he kills or by the scales in which he is weighing the souls of men, church artists were not always strict in their (super)natural history or distinctions. Seraphim are common, crowned, sometimes with fire (they were fiery with perfect love), occasionally with six wings. The censing beings and musicians are frequently angels of the third hierarchy. Cherubim survive the Reformation stan-

dardized as two wings with only a head, since they were distinguished by perfect knowledge.

Anglo-Saxon churches

More than 230 churches remain which are basically or in part Anglo-Saxon – 900 or more years old, that is to say, built between the 7th century and the Norman Conquest. Church-building and conversion went together, after St. Augustine's arrival in 597, and after the introduction of stonemasons from Italy, who built the first churches and taught new techniques to a people accustomed to build only in wood. From the first century of masonry and Christianity, down to 700, there are five churches to visit: the lonely box-like church across the fields from Bradwell-juxta-Mare in Essex, which St. Cedd built *c.* 663 on the edge of the North Sea and astride the walls of a FORT OF THE SAXON SHORE; Brixworth in Northamptonshire (*c.* 670–700); and, in surroundings of industrial nastiness, the churches of Escomb in Durham and Jarrow and Monkwearmouth in Tyne and Wear. Churches of the 8th to 9th centuries include Corbridge in Northumberland and Bardsey in West Yorkshire, but the Danish invasions of the 9th century interrupted church-building, and most of the surviving Anglo-Saxon churches belong to the years between 886, when King Alfred made peace with Guthrum and his Danes, and the Conquest. The imposing Northamptonshire church of Earls Barton, the Cambridgeshire church of Barnack, Barton-upon-Humber church, Humberside, the church and the neighbouring chapel of Duke Odda at Deerhurst, Gloucestershire, in the Severn valley, and the stark church of Bradford-on-Avon in Wiltshire, with its flying angels, were built in the 10th century. Some later churches of Edward the Confessor's reign (1043–66), are Langford in Oxfordshire with its tall and stiffly dignified carving of Christ crucified, and Bosham and Sompting in West Sussex. The grey tower of St. Michael's on the edge of the Cornmarket in Oxford, which seems worn out with existence, also belongs to this last Anglo-Saxon century.

The Anglo-Saxon core of a church is often concealed or modified by more graceful work of the 13th to 15th centuries. Towers may have a later belfry, naves may be opened up by aisles or traceried windows. But the clumsiness which Anglo-Saxon masons were only beginning to overcome by the mid 11th century usually protrudes and makes itself recognizable. Some usual distinctions of the Anglo-Saxon church are:

(*a*) Thin rubble masonry with a rough-and-ready look (as in St. Michael's tower, Oxford).

(*b*) Ill-proportioned naves, like narrow boxes, emphasizing height rather than length or width.

(*c*) Narrow, ill-proportioned doorways and window openings with clumsy semi-circular arches, flat lintels, or triangular tops of one long stone inclined against another.

(*d*) Long-and-short work, a primitive and characteristic way of strengthening the angles of a church, or a church tower, or the jambs of an archway, with long vertical slabs set between shorter horizontal slabs. Used early and late from the 7th century to the 11th, this long-and-short work is said to derive from the angle posts of construction in timber. By the middle of the 10th century English masons had devised a decorative way of dividing a surface (e.g. Earls Barton tower) which combined long-and-short quoins with long vertical strips or pilasters let into the wall.

Anvil clouds

Such clouds indicate distant thunderstorms. The rounded, splendid cumulus clouds of fine weather lose their firm shape on top and ravel into a cirrus of ice-crystals which often spreads laterally into the distinct likeness of a heavenly anvil with a pronounced beak or point to one side.

Apes

Apes carved in mediaeval churches, symbolized fraud and false pretensions, apes as men pretending to acts or functions of virtue, such as the ape in prayer, the ape doctor holding a bottle of urine.

Apple trees

Less particular about soil than plum or cherry, more reliable in yield than pear trees, apple trees in blossom around a village are so characteristic that it may be recalled that apples were eaten by the neolithic people, the first farmers and herdsmen of England, who visited the CAUSEWAYED CAMP or moot on Windmill Hill outside Avebury, in Wiltshire, four thousand and more years ago. Pips were found on pottery, possibly from native crabs which would have been sour in a neolithic no less than a modern mouth, but perhaps from the sweet fruits of *Pyrus sylvestris ssp. mitis* which the Windmill Hill people could have brought with them from overseas. This sub-species, native of south-east Europe and south-west Asia, is the parent of garden apples, and may have been grown already in neolithic Europe. Apples were held to be revivifying and rejuvenating, and there are stories to that effect from Irish and Norse mythology, as well as from the Near East. Loki, for instance, stole the apples which the goddess Ithunn kept for the gods to eat when they grew old, and gave them to the giants. The gods withered and wrinkled with age, and Loki was forced to get the apples back.

Apse

An Anglo-Saxon or Norman church rounded at the east end instead of squared – ending, that is to say, in an apse – recalls the early basilicas of Christianity. In this rounded part of the basilica the clergy celebrated the sacrifice of the mass, and the missionaries who came from Rome to Canterbury at the end of the 6th century naturally brought the apse and the basilican plan with them. Most Anglo-Saxon churches and most Norman churches were apsidal, but the Cistercian abbey-builders of the 12th century, in their severe style, made their chancels and chapels square-ended, which rapidly became characteristic of English churches. When churches were rebuilt or refashioned the rounded end (so common, for example, in French churches, Romanesque or Gothic) was seldom kept.

Aqueducts

Strictly speaking, aqueducts are conduits for conveying water from one point, such as a spring or river, to another, and not only the water-bridges that may be necessary on such a route. In this stricter sense the Romans in Britain devised aqueducts to towns, forts and mines. The Roman town of Dorchester

(Durnovaria) in Dorset was supplied by an aqueduct or open leat from the Frome a few miles away. Stretches preserved as an ancient monument can still be seen alongside a Roman road north-west of the town. Parallels of a later time are the 24-mile leat (begun 1585) bringing water from Dartmoor to Plymouth, which the town owed to the energy of Sir Francis Drake; and Hobson's Conduit (1610–14), which brought water from Nine Wells, near Trumpington, into Cambridge. Mine-leats and mill-leats are aqueducts in the same sense. There was a leat to the Roman gold-mine at Dolaucothi (Dyfed); and leats along valley sides to overshot water-wheels (*see* WATER-MILLS) were made by Anglo-Saxon millers before the Norman Conquest.

The great scenic aqueducts or water-bridges of the canal age are Telford's two iron and sandstone aqueducts on the Ellesmere (now Shropshire Union) Canal in Clwyd. The Chirk Aqueduct, finished in 1801, which caught the imaginative eye of the young artist John Sell Cotman (masterly watercolour in the Victoria and Albert Museum) is the shorter of the two, taking the canal by an iron trough over the Vale of Ceiriog on ten arches, with piers 65 feet high. The canal goes on through a tunnel and then, four miles from the Chirk Aqueduct and not far from Llangollen, crosses the Dee, more than 100 feet below, on an iron trough supported by the 19 loftier arches of the Pont-y-cysylltau Aqueduct opened in 1805.

Arrow-slits and gunports

Mediaeval castles until late in the 14th century were defended largely by bow and arrow. For firing the longbow the arrow-slits or firing-loops in the thick walls were long, narrow, vertical openings (as in Caernarvon Castle). For the crossbow they were either long with a small circular opening at the bottom or else in the shape of a cross – cross-slits – the branches of which end in round holes of the same small diameter. As artillery came into use in the 14th century the arrow-slit or firing-loop changed to the gunport. The first gunports (on the refashioned defences of Southampton *c.* 1360–70) are adaptations of the round-holed vertical arrow-slit, the embrasure inside having a bed for the cannon instead of sloping down from the hole. Gunports ending in larger holes with a 10-inch diameter, for larger cannon, appear about 1380 in the West Gate at Canterbury; and within a hundred years the ports became simply round holes widening inside to a flat bed to house the cannon. Sometimes round gunport and old cross-slit appear together in the same building. The final change, by 1500, was to large gunports with a square section, as in the Tudor coastal forts of south Devon and Cornwall.

Ash

One of the basic trees of country life, in hedgerows and woods, particularly common on chalk or limestone soil. It was regarded anciently and recently as a tree of great power, especially in healing and in repelling evil. According to Norse myth, Odin and his brothers, after creating the earth and the heavens, found two tree-trunks by the sea, which they turned into the first man and woman. The tree-trunk of the man was an ash. (No one knows the meaning of *embla*, which was the tree-trunk turned into the first woman.) Ash may have been thought powerful not only because its timber is so strong and smooth to the grasp and useful for handles of every kind of tool (and weapon), but because like the oak it attracts the lightning. So its virtue extends to its juice, its leaves, its fruits, as well as its timber. Ruptured children were passed through split ash saplings which were afterwards tied up, the rupture disappearing as the sapling closed and recovered. Cecil Torr in his *Small Talk at Wreyland* records asking a Devonshire father in 1902 why he had tried this 'cure' on his baby. The father said 'Well, all folk do it', and when Torr asked if in fact it did any good, the father clinched matters by saying 'As much good as sloppin' water over'n in church'.

Ashlar

This is usually freestone (stone easily sawn) in neat squared blocks used for facing a wall, in distinction to rubble (stone neither cut nor squared), to which it is often applied in a building. Ashlar is typical of sophisticated buildings, e.g. in the Cotswolds, from the 16th century onwards. Moorstone – surface granite – was also cut into ashlar for late mediaeval, Tudor and more recent buildings in Devon and Cornwall.

Asp

In church carvings, a winged two-legged snake, or asp, stuffing one ear up with its tail, signified Disbelief, (the deaf adder (Psalm 58) stopping its ear, charm the charmer never so wisely). The asp was believed to have a precious stone in its head. When men endeavoured to win this by enchantment, the asp put one ear

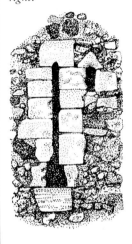

An early ARROW-SLIT *for crossbows at Framlingham Castle, Suffolk. These first appeared in Britain in the early 12th century and signalled the emergence of crossbowmen as a professional class of soldier in their own right.*

*A*mong the smaller AQUEDUCTS *constructed during the canal age, the single-arched span of the elegant Dundas Aqueduct is a work of classical proportions and detail. It was designed and built by John Rennie to carry the Kennet and Avon Canal over the River Avon near Bath.*

to the ground and stuffed its tail into the other, and was thus deaf to the spell.

Assart

An assart was a clearing in the old areas under forest law and often occurs in names of farms and fields, Sart Wood, Sart Farm, the Sarts, etc. It is a law term from the French *essarter*, to grub up. If someone wished to 'assart' some of his land in a forest area, he could do so only by royal permission and payment of dues to the Crown. John Manwood, one of the 16th century Justices of the New Forest, defined an assart in his *Treatise of the Laws of the Forest* as 'where a man doth fell and destroy his woods, and convert the soil wherein the woods did grow into tillage'. To do this without licence was 'the greatest offence or trespasse of all other against the vert or green-hue'.

Aumbry

A rectangular locker or recess in a church wall near the altar, or an altar site, sometimes with its original oak door. The chalice and other vessels for the mass were locked away in the aumbry (which may have a stone shelf), together with the chrism, or consecrated oil for christenings and for anointing the sick, the mass-books, and such relics as the church may have owned.

Aurora Borealis

The Northern Lights or Merry Dancers across the northern horizon are seen in the British Isles most frequently near the autumnal equinox (about 22 September) or the vernal equinox (about 21 March) in the early hours of darkness. They do not always shoot or dance, and wonderful coloured displays are uncommon. One is most likely to see a still arc of whitish luminescence. Streamers may appear nimbly shooting above the arc (as the poet Gerard Manley Hopkins saw them in a display at Edinburgh or on the Clyde in the last week of August 1871, towards the autumnal equinox, 'like breath misting and then being cut off from very sensitive glass'). Or the aurora may take the form of a crown shooting out rays. Displays increase in frequency the further north one goes. In Orkney and Shetland they are a commonplace; in the south of England displays average about seven a year. The Northern Lights are caused by streams of electrified particles emitted by the sun which spiral towards the magnetic pole and cause a glowing in the gases of the upper air. Auroral displays seen in Ireland after the death of St.

Colum Cille (Columba) in 596 or 597 were believed to be caused by angels carrying his soul across the sky to Heaven.

Avenues

Avenues of trees began to be planted early in the 17th century, expressing the formality and dignity of approach to the many new country houses of a newly rich class. They became more and more popular as the century wore on, producing this new sense of the word 'avenue' (from the French verb *avenir*, to approach, arrive). John Evelyn began his *Sylva* (1664) by explaining a list of words 'not as yet so familiar to every reader'. One of them was avenue, defined as 'the principal walk to the front of the house or seat'. But by that time many English avenues, for which 'walk' had been word enough, were already tall and stately. Various trees were used. Evelyn's favourites, widely planted by the evidence of his *Diary*, were the quick-growing species ELM and LIME, the lime trees being imported from the Netherlands. SYCAMORE, which also grows quickly, was planted, especially in the west of England, sometimes with BEECH (e.g. the half-mile double avenue of sycamores and beeches at the National Trust's Lanhydrock House, near Bodmin, Cornwall, planted in 1648), though it was a tree Evelyn disliked for the purpose. He also wrote in *Sylva* of the HORSE CHESTNUT being all the rage then for avenues in France, and advised the planting of plane tree avenues, the provision of which goes back to Rome and Greece. Horse chestnut avenues were common by the seventeen-forties, according to Philip Miller's *Gardeners Dictionary*, 1741.

Avon

The English adopted 'avon' as a RIVER NAME from the British language spoken round them and misunderstood by them. It means 'river', no more, no less. The British word was *abona*. The modern Welsh for river is *afon*, and is prefixed to the distinctive name, Afon Llyfni, Afon Dwyfor, etc.

Bally-

Frequent as the first element in Irish (and Scottish) place-names, Bally- is from the Gaelic *baile*, a hamlet or tribal cluster of houses. It corresponds to -TON in English names, TREF- in Welsh names, and TRE- in Cornish names. From the Irish *baile* or townland, the basic unit of Irish life, with its open field, the families moved in summer up to the BOOLEY HOUSES.

Barge-boards

Barge-boards, hung from the projecting 'barge' or roof-edge on the gable of a house, hide and protect the exposed ends of roof timbers. ('Barge', with sinister suggestion, comes from *bargus*, the mediaeval Latin for gallows.) Ornamentally carved barge-boards were commonly affixed to wooden-framed houses of the Middle Ages and the Tudor period and later (though the ones we see on such houses are not very often the originals). When eyes went back to the past in the romantic era, ornamental barge-boarding was revived and affixed to many villas and cottages, to give them a look of picturesque mediaevalism; and continued on Victorian housing, often the redeeming item about an otherwise hard-faced piece of builder's Gothic – often, too, with a debt to the Swiss chalet, Alpine holidays having become popular.

Barns

Both as word and object, barns pack much history into themselves. In Old English *bere-ærn* or *bern* meant 'barley-house', for storing the barley which was the chief crop of Anglo-Saxon farmers. It continued as the customary word for the chief storage building on the farm, whether the crop was barley, wheat or rye, etc. The kind of wood-framed thatched barn which went on being built into the 19th century, and so often survives, with aisles, and tie-beams from side to side, gives a look into something of remoter age, the Anglo-Saxon wooden hall which housed the family and retainers of the more powerful Englishmen before the Norman Conquest.

The tall double doors into a barn, on either side, allowed the entry of laden wagons (sometimes there will be an inclined plane up to the doors) and gave directly on to the threshing-floor of oak or elm planks two inches thick, firmly supported and very closely fitted. The draught between the doors lessened the floating dust and chaff raised by the thump of the flails, or threshals, on the corn. The presence of several barns on a farm is often explained by the need of a separate barn for each kind of corn that the farmer grew.

Monastic granges (*see* BARTON) and monasteries themselves were often equipped with durable stone-walled barns of great size, primarily for corn and grain. Big mediaeval barns of this kind are often loosely called tithe barns. But a barn is only a tithe barn if its function was to store the tithes or tenths of farm

produce in a parish. Even then it might have been built for monks or nuns; which demands an explanation of tithe, rector and vicar. Handing over tithes for the support of the parish priest had been made compulsory in England in the 10th century. Later it became common for a manorial lord to consign his control over the church and the benefice or 'living' of the priest (*see* PARISHES) to a monastery, cathedral or bishopric. These would add the greater part of the parish tithe to their own revenues, and would assign a smaller portion to a parish priest of their own choosing, who instead of being the priestly 'rector' or ruler of the parish, was the priestly substitute, or 'vicar' (Latin *vicarius*, a deputy). So a tithe barn might be built either by the parish priest usually as rector or by a monastery, cathedral or bishop as rector. The rights in a benefice were property; and when the monasteries were dissolved, the rights passed by grant to lay owners, who became 'lay rectors', and continued to enjoy the rectorial tithes, while vicars still received only the lesser portion. Collecting tithes in kind, in the shape of real tenths of corn and other produce, was irksome for both parties, and frequently tithe-owner and tithe-payers in a parish would agree on a cash substitute; which became general in 1836, when tithes in kind were abolished by law. So the need for tithe barns disappeared, though the fine buildings often remain, such as the Rectorial Barn at Church Enstone, in Oxfordshire, which was built in 1382. But 'rectors' and 'vicars' we still have, their parsonages alongside the church (often with a doorway in the wall between churchyard and parsonage garden) distinguished as 'rectory' or 'vicarage'.

Barony

In Ireland baronies are the mediaeval divisions of a county corresponding to the old hundreds of the English shire. They were originally the

The village of Old Warden in Bedfordshire was the Victorian creation of Lord Ongley. It is full of Picturesque details such as the BARGE-BOARDS *on this cottage gable.*

little kingdoms or chiefs' domains which existed, each with marked local differences, before the Anglo-Norman conquest.

Barrows

It seems the right thing emotionally that barrows, mounds over the remains of the dead, should be the most abundant of prehistoric monuments and mementoes. Heaping up a regularly shaped barrow of earth or cairn of stones over the dead who had been somebodies in life, whether their remains were dried, dismembered, reduced to ashes, or untouched, continued in these islands for some 5,000 years, from the neolithic to the English settlement.

c. 3000 B.C., and after. The first barrow-builders, immigrants originally from northern France, built 'long barrows' of earth, shaped rather like an enormous stone or flint axe. The dead, or accumulated bones of the dead, were placed under the thicker end, the butt-end, of the barrow. These barrows without chambers inside occur chiefly in Dorset, Wiltshire, Hampshire, Sussex, Yorkshire and Lincolnshire, on rolling chalk country, where the living grazed their herds and grew cereals.

Other immigrants sailed from western France and settled, either side, along the sea routes from Cornwall to Scotland, from the Isles of Scilly and the Severn estuary and

The Oxenford tithe barn, near Milford in Surrey, is strictly a fraud. Built by the famous Victorian architect and mediaevalist, Augustus Pugin, it nevertheless is true in all its features, such as the buttresses and pitch roof, to the mediaeval BARNS on which it is based.

Ireland to Orkney, and brought with them a different type of barrow, long, oval or round, with many variations, raised over actual tombs – that is to say, over chambers, or passages, or chambered passages, of huge stone slabs (now and again with some dry walling). These chambered barrows were family mausoleums, reopened repeatedly. Two splendid, now scientifically restored, examples are Wayland Smith's Cave on the Wiltshire Ridgeway, not far from Swindon, and the West Kennet Long Barrow, near Avebury.

Dolmens, free-standing stone chambers and passages, are now recognized as tombs of this kind which have lost their covering of earth or small stones (though some dolmens appear never to have been covered in that way, as if left incomplete).

Avebury and Stonehenge were founded by men who took their eventual rest in long barrows.

c. 2000 to 1000 B.C. In the Bronze Age new immigrants who added tools and weapons of bronze to the old armoury of flint and other hard stones introduced the smaller round barrows, which are so common throughout Britain.

The structure of these Bronze Age round barrows varies according to period and district. They may be encircled with banks, ditches or berms (a berm is a flat space or collar between ditch and barrow), or with all three. The shape ranges from inverted bowl (commonest of all) to bell or inverted saucer. Skeleton or body burial (sometimes in roughly hollowed lengths of oak tree) gave way to cremation. The remains, whether body, skeleton or ashes, might be placed in a grave, or in a small chest of stone slabs with a stone lid. The grave was at times protected from the overlying earth with a wooden structure like a hut (a 'death-house' or 'mortuary-house'). Ashes were covered over with a wide-mouthed earthenware urn, upside down.

Weapons and tools and food were put in for some kind of continued life after death, but 'treasure' in Bronze Age barrows is unlikely. Our Bronze Age forebears were neither rich nor very civilized, though gold objects have come from barrows of the richer chieftains of the more advanced Wessex culture centred on Salisbury Plain.

A flat top to a barrow may have been caused by the ancient collapse of the wooden death-house inside, a depression on top may be due to the ever-hopeful treasure-hunters or barrow-digging antiquaries of the past.

Barrows down to English times. What happened to the humbler dead is not known. Perhaps they were burnt, and perhaps no one bothered to preserve the ashes and bits of charred bone. Later in the Bronze Age, as if the habit of ritual preservation after death spread downwards in society, men were cremated and given urn-burial, stone-boxed, if there was stone available, in well-populated cemeteries. The cemetery habit persisted with British peoples of the Iron Age, and has never been lost. But round barrows were not altogether abandoned, and, perhaps *de rigueur* for the very grand and conservative (compare the grander tombs for the rich in churches or their grandiose mausoleums in the churchyard), continued to be raised to a lesser extent over Romano-British, Norse, Danish and Anglo-Saxon dead, burnt or entire, until the ancient barrow custom was abandoned under Christianity.

The very steep and tall Bartlow barrows on the Cambridgeshire–Essex border were raised over such Romano-British grandees, or rather over their ashes in glass bottles, along with a good many objects and utensils of bronze. Eastlow, a later Romano-British barrow at Rougham in Suffolk, south-east of Bury St. Edmunds, near a Roman road, contained a gabled 'death-house' of brick with a tiled roof, which in turn contained a body in a wooden, lead-lined coffin. English chieftains were often buried with considerable treasure for their life in death. The 7th century barrow at Sutton Hoo, on the Suffolk coast, which was excavated in 1939, provided the richest treasure ever discovered, though the only thing missing there was a body, as if the king or prince had been drowned at sea.

Barrow words and names and uses. The English had various heap or hillock words for naming barrows. Barrow itself comes from *beorg*, which survives in barrow names (as well as hill names), often as -bury, -borough or -bergh. Their special, more solemn word was *hlāw*, which in barrow names (as in Eastlow and Bartlow) is often -law or -low. In Wales *bryn* is the hill word commonly used for a barrow, which may be a *carn* if it is a barrow of small stones instead of earth. Norsemen and Danes talked of a *haugr*, which became the -howe of more recent speech.

A barrow, long or round, if it was conspicuous or conveniently placed, often came to be used centuries and civilizations later in a way which may be reflected in its name. 'Belas Knap', name of the celebrated Cotswold long

The Giant's Causeway, Antrim, N. Ireland, is reputed to have been built by the mythical Celtic hero, Finn Mae Cumhaill. It is Nature, however, that deserves the credit for the formation of these strangely symmetrical columns of BASALT.

'BARN' originally meant 'barley-house' and came to be used for the farm building in which corn or crops of any kind were stored, so barton, 'barley-farm', came to imply a farm good for corn, whether barley or wheat, and then (since the best corn-growing land on a manor was likely to be kept by the lord in his own hands, as his demesne) the lord's farm, which was worked for him by slaves in the early feudal centuries. A manor – and this was simply a change of lordship – would frequently be given or willed to a monastery for the good of the lord's soul. 'Grange' on the map is a later word which had the same eventual meaning. Borrowed from the mediaeval French for a granary, it meant a granary farm, the kind of corn farm which was a demesne, particularly such a demesne belonging to a monastery.

Basalt

Dark or darkish rock poured up as lava, basalt provides in its columnar forms, caused by slow cooling, one of the strangest of natural freaks. When Joseph Banks, president of the Royal Society, and a party of scientific friends on their way to Iceland discovered Fingal's Cave on Staffa in the Inner Hebrides on 12 August 1772, they thought they had at last found Nature acting as artist. 'Where is now the boast of the architect? Regularity, the only part in which he fancied himself to exceed his mistress Nature, is here found in her possession.' (Banks, in Pennant's *Tour in Scotland and a Voyage to the Hebrides*, 1772.) The tall hexagons into which the cooling lava had contracted and the shape of this sea-cave seemed to unite Gothic and Classic, and they were all the more delighted and satisfied to learn that the cave was named after Finn mac Cumhaill, the hero of Celtic myth, and the Fingal of James Macpherson's forged Ossianic poems which everyone was reading. So mingling land, sea, art, nature, past, present, this basaltic sea-cave became over the next sixty years the inspiration of poets, painters, composers (Mendelssohn crossed to Fingal's Cave in 1829, writing the first bars of his *Hebrides* overture the same day) and tourists.

Across from the Inner Hebrides, on the coast of Antrim (which is a plateau of basalt), Finn was also credited with building the Giant's Causeway, Ireland's classic bed of columnar basalt. Basalt (strictly speaking, dolerite) springs up from the sea on the Northumberland coast in hard, dark columns making coastal extravaganzas of startling regularity,

barrow at Charlton Abbots, looks as if it might come from some forgotten language as old as the barrow, but in fact it is Old English, meaning 'beacon mound'. Barrows elsewhere have been used as beacon sites. In some of the hundreds (old divisions of a county) the people fixed on a familiar barrow for their moots or monthly open-air courts. Gallows were frequently erected on barrows; also windmills; and frequently they have been regarded as the houses of elves and goblins, such as the North Country hobthrust. Wayland Smith's Cave, or Wayland's Smithy, the long barrow mentioned above, was regarded before the Conquest as the forge where Weland, the hero smith of Germanic legend, made swords and armour and jewellery.

Barton

Barton, in farm or village names, will be seen widely on the map, sometimes by itself, sometimes with particularizing words. Just as and supporting the splendid sea-castle of Dunstanburgh and the high-perched 16th century fort on Holy Island.

Basilisk

The basilisk, or cockatrice, is a mythical animal to be found in church carvings, with a crested bird's head and a serpent's tail. From a Greek origin (*basiliskos*, little king), the basilisk grew in malignancy and peculiarity in the Middle Ages. He was king of all the reptiles in the Libyan desert, was born of an egg laid by an old cock and hatched by a snake or a toad; and his glance was venomous and fatal, even from a distance, so he was carved as an aspect of Satan. A basilisk could be killed if regarded through a crystal bowl, which reflected his eye-venom back on to himself.

Bath stone

The famous yellowish building stone of the city of Bath, is an oolitic limestone, a consolidated deep-sea ooze of Jurassic age, mined mostly around Box and Corsham, in Wiltshire, where it occurs under the hills in beds up to thirty feet thick. It comes out of the mine soft and damp, and is easily cut and carved. Blocks are seasoned – dried of their 'quarry-sap' or 'quarry-water' – before they go into a building. The Romans mined it for building Aquae Sulis, their city of Bath, and transported it to other parts of Britain. Bath stone was used in the Middle Ages, and in the 16th and 17th centuries, and was then immensely popularized for town and country mansions by the rebuilding of Bath as a fashionable neo-Roman city in the 18th century.

Battlefields

Some battlefields allow one to picture the countryside as it used to be before so much of it was enclosed. A battle required space (especially when cavalry, beginning with the Battle of Hastings in 1066, became the dominant arm) and it is no accident that one talks of the *field* of battle, of Bosworth Field, Flodden Field, and so on.

Searching out the sites of the more ancient battles, of English against British, or English kings against each other, which were fought with smaller armies, takes one as a rule to the hill tops. Battles after Hastings take one frequently into the vales.

Such very old hill-top fields belong to an England in which valleys and forests on the heavy clays had still to be cleared. They

The greatest achievement of John Wood the Younger is Royal Crescent, Bath, with its instantly recognizable yellowish oolitic BATH STONE. *Built between 1767 and 1774 it is semi-elliptical in shape, with a magnificent sweeping wall of engaged columns standing on a one-storey plinth, the plinth being the entrance level of the house.*

include, above escarpment scenery which has not much changed, the site where the West Saxons beat the British in 556 at Beran byrg, which is Barbury Castle, hill-top fort on the downs above Swindon in Wiltshire; the field of Deorham (Dyrham, in Avon), in 577, where the West Saxons killed three British kings above the escarpment which drops from the Cotswold plateau towards Bristol; and the site of two battles above Alton Barnes and the Vale of Pewsey, in Wiltshire, by the dark long barrow of Adam's Grave (in those days Wodnesbeorg, Woden's Barrow), the earlier one fought between British and West Saxons in 592, the later one, in 715, between the kings of Mercia and Wessex.

Battles after Hastings were fought in a more and more thickly settled England of open fields and commons, considerably cleared of forest. Most of the important battles, English against English, in the Barons' War, the Wars of the Roses, the Civil War, took place on the Midland Plain, north-west of London and on the west side of the long hill escarpment which runs across England from the Cotswolds to Humberside. Battles against Scottish armies tend to be grouped in the open land of the north-eastern corridor between the Pennines and the North Sea, which is the best way of getting at England, or Scotland, the route of the A1 to Berwick-upon-Tweed.

Many battles were fought across flattish river land, e.g. Bannockburn, 1314; Towton, 1461; Tewkesbury, 1471; Marston Moor, 1644; Worcester, 1651; also Sedgemoor, last battle on English soil, 1685; and more than one stream or river, which guarded an army's flank, has gone red with the blood of horses and men – the Cock, for instance, alongside Towton Field. Other battlefields have been reputed for good crops. The hill outside Stratton in north Cornwall, where the Civil War battle of 1643 was fought, was so fertilized with trodden-in blood of horse and man that it produced 60 bushels of barley to the acre.

Another factor which helped to decide where army engaged army was the old system of Roman roads, on which quick movement from one part of the country still depended after so many centuries. Harold came south towards Hastings by a Roman road from London to Rochester and Maidstone to the coast, fighting and dying just to one side of it. Bosworth (1485) was fought on a Roman road out of Leicester, crossing the angle of Watling Street and the Fosse Way. Roman roads from York and Castleford, intersecting near Tadcaster, brought the Yorkist and Lancastrian armies to Towton Field.

Since armies were bogged in winter mud, nearly all the major battles were fought in a campaigning season between May and October. To get the best from a battlefield it should be visited in the month and round about the day, if they are known, of its lonely and lively – or deathly – drama. Sites which are decidedly evocative include Adam's Grave in Wiltshire, mentioned above, a piece of the purest and barest ancient landscape, south-west of Marlborough and south of the A4; Roundway Down near by in the same county, where Parliamentary troops were pushed over a nearly vertical escarpment on 13 July 1643 (outside and above Devizes, in the angle of A361 and A342, a wide shallow basin of wheatland, with green tracks and few hedges – though by the Civil War hedges were found useful as cover for musketeers); Marston Moor (2 July 1644) and Towton (29 March 1461 – an unusually early battle, fought in a snowstorm), close to each other in North Yorkshire, west and south-west of York, Marston Moor between A59 and B1224. Towton between A64 and A162, south of Tadcaster. On Towton Field the souls of the slain were prayed for in a long-vanished chapel. Many of the bodies were buried in the nearby churchyard of Saxton, including the body of Lord Dacre, a defeated Lancastrian, who lies there with his horse, under an heraldic tomb-chest. Flodden Field (Northumberland, near Branxton, south of A697 from Coldstream), in a wide border landscape between the blunt end of the Cheviots and the Tweed, is best visited in the autumn. It was an autumn battle (9 September 1513), fought when the district was brilliant with dead bracken, under bracken hills.

Bawns

Though not many bawns remain, they are some of the most telling of historical buildings in Northern Ireland. Strictly, a 'bawn' (from the Irish) is a walled or defended enclosure or farmyard. But, part for whole, it came to mean a fortified farmstead built by a planter (English or Scottish or one of the London Livery Companies) granted land in Ulster after the Flight of the Earls in 1607. A bawn – such as Dalway's Bawn, c. 1609, at Ballyhill, near Carrickfergus, in Co. Antrim, or Salters' Castle, c. 1619, built by the Salters' Company on the shore of Lough Neagh at Salterstown, near Ballyronan in Co. Derry – enclosed,

within a high rectangle of walls, a yard and a house across one end of it. At the corners were flanking towers, each with a conical roof. These flankers and the walls were liberally fitted with musket and pistol loops, eloquent of the position of the new planters in what had been one of the most Irish of all parts of Ireland.

Beacons

Beacons were much in the English mind from the start of troubles with France in 1337 to the time of the Armada. After the loss of Normandy in 1450 French raids across the Channel increased the fears of invasion; and when the Tudors built new coastal forts after 1538 they naturally concerned themselves as well about a better warning system. From 1539 they worked out more complex nets of inter-visible hill beacons, particularly from points between the Thames estuary and Land's End; by different combinations of fire, news could be conveyed along the coast and inland of an enemy being sighted, of an enemy closing in to shore, and of an enemy disembarking. Thus in 1560 beacons were arranged to bring men rapidly to the defence of Portsmouth, the historic entry into England: the firing of two master beacons at either end of the Isle of Wight would be followed by firing beacons on the mainland, which in turn would cause the lighting of beacons through Hampshire, Wiltshire, Dorset and Sussex, and then (if the simple fire code indicated the need for more men) through Somerset, Gloucestershire, Oxfordshire and Berkshire.

These schemes proved too difficult and fallible, and when the Spanish danger loomed the authorities in the far west relied on a rather simpler scheme of firing the beacons which would be a sign for mustering the trained bands at every parish church. On the sighting of the Armada in July 1588 the beacons were fired, at any rate along the Cornish peninsula, and were noted by the Spaniards.

Fire Beacon, rather than Beacon Hill by itself, is a common hill-name in Devonshire, reflecting these developments from the 14th to the 16th centuries (though the name is on record for one hill as early as 1200); and among Cornish beacons a 'Fire Beacon Hill' is to be found at Trevalga on the north coast, near Tintagel. (Beacon sites go up the Bristol Channel, in a splendid chain, as well as up the English Channel.) Once the Armada troubles were over, beacons were less carefully maintained. Carew wrote in his *Survey of Cornwall* (1602) that though nearly every Cornish parish was charged with a beacon, they were now watched 'secundum usum but . . . not greatly ad propositum'. From early in the 15th century beacon hills had also been selected with more system along the border, in Northumberland and Cumbria, to muster men against Scottish raids and invasions.

The gap between beacons, where the terrain allowed, was six to eight miles, the chains heading to a climacteric beacon at the most widely visible point of a shire, e.g. Lewesdon (993 feet) in Dorset, and on the Malverns the Herefordshire Beacon (1,114 feet) and the Worcestershire Beacon (1,394 feet). Faggots of brushwood or furze were often piled on the beacon site for fuel, to be lit sometimes on stone hearths or in a stone fire-turret such as survives on Culmstock Beacon in Devon. However, from the 14th century the standard hilltop gear was an iron fire-basket, or cresset, with a pitch-pot inside, raised up on a pole, to which one mounted by a pole-ladder.

Beacons were thought of again when Napoleon seemed likely to invade. In 1804 the accidental lighting of the beacon at Hume Castle in Borders (the starting-point of a Scottish chain since the 15th century) sent beacons flaring across the Lowlands and brought out the volunteers. There was some lighting of the beacons – of beacon bonfires – across country for Queen Victoria's jubilee in 1887, again for her diamond jubilee in 1897, and for Elizabeth II's coronation in 1953 and for her jubilee in 1977.

Beacon sites, Iron Age hill-camps and mapmaker's trigonometrical points frequently coincide, people boasting of the number of counties visible from the top. Cothelstone Beacon on the Quantocks (1,088 feet) is said to give a view of eleven counties, Stinchcombe Beacon on the Cotswold scarp (650 feet) a view of ten counties, and so on. Beacon was also the word for a warning fire maintained, often by a hermit, to safeguard or direct shipping. Thus a 'bekene' tower – a lighthouse — was built by a hermit at the mouth of the Humber, at vanished Ravenser, in 1428.

Beaver

It is worth discovering if any beaver place-names exist in one's neighbourhood. The European beaver, still living in Norway and in the Camargue, was not extinct in Britain when the first English settlers poured in during the 5th and 6th centuries and bestowed new names left and right on the countryside. Beaversbrook in a Wiltshire parish, Hilmarton, is the name of a farm on the edge of a stream rather small, one would think, for beaver lodges. (It is a name which later English migrants gave to settlements in Canada and the U.S.A.) Surrey's Beverley Brook (brook of the beaver's clearing) flows through Richmond Park. Beavers are better imagined in Nidderdale, on the Nidd at Bewerley (beaver's clearing), in North Yorkshire not far from Fountains Abbey; better still at Nottinghamshire's Bevercotes, which actually means beaver lodges (cotts, or huts), in the once wild country of Sherwood Forest, along the slow rivers Meden and Maun, which make marshy alder carrs or copses.

Beavers were animals which the English valley-clearers and valley-farmers would very quickly have wiped out, so beaver names are infrequent. In Wales they lasted many more centuries. Giraldus Cambrensis (1146–1223?) wrote that about 1,200 beavers were to be seen on the Teifi in Dyfed (where they made oak lodges), but nowhere else in Wales; though there were still, but rarely, beavers in Scotland. Hector Boethius, who died in 1536, knew of beavers on Loch Ness.

Beck

North-country for a brook or stream. To the southerner it always suggests a swift, noisy, rocky northern brook descending from wild country, and it is an Old Norse word by origin (*bekkr*) used by Danes and Norwegians. Just as the presence of foxgloves all of a sudden on a journey will tell you that you have left chalk or limestone for an acid soil, so names with 'beck' indicate that the country around was settled by Norse-speaking people in the 9th century, or later. The Old English words, besides *brōc* (brook), include *burna*, which gives us bourne and burn. 'Burns' flow eastward down from Cheviot and the moors, from the Scottish-named hills, laws and knowes, across Northumberland of the northern Angles. South-west, the other side of the Northumberland border, 'becks' tumble down into Teesdale and the Tees from the Norse-named FELLS.

Bedd-

In Welsh place-names Bedd- means grave, and the grave is usually a barrow, housing someone from myth or legend. Bedd Taliesin in Dyfed on the slopes of Moel y Garn (above A487, near Talybont) is a barrow with a stone box, believed to have been the grave of the ancient Welshman Taliesin, both real poet of the 6th century and the mythical bard of all wisdom. Bedd Arthur (Arthur's Grave), a barrow on the Prescelly Mountains, Dyfed, recalls the very ancient Welsh poem, 'Stanzas of the Graves', reciting the graves of heroes *E betev ae gulich y glav*, 'the graves that the rain wets'. Below Bedd Arthur, near Bryn-berian and near the moorland source of several streams, is a neolithic long barrow with a stone gallery or passage known as Bedd-yr-Afanc, grave of the water creature called an afanc.

Beech

A native tree of the dry limestones and chalks of south-eastern England. Caesar's statement in *De Bello Gallico* that Britain lacked the beech tree is demonstrably untrue, and so is the consequent belief that it was introduced by the Romans. But beeches were not common except locally; and so the species lacks that aura of associations and beliefs which attaches to oak, holly, ash, etc. Miller, in his *Gardeners Dictionary* (edition of 1741), speaks well of the beech, and recommends it for neat hedges around 'Plantations, or large Wilderness Quarters', which 'may be kept in a regular Figure, if sheared twice a year'. He remarks that its shade is believed 'to be very salubrious to human Bodies'. At the very beginning of his *Natural History of Selborne* (1789) Gilbert White gives what may stand for the 18th century judgement of this almost artificial-seeming neo-classical tree. Writing of the Hanger at Selborne, where the beech is certainly native, he says: 'The covert of this eminence is altogether beech, the most lovely of all forest trees whether we consider its smooth rind or bark, its glossy foliage, or graceful pendulous boughs.' Our present sub-Atlantic climate is too cold for the beech to maintain itself naturally in southern England.

Beehive huts

Beehive huts are best examined on a pilgrimage (a long journey, but worth it) to Skellig Michael, several miles out in the Atlantic off the Kerry coast, a rock-island up which one climbs by steps to a small Irish monastery of the 6th or 7th century, 545 feet above the sea and often just below a quiff of cloud caught on the heights of the rock. On this Irish counterpart to Mont-St-Michel or the Cornish St. Michael's Mount, the beehive huts or clocháns, shaped like one of the old straw skeps, are circular dry-walled structures narrowing to a corbelled roof, each with a stone-lintelled doorway and a stone-paved floor. Light is admitted by openings, and there are stone pegs protruding from the wall, on which the monks (probably two to a hut) hung their liturgical books in leather-thonged book-satchels.

Beehive huts of this kind constructed in this way (which might be square or rectangular as well as round) were once common in districts where suitable stone was plentiful. The type goes back (to judge from the same corbelling technique found in chambered tombs) to the neolithic centuries and continued to modern times. Such huts are recorded, not only in Ireland, but in Wales, Devon, Cornwall, the north of Scotland, the Hebrides and the Orkneys, in Brittany and elsewhere in France, for the most part in miniature, as adjuncts to the farm – pig-sties, milk-sheds, tool-sheds, hen-houses, etc.

Belemnites

Belemnites, which can often be found sticking out of chalk cliffs or the face in a chalk quarry, are fossils which formed around the internal shell of extinct cephalopods (the shell was enclosed in the cavity at the blunt end). Objects so sharp, regular and smooth, and apparently manufactured, inspired and required popular explanation. They were variously called thunderbolts, elf-bolts, elf-arrows, elf-spurs; and the names accord with Germanic tradition, i.e. they were the bolts discharged by Thunor, the thunder-god (whose name survives in Thursley in Surrey, Thundersley in Essex, etc.), or by elves who malignantly shot disease at men, horses and cattle, or they were the spurs worn by elves. Sir Thomas Browne in his *Pseudodoxia Epidemica* (1646), on belemnites and fossil sea-urchins: 'Terrible apprehensions and answerable unto their names are raised of Fayrie stones and Elves' spurs, found commonly with us in Stone, Chalk, and Marl-pits, which notwithstanding are no more than Echinometrites and Belemnites, the Sea-Hedg-Hog and the Dart-Stone'. Possession of belemnites guarded against attack by belemnites, like cancelling like, which was one of the regular principles of magic.

Belvederes

Belvederes are glazed lantern-rooms or turret-rooms projecting from the roof of a house to afford a view, as one may guess from the Italian word (*bello, bel*, pleasant; *vedere*, view). In Italian a *belvedere* is a look-out, turret, terrace, viewpoint. Leicestershire's Belvoir overlooking the famous vale means the same,

These 7th or 8th century **BEEHIVE HUTS** *are situated on the top of the monastery of Skellig Michael, off the coast of Kerry.*

'*The most lovely of all forest trees*', wrote Gilbert White of the BEECH. '*The Lady of the Woods*', *as it has also been called, the beech can provide spectacular forest views, such as this example in Burnham Beeches, though the dense shade produced tends to deprive the forest floor of undergrowth.*

ENCHES began to appear in English churches in the 14th century but only became general during the late 15th and early 16th centuries. The BENCH-ENDS, also known as butts, were cut from oak planks three or four inches thick and sawn vertically from sections of trunk to the length required. Though many of the subjects of the bench-end carvings were sacred, more secular themes were also depicted, such as this early 16th century bench-end carving of a miller and post-mill at Bishops Lydeard (below) or this representation of cloth-making (bottom) – again early 16th century – to be found at Spaxton Church, Somerset.

from the Norman era (Old French *bel*, and *vedeir*, a view), a name given by Benedictine monks. Look for architectural belvederes on late 18th century or early 19th century houses, when the moral and emotional attraction of views, or prospects, was strong. There are several, for instance, in and around Maldon giving sea-views over the flat Essex coast. When the Rev. Sir Henry Bate Dudley, journalist, pugilist, connoisseur and friend of Gainsborough, built an up-to-date, fashionably designed and very charming stuccoed addition to his rectory at Bradwell-juxta-Mare, in the seventeen-eighties, his architect capped the house with an Ionic belvedere between the chimneys, giving views over the flat Essex fields to the Blackwater estuary and to the North Sea by the Saxon church and Roman shore fort of Ythancaestir.

Ben

The word Ben, as in Ben Nevis, Ben Macdhui, etc., means peak or mountain, Gaelic *beinn*.

Bench-ends and benches

Oak benches with carved ends in a church usually belong to the early 16th century or the late 15th century. Mediaeval discomfort was on the way out, and more was made of sermons, so the bench came in. Then the Reformation substituted English for Latin in the services and brought priest and laity into closer communion in the nave: there was more to listen to, and more cause to sit, and benching the empty naves continued. The bench-ends were carved in simple or sophisticated style, squared off at the top (as in Somerset, Devon and Cornwall) or given the elaborate 'poppy-head' finials one sees often in churches in Norfolk and Suffolk. Subjects carved on top or sides, in the round or in relief, include saints and their symbols, the SEVEN DEADLY SINS, the SEVEN WORKS OF MERCY, the SEVEN SACRAMENTS, the INSTRUMENTS OF CHRIST'S PASSION, and the FIVE WOUNDS OF CHRIST (these last two especially common). Later, desire for comfort and dislike of draughts substituted the plainly made BOX PEW of the 17th and 18th centuries.

Bench-marks

These mapmaker's aids are to be seen cut into rock or stone, especially on such a building as a church, which no one is going to pull down. Each bench-mark consists of a wedge-like horizontal notch surmounting a broad arrow (the sign of the War Department, which

originally controlled the Ordnance Survey), and indicates an ascertained height or level on a line of levels. When a surveyor is 'levelling', or determining altitudes, he fits an angle-iron into the notch as a 'bench' or support for his levelling-staff. All bench-marks, with the height of each above mean sea level, are shown on large scale Ordnance Survey maps, such as the 1:1250 and the 1:2500 maps. A select number are marked on smaller scale maps. From the Ordnance Survey you can also buy a Bench-Mark List for your area.

Betws-

On the map of Wales, Betws- is a celticization of the Old English *bed-hus* (*gebed*, prayer), i.e. an oratory or chapel, in which prayers were said for the souls of the departed. Betws-y-coed, Chapel of the woods, Betws Garmon (also in Gwynedd), Chapel of St. Garmon; or in Shropshire, at 1,300 feet above the sea in Clun Forest, the church of Bettws-y-crywn, Chapel of the Sty.

Black-and-white houses

Black-and-white or 'magpie' houses, timber-framed, belong particularly to the west Midlands and the western counties from Herefordshire to Lancashire. Stone in these areas (much of it soft sandstone) was not always of good quality, and the forests west of the Severn provided excellent oak timber. So there developed at the close of the Middle Ages, and continued to the 17th and even into the 18th century, a specialized tradition of the house which is really a frame or box of timbers. In the timber-framed house, which was also built in other forest or woodland areas of England, it is the timbers, and not the walls, which carry the weight of the roof. The walling consisted of plastered laths, or interwoven wattle covered with daub, set between the vertical timbers, or 'studs'. In the western tradition the verticals or studs were more and more elaborately braced and criss-crossed and patterned; and the surface of the timbers was then blackened with pitch to protect them in this rainy western area. So the complex 'magpie' appearance evolved: black timbers, white plaster or daub between them. Elsewhere in England the oak timbers were not originally blackened, and in the forest districts of Kent and Sussex, for example, frame buildings were given a much less bizarre and more attractive look by close-set studding in its natural wood colour. A particularly lavish use of timber was often a sign of wealth.

Black-and-white tablets

Black-and-white tablets in churches are memorials which deserve attention for their often subtle proportions and lettering. These tablets of the 1780–1840 period are neo-classical. Reacting against the flamboyance of the late baroque and rococo monuments of the first half of the 18th century, which recited the virtues of the deceased with such immense complacency, the designers and their clients aimed to ally classical correctness and pathos. They wanted memorials which would be neat, elegant, and chaste, to use Regency adjectives. The elements are simple. A panel of white marble is set against a background of black marble, with sculpture in shallow relief. The white panel bearing the inscription may itself be emblematic (scroll, crumpled sheet of paper, sarcophagus, etc.). It may be a rectangle, an oval or a shield, surmounted emblematically by a draped urn, a weeping willow, a tree of life, a broken column, a figure of Grief with bowed head. The commonest emblem is the draped classical urn above a white rectangular panel, which suggested Thomas Hood's lines written when such neo-classicism was becoming old-fashioned:

Here's young Squire Ringwood's health, and may
    he live as long as Jason,
Before Atropos cuts his thread, and Dick Tablet,
    the bungling mason,
Chips him a marble tea-table, and marble tea-urn
    a-top of it.

– though as a rule the Dick Tablets of the period, up and down the country, were anything but 'bungling'. Compare with their products the rather flat Regency porches and doorways or the stucco façades of the Regency house. Fashionable towns such as Bath, Bristol and York were centres of the tablet trade.

Black house

Black-ceiled from the smoke of its peat fire on the open hearth, which gave an Indian-ink shine to the roof timbers and the underside of the thatch, the 'black house' was the crofter's cottage of the Outer Hebrides from Barra to Lewis, a long, low, one-storeyed rectangle of stone and thatch akin to the peasant houses of Iceland. The stone walls were built without mortar, and were double, with an infilling of earth. Low timbers on these very thick walls upheld a light roof of sods and straw or grass, tied down outside with straw ropes. Every year this blackened, soot-filled thatch was stripped off for manure. Small window open-ings revealed an earthen floor inside, and a wall-bed near the hearth, with its own little roof of sods to keep the sleepers dry and clean when drops of soot-water fell from the thatch in bad weather. Wordsworth, Coleridge and Dorothy Wordsworth stayed in a similar mainland cottage on Loch Achray in 1803. With pleasure, Dorothy recorded in her journal, they noticed 'the beauty of the beams and rafters gleaming between the clouds of smoke . . . Where the firelight fell upon them, they were as glossy as black rocks on a sunny day cased in ice.' Few, if any, black houses are now inhabited.

Blemya

Not infrequent in mediaeval carvings in church, perhaps as a symbol of gluttony, the blemya is a headless human figure with eyes and a mouth below his shoulders (as he appears in the 13th century Mappa Mundi, in Hereford Cathedral). He derives from the Blemmyae, an Ethiopian people, who have this legendary shape ascribed to them in Pliny's *Natural History*.

Bloomeries

Bloomeries were forges for producing slag-free bars or 'blooms' of iron. There was slag in newly melted iron because the furnaces had to be charged with layers of ore and charcoal; and the way to get rid of the slag was to bring the metal back to red heat and hammer it, or forge it, again and again. Iron Age, Roman, mediaeval and more recent bloomeries in old iron-producing forest areas, such as the Weald, the Forest of Dean and parts of Worcestershire, are often recognizable – if a plough has been over the ground – by the amount of iron-cinder turned up. If you notice brown knobbly bits of this iron-cinder or slag within the ramparts of an Iron Age camp (as at Kingsbury, near Purton in Wiltshire, or Saxonbury, near Rotherfield, Sussex), you will have hit upon a fortified site of ancient ironworkers. Water-wheels were employed in and after the Middle Ages to actuate the hammers and bellows, and in the wealden parts of Kent, Sussex and Surrey one can see the hammer-ponds built to impound the necessary water. Names such as Cinder Hill (very common in the Forest of Dean), Forge Wood, Hammer Wood, Furnace Wood, conjure a picture of ironworkers in forest glades and denes and their bloomery hammers, 'which beating upon the iron resound all over the places adjoyning' (Camden's *Britannia*, 1610).

Blowing-houses

Blowing-houses, to be seen here and there in ruins on Dartmoor and the Cornish moors, were the smelting houses of the moorland tinners from about 1300 to the 18th century. A stream diverted by a leat turned the overshot wheel in a pit alongside the house, and the wheel worked the bellows of the charcoal furnace, in which ore and charcoal were placed in alternate layers. The water-wheel also worked stamps or mills, or both, for reducing the ore to a fine powder, before it went into the furnace. As well as the bracken-grown tumble of pieces of moorstone or surface granite used to build the blowing-house, one may sometimes find granite mortar-stones in which the tin was broken up by the water-driven stamps, the round millstones of the 'crazing' or crushing mill, and slabs of granite with large rectangular depressions, which were ingot moulds for the molten tin. The ore for these old blowing-houses, which were called 'Jew's Houses' by 19th century tinners, was stream-tin from surface workings.

Blue of the sky

This desirable condition of the roof overhead is caused by the molecules of air scattering (mainly) the short waves of violet and blue light. Tennyson's

> drown'd in yonder living blue
> The lark becomes a sightless song

are April lines: the best, purest, deepest blue does not abound in dry summer when there are larger dust particles about in the air scattering more of the glaring brilliance of white light and toning down the blue, causing skies which are milkier and less attractive. In light between ourselves and darkish horizons, violet and blue are similarly scattered by the air, giving a blue look to distant and darkish woods, ridges, mountains, etc.

Bog trees

Often to be seen in upland peat-diggings, bog trees derive from open forest or scrub wiped out by the gradual formation of peat. The commonest species are birch, pine, alder and oak. SCOTCH PINE was dominant in the dry Boreal climate from about 9,000 to 7,000 years ago. From about 5500 to 2000 B.C. a wetter and warmer phase encouraged alder and oak, and the formation of peat-bogs. A dry phase c. 2000–700 B.C. was followed by a decline into a sub-Atlantic coolness and dampness which encouraged peat formation again (with human help), and continues to wrap us round. The peat preserved the remains of the trees it killed. In a Co. Donegal bog the deep-rooted stumps of ancient pines look and feel as if they had been living only a few years ago. Bog fir and bog oak retain their substance so well that they have been of great use in Irish life. Both have been fashioned into roof timbers. Bog oak has been made into furniture and utensils, slivers of bog fir have been woven into rope and used as kindling and for giving light. Ancient timber also comes out of the lowland peat of the Fens.

Bohereens

Characteristic of the townships and peasant farms of Ireland, bohereens, or boreens, are dry-walled lanes, narrow, seldom straight, often steep and brambly, and decidedly rough; better, as far as men are concerned, for hard bare feet than hobnails. They grew up, or were made, before wheeled traffic, and are in fact cow lanes (Irish *bóthairín*, little cow track) for conducting cattle through the home closes.

Bole hills

In the Peak District, hills (especially along the 'EDGES' of the MILLSTONE GRIT country) where the lead miners smelted their ore in a primitive way before wind-furnaces were introduced. They selected bolestids where the high hills were open to the prevailing south-westerly winds, and scooped out 'boles' (Old English *bolla*, a bowl), shallow bowls or saucers in the ground, which they filled with ore and wood. The pile was turfed over and the wind kept it alight. Bole Hill between Monyash and Bakewell looks down on a ring of old lead mines. The old bolestids are often marked by bare ground poisoned by the lead.

Booley houses

Booley houses, or traces of them, are found in mountain pasturings in Ireland. In summer, families moved with their cattle from their tribal villages (where the crops were growing in the unfenced field) to summer villages or groupings of summer huts in the mountains, in sheltered positions near streams. In these booley houses (Irish *buaile*, milking place) the summer dairying was done, butter and cheese were made, young and old feeling a sense of freedom and release. As in other mountain countries they were practising 'transhumance', the temporary change of house and activity which took the Welsh family and their cattle from the *hendref* (old farm) to the mountain HAFOD or *hafoddy*, the Scottish family to the

SHIELING, and the Norwegians to the *saeter*. To the English, booleying seemed peculiar and undesirable. Edmund Spenser the poet, who had land in Ireland, maintained (in *A View of the Present State of Ireland*, 1595) that people practised 'mischeives and villanyes' in the booley, thinking themselves 'halfe exempted from lawe and obedience, and having once tasted freedome, doe, like a steere that hath bene long out of his yoke, grudge and repyne ever after to come under rule agayne'. He would hardly have approved of the modern family transference to summer bungalow and holiday camp. The booley houses on the mountain were rectangular, oval or round, built of sods, or of stones, with a roofing of heather; they usually show as small mounds. Booley (-voley, -vooley, etc.) is common in place-names.

Bosses

Bosses, the large rounded knobs or protuberances which key the intersections of ribs in a church roof, either in wood or stone, gave the mediaeval carver opportunities for limitless virtuosity in compact design. The emblems, symbols, biblical characters and events, faces, grotesques, etc., are often too high for a clear or comfortable view without field-glasses or a mirror (which is a piece of equipment worth taking in a car). English carvers took, as a rule, the whole convex surface of the boss as something to be ornamented, whereas abroad the boss is often carved with more monotonous effect as a flattened disc.

Bottle seals

Seals or medallions of blackish glass, often dug up around old houses, have become detached from wine bottles. They are commonly marked with the owner's name, initials, arms, crest, etc., and with the date (probably the date of manufacture in local GLASSHOUSES, often in the woodlands, not the date of bottling). In England the wine bottle, dumpy, with a shortish neck and wide base, came into general use early in the 17th century, to be succeeded in the 18th century by the taller cylindrical bottle of a shape for binning. Both kinds were supplied with these seals, partly as a practical measure of ownership and identification – since a sound wine bottle can be used again and again – partly no doubt as a symbol of status and snobbery. The seal – and the bottle – were taken from France. Bottles with seals were made for wine merchants and innkeepers as well as for lords, squires, parsons and others,

and were still being made in the 19th century. Sheelah Ruggles-Brise's *Sealed Bottles*, 1949, gives much information.

Boulder clay

Boulder clay was laid down when the glaciers of the Ice Age melted. Moving with vast weight and grinding power, the glaciers had scoured earth and rocks into a mixture geologists vividly call 'rock flour', mixed with smaller and larger pebbles. This was transported, and deposited, in the end producing that rather smoothed landscape characterizing much of the Lowlands of Scotland, or the north Midlands; or much of Norfolk and Suffolk, where the boulder clay overlies the chalk. The clay itself can be examined along the coasts (east and west coasts from Wales and East Anglia to the north), where the sea has cut it back to a cliff. The cliff breaks and dribbles to the beach, and the sea washes out pebbles and lumps of rock, often of distant origin, and makes (for instance, along the splendid beach of Porth Neigwl on the south coast of the Lleyn peninsula) odd little rolls of clay filled with coloured grains of rock.

Boundary banks and ditches

Long, apparently pointless, ditches and banks in your neighbourhood may be prehistoric (*see* DYKES), or mediaeval; and if they are mediaeval they may be ancient estate boundaries or park boundaries. To dig and heap up, after all, is the obvious way to delimit: it depends only on having the labour, which great mediaeval lords could command cost-free. An estate boundary may belong to the 13th century, a busy time for the aggrandizement and settlement of properties. Along the crest of the Malverns, for instance, one can see the Shire Ditch, continuing as the Red Earl's Dyke, cut by the very powerful dictatorial Gilbert de Clare, Earl of Gloucester (1243–95) – whose body 'was of a very ruddy and blody color' – to mark the boundary between his hunting grounds along the east of the Malverns and those of the Bishop of Hereford along the west of the ridge. Other banks and ditches marked lengths of boundary between one great Anglo-Saxon estate and another. Sometimes one sees little more than a not very straightly ruled ditch, with its bank worn away. Sometimes the bank remains high and the ditch fairly deep, giving the appearance of an isolated stretch of sunken lane.

Park banks and ditches, when they are traced, very obviously enclose their areas

*T*he Devil is here depicted on a roof BOSS *in Southwark Cathedral, swallowing Judas Iscariot – whose skirt and feet are still visible.*

A BRASS-*rubbing of a cross-legged knight from the tomb of Sir Robert de Bures (c. 1320–30) at All Saints Church, Acton, Suffolk.*

(which may be smaller than one would expect), the mediaeval lord, under royal licence, having built a running mound (which was palisaded) to shut in the deer he required to augment his winter supply of meat. The later walls surviving around a deer park (e.g. at Raby Castle, Durham, and Sudeley Castle, in the Cotswolds) give some idea of the height required in the mediaeval combination of bank and palisade. W. G. Hoskins's *Making of the English Landscape* (1955) and *Provincial England* (1963), and O. G. S. Crawford's *Archaeology in the Field* (1953) give help in recognizing and interpreting these banks, ditches and enclosures. They differ from prehistoric dykes by fitting in more or less with the neighbouring field boundaries – i.e. they belong to the settlement we inherit.

Box pews

Box pews, or 'square pews', wainscoted and with doors, were set up in churches in the 17th and 18th centuries to make attendance at services less draughty and lethal. In a church where they survive (such as Old Dilton, near Westbury, in Wiltshire), it will be seen that the box pews are arranged so that the congregation faces, not the altar (in some of the pews they might have their back to it), but the pulpit and the prayer-desk, in the nave, from which the post-reformation service was conducted. Certain of the box pews were family corrals, upholstered, curtained and comfortable; and with extra grandeur the squire and his family not infrequently occupied an enclosed parlour pew (sometimes in an old CHANTRY CHAPEL), with a fireplace and furniture, entered by a private doorway from the churchyard or the manor-house grounds. In Draycot Cerne church, near Chippenham in Wiltshire, a memorial of 1767 looks down on to the parlour pew of the Longs, whose great mansion stood alongside, and remarks on the 'amiable condescension' of Sir Robert Long, who had flown no doubt to another parlour pew in Heaven.

Brasses

Brasses are effigies of the dead (or effigies for the dead, since they do not attempt likeness) designed on the flat in imitation of the three-dimensional tomb. They seem to have developed in Flanders (where there was a lack of good stone for sculpture) about the beginning of the 13th century, and they soon evolved into large tomb-length rectangles of a finely engraved complexity. Cheap or not

compared with the coloured and gilded figures on a tomb-chest, brasses quickly created a fashion, and were duly laid over grandees both temporal and spiritual. English designers preferred a still cheaper variety of brass, which combines with excellent effect small pieces of engraved metal separately inlaid in a slab (usually of blue Tournai stone). Either kind may more or less exactly imitate the details and ensemble of a tomb-chest. A canopy will be engraved over the figure, his feet will rest on a lion or a dog, and he will be surrounded by angels or mourners or heraldic shields, and the whole may be enclosed, as on a tomb-chest, within a border which itself encloses an inscription.

Abroad, the earliest known brass is one in Germany of 1251. In England (where more mediaeval brasses remain than in all the rest of Europe), the oldest to survive is the famous brass of 1277 to Sir John Dabernoun, at Stoke d'Abernon, in Surrey. After the 15th century the English craft declined until brasses became at the finish the small scratchy plates of a decadent folk-art commemorating quite humble characters.

–breck

When found in place-names in Yorkshire, Lancashire and the Lakes, –breck can usually be taken to mean a hill or hillside (Old Norse *brekka*). It is one of the sign-words, like FELL, of areas settled by the Norwegians.

Brick

Though the Romans used their tile-like red bricks (which can be seen, 12 to 18 inches long and rather more than an inch thick, in excavated remains of Roman villas and fortresses, and re-used, where there was a Roman ruin to be quarried, in the mediaeval walling of churches), bricks were little made again in England until the 14th century. Brick architecture in the Low Countries then began to be followed here and there along the east coast, around Hull, in Norfolk and Suffolk, and in Essex. For a long while brick remained a material for the grander purposes of church, mansion (and Cambridge college), spreading slowly but with economic inevitability into other districts. Baking bricks was easier and cheaper than quarrying and shaping stone. Bricks could be baked on the spot from the clay removed in digging foundations; or they could be made in small local kilns, obviating transport of stone from distant quarries on poor roads. Standardized to the grasp of the mason's fingers and thumb, bricks were easier to build with as well as cheaper; and gradually they worked down from mansion to smaller house, and even to cottages by the end of the 18th century. The East Anglian halls or mansions in Tudor brick come as a surprise in colour, grace and charm, e.g. Oxburgh Hall Gatehouse (*c.* 1482), south-west of Swaffham, and East Barsham Manor (early 16th century), north of Fakenham, both in Norfolk.

Bridges

The shape of the arch or arches of an older bridge will indicate more or less when it was built, since bridge-arches conform to the arch-shape customary at any time in other buildings. Bridges with rather narrow pointed arches are likely to be 13th or possibly 14th century. Bridges with 'four-centred' arches, with a flatter profile (as if the four curves which make up the arch were each drawn from different centres placed at the four corners of a square), are likely to belong to the 15th century. Bridges arched in a still flatter shape (as if drawn from four centres marking the corners of a rectangle) will be Tudor or Jacobean. Bridges with semicircular arches are likely to be 18th century. Bridges of the 14th and 15th centuries are often ribbed under the arches. This is a rough guide to old bridges still

ℬOX PEWS not only provided comfort in draughty churches but also lent a certain aesthetic charm, as in this example in the Holy Trinity Church, Goodramgate, York. Internally it is one of the most picturesque churches in York. Pews of many dates are grouped around the two-decker pulpit installed in 1785. The stained glass in the background is 15th century York School.

*T*he stark beauty of *Clapper* BRIDGE, *Postbridge, Dartmoor, as it spans the River Dart near the Princetown– Mortonhampstead road. The bridge, which probably dates back to the 13th century, is constructed of monolithic slabs of granite (the clappers), each about 15 feet long. The name Postbridge is derived from the granite posts set up in the area to guide travellers to this bridge in bad weather conditions.*

in use or superannuated alongside a modern road-bridge.

The 13th, 14th and 15th centuries were a great constructional time, when bridge-building was considered a godly and neighbourly act. Many difficult fords and ferry passages were bridged for the first time, and many decayed wooden bridges were renewed in stone. If they have not been enlarged, these older mediaeval bridges will have a roadway about 12 to 13 feet wide. Notice the cutwaters, the triangular wedges of masonry finishing off the piers, which divide the current and protect the piers from ice or timber coming down with a flood. Sometimes these are built only on the upstream side. On later mediaeval and Tudor bridges – especially the long ones – the parapets are often carried out over the cutwaters to give V-shaped spaces into which foot passengers can squeeze when a wagon or cart goes by – or nowadays a car.

Wheeled traffic was less common than one thinks until late in the 18th century, when road surfaces were improved, a fact which explains the survival of so many packhorse bridges, mediaeval, Tudor, 17th or 18th century. A packhorse bridge alongside the ford, which the packhorse trains still splashed through when the stream was low in summer, will have an immediately distinctive width of about $3\frac{1}{2}$ to $6\frac{1}{2}$

feet. Frequently it will have exceptionally low parapets, or none at all. Higher parapets would have interfered with the burden fastened on either side of the pack-saddle.

The narrow clappers, or clapper bridges, of Cornwall, Dartmoor, Exmoor, North Yorkshire, etc., made of large slabs of stone (the word is from the Mediaeval Latin *claperius*, a heap of stones), are simply packhorse bridges of a primitive kind, as old – some of them – as the Middle Ages, but no older. The 13th century is the date advanced for the famous clapper of granite slabs at Postbridge on Dartmoor. Another was built on Dartmoor as late as 1780. The sequence must often have been ford, stepping-stones, and then clapper, as one may see on several Dartmoor streams. On the Meavy, north of Plymouth, the narrow Marchant's Bridge, above stepping-stones and a ford, was trodden by the packhorse trains of merchants who sold their goods at the nearby Marchant's Cross. A clapper and a later packhorse bridge keep company by a ford at Linton, in Wharfedale, in North Yorkshire. At Wycoller, under the moors in north-east Lancashire, between Haworth and Colne, ford, stepping-stones, clapper and two-arched packhorse bridge persist side by side. Clappers of smooth slippery stone, without a parapet, were obviously a hazard to be superseded when possible.

The Romans built many road bridges, long and short, some with stone piers, with cutwaters, upholding a wooden superstructure, some altogether of timber. Scattered stonework and piles driven into river-beds have often been found.

Brigid's Cross

On 31 January, the eve of the feast of St. Brigid, the Irish plait green rushes into the three-legged swastikas or lozenge shapes of the Brigid's Cross. The crosses are stuck up in cowsheds and in cottages, where they show up against the smoke-carboned thatch, to avert evil of every kind (including lightning). They are – or should be – renewed every year. Brigid, the blessed Bridie, the 'Mary of the Irish', St. Bride in Scotland and England, St. Ffraid in Wales, is supremely a country saint, and is held to be a christianization of an Irish mother-goddess. So she is concerned with birth and increase, with cattle, milk, butter, the spring of the year. The Brigid's Cross is a magic sun or eye with analogies in other parts of the world, and one of the blessed Bridie's flowers is the dandelion, the sun of the spring

Ashness Bridge, a packhorse BRIDGE, *near Grange-in-Borrowdale, Cumbria.*

meadows, the stem exuding a milk believed to nourish young calves.

Brochs

Brochs provide sufficient reason for a long holiday journey to the north. Excavations in progress from year to year should find out more about these odd buildings, but it seems that they were built and lived in between about 100 B.C. and A.D. 100 by farming and fishing people of the Iron Age who found themselves in need of tower homesteads or fortified homesteads – British immigrants who had moved up from the eastern lowlands and Northumberland under pressure from Belgic invaders farther south in Britain. Centuries later their tower-houses were named brochs (from Old Norse *borg*, a fort) by Viking settlers or travellers. Brochs are to be found as far south as Wigtown, on the west coast of Scotland, with notable concentrations as you go north, in Skye, Ross and Cromarty, Sutherland, Caithness, and then Orkney and Shetland. On the south-east coast there are brochs in Berwickshire, Selkirk, Midlothian, Fife and Angus. Quite a number are delightfully situated on rocky knolls overlooking the sea. Shetland scores in that way with the famous broch of Mousa, more than 43 feet high. In the Highland Region, Dun Troddan broch and Dun Telve, both near Glenelg, are 33 and 25 feet high. Dun Carloway on Lewis, 15 miles from Stornoway, goes up to 30 feet. The hollow, galleried, mortarless walls of a broch, built of large slabby stones, may be as much as 15 feet thick, the inside diameter as much as 40 feet, giving room to live inside, in huts built against the circumference of the wall, as if a broch had been a shrunken or constricted hill-fort. The single door was secured by a bar fitting into holes on either side of the doorway. With the bar in place, brochs must have been nearly impregnable. The walls were fireproof, too thick to batter down, and too steep to scale. Richard Feachem in his *Guide to Prehistoric Scotland* (1963) compares the broch-dwellers to 'the tender meat of a crustacean secure within the hard shell': Fort Crab, Fort Lobster.

Bullauns

Bullauns in Ireland (Irish *ballain*, cup) are round basins in stones, artificially made, associated with particular practices and beliefs. Most of them (there may be several on one stone) are probably ancient mortars for grinding or pounding grain, etc., and they often

occur at Dark Age monastic sites, for instance, St. Laïsrén's monastery on Inishmurray, off the Sligo coast. Some bullauns have been made deeper – or perhaps made – by the practice of turning large pebbles in them to enforce a curse (the pebbles are turned three times against the sun). Water that collects in a bullaun is thought to have healing power, and bullauns are also connected with fertility. It has been suggested that these practices descend from the fertility religion probably expressed in prehistoric cup-and-ring carvings on outcrops of rock and on stones in chambered barrows.

Burh

Old English for a place with defences, burh is the word which changed form and meaning into 'borough', for a town (though -borough at the end of a place-name may mean hill, from *beorg*). Our Anglo-Saxon ancestors used *burh* when they spoke of an old hill-fort or camp (such as the great Iron Age fortresses of Badbury in Dorset or Cissbury in Sussex). But they made burhs of their own, especially when trouble with marauding and invading Danes occupied them in the 9th and 10th centuries. In Wessex, Alfred's kingdom, they threw up ramparts of earth or stone around conveniently placed settlements where people from the countryside could take refuge from the Danes. A few of the towns which developed from such burhs still lie inside their anti-Danish defences. Wareham in Dorset is almost enclosed by the tall earth ramparts called Wareham Walls. Wallingford, near Oxford, at a crossing over the Thames, is partly enclosed in earthworks. Cricklade in Wiltshire, on another Thames crossing (and on

The Dun Carloway BROCH, *or fortified homestead, on Lewis, Scotland.*

a Roman road), lies inside a rectangle of burh ramparts which were originally faced with stone. Lydford, on the fringe of Dartmoor, was another of Alfred's burhs, but here the fortifiers needed only to pile up the tall rampart which cuts off the Lydford promontory from one gorge to another. The Anglo-Saxons reckoned that in their burhs four men were required for the defence of each $5\frac{1}{2}$ yards of rampart.

Bustards

In the British Isles the extinct bustard is an archaeological witness in his museum case, like a flint axe or a cannonball. The last bustards of resident British stock survived till *c.* 1825–32 in East Anglia and on the Lincolnshire and Yorkshire wolds. On Salisbury Plain, which had been their headquarters, and where they had no doubt been familiar to neolithic and Bronze Age shepherds, they died out rather earlier, *c.* 1810–20 (see the stuffed bustards in the Devizes and Salisbury Museums). These shy birds, strong running, strong flying, large as turkeys and as good to eat, belonged to England before enclosure – to the Salisbury Plain described by John Evelyn in the 17th century, 'that goodly plaine or rather Sea of Carpet, which I think for evenesse, extent, verdure, innumerable flocks, to be one of the most delightfull prospects in nature'. Enclosure altered this and other goodly plains, gradually transforming and reducing the bustards' habitat. Their decline seems to have begun as early as the 16th century, and to have been hastened by the hoeing of winter wheat which disturbed them in the breeding season.

Butts

Low earth mounds in village closes or fields near the church may have been butts for archery practice, and the probability will be strengthened if the field is still called the Butts or Butt Close. There may be two low mounds, against which the targets were set, about 200 yards apart in a straight line. (On farms, though, a similar field name may imply a butt-end strip of land against a boundary.) English power in the Hundred Years War depended so much on the longbow, which was a tricky weapon to learn, that statutes provided for butts and practice in every village and town, and for more than a century after the introduction of firearms in the mid 15th century the use of the bow continued to be thought the *ne plus ultra* of manliness and patriotism. Flodden Field in 1513 was the last mediaeval battle, the

last battle in which bowmen were important. Nearly thirty years later the possibility that the French might invade made authority insist once more on butts in every village and longbow practice on Sundays and holidays (1541), a provision which went with the building of new forts along the Channel and an overhaul of the system of BEACONS. As usual, the military mind was conservative and slow. In 1549 the young Edward VI had to hear the elderly Latimer preach a splendidly fatuous and bloody sermon on the bow, which 'hath ben Goddes instrumente whereby he hath given us manye victories agaynests our enemyes', and on the negligence of justices of the peace 'in executyng the lawes of shutynge' – i.e. keeping up butts and practice – now that everyone had taken to 'horynge in townes, instead of shutynge in the fyeldes'. For another fifty years or so authority continued the pretence that butts and bowmen were indispensable.

Bwlch

A Welsh word which surprises the Englishman on signposts, bwlch means a gap or pass. Out of the high mountain district a familiar example is Bwlch in Powys, where the A50 mounts up through gap and village between hills, taking the route of a previous Roman road. Bwlchgwyn, the quarry village of the White Pass, in Clwyd (on A525), was used by the Roman road from Chester to Bala Lake.

-by

At the end of a place-name, -by is commonly from the Old Norse *by*, a farm or village. It is the name-ending (in contrast to the -TON of Anglo-Saxon counties) typical of the counties in the north Midlands and the north-west which were settled by people of Scandinavian stock.

Cadaver

Cadaver (Latin for corpse) is the name given to grisly effigies of the dead on their tombs. Men were more than usually obsessed by death and decay after the early years of the 15th century. Epidemics swept through Europe (plague, then sweating sickness, or the 'English Sweat'). Sermons were preached and poems written on death and worms, Death was personified as a grasping skeleton arresting all sorts and conditions of men, the Dance of Death was engraved and painted (sometimes in the large on the outside of a prominent building as at Basel or in Venice, on the Grand Canal); and the cadaver, the dead man in his shroud, was commonly figured on brasses and in stone. In Tewkesbury Abbey, for example, an unknown monk or abbot of the 15th century is sculptured under a canopy as an emaciated cadaver on the verge of decay. Large worms – *humiliatus sum vermis*, by worms am I abased – slither around his knees, a toad crouches in the folds of his shroud, a mouse nibbles his fallen belly and a snail creeps between his arm and his prominent ribs. 'As I ye shall be' is the message of such cadaver tombs and brasses.

Cair-

Cair-, Caer-, Car-, in place-names in Wales and Cornwall, the Marches and the north-west, means a fortified place, a hill camp, a fortified homestead. Names with Caher- in Ireland have the same meaning.

Canals

Canals come into historical focus if they are thought of as artificial rivers, without shallows or currents, extending the old system of water transport on which our ancestors depended before the revolution of road and railway. In the long era of roads transformed so easily into sloughs of mud it was quicker, cheaper, and more reliable to carry goods for any considerable distance by sea, and then up the rivers. For example, in the Middle Ages it paid to ship limestone from Devon or Caen in Normandy to building sites in the south-east, though there were inland quarries nearer to hand. Our major 18th century canals were conceived as waterways joining and extending the ancient riverways, which themselves had been much improved by flash-locks and then pound-locks with gates (*see* LOCKS) since the 16th century. James Brindley (1716–72), the great canal engineer, planned in this way to link the Mersey, the Trent, the Thames and the Severn, in imitation of the 17th century canals linking the rivers of France. Our canal era began splendidly in 1761 with the Duke of Bridgewater's canal from the Worsley coal-mines (Brindley's first canal), and finished, or dwindled miserably, in the opening decade of the railways, 1830–40. Actually, the oldest of our canals, built as fen drains by the Romans, are the Car Dyke, from the Nene at Peterborough to the Witham at Lincoln, and its continuation, the Fossdyke (still navigable), from the Witham to the Trent.

In canal exploration things to note include AQUEDUCTS, INCLINED PLANES, tunnels, lock flights, side cuts, wharves, canal basins and the

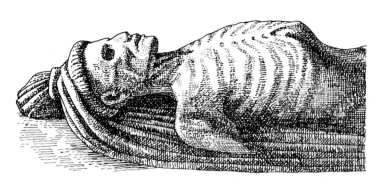

late 18th century and Regency architecture of canal bridges, warehouses, bargemen's inns and lock-keepers' cottages. Also storage reservoirs for maintaining the water level. Note as well cast-iron mile-posts, and the grooves which tow-ropes have scored in bridge or tunnel masonry.

Carn

In Welsh and Cornish, as in Gaelic and Irish, carn originally meant a pile of stones. So carn, or cairn as the word became in Lowland Scots, may also mean in place-names and ordinary speech something that looks like a pile of stones, a rocky hill or hilltop or mountain, or a pile of stones of some special kind, a barrow made of stones instead of earth, stones heaped up for a memorial or to mark a path or a boundary. Some carns were thrown up to give extra height to a look-out point (*see* TOOT-HILLS), some as aids in surveying.

Cashel

In Ireland the cashel (Irish *caiseal*, from Latin *castellum*) is a homestead of the Early Christian era, strongly fortified with round drystone walling, often with a SOUTERRAIN inside. It is a grander version, a chieftain's version, of the humbler rath or ring-fort with earthen ramparts. Cashel walls sometimes surrounded an Irish monastery, e.g. St. Mo-Chaoi's monastery on Mahee Island, in Strangford Lough, Co. Down.

Cassiopeia

Cassiopeia circles round the north celestial pole, one of the constellations we can always see, and one of the most easily recognized for its position and its W shape (in summer – in autumn and winter it reverses above the Pole Star into an M). It commemorates Queen Kassiopeia, mother, in Greek myth, of Andromeda. When she bragged that she and

A detail from a particularly macabre CADAVER from the tomb of Sir John Golafre (d. 1442), Fyfield Church, Berkshire.

her daughter were more beautiful than the daughters of Poseidon the sea god, Poseidon sent the sea-dragon, which was about to eat Andromeda on her rock when Perseus appeared and rescued her, her parents having agreed that the two should marry. Kassiopeia tried to go back on the bargain, and was eventually set in the sky by Poseidon, tied down in disgrace, as we see her, in a market basket. Various peoples have also thought of the constellation as a leg, a key, a kneeling camel, a stone lamp, and a woman in a chair. James Joyce has a nice fancy in *Ulysses* that the W of Cassiopeia was Shakespeare's initial in the heavens, regarded by him as he walked back from nights with Anne Hathaway, and that the famous nova which appeared in Cassiopeia in 1572, visible by day and night, was 'a star, a daystar, a firedrake' rising at his birth (in fact, eight years after his birth).

Castles

Like brochs, raths, hill-forts, crannogs, burhs, peles, and moated homesteads, castles were an expression of insecurity, though on a grander scale – the insecurity of power. They began as Norman strongholds (*see* MOTTE-AND-BAILEY) in the conquest of a hostile population: they fell out of use with the coming of artillery, security, and strong government at the centre (though many picturesque castle houses came to be built for rich men in the romantic era, for instance by the architect John Nash). Some of the grandest and strongest mediaeval castles, naturally enough, survive in districts where insecurity was longest lived, where Anglo-Norman and English kings, overlords, and lords still had most to fear, in Wales, the Marches, Northumberland, and Northern Ireland.

The castle was a crustacean's shell: a normal life went on inside. So one sees, not only the special features of defence, but such necessities of living as chapel, storehouses, a hall for retainers, stables, wells, fireplaces, 'GARDE-ROBES' or privies, often jettied from the walls over ditch or moat, into which everything dropped; also the lord's WATER-MILL and DOVECOTE outside, his PARK for a winter supply of venison, and his FISHPONDS. Castles looked much more striking in the mediaeval landscape, since they were whitewashed or colour-washed, people in the Middle Ages not having our taste for surfaces of raw stone.

Some special castle words and features which deserve clarification:

Motte, earth mound of the early invasion castles of earth and timber, supporting the lord's quarters. The motte was sometimes preserved in rebuilding and capped with a round tower or shell keep in stone.

Bailey, or ward, the courtyard or space within the outer defences, and thus within the –

Curtain, or *curtain wall*, enclosing wall strengthened with mural towers which projected to allow defence left and right along the wall. The subsidiary buildings were generally set against the inner face of the curtain. The lord and his family, however, lived more securely in the –

Keep, or *donjon* (from Latin *domnionem*, lord's quarters), the usually rectangular main tower, of special defensive strength, which was substituted for the earlier motte.

Gatehouse, the towered defences of the single entrance to a castle, from which a portcullis (Old French for 'sliding door') or iron-bound timber grating was let down in grooves in the stonework, to bar the opening.

Moat, or *ditch*, around the castle, to keep attackers away from sapping or breeching the walls. All the better when water was available to fill it. It was crossed by a bridge which tipped up on an axle, the top fitting back into the gatehouse wall.

Crenellation, the notch-like rectangular gaps or openings (*crenelles*, from Latin *crena*, a notch) in the parapets or battlements, giving towers and curtains their indented look.

Arrow-slits, and *gunports*, wall openings for shooting and light.

Slighting. Castles, after siege and capture in the Civil War of the 17th century, were 'slighted', i.e. razed or rendered useless by blowing them up. The huge leaning fragments of Corfe Castle in Dorset, blown this way and that, remain as an example.

Cathedrals

With their towers or spires visible far around the countryside, cathedrals are the great mother churches of a diocese, in which the bishop has his *cathedra*, or throne. Bishops were responsible for the building of most of our cathedrals. After the Conquest many of them were made into abbey-churches, i.e. they were served by Benedictine monks instead of secular clerks (clergy not shut away from this world under monastic rule). The great churches of a few abbeys (e.g. Peterborough, Bristol, Gloucester, Chester) were transformed into cathedrals at the Reformation. So cathedrals often preserve monastic specialities – e.g.

The village of Dunvegan, whose CASTLE *bears its name, is situated to the north-west of the island of Skye in the Inner Hebrides. The castle is the seat of the Macleod chiefs and, although parts of it are reputed to date from the 9th century, its massive four-square towered pile definitely shows traces of rebuilding from the 15th to the 19th century. It has many of the traditional features associated with castles — a moat, 10-foot thick tower walls, and crenellated parapets and battlements.*

Founded as a Christian church in the 7th century by Bishop Mellitus, St. Paul's was endowed by Ethelburt, King of Kent. It was burnt down and replaced by a Norman CATHEDRAL *which became known as Old St. Pauls. This building was in turn burnt down in the Great Fire of London in 1666 and the present cathedral was built on the site by Sir Christopher Wren. This view of the official seat of the Bishop of London, whose throne may be viewed inside the cathedral, is taken from the house where Wren lived while St. Pauls was being built.*

Gloucester preserves the LAVER, where the Benedictine monks washed in the morning and before eating, and the alcoves along the sunny northern side of the CLOISTER in which each monk had his carrel, or study desk; Bristol keeps its REFECTORY, night stairs, and dormitory building, or DORTER.

Causewayed camps

Causewayed camps are one of the enigmas of prehistoric antiquity. Many have been discovered in the south of England, most of them on the chalk, and on hills, two also on low ground in the Thames valley; and finds have proved that they belong to early neolithic times – the era of the first stockbreeders and farmers – together with long BARROWS and FLINT MINES. One causewayed camp has been carbon-dated to *c.* 3480–3000 B.C. The hill examples show worn traces of pits and ramparts arranged in one or more exact circles around an open area, with apparent causeways leading into this area from the outside. Bones of cattle and other animals have been found in the pits, which are flat-bottomed. But the sites appear not to have been occupied except intermittently or seasonally. This seems to rule out a view that they were villages, made up of huts partly dug into the ground. It was then supposed that they were corrals, in which cattle were rounded up in the autumn, some to be slaughtered (since they could not all be kept through the winter), while the new calves for stock were marked – with a nick in the ear –

and, when necessary, castrated. A third and likelier view sees in the causewayed camp a fair ground (where the assemblies perhaps remotely forewent the various isolated downland fairs – as on Tan Hill, in Wiltshire, not far from the famous causewayed camps of Knap Hill and Windmill Hill, near Avebury – which lasted down to this century?). Every kind of business would be transacted between assembled families of the tribe, goods would be exchanged, ceremonies and rites would be performed – and animals killed for feasting and jollification. Whatever was the exact reason for providing the pits, the material removed in digging them was thrown out and up on to a bank which defined the internal area, the 'causeways' being no more than the spaces naturally left between pit and pit. One may suppose that the population grew and that more people came to the 'fair', the pits filled up with food refuse, and a second ring of pits was added, with a second bank, giving more room, and a third with a third bank. Eventually, after being in use for six centuries or thereabouts, these old centres may have been abandoned for the more elaborate HENGES.

Causeways

Causeways, or causeys, raised paths of earth and stone, were not infrequently built in the Middle Ages and later, as works of piety and convenience, often as the approaches to a bridge. Causeys (the word is from the mediaeval French, familiar to motorists in the modern warning *chaussée déformée* – roadway distorted – over more kilometres than one cares to think) were neatly defined by Thomas Fuller in *The Worthies of England* (1662) as 'bridges over dirt', which applies equally to the celebrated Maud Heath's Causey, for $4\frac{1}{2}$ miles outside Chippenham, in Wiltshire, built and maintained still from the endowments of a 15th century widow, and to the 'Causey to Hell Gate' in *Paradise Lost*, which those notable engineers, Sin and Death, built over Chaos from Earth, a super causey –

> . . . a passage broad
> Smooth, easie, inoffensive down to Hell.

Mediaeval causeys on monastic estates remain in the Fens and on Sedgemoor, where the A361 from Glastonbury to Taunton uses the Greylake Fosse built for the monks of Glastonbury. Causeys were perhaps suggested by the raised agger of ROMAN ROADS, which were often named as such (e.g. Long Causeway, in the Peak; Devil's Causeway in Northumberland; Chute Causeway in Wiltshire, on the Roman road from Winchester to Cirencester). The Welsh for causey is *sarn*, also applied to Roman roads, such as Sarn Helen.

Caves

Caves are best and most numerous in LIMESTONE, which is subject to hollowing action, chemical (solution of the calcium carbonate which makes up the rock) and mechanical. If they were dry, without streams, limestone caverns offered early man safe and durable shelter – and walls to decorate. But so far no cave in the British Isles has been found with Upper Palaeolithic paintings or engravings. Much of limestone Britain was under ice, the hunting population was small, and it seems unlikely that cave art of the French or Spanish kind was much practised so far north. All the same, British caves were occupied as homes or shelters from the Upper Palaeolithic to fairly modern times (particularly in the Iron Age and in the Roman centuries), and several of them have been important archaeologically. The first burial of a palaeolithic hunter to be found (1823) was in the floor of Goat's Hole in south Wales, and it was the discovery in Kent's Cavern, Torquay (1825), of flint tools sealed in with fossilized remains of extinct animals that first indicated the extreme antiquity of man and upset biblically derived dogmas of Creation and Flood and the age of the world.

British caves have sounded to the clack of Iron Age looms, and (caves in Somerset, Antrim, Fife, Skye) to the ringing of the anvils of Iron Age smiths. In the north, as some cave names show (Thirst House, in Deep Dale, Hob Thirst Hole in Monsal Dale, both in Derbyshire; Hobthrush Hall, Over Silton, North Yorkshire, etc.), caves were often believed to be the homes of savage thyrsts and milder hobthyrsts or hobthrushes. Thyrsts (*thyrs* in Old English, *thurs* in Old Norse) were demonic giants or giant demons of Scandinavian or Anglian mythology, dwindling into the hobthyrsts or drudging goblins of the farm.

Unquestionably the best cave areas, in which caves have been valued for their scenic, traditional and romantic distinction, are the North Yorkshire limestone in the area of Ingleborough, Pen-y-ghent, etc., and the Derbyshire limestone. Both areas abound in what the cave specialist calls 'caves of debouchure', i.e. caves which have, or had, streams flowing from the mouth, which adds greatly to the charm and mystery of cave entrances, some of which may be coloured with orchids in early summer, hung with ivy, and filled with different colours of light according to weather and time of day.

Cedar of Lebanon

John Evelyn is credited with introducing this tree of the English country house, more than any other a tree of serenity (and status), towering and dividing and extending its horizontals. He wrote of it in *Sylva* (1664): 'But now after all the beautiful and stately trees, clad in perpetual verdure, should I forget the Cedar, which grows in all extreams . . . for so it does on the mountains of Libanus, from whence I have received cones and seeds of those few remaining trees. Why then should they not thrive in Old England? I know not, save for want of industry and trial.' Industry and trial followed; and enough Cedars of Libanus were about for Miller in his *Gardeners Dictionary* (1741 edition) to complain that they were too often being shorn into pyramids, instead of being allowed to grow normally, their branches level 'like a green carpet', waving with the wind, and making 'one of the most agreeable Prospects that can terminate a Vista, especially if planted in a rising ground'. Cedars of Lebanon suited the country-house feeling of actual and moral lordship, as if both Solomon and the Psalms were rooted within view of porch or portico – 'the trees of the Lord are full of sap; the cedars of Lebanon, which he hath planted'. By mid-nineteenth century, hall or manor-house and the Cedar of Lebanon were emotionally inseparable, as in Tennyson's *Maud* (1855), in which the lover addresses the cedar in the hall garden –

> O, art thou sighing for Lebanon
> In the long breeze that streams to thy
> delicious East . . .

Cefn

Common in Welsh names of hills and mountains, cefn means a back, or a ridge like a back. Thus Cefn-brîth (Clwyd) means literally 'Speckled Back'.

Celtic saints

Parishes, churches, chapels, holy wells, in Cornwall, Wales and border districts, often bear the names of unfamiliar saints, many of them outside the Roman calendar. These were the saints, holy men, or hermits of Celtic Christianity, who flourished in the 5th to 7th centuries, passing to and fro between Wales, Cornwall and Brittany, and having some contact with Ireland. While their Anglo-Saxon neighbours were still heathen, they founded little monastic communities, churches and chapels, not infrequently on islands in the Atlantic (*see* LLAN-). Celtic saints who have churches in Wales, Cornwall and Brittany include the great St. David of the 6th century, St. Peulin, or Paulinus (of various sites in Wales, where he was born, including Capel Peulin in Llandingad, Dyfed, and Llangors in Powys; St. Paul near Penzance in Cornwall; St. Pol-de-Léon in Brittany, where his bell named Hirglas and his head are preserved in the cathedral, and the nearby Ile de Batz, where he died in 573), St. Carantoc (of Llangranog, Dyfed; Crantock in Cornwall and Carantec in Brittany); and St. Patern (of Llanbadarn Fawr, Dyfed, in Wales; north and south Petherwin, in Cornwall; and Vannes, in Brittany). Irish saints tended to have more to do with their Gaelic brethren in Scotland and the north-east, though St. Brigid was honoured in Wales (as St. Ffraid), Cornwall, Devon, Cumberland (now part of Cumbria) and Brittany, as well as in Scotland and her own country (*see* BRIGID'S CROSS).

Centaur

Half horse, half man, the centaur was a Greek invention, or projection into imaginable form of stallion-like violence. But the centaur as bowman (Sagittarius), shooting an arrow at lion or dragon, appears in church sculpture as a symbol of Christ mounted on the horse of his vengeance against the Jews and slaying evil or harrowing hell. This centaur bowman is to be seen on MISERICORDS, BOSSES, capitals, FONTS, and TYMPANA (e.g. Kencott, Oxfordshire) over the main door into the church.

Chalk

A limestone (i.e. a rock largely made up of calcium carbonate from the shelled creatures of ancient seas, which can be 'burnt' or calcined into lime, or calcium oxide), varies in degree of softness and in tones of white and grey. The white Upper Chalk is a great scenery builder, or rather has been moulded by time into swelling scenery such as that of the Yorkshire Wolds and the downlands of Wessex and the south. Since it drains quickly and affords a dry living and was anciently covered with scrub rather than forest, chalk country was favoured by early immigrants, the first nomadic stock-raisers and farmers of the neolithic, the Bronze Age peoples who raised round barrows over the remains of their dead, and the Iron Age farmers who retreated into ramparted farm-steads or hill-forts. For some 5,000 years sheep and cattle have nibbled the grass of the rolling chalk hills and kept them characteristically smooth.

Driving through the countryside, it is often possible to tell at a glance where a chalky soil begins and ends from the disappearance or sudden appearance of certain obvious plants and flowers which dislike or like the presence of lime. Broom, foxglove and bracken are lime-haters, ending abruptly with chalk or limestone. Old Man's Beard demands lime and festoons tree and hedge along chalky or lime-stone lanes (especially in the south). The blue Meadow Cranesbill in summer beautifully characterizes chalk country, for instance around Salisbury Plain, and in Northern Ireland suddenly becomes abundant with the chalk around Dunluce Castle, Co. Antrim (where it is called the Flower of Dunluce). Chalk from gleaming hillside pits (which like chalk cliffs are always worth searching for fossilized sea-urchins and belemnites) has been quarried for centuries to burn into lime for sweetening acid fields and for making into the now outmoded lime mortar.

From the Middle Ages to the last century chalk for buildings – often known as clunch – was quarried in many counties from the hard, mainly greyish, beds of the Lower Chalk, sawn into blocks, and dried out before the building began. It lasts well (so long as eaves project far enough to keep it clear, more or less, of rain), and was much used with dressings of brick, or on a footing (in Wiltshire) of sarsen stone. But the rather dingy grey-white of such chalk in churches, farmsteads, cottages, turns a dingier grey in damp weather.

Chancel

The holiest and most secret part of the medi-aeval church, enshrining the main altar. Here beyond the chancel arch and the rood screen, which excluded the laity, the priest performed the offices. The reformers of the 16th century did not unite NAVE and chancel. They kept the screens and the wooden TYMPANA on which the Last Judgement or DOOM had been painted (these were usually destroyed towards the middle of the nineteenth century), but they brought the laity into the chancel for the celebration of the Eucharist.

Chantry chapels

The rich and illustrious who hoped to find a way to heaven would often leave property to establish and endow chapels of a special kind, to be built in churches around their tombs and effigies. They had much to fear after a possibly unvirtuous life. Prayer might help them to escape the avenging judgement of Doomsday, illustrated in the DOOM PAINTING, it might ease the cleansing journey of their souls through purgatory, which can be so well understood from the purgatorial terrors of the Lykewake Dirge (from North Yorkshire):

> If meat and drink thou ne'er gav'st nane,
>   Every nighte and alle,
> The fire will burn thee to the bare bane,
>   And Christe receive thy saule.

So in these chantry chapels priests were to chant masses for their souls, and keep candles burning, for all time, and thus help to bring them to eternal rest – *Requiem aeternam dona eis, Domine*.

Inside the great cathedrals and great Benedictine churches (Wells, Winchester, Salisbury, Tewkesbury, etc.) the chantry chapels are often, so to say, little churches inside the big one, little cages of stone, fan-vaulted, and walled with the most delicate tracery, enclosing prince, earl, bishop, abbot. In smaller churches there was seldom room for these separate structures, and in that event a chantry might be devised by screening off a part of the church or building a chapel out from the walls of the chancel or the nave. A very splendid chantry of this kind is the Beauchamp Chapel on the south side of St. Mary's, Warwick, built in the 15th century (the great age of chantries) around the tomb of Richard Beauchamp, Earl of Warwick, whose effigy raises two long-fingered hands to a carving of the Virgin Mary in the roof. Figures pray and weep for him round the tomb, and there was formerly a Doom painting on the wall. The Earl had directed in his will 'that there be said every day, during the world, in the aforesaid chapel . . . three masses'. But the perpetuity provided for in chantry chapels came sharply to an end in 1547 when they were dissolved and their endowments forfeited to the Crown.

Chapels

By strictest definition there are two chief kinds of chapel, the screened-off portion of a church or a cathedral, dedicated to its own saint (this may be a chantry), or the more or less private oratory attached to a palace, castle, mansion, college, almshouse, hospital, etc. The word derives from the *cappella* or cape of St. Martin

he Beauchamp Chapel in St. Mary's church, Warwick, is a superb example of mediaeval work. The monument to Richard Beauchamp, Earl of Warwick (c. 1450), in this CHAPEL, *shows him with his feet resting on a lion, implying that he died on the field.*

of Tours, which he divided with the beggar. This most revered relic was kept in a portable shrine, after which an actual building enshrining relics was known as a *cappella*, served by a *cappellanus* or chaplain. Particularly in the 14th and 15th centuries it became a mark of standing to have one's own private chapel (which the bishop had to license for divine service), along with a chaplain to do the serving. Of the many which survive, some are practically or altogether part of a mansion, e.g. the 15th century chapels at Bradley Manor (Highweek, Devonshire) and Cothele House (Calstock, Cornwall), both of them mansions belonging to the National Trust. Other chapels were built alongside the mansion. Where the mansion has disappeared, or dwindled to a farmhouse, the chapel may exist today only as a cowshed or barn.

Chapter-house

The often elegant and airy chapter-houses of CATHEDRALS or MONASTERIES were built for the daily meetings at which the members of the community discussed their affairs, confessed their sins and shortcomings, and heard the names of benefactors read out for remembrance. The proceedings opened with a chapter of the Scriptures or some religious book, so the meeting was the 'chapter' and the hall the 'chapter-house'. Always adjoining the church, chapter-houses were at first rectangular, as at Bristol and Ely. Cistercian austerity kept to rectangular chapter-houses (Furness Abbey, Fountains Abbey, etc.). But it was easier to hear what was said and read in the polygonal chapter-houses, vaulted with wonderful elegance and virtuosity from a central pillar, which were built in the 13th century.

–chester, –caster

Most often at the end of a place-name, –chester or –caster indicates usually that the place was a walled Roman town, within such walls as one still sees around the modern emptiness of Silchester (which means the *ceaster* with sallows, i.e. sallows growing on the ruined walls, as they still do). The Anglo-Saxon settlers borrowed their word *ceaster* from the Latin *castra*, a camp or fortified place, perhaps from the actual Latin they heard spoken in the cities in the earliest years of infiltration. Thus Bath was called *Bathanceaster*, the Walled City of the Bath or Spring; and 'The Ruin', the Old English poem which is probably about Bath, speaks of the wonder of the wall-stone, the hot spring and courtyards within the bright breast of the wall, which has fallen with the towers and the gates. Some former Roman towns or forts were renamed after the Anglo-Saxon headman (or so it seems) who moved in with his people. Chichester in Sussex is Cissi's *ceaster*, Rudchester (Northumberland), Rudda's *ceaster*.

Chest-tomb

Inside a church or outside in the graveyard a chest-tomb or tomb-chest is a stone box placed over a grave as a form of memorial on its own, which was suggested by the stone base which upheld the more costly effigy engraved on brass or carved in stone. Chest-tombs were set up in mediaeval graveyards, though not a great many are left. Yorkshire has two celebrated ones: the chest-tomb at Saxton (N. Yorks) over the Lancastrian leader Lord Dacre, killed near by in the battle of Towton, 1461, and buried upright alongside his horse ('The Lorde Dacres slayne at Towton feld is buried in Saxton church yard, and hath a meane tumbe' – John LELAND), and the earlier chest-tomb of the 14th century in Loversall church-yard (S. Yorks) near Doncaster, ornamented with patterns of window tracery. With changes of style and ornament chest-tombs continued popular till the early years of the 20th century.

Chine

Chine (from an Old English word *cinu*, a cleft) is used in the Isle of Wight and Dorset to describe curious, dramatically unstable little ravines cut through soft cliffs of sand and clay by streams running seaward. Slips and falls can turn a once picturesque chine (Blackgang Chine, for instance) into a muddy mess. Chines at Bournemouth were the habitat of a giant earwig now probably extinct in Britain.

Chipping

Chipping in the names of country towns usually means 'market place' or market (from the Old English *cēping*), as in Chipping Sodbury in Avon, a town serving a wide market area. A merchant or trader who brought his goods to a 'chipping' was a *cēap-mann* or *ciep-mann*, i.e. a chapman.

Chi-rho

Monogram of the first two Greek letters of the name of Christ, the chi and the rho, found on Celtic Christian monuments of the Dark Ages. In Cornwall, for instance, the Chi-rho is carved on the stone at St. Endellion, on Doyden Headland, commemorating a certain Brocagnus. The Chi-rho also occurs with the figure of Christ on the 4th century TESSELLATED PAVEMENT from Hinton St. Mary in Dorset, now in the British Museum, and on wall plaster of the Lullingstone Roman villa. This monogram preceded the cross as a common symbol of Christ and was said to have appeared to Constantine in a dream.

Choir

In the great conventual churches and cathedrals the choir is the part of the church where the members of the religious community had their stalls and sang the offices, divided from the nave by the choir screen (*pulpitum*). It was Victorian clergy who introduced into the chancel of the parish church what we now think of as the 'choir', complete with stalls of oak or pitchpine for surpliced singers.

Chrisoms

Chrisoms, or chrisom-children, are often imaged with their mothers or in their mother's arms on tombs and brasses, especially of the Tudor period: they are children who died in infancy, shown swaddled over the chrisom-cloth which surrounds their heads (and shrouded them under the swaddling bands). This chrisom-cloth, our modern christening robe, was worn for a month after the sacrament of baptism. In the service (see Edward VI's First Prayer Book of 1549) the child was first baptized with water, after which the priest 'put upon him his white vesture, commonly called the Crisome', saying 'take this white vesture for a token of the innocence which by Gods grace in this holy sacramente of Baptisme, is given unto the'. The priest then anointed the child with the mixture of oil and balm, which was itself the chrism, chrisom or cream (from the same word), chrisom coming to be used in short for both the chrisom-cloth and the chrisom-child.

*T*he CHI-RHO *monogram (above) is from the handle of a silver strainer which belongs to the earliest known group of Christian silver, dating back to the 4th century AD.*
A CHRISOM *on brass, (1520), which can be seen at Chesham Bois church, Buckinghamshire.*

The CHURCH TOWER *(below) of St. Mary's church, Stamford, Lincolnshire, has a distinctive broach spire which includes a profusion of gabled dormers.*

A CHURCHYARD CROSS *at Patrick and Columba, Kells, Co. Meath, Eire.*

Christ of the trades

A mediaeval painting on a church wall of Christ surrounded by hammers, axes, saws, scales, scissors, sickles, etc., and showing his wounded hands and feet and side, warned parishioners who wouldn't rest from their trade on Sunday of the sorrow they inflicted on Christ: their tools kept his wounds open and bleeding. There are examples at Hessett, in Suffolk, and at Linkinhorne and Breage in Cornwall.

Church houses

Church houses, built alongside church or churchyard, survive in some villages from the early 16th century. They were maintained by churchwardens for parish festivities, especially the church-ales on Sunday evenings, at Whitsun, Easter and Christmas, when the parishioners enjoyed strong beer brewed in the church house from gifts of malt, and sold for the upkeep of the church, the service books, etc., and for helping the poor. John Aubrey wrote of the spits and crocks which had been kept in the church houses, where the householders 'met, and were merry, and gave their charity', adding 'The young people were there too, and had dancing, bowling, shooting at butts, etc., the ancients sitting gravely by and looking on.' These church-ales (which robustly foreran church socials and bazaars) were frowned on after the Reformation by the Puritans and the magistracy, and within a hundred years church houses gradually disappeared, and with them the ales 'in the whiche with leapyng, daunsynge and kyssyng', according to a complaint made to Henry VIII, 'they maynteyne the profett of the churches'. Some church houses became ale houses pure and simple.

Church towers

These originated, not as defences or refuges, as one might think, but simply as a housing for bells lofty enough to float their sound to a wider circle of town or country. They were invented in northern Italy in the 9th century. A century later, before the Norman Conquest, the Anglo-Saxons developed our characteristic tower at the west end of the church, first of all by enlarging small tower-like churches. A new nave was extended to the east and the original lofty rectangular nave was heightened to a belfry (Barnack church, Cambridgeshire). From that beginning the western bell-tower rapidly became a looked-for and more or less essential element of every new church – if the builders could afford it. If they couldn't, they would equip a church with a small bell-cote or bell-turret on the western gable, as on many little Welsh churches. Technique was much improved by the experience of building castle towers after the Conquest, and bell-towers grew in height, splendour and architectural sophistication, especially in the 15th century in counties (e.g. Devon, Somerset, Norfolk, Suffolk) which became rich on wool and cloth. Central towers originated in the 'lantern' raised above the crossing, or intersection of nave, chancel and transepts in transepted churches, which would otherwise have been a poorly lit area of the church.

Spires capping a tower combine style, or Gothic feeling, with function. They were a sensible means of roofing a bell-tower in latitudes where snow was always a winter possibility, but they were also made to rise in a delicate thinness, so that in a late 13th or early 14th century church the spire outsoared the whole multitude of lesser spires or pinnacles, inside and out, which gave a Gothic upwardness or verticality to buttresses, gables, shrines, chantries, canopies, niches, etc. Spires in England were known as broaches from their resemblance to the mediaeval cook's sharppointed broach or spit, though 'broach spire' has come to mean the usually octagonal spire into which the square tower seems to contract, without the interruption of a parapet, triangles of masonry sloping and splaying inward from the corners of the tower to the spire itself.

Churchyard

Burial in the churchyard or burial ground of the parish cannot be denied to the corpse of any parishioner, no matter what he was in life, or what his beliefs were. The parish priest, or incumbent, owns the churchyard as he owns the church (both are part of his freehold), in joint possession with the parish church council. The council maintains it, the parson controls it. But he does not own the gravestones or other memorials. Every memorial belongs to him who sets it up or to his successor; who can take action of trespass against removing it or defacing it. By resumption from general custom the grass that grows on the churchyard and the graves belongs to the parson as a part of his endowment – which was of some consequence when parsons kept their own cows and horses and farmed their own glebe. Not infrequently – though it was against church law – the parson or sexton grazed animals in the churchyard, which in any case was not always well fenced. So well into the last century graves were pegged with lengths of osier and bramble. Though churchyards are consecrated ground, note that even now there may be fewer graves on the north side of the church, which was anciently regarded as the dangerous side more open to the activity of demons.

Churchyard crosses

From early times before the Norman Conquest, crosses were commonly erected in churchyards, usually on the south side of the church. There is some evidence that the churchyard cross descends from crosses originally set up to mark meeting-places for worship, churches afterwards being built alongside; but they were *de rigueur* in the mediaeval churchyard for the complex procession on Palm Sunday, which left the church carrying 'palms', preceded by a blood-red wooden cross and two banners. At a first station the gospel was read. The bloody cross then gave way to a silver cross carried in front of the Host and the relics which belonged to the church, and after a mass at the foot of the churchyard cross, the cross itself was wreathed with the palm branches, which might be yew, sallow, or box. A third station was made at the entrance to the church, where the Host and the relics were held up over the heads of the procession, everyone bending his head as he entered. The fourth and last station was made in front of the rood. The crosses are of many dates and kinds, wheel-headed crosses in Celtic areas, Anglian crosses with carvings up the shaft (especially vine-scrolls – 'I am the true vine', Gospel according to St. John 15. 1) in the north; and later and most frequent, crosses on tall shafts surrounded with steps, on a round, square or octagonal plan. Often only the steps and the socket-stone of the cross remain. Many were beheaded at the Reformation, since the shaft commonly upheld, not a Latin cross, but a tabernacle carved with 'Papist' images, i.e. a figure of Christ crucified on one face and of the Virgin on the other, often with a saint carved on each of the narrower sides. The plain or canopied niche frequently cut into the socket-stone was provided to house the pyx (containing the reserved Host) in the Palm Sunday mass.

Crosses were set up for other purposes outside the churchyard. Some along routes to church were spaced at intervals to give bearers a rest when they were carrying a corpse to a funeral. The corpse was set down at the foot of the cross and prayers were said. Some marked the limits of property, especially church property. Some marked a track across difficult country (crosses of both these kinds are to be seen on Dartmoor), or a ford. Some were set up in market-places. Other early crosses (especially of the wheel-headed Celtic type) are commemorative, such as the 11th century wheel-headed cross near Carew Castle, east of Pembroke, Dyfed, commemorating a King Maredudd.

Cider mills

Cider mills, with tall stone wheels which revolved on edge, singly or in pairs, in the circular trough of a round stone base, are often to be seen in cider-making areas of south-west England, and in Normandy, from which they were perhaps introduced in the 12th or 13th century, along with the word cider (Old French *sidre*). Wheel edge and trough are grooved. These cyclopean mills are often mistakenly called 'cider presses', though their function, with horse or formerly oxen drawing the wheel, which was attached to a central pivot, was to break the apples before pressing, the apples undergoing, like grapes in the *vendange*, a two-stage process of crushing followed by pressing under weights. In the southwest of England (as in Normandy) the mills are usually of granite.

Cirrus

(Latin for a lock of hair), our top cloud roof, five miles or so up, formed not of vapour, but of minute crystals of ice. Cirrus may spread out like a skin over the sky, taking brilliance and clarity out of a summer day; it may be in sheets, bars or waves, or wisps, may be frayed out into 'Mare's Tails', or appear to be divided into fish-scales or 'Mackerel Skies' (caused

A disused CIDER MILL *in a Hereford orchard, composed of a stone wheel and harness. The apples would have been crushed between two heavy stone wheels, to one of which a horse was harnessed and made to walk slowly round the mill as the apples were loaded.*

when layers of waved or barred cirrus criss-cross over one another). Sheets of cirrus are responsible for the great cloud haloes round sun or moon, the ice crystals catching the light. Note that lofty cirrus and clouds nearer earth often traverse the sky in different directions, impelled by different wind streams.

Cistercian abbeys

Such abbeys need to be emphasized in a country book, since the monks of the Cistercian order rejected town for country, and populous country for remoter valleys, which were wilderness in the great founding decades of the 12th century. Their aim was to pray and work in austere uninterrupted simplicity (though the heavier agricultural work was done by the more numerous lay brethren, not by the choir monks). The earlier ruins of the Cistercian abbeys in England, Wales, Ireland and Scotland (always dedicated to the Virgin) show how they rejected the over-complex and ornamental for a severe architecture with simple capitals and a square end to their churches (e.g. Buildwas Abbey, Shropshire). They preferred plain carving and plain glass, and preserved the rectangular CHAPTER-HOUSE. The valleys they discovered, cleared and cultivated, show a sunny balance between economic suitability and a delightful calm, which does seem to offset a little of their sternness: below, a well-watered level, neither uncomfortably wide nor claustrophobically enclosed; above, the hills which afforded sheep walks for their supporting trade in wool. This careful selection of abbey sites makes it pleasant and instructive to visit not only the abbeys which still have plenty to show of the claustral buildings (e.g. Fountains, Rievaulx, Byland, under Yorkshire hills; Tintern, in the Wye valley; Cleeve, under the sheep walks of Quantock; Melrose, in Scotland; or in Ireland, Jerpoint, Kilcooly, Holy Cross, Mellifont, Boyle), but to visit as well Cistercian valleys where little or nothing is left except stumps of masonry or green ridges under the level turf – and the stream or river which was essential to the sheep-ranching activities of the abbey.

Notice in the plans of the Cistercian abbey how provision was made – severity or no – for a 'warming house' between the REFECTORY and the monks' quarters, where the brethren defroze or dried their clothing after their winter work in frost and rain and snow. Warming houses can be seen at Byland and, better, with two great hearths, at Fountains.

Clapper bridge

A narrow bridge of stone slabs (see BRIDGES) or sometimes a stone causeway by a road.

Clay pipes

Clay pipes dug up in the garden, etc., may be dateable by shape and – sometimes – by the maker's initials, name or mark. Here is a rough guide. The pipes of Queen Elizabeth's day, when tobacco was taking hold, follow the Indian shape, the pipe which was passed from hand to hand. Bowls are small, not much thicker than the stem, and they do not have a spur or a projecting step underneath. After 1620 or thereabouts bowls become larger, often have an incised rim and always a spur or step. This is the pipe of the individual smoker, with its foot rest. Up to the end of the 17th century the plane of the top of the bowl slopes forward and is not parallel with the stem, as it is in pipes of the 18th and 19th centuries. Some clay pipes of Victorian date imitate the shape of the briar pipe with or without a spur under the bowl. Pipes are sometimes marked on the side of the bowl, on the step, or on the stem, with the maker's name, initials, or mark, and sometimes with the actual date.

The London Museum can usually tell you what the initials stand for, and where and when the maker worked.

Clerestory

In mediaeval churches, the upper part of the walls, especially along the nave, raised above the roofing of the aisles to provide extra window space.

Clints

The Yorkshire and North Country word for one of the peculiarities of the mountain limestone – exposed, more or less level, pavements of limestone weathered along the joints into cracks or 'grikes', which may go down quite a long way into the rock. (Strictly, clint, which comes from the Old Danish, meant the sheer cliff-like edge to such a pavement area.) Moss often turns the pavement into a firm, noiseless carpet. Woodland flowers grow

Over periods of time CLAY PIPES *changed and developed. They can be identified and dated by such features as the shape of the bowl, the presence of a pedestal or by their protruding spurs and stem.*

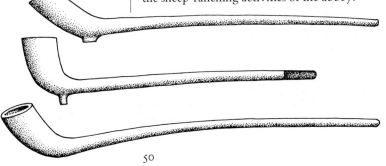

The ruins of Melrose, a CISTERCIAN ABBEY, in Borders, Scotland. Although it was founded in 1136 by David I on the site of an old monastery, most of the remains visible today date from the 15th century and include some remarkable decorative work and figure sculpture.

down in the shade of the grikes, from nettles to wood-anemones, bluebells, or even lilies-of-the-valley. Trees, especially lime-loving ash trees, grow out of the pavement, the surface roots tight like long claws around the divisions of the rock. After rain, the grey clints reflect the colour of the sky, and can turn deep red at dawn or sunset. Some of the most extensive clints surround the neighbouring mountains of Ingleborough and Whernside in North Yorkshire.

Clitters

A curiosity of Dartmoor and the Cornish moors, clitters, or clatters, are grey lichenous ridges or bands of broken GRANITE, large blocks and smaller ones, set at awkward angles. Walking or clambering across a clitter isn't easy, as anyone will know after an exploration of Wistman's Wood where the celebrated dwarfish oaks grow out of a clitter, or after searching a clitter for ferns. Clitters were formed by an ancient disintegration of granite outcrops in extreme cold, the blocks falling on to snowdrifts frozen hard against the tors, and shooting off downhill.

Cloister

By the cloister, the covered vaulted alley enclosing a rectangular yard or garth in the centre of a monastery or of the buildings of an abbey-cathedral, the monks could walk (though not talk – that was forbidden in the cloister) between their great church on the north side and the CHAPTER-HOUSE, the sacristy (where the vestments and service vessels were stored), the parlour (which was a small talking room), the day stair, the LAVER, and the REFECTORY, where they dined. The arcading

around the garth was usually glazed, so the monks were out of the wind as well as the rain. On the northern sunny side they read and worked at their carrels (see CATHEDRALS) during the afternoon. A cathedral cloister today, secluded, reposeful, leading nowhere, hung with 18th century and Victorian memorial tablets, and perhaps filled up with a cedar, gives a wrong and rather romantic impression of what used to be a busy centre of communications, pit-a-pat with sandals.

Clon-

In Irish place-names Clon- means meadow or pasture, from the Irish *cluain*: thus the ancient Christian centre of Clonmacnoise, in Co. Offaly, means 'pasture of Nóis's people'.

Close

MONASTERIES and their subsidiary buildings were shut behind high walls with a gatehouse and lesser gates – enclosed, that is to say, in a close, the word we use for similar precincts around a cathedral, where the clergy, as at Wells and Salisbury, followed the monastic example. According to wealth and size, monastery walls might enclose many acres (allowing room for infirmary, graveyards, fish-ponds, orchards, vineyard, dovecote, storehouses, etc.) or only a few.

Cloughs

In the moorland country of the north, Derbyshire, Lancashire, Yorkshire, etc., little rough steep-sided ravines, gullies, gutters, with a stream tumbling through the rocks.

Coade Stone

Remarkably hard, weather-proof artificial stone made from *c.* 1769 to 1836 in the factory of Dorset-born Mrs. Eleanor Coade (d. 1820) and her successors, at Lambeth. Using designs by neo-classical architects and sculptors, the factory turned out statues of nymphs and river gods, garden urns and vases, doorways, porches, gate-piers, reliefs to set in walls, chimney-pieces, churchyard table-tombs, church monuments, and even fonts – work for outside and inside alike. The quality was exceptional, and objects cast in this artificial stone (often signed E. and W. Coade, or Coade and Sealy) exist in houses and gardens, etc., all over Britain.

The composition of Coade Stone was a mystery until an analysis (*Architectural Review*, Nov. 1954) proved that it was made by heating china clays mixed with finely ground quartz,

A typically picturesque COB *cottage, with ivy-coloured walls – though the brick chimney is obviously of more recent construction than the rest of the building.*

flint and glass, no doubt an early outcome of Cookworthy's discovery of china clay and china stone in Cornwall.

Cob

Many cottages, farmhouses, farm buildings, garden walls, vicarages, even manor-houses, in Cornwall, Devon and Dorset, are made of cob, a mixture of earth and chopped straw (and sometimes cowhair or horsehair). The thick walls were built up wet layer by layer, often on a footing of moorstone or boulders; and were then whitewashed, as a rule, and given a water-repelling band of tar around the base. Once the thatch overhead has gone, cob rapidly washes down and away. But it can last for centuries. Fifteenth century portions of the manor-house at Trelawne, in Pelynt, in East Cornwall, were found to be of cob; a Dartmoor cob cottage was dated by a coin in one of the walls probably to the last decades of the 13th century.

Cockshoot

Cockshoot (or Cockroad) is one of the common minor place-names of the countryside, especially in old woodland or forest areas such as the Forest of Dean and its borders. The cock was the woodcock, the shoot or road was a clearing through which woodcock made their swift evening flight from wood to marsh, banging into nets stretched across the end of the shoot, which was also known as a cock-glade. Woodcock were taken in this way from the 13th century, or earlier, to the 18th century.

Coldharbour

Another of the common minor names of the countryside. Harbour in its mediaeval form often meant a place where one harboured, i.e. a shelter or an inn; its original Old English meaning was a place where an army (*here*) was harboured or quartered, just as *hereford* (Hereford, with a ford over the Wye, on the battle route to Wales) was an army ford; or a 'herepath' (often surviving as an ancient road name), a road taken by armies, i.e. an important through way. So it has been asked if the many Coldharbours had anything to do with inns or shelters along Roman roads. Coldharbour seems usually to have been a recently bestowed ironical name for a cold shivery place which in fact does not give any harbour or shelter. Yet sometimes the other explanation may apply, not only to Coldharbour, but to some places called Caldecote, a parallel name for a cot, inn, or shelter in cold places, and some called Folly (which does not always signify an architectural folly, and may mean a shelter made of branches). At any rate, in the Midland counties of Bedfordshire, Buckinghamshire and Hertfordshire the Coldharbours, Caldecotes and Follies have been plotted in relation to Roman roads (*Roman Roads in the South-East Midlands*, by the Viatores, 1964), with results which do suggest a connection (though not a Roman one) with the old road system, as if road shelters were not infrequently improvised.

Colonia

In Roman provinces a *colonia* was a town settled with those who had the full rights of Roman citizenship, in contrast to native towns. In Britain only four towns were of this dignity; York (Colonia Eburacensium), and three which were founded for retired soldiers of the Roman army – Colchester (Colonia Victricensis), founded in A.D. 49 alongside the native town of Camulodunum; Lincoln (Lindum Colonia), founded *c.* A.D. 92, for old soldiers of the 9th legion; and Gloucester (Colonia Nervia Glevensis), founded for old soldiers of the 2nd legion in A.D. 97. The word *colonia* survives in Cologne, which was the Roman Colonia Agrippensis.

Commons

A major relic of the ancient English system of husbandry, commons prevailed for more than a thousand years before the enclosures (*see* FIELDS) of the 18th and early 19th centuries – a system older than the Norman Conquest, older than the manors as they were organized after the Conquest, yet integral to them. Villages lived communally by crops and by livestock. Crops were grown on the strips which the villagers held in the open field, the livestock was grazed for much of the year on the undivided common. The common might belong to the lord of the manor (and may still belong to him, if he exists), but the villagers enjoyed the various rights or 'estovers' necessary to their livelihood, not only the right for each man to graze so many sheep, cattle, pigs, geese, asses, horses, but the right to collect firing, fencing, hedging, bedding for animals, and so on. Naturally it was the poorer land or waste land (as a common often appears to be to this day, with its rounded clumps of blackthorn or may or brambles, and its scattered oaks) – the land further away from the village, the church, and the hall, which did not repay

Dartmoor covers an area of over 200 square miles, much of which is privately owned. It was created a National Park in 1951 and, although the public is allowed access to it, only those eligible for 'common rights' can use the 'COMMON' land for dwelling or grazing.

cultivation. Common land is of all kinds, according to terrain: it may go with town as well as village, it may be heath, scrub, wood or semi-woodland, fen, or moor.

Communion rails

Communion rails were introduced from the open baroque churches of the Continent, and came into use in English churches late in the 16th century. They became the rule when altars were set against the east wall. This was first done in Gloucester cathedral: Laud, when he became Dean of Gloucester in 1616, having moved the altar as far east as possible. After the Reformation, the altar had either been left behind the chancel screen, the parishioners coming into the CHANCEL and kneeling round it for the Eucharist, or had been moved outside the screen into the NAVE – with unfortunate results. Dogs strolled into the church and lifted a leg against the altar. Schoolchildren, workmen, church-wardens used the altar as a convenient table. So it was moved to the far end of the chancel, against the east wall. Wooden rails, their uprights set close enough to keep out the offending dog, were built from side to side of the chancel. The railing set the altar apart, reminded the parishioners that it was God's table, to be approached with reverence, and also aligned communicants in a decent and orderly way, leaving the priest enough space to move between communicants and the altar. So altar rail became 'communion rail'.

Conjunctions

Conjunctions – near conjunctions – of planet and moon (especially crescent moon) or planet and planet, brief unfamiliar twinnings in the night sky, are something to watch for, even if devoid of their old astrological significance. One may look up at them without having to heed the sensibly sceptical remark in Gerard's *Herbal* of 1597, 'who would look dangerously up at Planets that might look safely down at Plants?' Astrologically a conjunction was fateful if two bodies were not necessarily close, i.e. if they were in the same longitude, not the same longitude and latitude, in one or another sign of the zodiac (the band of constellations along the sun's path, each with its sign).

Consecration crosses

Such crosses were a defence of the mediaeval church against demons and the Devil. Each inside a circle, they were carved or affixed in metal or painted, usually in red, on the exterior and interior walls, three to a wall, or twelve

One of the remarkable, broad-faced, broad-haired CORBEL *heads that support the inner voussoirs of the 14th century church of St. Ippollitts, Hertfordshire. The church was rebuilt in 1879, carefully re-using old materials and motifs, including the corbels.*

inside and twelve outside (though few complete sets now remain). Look for them at a height of seven to eight feet, where they were placed to be out of reach of damage or defilement. With each cross a bracket was fitted to hold a long candle. When the bishop arrived to consecrate a newly built or rebuilt church, he had to climb up a ladder to every cross with its tall lighted candle, and anoint it by tracing out the cross with a thumb dipped into chrisom (*see* CHRISOMS), saying each time *Sanctifecetur hoc templum,* Blessed be this church, while the clerics below sang a biblical anthem on the building of the Temple with precious stones. After this, burning incense was waved under every cross. Mediaeval pronouncements say the crosses were intended to scare away devils, to signify the victory of Christ, and to recall the Passion. The twelve candles were the twelve apostles who were the light which lit up the world.

Conyger

Conyger, the obsolete name for a rabbit warren (Old French *coninière,* a rabbitry, a place for conies), survives from the Middle Ages in such place-names as Conigre Farm, Coniger Hill, the Coniger, Conigre Copse, recalling the peculiar history of the rabbit in Great Britain. In the Middle Ages a rabbit warren was something to note (as rabbit burrows are again, now that myxomatosis, introduced in 1953, has reduced the rabbit population). Rabbits had been brought over from Normandy late in the 12th century and conygers established by lords of the manor, often near their manor-houses, sometimes on a warm hill slope, sometimes on an island with its convenient fence of water (there were 14th century rabbit warrens on the Dyfed islands of Skokholm, Skomer and Middleholm). Rabbits were reserved (warren is from the Old Norman French for a game preserve) long after they had spread from the conygers, and tenants were not free to kill the rabbits on their land until the passing of the Ground Game Act of 1880. Frequently conygers were made in the shape of long mounds – 'pillow mounds' – several of them close together, which can sometimes be detected on open ground. Or conygers may consist of a single mound hundreds of yards long; as on one north Wiltshire manor, where the warren, in a Conegar Copse, adjoins the demesne of the long-vanished manor-house, a mound more than 20 feet wide, more than 300 yards long, and still 4 to 5 feet high.

Coombs

Coombs are a characteristic land form in the Downs, short, wide, blind-headed valleys cut back by the sapping of springs along a line of weakness. Many were greatly enlarged at the end of the Ice Age when the sub-soil was frozen for much of the year and saturated masses of frost-shattered debris sludged out of the coomb mouth, to remain as fans of Coomb Rock, as well seen in the cliffs round Brighton. It has been proved that the whole of the huge coomb of the Devil's Kneading Trough, near Wye, in Kent, was cut within 500 years.

Corbels

Corbels (Old French *corbel,* a raven, because they were often cut to a shape suggesting the thick beak of a raven) are stones projecting from a wall to serve as brackets or supports. Whether single or in rows, they lent themselves to carving, especially in churches. Norman churches often have a row of corbels upholding a *corbel-table* (i.e. a course brought forward along the top of a wall to mask the eaves) carved into symbolic heads and grotesques, so that the eye runs along intrigued from one fantasy to another. For instance, the table or 'tabling' round the little Norman church of Kilpeck, Herefordshire (built *c.* 1140), is supported on corbels cut into heads and shapes, among them the AGNUS DEI, a rabbit with a hound, the hydrus entering a crocodile by the throat (Christ descending into hell, from which he will break out as the hydrus broke out of the crocodile), and even a SHEILA-NA-GIG.

Corn dollies

In most, probably all, parts of Britain, making corn dollies endured unselfconsciously until farming began to be mechanized in the 19th century. On each farm the last stems were plaited, as they stood, into the dolly. Sickles were then thrown at the dolly till it was severed. The dolly was preserved on the farm until spring and then given to the cows, or the horses when ploughing began. The custom was probably debased from a belief, attending the invention of agriculture in the Middle East some 7,000 years ago, in a fertility goddess living in the cereal plant and kept alive in this way through the dead of winter, despite the harvest. Names for the dolly are the Mare (Midlands), the Neck (south-west counties), the Kirn Baby (northern counties), the Hag (Wales) and the *Cailleach,* i.e. hag or old woman (Ireland and Highlands).

'Cornish' crosses

The kind of cross now frequently placed in graveyards outside Cornwall, made of Cornish granite, is not exclusively Cornish by origin. The ancient wheel-headed cross belongs to all the Celtic countries, and was set up in Cornwall, Wales, Ireland, Man and Scotland over a long period from the 9th century, or earlier, to the 13th. The wheel cross derived from the wreath-encircled form of the CHI-RHO (the monogram of the first two letters of Christ's name in Greek) which was carved on Gallo-Roman and Merovingian stone coffins in the south and south-west of France, an area with which the Celtic countries maintained traffic by sea.

Corn-kilns

In Ireland, the Highlands and the Western Islands, where the harvested corn had too much moisture, corn-kilns were used for drying the grain before it was ground in QUERNS or pounded into meal. Some were round pits in a hillside, lined with stone and roofed with thatch. A flue brought the heat up from a turf fire at a lower level. Others (e.g. several on the mountainside above the lakes of Glen Lough, Co. Donegal) consisted of floors dug out under boulders and slabs and smoothed with clay. Difficult to spot, such kilns were used to dry barley for making potheen (unlicensed whiskey) before the potheen distillers took to treacle instead of barley.

Corn weeds

Corn weeds, where they continue from season to season either because of poor farming or special conditions of soil and habitat, are among the antiques of the countryside. There is evidence that some were introduced *c.* 3000 B.C. by our first farmers, or scratching cultivators, of corn – e.g. White Campion (*Melandrium album*); and Corn Marigold (*Chrysanthemum segetum*), which originated in western Asia. The true Cornflower or Bluebottle (*Centaurea cyanus*), which has now practically vanished from cornlands, and the rapidly decreasing Corn Cockle (*Agrostemma githago*) are both species which prefer a warmer and drier climate than ours. They may be native, like the corn poppy, but the cornfield gave them reduced competition and an open habitat where they could endure as long as the seeds were not sifted out of the seed corn. In the

The Field Poppy (Papaver rhoeas) is a native CORN WEED *which grows from June to September. To see it growing in a wheatfield, as it is here, is becoming a less and less common sight.*

Mediterranean and Near Eastern civilizations the corn poppy was held in respect as the inseparable and essential companion of wheat, to the Assyrians. 'Daughter of the Corn', to the Latins a plant sacred to the corn goddess, Ceres. Other corn weeds provided marginal food, e.g. Corn Spurrey (*Spergula arvensis*) and Black Bindweed (*Polygonum convolvulus*), which both contributed to the last meal of the celebrated Tollond Man, hanged and thrown into a Danish bog in Iron Age or Roman times and recovered intact in 1950. Weld (*Reseda luteola*), actually sown with barley and oats by some 18th century farmers, was used as a yellow dyestuff as early as the neolithic period. Another corn weed to be regarded with retrospective concern is Stinking Mayweed or Mathen (*Anthemis cotula*), a plague-plant of farming before machines, which caused the most intense blistering on the faces, arms, and bodies of harvesters.

Corrie

A corrie, from the Gaelic *coire*, a cauldron, is a rounded, more or less cauldron shaped, hollow with steep sides scooped out in the mountains by ice and compacted snow in the Ice Ages. Corries often hold a small lake or TARN, such as Wilson's Pool under the scooped-out precipices of Cader Idris, or the lochan (small lake) of Coire an Lochan, under Braeriach in the Cairngorms, Scotland's highest lake (3,250 feet above sea level).

Cotswold stone

Cotswold stone, the material of churches, manor-houses, farmsteads, barns, villages, towns, roofs, bridges, stiles and field walls on and around the great Cotswold plateau, mainly in Gloucestershire, is an oolitic limestone which has been quarried for centuries, and was even used in the walling of neolithic chambered tombs. Much of the dry walling across the Cotswold slopes and levels is made from the top bed of rough shelly limestone, from the surface pits which are to be seen on every Cotswold farm. For the best building quarrymen have to go down to a deeper bed of freestone (*see* ASHLAR) often exposed in the Cotswold escarpments. The combination of limitless supplies of this good stone with wealth from wool and cloth gave rise to the Perpendicular, Tudor and Jacobean traditions of Cotswold building which persist unbroken. *Quarrere* and *quarelle*, the mediaeval words for a quarry, give Cotswold many of its minor place-names such as Quar Ground, Quarl Mead, Quarrel Hill, Slat Quar, Tile Quar (the last two referring to stone roofing tiles).

Cottage orné

Look for *cottages ornés* in districts to which well-to-do families of the 1800–1830 period were drawn by the summer charms of the picturesque, inland or marine, particularly in the resorts of south Devon and the Isle of Wight, and in, and along the edges of, Wales, a country which exerted a strong historical–picturesque pull on our Regency ancestors. The *cottage orné* inclines to length rather than height, ornamental verandas, ornamental 'Gothic' detail (e.g. BARGE-BOARDS) set off by white, smooth-surfaced walls, in which summer access is given by pointed French windows. They are frequently thatched, and windows may be edged with brilliantly coloured glass. MONKEY-PUZZLES (introduced in 1795) are sometimes planted in front. A picturesque exterior accorded with the picturesqueness of the (original) prospect and surroundings, the Regency or Early Victorian family enjoying an architectural simplicity-with-elegance, in the holiday simplicity of seaside or country life. Sidmouth, in east Devon, as a Regency and Early Victorian family resort (where shops specialized in polished jasper, agate, chalcedony and cornelian from the beaches, and families indulged in the marine biological searching of rock-pools), still retains a wealth of *cottages ornés*.

Country houses

The era of the great country houses we now enjoy visiting began with one Welshman, Henry VII, and ended with another, Lloyd George, in his revolutionary budget of 1909. In the Tudor security which followed the battle of Bosworth (1485), the mediaeval idea of the castle died away, and conditions of a damp and windy life inside defensive battlements and moats became unnecessary and unendurable. The old rich crept out of their crab-shells, and from uncomfortable strength joined with the new rich in surroundings of an enjoyable ostentation, which was to be contrived, according to the styles of each period, for some three and a half centuries. The carve-up of monastic spoils also gave a fillip to country-house living.

Every county shows its own examples. Readers will find an admirable brief conspectus of the way country houses developed in a single county, from the 16th to the 19th century, in W. G. Hoskins's *Leicestershire* (1957).

Twenty years of agricultural depression from 1875 to 1895 and changes in taxation – the introduction of death duties on agricultural land in 1894, the hugely increased death duties and supertax of Lloyd George's 1909 budget – undermined the accumulation and transmission of excessive wealth, and weakened a country-house class which had increased in idleness, intellectual backwardness and social irresponsibility. (In 1883 more than half of the acreage of England and Wales was owned by 4,217 people.) But as one walks around the more than 800 country houses now open to the visitor – see the yearly handbook, *Historic Houses, Castles and Gardens in Great Britain and Ireland* – one has to be grateful for the abilities of the architects and garden designers and the opportunities given to them from the 16th to the early 19th century, strongly as their work may contrast with the taste, or lack of it, which the landed interest so often displayed in their furnishings and treasures.

Crannogs

Crannogs are more or less round, or round, artificial islands in lakes in Ireland and Scotland, on which a homestead or farmstead was built. They were steadings defended by water instead of ditch and rampart. Some have been found (and a few excavated) in marshy ground which was once a shallow lake, others are still platforms on the water. A few go back to the Bronze Age, some to the Iron Age, most to the insecure time of the Viking raids. Some Irish crannogs (they are vastly more numerous in Ireland than Scotland) went on being used into the Middle Ages, or later still, house succeeding house. Crannogs (from Irish *crann*, a tree) were made by piling up peat and faggots and timbers and stones inside a ring of stakes (or sometimes a ring of stones). There might be a faggot causeway to the land, cunningly placed just below water-level; and a little harbour to one side of the crannog for dug-out canoes.

Cressets

What we now call a 'cresset' is not infrequently to be seen preserved in a church or the precinct of a monastery. Strictly, these multiple stone lamps should be called cresset stones, since they contain 'cressets', i.e. receptacles for holding fat or grease (French *graisse*, Old French *craisse*, so *craisset* or *cresset*, for a grease holder). Monastic and other cressets are small or large, portable or too heavy to move. A large cresset stone may have a dozen holes, a small one may be four-holed or three-holed. The cresset-holes were charged with fat from the monastic kitchen, and each one had a floating wick. Cresset was also the word for iron fuel-holders or fire-baskets held aloft on a pole, fixed, as in BEACONS, or capable of being moved.

Crofts and crofters

In ordinary English usage a croft is a small enclosed piece of land, a small field (*see* FIELDS). It is in the Highlands and Islands that croft, and so crofter, became special words. From the late 18th century the Highland peasants were subjected to a revolution upsetting the old life of their communities or 'townships': the landlords introduced sheep farming, the old cattle grazings were taken over, and, instead of tilling their arable in common, the Highlanders (often cleared into new barren townships along the coast) were allotted individual 'crofts' or arable smallholdings, becoming poor 'crofters', forced over the years into a system of husbandry alien to their traditions and their habitat, which led to poverty, emigration, and the depopulation of the old Gaelic lands.

Crop-marks

It was noticed long ago that the buried foundations of walls affect the look of the vegetation overhead, so making a kind of surface print, or plan. Contrariwise, deeper instead of shallow soil, richer and damper, on top of a now invisible ditch or pit produces darker green, healthier vegetation. In grass or corn, crop-marks of the kind reveal – from the air especially – the often complete and exact plan of neolithic HENGES, ancient enclosure sites, barrow sites, sites of farmsteads and fields of the Iron Age, Roman roads, lost mediaeval villages, etc.

Cross-legged knights

That all mediaeval tomb effigies of knights in armour with one leg crossed over another represent Crusaders is a notion at least as old as the 18th century. The crossing of the legs was supposed to be a sign that the knight had taken the cross. But, confined to English monumental sculpture, this was a way of varying the stiff, straight-legged posture of the unrobed effigy, a stylistic not a symbolical innovation which was introduced *c.* 1240 and lasted till *c.* 1350.

Crown-glass

Window panes with the blemish of a crown or knob in them are survivals, if genuine, of a pre-industrial technique which lasted until the eighteen-thirties. Up to that time window-glass was made by blowing out globes of molten glass which were then fixed by a knob of glass to an iron pontil or punty, or spinning rod, and detached from the blowing-iron.

With a hole in it where the blowing-iron had been, the globe was heated once more, and whirled on the pontil until the hole opened up, and the globe was transformed into a disc. Cutting the window-glass from the pontil left part of the knob or crown behind, as an unavoidable blemish. The cheapest panes were those with the crown.

Crucks

Crucks (i.e. crooks) are incurving timbers, pairs of reversed blades, each pair cut from a single tree, which form a series of arches upholding the ridge-beam of a primitive type of timber-framed cottage or farmhouse or barn. The gable of a cottage usually shows the end pair of crucks. Existing cruck cottages have generally had a storey inserted to provide for bedrooms, but as built they were halls open to the roof, and the point of the crucks, curving inwards from ground level or from a stone footing some way up the wall, was to provide space as little obstructed as possible down the sides and with plenty of room overhead. Distribution of cruck buildings (they are not to be found between the Humber and the Wash, in East Anglia, in Essex or across the Thames in the south-east) suggests that they continued to be built – up to the 17th century or later – in Welsh districts or where a British element had been left behind in the population, i.e. that the cruck technique was British in origin, and older than the Anglo-Saxon settlement. Even now cruck cottages are more plentiful than they are supposed to be, especially west of the Severn and in villages of the old forest country of the Midlands.

Crypts

Crypts were built to house the tombs and relics of saints and are found as a rule under the east end of churches near the high altar. Under the great cathedral churches they were made large to afford room for pilgrims. English churches with crypts include the priory church at Hexham (crypt of 7th century, built of Roman brick); Repton, Derbyshire (10th century); Wing, Buckinghamshire (11th century); and Lastingham, North Yorkshire (11th century), which housed the relics of St. Cedd.

Cuckoo pen

Small hillside or hilltop crofts or occasionally earthworks in Oxfordshire and especially Gloucestershire, and other counties, have the name Cuckoo Pen. A joke name – here the cuckoo was walled round, but flew away because the hedge was too low – from the folktale preserved in *The Merry Tales of the Mad Men of Gottam* (1630): 'On a time the men of Gottam [Gotham, in Nottinghamshire] would have pinned in the Cuckoo, whereby shee should sing all the yeere, and in the midst of the town they made a hedge round in compasse, and they had got a Cuckoo, and had put her into it, and said, Sing here all the yeere, and thou shalt lacke neither meat nor drinke. The Cuckoo as soon as she perceived her selfe incompassed within the hedge, flew away. A vengeance on her said they, We made not our hedge high enough.'

Cumulus

Cumulus (Latin for pile or heap), the large snowy clouds typical of the summer sky, snowy domes with a flat horizontal base. They are occasioned by bubbles of warm air rising in the morning, expanding, and then condensing their moisture as they cool. In the evening they melt innocently away. But these noble travellers in the blue sky may develop into thunderclouds (cumulonimbus), in which event dark horizontal bars of stratus or layer cloud show against their whiteness, the dome flattens in a lopsided way into an ANVIL CLOUD, the horizontal base frays and blurs, and often appears to be dropping veils of rain (VIRGA). They also change into the long rolls of stratocumulus.

Cursus

An unexplained kind of earthwork of *c.* 2500 B.C. (generally visible only as CROP-MARKS) consisting of low, more or less parallel banks 150 to 400 feet apart, enclosing what was perhaps a racecourse or a processional way. They are often associated with HENGES and long BARROWS, as at Stonehenge, where the (visible) cursus is $1\frac{3}{4}$ miles long and 300 feet wide. The most extraordinary is the Dorset Cursus, extending six miles across Cranborne Chase, one of the areas of Britain richest in archaeological monuments and enigmas. The best section runs on the south side of A354, the road from Salisbury to Blandford, from a little south of Pentridge to a long barrow on Gussage Hill.

Cwm

Welsh for a valley. It descends from an earlier British word which our English ancestors in the hill-country of the south-west borrowed from their British neighbours, and transformed into coomb. (In Welsh, w is an oo sound, short as in *cwm*, or long.) *See* COOMB.

Dale

A valley (from the Old Norse *dalr*), dale is generally a North Country word, the word which the Scandinavian settlers used in England (in the Lake District, the Yorkshire Dales, etc.), as they had in Iceland, where every valley is somebody's *dalur*, or the *dalur* of some particular river or natural feature. The English settler's word was *denu*, a dene, or *cumb*, a coomb (*see* CWM).

Danes' fences

In Northern Ireland, ancient field-fences of uncertain date built of stones between stone uprights (sometimes only the uprights remain). Like much else, they are popularly ascribed to the 'Danes', the 9th and 10th century Scandinavian raids and settlements in Ireland having left behind a vast amount of folk belief about the 'Danes', their violence and cruelty, their homesteads, their treasures, even their power to turn humans into frogs.

Date stones

Date stones are something to look for on farmhouses, or farmhouses which may have declined to the status of a labourer's cottage. With initials and the year neatly carved in raised lettering, set in the wall or above the main door or high on the chimney stack, such a stone – if the date fits – may indicate a new home built during the first great housing revolution between the fifteen-seventies of Queen Elizabeth I's reign and the Civil War, a period of increased rural wealth and comfort. The chimney stack in which the date stone is so often fixed is likely to have been the yeoman's especial pride; probably he had neighbours who were living in mediaeval hovels of a few rooms, or even a single room, with a roof hole instead of a chimney, and no glass in the windows.

Death's-head

A skull carved or engraved on memorials, brasses and gravestones as an image of death, over which one will triumph at the resurrection, common from the death-obsessed period of the Tudors down to the 18th century. According to the great *Oxford English Dictionary*, the expression death's-head is first found in Shakespeare, Falstaff calling Bardolph's face 'a Death's-head, or a Memento Mori', and Portia saying she would rather be married to 'a death's-head with a bone in his mouth' – she was thinking of that common form of death's-head, a skull with cross-bones.

*Wensleydale
is the largest
and least industrialized
of the Yorkshire* DALES.
*The view here was
taken near Hawes,
looking south over the
gentle hills traversed by
drystone walls. The
population of the North
Yorkshire Dales has
been supplied for several
centuries by a series of
small market towns,
such as Masham and
Askrigg, which were
connected by a network
of small roads. Many of
these roads still survive
and now carry motor
traffic, like the one in
the foreground of this
photograph.*

Deer roasts

Found in some parts of Ireland, Wales, Scotland and England, deer roasts are on the surface no more than hard horseshoe mounds, with the open end on to a stream, single or in a group. A few stones may be showing, small and broken, with a reddish look as if they had been many times in a fire. Mound, stones and stream indicate an ancient cooking site, though what was cooked was not necessarily venison. It has been found by excavation that the elements of a deer roast are a stone-laid hearth, within the horseshoe of burnt stones and charcoal, a tent-shaped hut or shelter alongside, and between the hearth and the stream a trough-like pit which was lined with planks or a hollowed length of tree. The trough, which would take as much as 100 gallons, was filled from the stream, and the water boiled by transferring heated stones or 'pot-boilers' from the hearth. Anyone who has attended a village pig-killing may surmise that what went on was not so much a boiling and roasting of meat as preparing carcasses for smoking and salting – scraping them and shaving them with the aid of the boiling water, and immersing the parts to be smoked in the warm brine, with which the trough would be recharged. Loins, hams, etc., would then have been smoked in the tent. The age of these cooking places (called 'deer roasts' from the Irish *fulacht fiadh*) is uncertain. Some may be as old as the Bronze Age, but the method may well have lasted into historic times. The many Irish examples are most of them in Co. Cork, Co. Waterford and Co. Kilkenny. English deer roasts have been found in Norfolk, Cumbria, Warwickshire, Shropshire (e.g. by the pool alongside the hillfort of the Berth, at Baschurch, north-west of Shrewsbury, where there are three side by side, cut back into the hill). In Wales they range from Gwynedd in the north to Dyfed and Glamorgan in the south. In Dyfed they are frequent on streams in the Llandilo area; and round Red Roses, south of Whitland, where four have been marked with stone pillars.

Demesne

From *dominicus*, 'belonging to a lord', the farm on a manor (frequently today the 'home farm') which a lord kept in his hands.

Deserted villages

Deserted villages, now recognized as a sealed-off store of information about how men lived and how society worked in the mediaeval countryside, are very abundant in the east Midlands (Oxfordshire, Buckinghamshire, Warwickshire, Leicestershire, Northamptonshire), in Norfolk, on the Lincolnshire Wolds and in the east and north of Yorkshire – in districts, above all, where it paid the landlords of the late 15th and early 16th centuries to remove the farmers, let the villages fall to ruin, and enclose the village FIELDS – the open fields – for sheep and wool. Thus, on 2 October 1494, sixty inhabitants were turned off their farmsteads at Bittesby, between Lutterworth and Watling Street, by the Earl of Shrewsbury to make exclusive room for sheep and cattle. Not all the villages taken over in this way were viable communities. Some had weakened and decayed over the centuries and could scarcely manage to maintain the open fields. The landlords gave them the *coup de grâce*. Other villages died of their own accord, because they had been badly sited on marginal land. A deserted village usually shows up on the ground. The main street and the side lanes are visible as hollow trenches under the turf. Small rectangles of the tofts, or bank-fenced house-places, and long narrow rectangles of the bank-fenced crofts behind them can be seen. There may be a windmill tump; there may be a few stumps of an abandoned church, or occasionally the church may survive (as at Lowesby, east of Leicester, where the village was reduced to the church and the manor-house). And round the deserted village, evening light, which adds shadow to the mounds, will also emphasize the old ridge-and-furrow (*see* FIELDS) of the farm lands which were made over to sheep.

Devil

As God's enemy and opposite and as the enemy of man, the Devil appears in many guises in church carvings and paintings – e.g. as dragon, ASP, AMPHISBAENA, BASILISK, APE, LION, FOX, wolf, and Leviathan, the great mouthed whale of the Book of Job (*see* HELL MOUTH). The first four, whether winged or legged or tailed or all three, belong to a serpentine family, and go back in the first instance to Genesis and Revelation. It is the poisonous nature of snakes and the story of the Fall which shape the Devil into a serpent – 'The serpent beguiled me and I did eat' (Gen. 3. 13); it is Revelation which makes him into a dragon – 'And there was war in heaven: Michael and his angels fought against the dragon . . . And the great dragon was cast out, that old serpent, called the Devil, and Satan, which deceiveth the whole world' (Rev. 12.

*T*his finely carved wooden boss in Westminster Abbey dates from the mid-13th century and depicts a battle between a man-lion and the DEVIL, in the form of a dragon.

7–9). The dragon slain by St. Michael (feathered archangel, with wings) and by St. George (saint, without wings) is the commonest church devil. Both St. Michael and St. George tread on the dragon (and on the lion as well). This is giving shape to sentences in Psalm XC in the Vulgate (in the corresponding Psalm 91, in the Authorized Version, the translation is different) which runs: 'Thou shalt walk on the adder [i.e. the asp] and the basilisk, thou shalt trample underfoot the lion and the dragon.' What is apparently – and very curiously – an example of the trampled dragon may be seen in the porch of Tredington church in Gloucestershire, in the shape (now a little crushed and broken) of an ichthyosaurus in one of the floor slabs – Satan trodden under the feet of everyone who enters the church.

Dewponds

Dewponds which no longer hold water are now more frequent than dewponds which function: one sees them as round, grass-grown saucers on the sheep uplands of Sussex, Hampshire, Wiltshire, Dorset, and a few other chalk areas. Such ponds – the word dewpond and the false notion that they are filled by dew were invented by sentimental antiquarianism in the mid 19th century – were specially devised to retain water on porous chalk hills. The pond-maker chose, where possible, a shallow basin which would collect the rain, and at the lowest point he hollowed a round pond which was carefully lined with impermeable clay and topped with a protective layer of flint or other stones. When the clay lining dries out and cracks, or when it is damaged, the 'dewpond' ceases to hold. There is evidence (see O. G. S. Crawford's *Archaeology in the Field*, 1953) that Anglo-Saxon and prehistoric ponds were dug (or enlarged) in naturally impervious pockets of clay, but no evidence at all of the ancient manufacture of artificially lined 'dewponds'. Many of them are modern, some may be as old as the 17th century. Fostered by sentimental poets and romancers including Kipling and Eleanor Farjeon, the myth of the dewpond was destroyed in A. J. Pugsley's *Dewponds in Fable and Fact*, 1939.

Dissenting chapels

Dissenting chapels in villages and hamlets and small towns have a tradition of simple building going back to the last decades of the 17th century. 'Meeting-house' describes them more exactly than chapel, whether they were built earlier by the Quakers or the Independents, or

later, from mid-eighteenth century up to the eighteen-forties and fifties, by the Methodists, and especially, after 1810, the new Primitive Methodists, whose movement fanned from Hugh Bourne's famous camp meetings on Mow Cop, on the Staffordshire–Cheshire border. A thatched meeting-house in the Wiltshire village of Horningsham, dated 1566, is said to be the oldest free church in England, built for Scottish Presbyterian masons employed between 1566 and 1579 on the great neighbouring mansion of Longleat. Otherwise there remain few meeting-houses older than 1700. Built by poor congregations who did not look for religion in externals or external symbolism (their imagery – see Bernard Manning's *Hymns of Wesley and Watts* – was in hymn and sermon), the typical chapel or meeting-house of the 18th century was rectangular, with pulpit, and a gallery for maximum accommodation. Frequently the rectangle was not so deep as broad, with two doorways in the broad front, one for men, one for women, who sat on different sides. Village or country Methodist chapels, with their communion tables and railed-off communion area in front of the pulpit, are sometimes of this plan, sometimes long rectangles – either way, like all dissenting chapels, plain enclosed spaces in which the preacher sees everyone and is heard and seen by everyone. Neo-Gothic and Victorian Renaissance came into the village chapels, but until the eighteen-forties and even the eighteen-fifties they usually retain the simple (and cheaper) round-topped windows derived from the larger Georgian or Regency chapels which were familiar in the large towns. In scale and material these unpretentious rural chapels are often appropriate to their site, which is not infrequently a waste corner no one wanted, an old cottage garden, or a length of road verge which was quietly appropriated. Village chapels often go in pairs, the first simple chapel, all that the infant congregation had been able to afford, and its later and sometimes pompous mid-Victorian or late Victorian replacement, the 'second chapel'. Nowadays the one is often a cottage or a store, the other a garage.

Dolmens

Dolmens are the stone chambers of neolithic tombs (*see* BARROWS), most of them originally covered with a mound of earth or stones, which has worn away in the course of some 4,000 to 5,000 years. Archaeologists do not like the word dolmen, which comes via the

French, apparently from the Cornish for 'hole stone', i.e. a capstone held up by the vertical stones, so that it leaves a space or hole underneath. But that is no reason why we should be bullied into dropping so useful and pleasant a term. The earlier word was cromlech – Welsh for 'bent flagstone'. English belief has connected dolmens with giants, fairies, goblins, etc. Irish dolmens were held to be giants' graves; also the beds in which the young lovers Diarmuid of the Bright Face and Gráinne (Grania) slept, when they were pursued by Finn after eloping from Tara. Antiquaries in the 17th and 18th centuries, familiar with the post-Reformation altar table, were convinced that dolmens were the altar tables on which British Druids had offered up human sacrifice (*see* 'DRUIDICAL' REMAINS).

Doom paintings

The Doom or Last Judgement, in churches, was commonly painted on a wooden tympanum fitting the chancel arch above the rood screen, or on the wall itself above the arch. The CHANCEL (beyond the arch) was reserved for the clergy in the Middle Ages: the laity, in the NAVE, looked eastward to the ROOD, or great rood, the figure of the crucified Christ above the screen, and saw, as a background to this earnest of salvation, the terrible prospect of the Doom or Judgement which awaited them – typically a scene in which Christ presides in majesty, flanked by the buildings of the Heavenly Jerusalem, while below him the graves give up their dead, and the naked souls are weighed by ST. MICHAEL and received by angels into bliss or forked by devils into the wide, fiery, scarlet mouth of Hell. Dooms were painted over at the Reformation, when the laity were admitted into the chancel for the Eucharist, and then often dismantled and destroyed in the Early Victorian period, when nave and chancel were opened into one long vista.

Dorter

In monastery ruins the dorter, or first-floor dormitory of the monks, on the south side of the cloister, has generally disappeared. It was a long room (which came to be divided up into cubicles), with a low window for each bedstead. The dorter communicated with the night stair (a wonderful and rare example of the night stair survives in the priory church of the Augustinian Canons at Hexham, in Northumberland), leading down into the south transept of the church. By this stair the monks

descended in the early hours before dawn, for the first of the offices. By the day stair, the sleepy monks came up from the cloister to the dorter for a rest after they had eaten in the middle of the day. The ruins of Cleeve Abbey, on the seaward side of the Quantocks in Somerset, preserve both the day stair and dorter.

Dovecotes

Free-standing buildings of stone, brick or even cob, dovecotes were appendages of a manor-house or the demesne farm which the lord kept in his own hands. Introduced from Normandy, the mediaeval dovecotes were round with a cone-like roof or beehive shaped. The circular shape allowed the internal fitting of a potence or pair of ladders revolving at a touch on central pivots, so that the fat squabs or young pigeons could be taken from the nesting holes quietly and without fuss. (Potences more often survive in the great dovecotes attached to châteaux in France.) Such round, tower-like dovecotes were known to the Romans – they are described in detail by Varro in his *Rerum rusticarum libri iii* written in 37 B.C. – and they extend to Iran, where they are still in use to provide pigeon dung for growing melons. Forbidden to

manorial tenants, dovecotes were part of the scheme of domestic economy (including CONYGERS, PARKS, FISHPONDS) enjoined by the scarcity of fresh meat in winter and spring. In a famous poem (see J. P. Clancy, *Mediaeval Welsh Lyrics*, 1965) the Welsh poet Iolo Goch (*c.* 1320–*c.* 1398) pictures the layout of Owen Glendower's manor at Sycharth, in Clwyd, the vineyard, the orchard, the lime-washed castle, the conyger, the deer park, the

> Fine mill on smooth-flowing stream;
> Dovecote, a bright stone tower;
> A fish-pond enclosed and deep,
> Where nets are cast when need be.

Later dovecotes were of various patterns, square or rectangular (frequently shaped at the top like a lectern), octagonal, and so on. It was the new turnip husbandry of the 18th century, allowing the plentiful overwintering of cattle, which brought them into disuse.

Downs

A *dūn* in Old English was a hill, varying in size from less than Oxfordshire's Faringdon (*fearn dūn*, or fern hill, the sandy, once bracken-covered, hill above the town, covered now with nursery plots and crowned with pines and

a PROSPECT-TOWER) to Snowdon, the snow hill or snow mountain (which the Welsh call *Eryri*). By the Middle Ages a *doun*, though often a hill, had also become a word for rolling sheepwalks, the 'turfy mountains where live nibbling sheep', the rainbow-arched 'unshrubbed down' of Prospero's interlude in *The Tempest*. More and more in the plural, downs became the special word for the rolling, smooth-nibbled, upland chalk country of the south, from Kent to Dorset—as in a poem written to be sung by shepherds to the Queen of England when she paused on the chalk uplands outside Devizes in Wiltshire, on her way back to London, on 11 June 1613:

> Our comfort is thy Greatness knowes
> Swarth faces, coarse cloth gownes
> Are ornaments that well become
> The wide, wild houseless Downes.

Drom-

Drom-, Droom-, Drum-, in place-names in Ireland and the Highlands, means a ridge, from the Irish and Gaelic *druim*. It can be a mountain ridge (the Welsh equivalent is *trum*, as in Trum-y-Ddysgl, Ridge of the Dish, 2,329 feet, or the huge whaleback of Drum, 2,528 feet, in north Wales), but usually it is the kind

A view of the Wiltshire DOWNS *from White Horse Hill, near Kingston Lisle, Wiltshire. The low-lying hills in the foreground can support crops and the higher land provides pasture for sheep to graze.*

An aerial view of a DROWNED VALLEY – *the mouth of the River Helford, in Cornwall.*

of ridgelike little valley hill geologically known as a DRUMLIN, a little *druim*.

Drove-roads

Drove-roads, driftways or drifts were the untolled routes by which cattle from the Highlands, cattle from Ireland (shipped over to Portpatrick in Dumfries and Galloway), cattle from Wales, etc., were driven to the English fairs and grazing grounds, where they were fattened before going on to the cattle-markets such as London's Smithfield. The great era of the drovers was the one of increasing English population from the 16th to the early decades of the 19th century, before the coming of the railways. Highland cattle and cattle from the remotest of the Islands – especially after the Union of the Kingdoms in 1707 – took the driftways through the glens and over passes to great Lowland 'trysts' or fairs, especially at Falkirk and Crieff, north-east of Glasgow, where sellers and dealers met. Shod with cues, crescent-shaped shoes for each segment of the hoof, the cattle made ten to twelve miles a day; and the long journey continued slowly down the length of England, principally to the great

October fair on Bullock Hill at Horsham St. Faith, north of Norwich (the last St. Faith's Fair was held in 1872), from which the cattle were distributed to the fattening meadows. Cattle from north Wales lowed their way to Barnet Fair, 'the largest in England for horned cattle', north of London. Cattle from south and central Wales went to fattening grounds on the Midlands side of the cattle fairs at Tewkesbury, from which Barnet Fair could easily be reached. The drovers kept to the free roads, including the old green roads and tracks, avoiding as far as possible the new gated turnpikes which they could use only by paying a toll per beast. Celebrated drove-roads include the green and now lonely Sewstern Lane (also known as the Drift) along the Leicestershire – Lincolnshire border, used by Scottish drovers *en route* for Stamford and the Midlands, and the Welsh Road, now a minor road, going across Warwickshire from Kenilworth south-east into Northamptonshire, and used by droves and drovers from north Wales. Inn names (e.g. The Drovers Call, The Highland Laddie, The Scotsman's Pack) often indicate drovers' routes or destinations.

Drowned valleys

Drowned valleys, which make some of the most placid of estuarine scenery (e.g. the tidal waters of the Fal and the Fowey in Cornwall, the Dart in Devonshire, Milford Haven, Solva and Porth Clais in Dyfed, and the long inlets in the south-west of Ireland), are the results of shifts in the relative levels of land and sea. The formation of the great ice-sheets of the glacial period lowered the sea level and the rivers cut their valleys down steeply to a lower depth, only to have them drowned or flooded inward from the mouth when the sea level rose at the melting of the glaciers, coupled with some tilting and lowering of the land. The visible sides of a drowned valley or 'ria' (the Spanish word for such river mouths along the north coast to the corner of Spain) show the profile one finds when a river valley has been flooded for a reservoir.

'Druidical' remains

'Druidical' remains do not exist. As late as the nineteen-thirties the B.B.C. broadcast a talk connecting Stonehenge with the Druids, and 'druidical' still creeps into daily journalism and some guidebooks as an adjective for stone circles and tombs. Not much is known of the historical Druids. Fewer than twenty classical authors mention them as a class of supreme hierophants in Gaul, where they were suppressed by the Romans. Caesar, in *De Bello Gallico*, is the chief authority. They were variously said to believe in the transmigration of souls, to sacrifice murderers, to study the objects of the night sky, to instruct candidates in lonely valleys and caves, and to believe in the sanctity of OAK and MISTLETOE (especially mistletoe which grew, as it rarely does, on oaks). Caesar wrote that the Druids originated in Britain. Tacitus records the military slaughter of the Druids of Anglesey in A.D. 60, and the felling of their sacred woods. Druids in the Irish sagas, such as the story of Diarmuid and Grania, show the importance of their role in Ireland before Christianity.

For patriotic reasons, French, and then English, scholars in the 16th century exalted the Druids as witness that their ancestors had believed so early in the immortality of the soul. Tudor and Jacobean antiquaries became more curious and speculative about British origins and ancient monuments; and before the end of the 17th century Druids and stone monuments between them supplied complementary answers to the two questions of where these once powerful priests conducted their rituals and what had been the function of stone circles and DOLMENS. In 1695 it became widely known that the Wiltshire antiquary and F.R.S. John Aubrey considered Avebury and Stonehenge (*see* HENGES) to have been temples of the Druids; and by this time dolmens or cromlechs were thought to have been Druid altars. Before long, the bearded, venerable, patriarchal, philosophical long-robed, mistletoe-slicing Druids were made responsible not only for circles and dolmens, but for STANDING STONES, LOGAN ROCKS, ROCK BASINS, even caves. In 1747 the architect John Wood of Bath convinced himself that Bath, with its hot spring, had been the seat of the original Arch-Druid, that his under-Druids had their headquarters in the stone circle of Stanton Drew, near Bristol (*Drew*: evidently Stanton of the Druids – though it was really the Stanton, or 'Stone farm', which had belonged in the 13th century to a man named Drogo). He also thought that the stones of Stanton Drew had been arranged as 'a stupendous Model of the Planetary World', and had been dug out of the great cavern of Wookey Hole in the Mendips, in the course of enlarging the cave where the Druids conducted their initiations.

Outlined on the backward horizon, and lit both by their wisdom and sacrificial flames, Druids conveniently filled a vacuum in the mind. A more sceptical outlook in the 19th century began the divorce of Druids from 'Druidical remains', which was completed when archaeology in this century showed that dolmens and Avebury belonged to the neolithic era and Stonehenge mainly to the Bronze Age, antedating by many centuries the Iron Age arrival of Celtic peoples in Britain. Perhaps some traces of 'druidical' thinking are still present in archaeological insistence that HENGES must have had to do with ritual and religion. For the Druids and the Druid mania, read Sir Thomas Kendrick's *The Druids*, 1928; A. L. Owen's *The Famous Druids*, 1962; and Stuart Piggott's *William Stukeley*, 1950.

Drumlins

Drumlins are small, rounded, ridge-like and egg-like hills of glacial drift, of which a congregation or swarm may be found in a once glaciated valley, each egg-like drumlin following the direction of the ice-flow. In early summer the grass on drumlins is often pink with orchids, ragged robin or bistort. Drumlin is an Anglo-Irish word (a little *druim*, or ridge), and drumlins abound in fantastic

number across the north of Ireland from
Down to Sligo, interspersed there as elsewhere
(Scotland, Yorkshire, etc.) with eskers (from
the Irish *eascra*. The Scottish word for an esker
is a kame, i.e. a comb), longer narrow ridges of
sand and gravel which formed the beds of
streams in the melting glaciers.

Drystone walling

Drystone walling – 'dry' because no mortar is
used – depends upon ready supplies of loose
surface stone, or stone which can be quarried
without too much trouble, and is of much
greater antiquity than one would think. The
essence is gravity and good bedding, an inter-
placing of the stones, whether they are flattish
or lumpy, so that weight, friction and position
hold them in place without an inclination to
spread. Even if the foundation sinks, and the
wall with it, the stones remain interlocked and
the wall is undamaged. It was said that every
stone 'did its duty by its neighbour'. Nowadays one sees old or new field walls in which
this principle has been neglected. The top
course has been fixed with cement, the wall has
sunk, and the cemented course has remained
unsupported in the air and has then collapsed.
Very neat drystone walling occurs in neolithic
chamber tombs, reaching an extraordinary
refinement and exactitude in the great tomb of
Maeshowe in Orkney. Down the centuries
drystone techniques remain familiar in Iron
Age and Dark Age buildings in the stony
areas – often the fringe areas – of the British
Isles, in RAMPART FARMSTEADS, BROCHS,
BEEHIVE HUTS, etc.

Where surface stone is abundant, prehistoric
field fences were sometimes dry-built (there is
evidence of prehistoric field divisions on the
Cotswolds), sometimes with smaller stones
infilled between uprights, only the uprights

now remaining. Bronze Age alignments of this kind can be seen, for instance, in the granitic Isles of Scilly, some of them, owing to a later submergence which divided a large island into small islands, continuing from a heathery hill-side down under the sea. To pile up stones is less trouble than to dig and pile up earth, which is one reason for the abundant stone-walling in Ireland where the agricultural and social system demanded small plots around the homestead. Moreover, such plots needed to be cleared of stones, which was conveniently done by building them into walls.

In England the fillip to drystone field wall-ing came with the enclosures of the 18th century and the abandonment of the old system of open field and common, when the Cotswold plain was divided up with oolitic limestone walls of the most sophisticated craft, the COTSWOLD STONE having been quarried from just below the surface. The same revolu-tion subdivided the mountains and moors of the Craven district (North Yorkshire) into its immense geometric grid of walls of grey limestone derived not from quarrying, but from the naturally split layers of limestone 'pavement'.

Dun-

In Scottish place-names, Dun- (Gaelic *dùn*, *dùin*) means a defended site, large or small, historic or prehistoric; as in Irish place-names, Dun-, Down-, Doon-, Don-, from Irish *dùn*, e.g. Downpatrick, which is St. Patrick's Fort.

Dunes

Hillocky ridges of sand blown up from sandy bays and beaches, dunes are great engulfers – and revealers – of the past. Piling up to a depth of fifty or sixty feet and moving inland (though nowadays they are usually controlled and fixed), they have buried prehistoric settle-ments, Roman roads, Dark Age and medi-aeval churches and villages, etc., which have sometimes come to light again with sub-sequent breaching and erosion. Examples in-clude the neolithic settlement of Skara Brae, at Sandwick, in Orkney; in south Wales, an old church lost in Penmaen Burrows in 1528 and rediscovered in 1861, Theodoric's Hermitage, covered by Crymlyn Burrows in 1227 and found in 1898, and the old borough of Kenfig, with a stretch of the Roman road from Cardiff to Neath, lost under Kenfig Burrows in 1344; and in Cornwall, the little Dark Age church of St. Piran, overwhelmed by Perran Sands and abandoned about 1100, found again in 1800

and then in 1910 encased in concrete, among its ragwort yellow dunes.

The words for dune (itself a sandhill word we borrowed from the Dutch) vary around the coast. Dunes are 'burrows', usually, from the Old English *beorg*, a hill. In Norfolk around Holkham and Scolt Head, they are 'meols' or 'meals', which is the Norseman's name (Old Norse *melr*), to be found on the Lincolnshire coast (Ingoldmells, i.e. Ingiald's dunes), and across country on the Lancashire coast (North Meols, Cartmel). In Cornwall a dune is a 'towan', in Wales a *tywyn* or *towyn* (along the sand-blown coast of south Wales

English 'burrow' and Welsh *tywyn* and *towyn* co-exist on the map). Along the Northumberland and Scottish coasts dunes are 'links', from the Old English *hlenc*, a ridge; which – since the Scottish speciality of golf was played on the stabilized dunes of the Firth of Forth – has given us the term (golf-)links. The advancing, devouring action of dunes can be understood if one looks at them in profile. Towards the prevailing wind they have a more or less gentle incline, with a steep slope away from the wind. The sand is blown up the incline, and drops down the slope, so that the dune all the while drives forward.

Duns

Duns in Scotland (*see* DUN-), in archaeological usage, are fortresses or little fortified homesteads of a special kind scarcely less fascinating than the BROCHS, to which they may be related. They are ovals or circles as a rule of drystone walling, forty to fifty feet in diameter. The walls are very thick, sometimes with galleries inside them, and steps up to the top of the wall; and corbelled entrances which had barred wooden doors. Often they are perched on outcrops of rock, on windy knolls, ridges, headlands, which were difficult to attack and gave a good view of likely

The crests of the sandhills seem almost to be mirrored in the crests of the waves along these sand DUNES *at Winterton-on-Sea, near Yarmouth, on the Norfolk coast.*

attackers. Duns occur from Dumfries and Galloway in the south-west, up the west side of Scotland to Strathclyde, Tayside, the Hebrides and the Highlands. They seem to have been built first of all in the Iron Age, though several of them (perhaps most of them?) went on being used in the Dark Ages or later still. Should you care to visit one in *situ*, remember to ask to be guided to the 'doon', not the 'dun' as in dunderhead.

Dykes

In the shape of earthen dykes the sense of property, communal or more or less personal, has scarred most areas of Britain. A dyke is negative and positive: if you dig a trench, you leave a ridge; if you build a ridge, you leave a trench. With the two together, if the trench is deep enough, the ridge high enough, you create a very effective defence-cum-boundary – at any rate, a permanent passive defence (that does not have to be manned all the while) against the wholesale driving off of herds and flocks, and a boundary which tells each population where they ought to be and stay.

There are pre-Roman dykes on the chalk grazing lands of Wessex (e.g. Grim's Ditch, on the Dorset side of Salisbury) and East Yorkshire. These are rather to be thought of as remains of outsize field fences or ranch fences, as old as the late Bronze Age. Also in the late Iron Age, dykes were built in front of Belgic settlements (Wheathampstead, Colchester, St. Albans), and to bound or defend grazing pounds in Oxfordshire (another Grim's Ditch) and Sussex.

The prototypes of the greater running earthworks were Hadrian's Wall of seventy-two and a half miles across the waist between the Tyne and Solway Firth, built A.D. 122–8, part in turf (later rebuilt in stone), part in stone, and maintained for two and a half centuries; and to the north again, across the narrower waist between the Firths of Forth and Clyde, the turf-built Antonine Wall (A.D. 142) of thirty-seven miles, ultimate defence of the Roman Empire, which now shows more as trench than rampart. These were *limes*, which were built along other bounds of the Roman Empire, defensive limits or frontiers, differing from the crude dykes of later centuries less in basic function than in engineering skill and elaborate military arrangements for watch and ward.

Both these great Roman works exemplify one thing about community or property dykes: that the ditch or trench is on the outside, or far side, from which trouble was to be expected (the ditch to the north of Hadrian's Wall was 27 feet wide, the ditch north of the Antonine Wall 40 feet wide and 12 feet deep).

The great phase of dyke building came in the time of the Anglo-Saxon kingdoms before there was a united England, English ditch and rampart boundaries to explore including Wansdyke, in its Wiltshire downland lengths; Offa's Dyke; and the immense East Anglian dykes.

Wansdyke (*Wodnes dic*, dyke of the god Woden) used to be thought a single earthwork running from Wiltshire into Somerset, but it seems to divide into two separate earthworks, an eastern dyke of about fifteen miles in Wiltshire (particularly bold and big on either side of A361, the road from Beckhampton, near Marlborough, to Devizes) and a western dyke of seven miles in Somerset. In its eastern portion it has been explained as a sub-Roman or British work of the 5th century built to keep Saxon settlers in the Thames valley out of the valuable grazing and corn lands of Salisbury Plain. But the eastern portion may have been built *c.* 592, across the Ridgeway, as a boundary between two West Saxon territories; and the western portion later still, *c.* 628, across the old Roman road of the Fosse Way, to protect West Saxons from Mercians.

Offa's Dyke (very fine on bald hills near Clun in Shropshire) divided Mercian from Welsh territory for more than 120 miles, and was the work of Offa, king of Mercia, *c.* 785 (ditch on the Welsh, or west side). By keeping the Welsh and Mercians apart it seems to have ended a long period of intermittent warfare.

The East Anglian dykes, short but extraordinarily impressive (Devil's Dyke on Newmarket Heath, Fleam Dyke, slap across the Icknield Way, the modern A11 to Newmarket), were probably built by the East Angles in the 7th century to keep the Mercians from raiding into their territory up the Icknield Way (ditches on the Mercian side).

Irish dykes of the same structural family are the long Black Pig's Dyke, or Black Pig's Race, or Worm Ditch or Dúnchladh (variously ascribed to a dragon, or worm, and a supernatural pig), which nearly cuts off Northern Ireland by a wrigglesome route from Castleblayney in Co. Monaghan to Bundoran in Co. Donegal (ditch on the south side); and the Danes Cast (good stretches south of Armagh, and near Scarva).

A characteristic of all these later dykes is that the builders stopped short when they came to terrain or natural features (often existing no longer) which served on their own account as boundary or defence. The Cambridge dykes blocked the dry open passage between thick forest and soft fen; the Black Pig's Dyke often breaks off at a lake; Offa's Dyke and Wansdyke are gapped in similar ways.

Eagles

Eagles, carved in churches (e.g. on 15th century FONTS, or as the bird of LECTERNS, holding up the Bible), symbolize St. John the Evangelist. The four beasts around the throne (Revelation 4. 6, 7) were identified with the four evangelists, and the fourth 'was like a flying eagle'. The symbolic message of the eagle was enriched from St. John's Gospel and the mediaeval Bestiary. The Gospel opens with the Word, and with the Light, the Bestiary tells how the eagle renews itself in old age by flying up and gazing into the sun (which was Christ), burning away its dim-sightedness and old feathers, and then flying down and dipping itself in the freshness and purity of a fountain.

Eagres

Eagres, or bores, rush up the Severn and the Wye, the Humber, Trent and Ouse, and the Solway Firth (and the Amazon, *inter alia*). The incoming tide or tidal front, momentarily checked in the shallows by the down-flowing river water, rears up from shore to shore and then runs noisily forward as a tidal wave or series of waves. Eagre is the Old English *ēgor* or *ēagor*, a poetical word for a flood, or full tide, appropriate to the heroic nature of the inland wave; it gives its name to Averham in Nottinghamshire, anciently *aegrum*, 'at the floods', which stands, with its church, near the uppermost limit of the Trent tides and eagres. Bore is from the Old Scandinavian *bara*, another poetical or heroic word, meaning wave or billow. The advance of a bore is a strange, intimidating thing to see, 'equally terrible', wrote Thomas Fuller in his *Worthies of England* (1662), 'with its flashings and noise to the seers and hearers, and oh, how much more then to the feelers thereof'. On the Severn it is seen at its best along the eight miles below Gloucester. F. W. Rowbotham's *The Severn Bore*, 1964, an admirable natural history (and time-table) of the great wave, instructs one on how to avoid the crowds and observe the bore in solitude. It is perhaps most dramatically seen when it appears all of a sudden round a bend like a second river on the river's back, and thrusts angrily yet smoothly up the narrows with all the tide behind it. The highest and most formidable of the Severn bores have their double occurrence on about twenty-five days of the year, impelled by the high equinoctial tides of February to April and August to October. The eagre on the Trent, impressive (but less so than the Severn bore), is best watched where the Roman road from Lincoln to Doncaster crosses the river at the Roman station of Segolecum – Littleborough, in Nottinghamshire, some eight miles east of East Retford.

Earthquakes

A visitor to Little Wigborough church, standing alone in the very mild low coastland of Essex, will read with surprise a brass tablet saying that the tower was overthrown by an earthquake in 1884, and rebuilt. (A shattered gravestone remains from the fall.) This was the most severe British earthquake on record, the Colchester Earthquake, which damaged twenty churches and more than 1,200 buildings, caused earth cracks across Mersea Island, and necessitated a Lord Mayor's Fund to help with the rebuilding. Most British earthquakes (more than 1,200 have been recorded since A.D. 974 – see Davison's *History of British Earthquakes*, 1924) have been due to slips along a fault, e.g. along the Great Glen Fault in the Highlands, which produced the sharp Inverness Earthquake of 1816, and the Highland Border Fault, which has made the small country town of Comrie, between Crieff and Loch Earn, in Tayside, the most earth-rocked place in Britain (though the rocking has seldom been severe). Earthquakes are several times mentioned in the *Anglo-Saxon Chronicle* (e.g. one on the eve of Michaelmas, 1119, felt most of all in Gloucestershire and Worcestershire). If few people have ever been killed, churches especially have suffered. An earthquake of 1185 cracked the fabric of Lincoln cathedral. St. Michael's church on Glastonbury Tor in Somerset was overthrown in 1275 (11 September), and a shock in 1248 brought down the vaulting in Wells cathedral. Effects have been various. British earthquakes have been marked by 'seiches', or oscillations of water surfaces (one of the Comrie earthquakes, in 1789, cracked the ice on an ornamental water). A shock in 1580 brought down part of the cliffs at Dover. The sharp earthquake in north Wales in 1903 set the stones rolling on screes in the Snowdon neighbourhood. The

Hereford Earthquake of 1896 (17 December, 5.32 a.m.) knocked down chimneys and was felt over 115,000 square miles: 'Cats noticed the shock to a distance of 22 miles, cattle to 34 miles, horses to 83 miles, and poultry to 91 miles. Dogs barked at a distance of 109 miles. Small birds were frightened at 108 miles, and pheasants crowed at 145 miles' – and roosting birds were shaken out of the trees and killed by falling in their sleep to the ground. Earthquake sounds in Britain have been noticed as being variously like blasting or gunfire or thunder, the moaning and roaring of the wind, the quick staccato passage of wagons or heavy traffic and so on.

Earth-shine

Dorothy Wordsworth in her Grasmere Journal for 8 March 1802, wrote of the exceptionally strong earth-shine or earth-light she had just seen on the moon, i.e. the faint illumination of the dark portion of the moon, between the arms or cusps of the new moon, by light reflected from earth: 'On Friday evening the moon hung over the Northern side of the highest point of Silver How, like a gold ring snapped in two, and shaven off at the ends, it was so narrow. Within this ring lay the circle of the Round Moon, as *distinctly* to be seen as ever the enlightened moon is. William observed the same appearance at Keswick, perhaps at the very same moment, hanging over the Newland Fells.' The terms 'earth-light' and 'earth-shine' for this curiously moving phenomenon were coined after her time: she knew it, and Samuel Palmer, who made several imaginative drawings of crescent and earth-shine some twenty-three years later, knew it, as the Old Moon in the New Moon's arms, and it was considered the surest sign of bad weather, of the moon storing up and then unloading her moisture (as in the ballad of Sir Patrick Spens, where it foretold the dark sky, the loud wind and the fatal gurliness of the North Sea). What appears to us as a faint light on darkness is the moon's counterpart of our own moon-light or moon-shine, earth-light on the moon being much stronger than moon-light on the earth and making itself just visible to us, in return, across some 239,000 miles. But the intensity of earth-shine varies according to the condition of earth as a reflector.

Easter sepulchres

In churches a cross, an image of Christ, and, on the breast of the image, the reserved Host, were sadly 'buried' on Good Friday, the day of the Crucifixion, in an Easter sepulchre in the chancel. Candles were lit around the sepulchre, watchers kept vigil. Then on Easter Day, the happy day of the Resurrection, the Host and the Christ were taken out, and carried to the altar, to the sound of an anthem. The Easter sepulchres were usually separate structures of wood, very richly decorated and coloured. But in some churches a permanent sepulchre was built into the chancel wall, sometimes elaborately carved with foliage, the three sleeping soldiers, the three Marys, the Resurrection, and the Ascension.

Echoes

Echoes, especially multiple or polysyllabic ones, were much sought after by the natural historians and county writers of the 17th and 18th centuries. John Aubrey complained of the absence of polysyllabic echoes in Wiltshire. Robert Plot in his natural histories of Oxfordshire and Staffordshire wrote of the 'discourse with the Nymph Echo' (he was very pleased with an echo at Tatenhill Church in Staffordshire, which returned five syllables at a distance of seventy yards). In his famous *Natural History and Antiquities of Selborne*, Gilbert White wrote at some length of echoes and 'anathoths' – the anathoth being the point to which an echo returns. He and his friends spoke lines from Virgil to an echo near Selborne capable of returning ten quick syllables of Latin verse and four or five slow ones. These classically educated enquirers into nature were familiar with Ovid's account of how Echo pined away for love of Narcissus, losing her body, but not her voice, changing to bones, which changed to rock, which went on speaking when spoken to. But if they liked the idea of this Greek nymph in the English countryside, they were also concerned with acoustics, measurement and explanation, and what they called the *centrum phonicum*, the sound-centre from which the noise or voice was returned.

The most famous echo in the British Isles – at Killarney, where the bugle is blown from a boat in between the lakes, and the glens reply – was responsible for Tennyson's 'Blow, Bugle, Blow' (Tennyson having heard the bugle and the reply in 1848) and so for the music to the poem in Britten's *Serenade for Tenor, Horn and Strings*. There are traces here and there of an earlier Scandinavian and Anglo-Saxon belief that the echo was the voice of dwarfs (who were supposed to live in rocks). The striking echo at either place gave the name Dwaraden, 'dwarf dene', to a valley in Yorkshire, and the name Elvendon, 'elves' hill', to a valley and farm at Goring-on-Thames, in Oxfordshire.

Edges

Edges, or escarpments, long inland slopes or cliffs across country, have mostly been caused by the tilting of layers of fairly resistant rock (CHALK, LIMESTONE, MILLSTONE GRIT, etc.): the layers, or strata, dip backwards, and weathering has cut, and goes on cutting, a face. Edge was the word our ancestors used – very appropriately – for the sheer black escarpments of Millstone Grit where the Derbyshire moors drop to the Derwent – Stanage, Burbage, Millstone Edge, Froggart Edge, etc., now much favoured by climbers (see *The English Outcrops*, by Walter Unsworth, 1964); or for the grim Blackstone Edge climbed by the paved Roman road between Rochdale and Halifax. The word was also used of the long escarpment of the Cotswolds, as in Weston-sub-Edge, Wotton-under-Edge, or Edgehill which looks down to the battlefield of the Civil War.

Eglwys

Eglwys in Welsh, eglos in Cornish, place-names, is 'church' (e.g. Eglwys y Drindod, Gwent, 'Trinity church'; Lanteglos, in Cornwall, 'valley church'), the Romanized Britons having borrowed the Latin word *ecclesia*.

Eleanor crosses

Queen Eleanor, the Spanish wife of Edward I, died at Harby in Nottinghamshire, near Lincoln, on 29 November 1290. Her bowels were buried in the Lady Chapel of Lincoln Cathedral and her body was then carried to Westminster Abbey for burial. Where it rested for the night on its cross-country journey, the Eleanor Crosses were set up, between 1292 and 1294, in accordance with her will. Each was an elaborately storeyed design, with pinnacles, crockets, canopies, shields, and statues representing the Queen. Three survive at Waltham Cross, in Hertfordshire, at Hardingstone, on the outskirts of Northampton, beside A508, and in the village of Geddington, north-east of Kettering in Northamptonshire, just off A43.

Elephants

Frequent in church carvings (and usually carved very inaccurately), elephants were held to be images of Adam and Eve, in and out of Paradise. According to legend, elephants were so free of carnal desire that they mated only once in a lifetime. Adam and Eve in Paradise were innocent like the elephants and had no knowledge of evil or of the source of carnal pleasure until Eve ate of the fruit. Elephants were said to fear dragons so much that they only gave birth in the security of a pool.

Elm

Since *c.* 700 B.C. the elm has been one of the commoner trees of our dampish climate, essential to life, along with ash for handles and oak for almost everything. Though it burns slowly and poorly and though its sap-wood decays quickly and its heart-wood is more liable to woodworm than the harder oak (the favourite timber from prehistoric times), it must have been discovered early that it lasts well as clap-boarding in the open air, and exceptionally well in contact with water. Salters and millers made sluices of elm board. On the farm it was used not only in shed and barns, but for troughs, and for the barrels of pumps, one end in the open air, the other down the well. Elm water-mains, hollowed out of trunks, were standard in towns until the 19th century and had a long life underground. Special uses apart, elm was really the poor man's oak (though – coffins for everybody being a fairly recent innovation – he wasn't buried in elm until modern times). The name Warwickshire Weed for elm marks it as the characteristic hedgerow tree of the Midlands – until the modern epidemic of 'Dutch' elm disease – blunt and dark and tall in the sky in English summer scenery, but with a prosaic reputation.

Enclosure roads

The Parliamentary enclosure of the great open fields of the English village in the 18th and 19th centuries (*see* FIELDS) often made it necessary to have new roads between village and village in place of the open tracks and paths, which had zigzagged between the furlongs of unenclosed arable. Enclosure roads of this kind are straight, often for several miles, and easily recognized by the wide strips of grass left and right of today's hard ribbon of surfacing. A customary width from hedge to hedge was forty feet, specified in the enclosure awards to allow traffic to wind about and avoid the waterlogging and deep ruts of winter. Since hard surfacing began, the grass verges have been a godsend to the gypsies, and have sometimes been enclosed by squatters, who have built cottages and given themselves long, narrow potato grounds, or by farmers. Local roads with an excess of sharp turns often date from enclosures of the 16th and 17th centuries.

*O*ne of the three ELEANOR CROSSES *to have survived of the original twelve. This hexagonal monument at Waltham Cross was constructed by Nicholas Dyminge de Reyne and Roger Crundale and sculpted by Alexander of Abingdon. It was begun in 1291 and since then has been heavily restored, notably in 1833 and again in 1883.*

Epitaphs

Epitaphs on church monuments and on grave-stones were collected in Victorian and Edwardian days for their quaintness or their eccentricity and incongruity in face of death, a superior approach. Like the monuments which carry them, they are more rewardingly examined for the expressive excellence they often show (especially in the early 17th century) and for the social and religious attitudes they proclaim.

The mediaeval epitaph or inscription tends in its Latin and its Gothic lettering to be short, practical and informative – names, dates, lord-ships perhaps, and customary requests that the reader should pray for the souls of the departed or hopes that the souls will meet with God's mercy – *quorum animabus propicietur Deus*. The epitaphs or inscriptions are a small, relatively modest part of the monuments, which, with their figures in flat or round, on brass or in stone, are designed with conspicuous dignity.

The post-Reformation epitaph becomes more personal, florid and this-worldly, just as the monument, under Renaissance influence, is more often a coloured display of position and lineage, with more heraldry, and less respect for its architectural relationship to the church. Poetry rather than design having become the characteristic art after the Reformation, verse epitaphs abound. They begin to assume that rank and power ensure goodness and a good reception in the world to come – an attitude often more endurable in the skilled verse of the later Tudor or Jacobean period than in the orotund verse or prose of 18th century epitaphs. Shakespeare is reputed to have written the epitaph on the tomb of Sir Thomas Stanley (d. 1576) in Tong church, in Shrop-shire:

> . . . Not monumentall stone preserves our fame
> Nor sky aspyring piramids our name
> The memory of him for whom this stands
> Shall outlyve marble and defacers hands
> When all to tymes consumption shall be geaven
> Standly for whom this stands shall stand in
> heaven.

The righteousness of dead selves extended or descended from grandees to businessmen, as in the epitaph to Thomas Hulbert, cloth merchant, of Corsham, Wiltshire (d. 1632):

> A loveing Neighbor, & a Master milde
> Who never did the needy poore contemne
> And God enrich't him by the hands of them.

But it is also true that verse epitaphs of the early 17th century often have a lyricism and

This summer scene on the River Test at Mottisfort, Hampshire, shows the EDGES *or escarpment of the South Downs in the distance.*

feeling which may be said to stem from the lyricism of Shakespeare's *Hamlet* (published 1603) with no more than a hint of the smell of Yorick's skull. Even in remote churches verses may be found combining delicate rhythm, humility, dignity and an imaginative sense of the charm of the lost world as well as the postulated New Jerusalem. A collection of such epitaphs would add to English poetry.

Eighteenth century epitaphs – florid verse, or florid prose often composed by poets – frequently make outrageously bland claims for the dead who are clearly conducted to heavenly manor-houses of the best modern style. This has prejudiced parsons and topographers against the formal elegance and beauty of the monuments. The religious revolutions of the late 18th and early 19th centuries reduced both epitaph and monument to a less exaggerated prose. But inscriptions and monuments alike declined rapidly into the mannerisms and clichés of a belief fossilizing into social convenience.

Evening (and morning) star

This is the planet Venus, brightest of the planets in our system, to be seen with emotion in sole proprietorship of the sky after the sun has gone down, and perhaps with extra emotion – since we are usually in bed at such hours – when she is observed in sole possession of the sky in the morning twilight before sunrise. An almanac or the monthly sky-guide in the newspapers tells one when to look for that wonderful sight, the conjunction of Venus and the horned moon. This brightest object in the sky after the sun and the moon will throw shadows, best seen on smooth surfaces – e.g. when Venus at her nearest and brightest shines through a window. (Gilbert White, at Selborne, 8 February 1782: 'Venus *shadows* very strongly, showing the bars of the windows on the floors. and walls.' 9 February: 'Venus sheds again her silvery light on the walls of my chamber, etc., and *shadows* very strongly.') Our respect for Venus as the star of love is one of the exquisite things we owe to Mediterranean civilization. The Romans made the identification of goddess and planet, but there are two partners to love, and the Greeks thought of Evening and Morning Star rather differently as beautiful young men with torches: in the evening Hesperos (Vesper in Latin), the *Hesperos Aster* or Evening Star; in the morning Phosphoros (Lucifer in Latin), the *Phosphoros Aster* or Light-Bearing Star, son of Eos, the sexy goddess of the dawn.

-ey

-ey, -ea, -y, at the end of many place-names signifies an i-(s)-land, from the Old English *ēg* or *īeg* – Sheppey, sheep island; or it may come from the equivalent word *ey* which the Norsemen used – Lundy, puffin island. Essex and the Fens are rich in English island names: Mersea, sea island, Beckney beacon island, Whittlesea, Wittel's Island, Ely, eel island, etc. The Norse raiders and settlers had another island word, *holmr*, which they gave to Steep Holme and Flat Holme in the Bristol Channel, Humberside's Axholme (Haxey Island), and the various little holmes afloat in Windermere – Lady Holme, Longholme, Crowholme, etc.

Eye-catchers

Eye-catchers originate in the 'improving' landscaping movement of the 18th century (which really did improve), with its related feeling for an ideal of the Middle Ages. When a landlord improved his estate with planting, clearing and the creation of landscapes, he would select a focal point in a view, building something there to direct and catch the eye and bring it to rest. In this way uniformity was broken, and distinction added to the landscape. 'When a wide heath, a dreary moor, or a continued plain is in prospect, objects which catch the eye supply the want of variety; none are so effectual for this purpose as buildings' (Whately's *Observations on Modern Gardening*, 1770). As likely as not the building would be an imitation Gothic affair. The earliest eye-catchers were façades only, screens giving the appearance of ruin, castle, bridge, etc., such as the pinnacled sham gateway at Steeple Aston, designed by William Kent *c.* 1740, to accent a monotonous north Oxfordshire landscape, or the Shobdon Arches, Hereford and Worcester, built on a ridge in the seventeen-fifties out of the Norman carvings of the demolished church at Shobdon. Such screens took on substance and turned into more than façade (Dunstall Castle, *c.* 1750, Croome d'Abitot, Hereford and Worcester; Ralph Allen's sham castle, 1762, on Bathwick Hill, Bath; Rothley Castle, 1776, on the Northumberland moors).

Fairs

Fairs (we borrowed 'fair' in the Middle Ages from the Old French *feire*) are so called because they were ordained to take place or begin on *feriae*, the feast days or holy days of saints. On saints' days, which were also conveniently memorable dates in the calendar, men had time off from labour (holy days becoming

holidays) and were able to trudge or ride in to the mixed business, fun and sociability of the fair. Fairs every so often were a necessity of life, until railways, roads and efficient postal services came to change the towns and the way in which goods were distributed; and most of them originated in the 13th and 14th centuries along with the new towns or seignorial boroughs established by manor lords. They hoped to do well from the tolls of the frequent markets (*see* MARKET CROSSES) in the town and the larger, less frequent (usually annual), fairs, to which goods were brought from all over the country. A fair, as an exclusive right, could be established only by a royal charter, which specified its date and its duration. Once he had his charter and his fair, the lord of the fair would often farm his rights out to a lessee, who paid a rent, and made what he could out of the tolls, providing the necessary booths, hurdles, utensils, etc., which were kept in a fair house. Fairs – complete with fair house – might be in the open countryside as well as in the towns and the larger villages. Thus in Wiltshire, until the years before the First World War, Tan Hill Fair or St. Anne's Fair for sheep was held in lofty isolation on the Marlborough Downs, on St. Anne's Day, 6 August, St. Anne being the patron saint of the parish church hundreds of feet below in the valley.

Such 'charter fairs' for the sale of goods or beasts differed in their primary function from the 'mop fairs', or 'statutes' or 'statute fairs', several of which still go on as fun fairs (e.g. the Marlborough Mops in October). These go back to statutes of the early years of Elizabeth I's reign which ordained meetings in every hundred for settling wages and disputes about employment, and finding masters and servants. They were 'mops', so it is said, because servants signified the jobs they were after by carrying the instrument of their trade, mop, flail, etc.

Farm

Farm for a holding of agricultural land, and farmer, for the man who runs it, are fairly modern words which came into use when the open fields of the village (*see* FIELDS) in which each man had his scattered strips, began to give way in the 16th century to enclosed, compact holdings, for which a fixed rent, a *firma* in the lawyer's Latin, a 'farm', something fixed or confirmed, was paid by the tenant to the landlord. 'Farmer' gradually superseded the older descriptions, 'yeoman' for the free tenant or owner, and 'husbandman' – the husbandman having been the unfreed cultivator or peasant, the villein of the manor holding his house and his land by service to his lord.

Farmhouses

Farmhouses seldom date back beyond, or as far as, the 16th century. The mediaeval farmer or husbandman had lived in hovels frequently built of COB, consisting of a single room without ceiling, with a central hearth, windows without glass, and an earth floor. These gave way in the last decades of the 16th century, and the early years of the 17th century – in Shakespeare's time, when wealth and population increased – to farmhouses of stone or timber with chimneys, glazed windows, and two rooms, a hall for general family use and a parlour for sleeping. Such Elizabethan farmhouses may survive, sometimes altered or enlarged out of immediate recognition, sometimes downgraded a long while ago to workmen's cottages which are now often condemned or abandoned. Advance in

comfort and extra rooms continued till the Civil War, and then on the same lines till the end of the 17th century. Upstairs chambers were devised, a kitchen and buttery were often added. The changes, difficult to work out, impossible to reduce to a formula, and varying district by district, are described by M. W. Barley in a pioneer book, *The English Farmhouse and Cottage* (1961). This book emphasizes that the improved farmhouse of the 17th century in stone or brick or timber reflected the England of the open field village (*see* FIELDS) and subsistence farming carried on in the old ways by the family: the farmhouse was still rooted in the mediaeval past, the mediaeval organization of country life; and its fabric, however changed, was still related to Gothic ways of building.

Enclosure in the 18th century began to

*O*ne of the most famous FELLS, or mountains, of the north-west of England, is the Norse-named Scafell, in Cumbria.

spatter more of the countryside with substantial new farmhouses away from the village – houses influenced by the new Classical modes and reflecting the new wealth and social position of farmers, each with a consolidated farm in the new manner, farmed on new principles. In the villages the thatched 17th century farmhouses, so often abandoned to the farm labourers, were frequently divided, as one may still see them, into two homes.

Fell

In the English of the north-western counties, a mountain, from the Old Norse *fell* or *fjall*. It is pre-eminently a word of the districts peopled by the Norwegians (Snaefell, in the Isle of Man, Scafell in Cumbria, Mickle Fell, Durham's highest point).

Fenland ditches

Like the Cambridgeshire fenmen characterized in Camden's *Britannia* as 'a kind of people according to the nature of the place where they dwell rude, uncivill, and envious to all others . . ., who stalking on high upon stilts, apply their mindes to grasing, fishing and fowling', marsh people have been conservative in their once 'drowned lands', and have preserved special words for the one obvious feature of their lives and landscape – the drainage ditches. Sedgemoor and south-western marshes along the Severn keep the word 'rhine' ('reen' in Gwent), from the Old English *ryne*, a water channel. Also the word 'gout'. Romney Marsh, much of it reclaimed between the 13th and 16th centuries, has its great 'sewers', like the Fens, where drainage was controlled by a Session of Sewers, 'sewer' (from the Old French) keeping its original meaning, pleasanter than the one it has today.

The Fens proper retain the richest vocabulary of man-made water channels. 'Dykes', 'lodes' and 'eaus' are from words which would have been familiar to Anglo-Saxon fenmen ('eau', from the Old English *ēa*, a stream, has nothing to do with foreign engineers). 'Leams' and 'cuts' – as well as sewers – were terms used by fenmen in the Middle Ages. 'Drain' came into use in Tudor times. 'Level', of the great extents of marshland, not only in the Fens, is a word that came in with the great reclaimers of the 17th century. Fenland water-channels often preserve the memory of the reclaimers and improvers, e.g. Morton's Leam cut in 1478–90 by John Morton (when he was Bishop of Ely) to take the surplus waters of the Nene seaward from Peterborough, or

Popham's Eau from the Nene to the Ouse cut in 1605 by a London company under Lord Chief Justice Popham.

Ferme ornée

Invented in the seventeen-thirties by Philip Southcote, the *ferme ornée* was a modest combination of house and grounds (or landscape garden) designed to suggest the pastoral delights, blending 'the useful with the agreeable'. Southcote contrived his *ferme ornée*, Woburn Farm, near Chertsey, out of 150 acres of Thames meadowland, with careful planting of trees, a winding walk and some winding water, cunningly arranged views of villas and villages and fields of corn, bringing near to his Gothic house the lowing of cattle and the bleating of sheep and the cackling of hens – 'the beauties which enliven a garden are everywhere intermixed with the properties of a farm'.

This famous little paradise laid out in the years after 1735 was imitated, and became popular for the moderately well-to-do in Surrey, Kent and the Isle of Wight in the early decades of the 19th century, when the house was often built in a rustic fanciful Gothic, with BARGE-BOARDS and verandas, and frequently a steep thatched roof. In 1848 the *ferme ornée* was described as differing from a common farm 'in having a better dwelling-house, neater approach, and one partly or entirely distinct from that which leads to the offices. It also differs as to the hedges, which are allowed to grow wild and irregular, and are bordered on each side by a broad green drive, and sometimes by a gravel walk and shrubs.' The *ferme ornée* of the 18th century had contracted to a more genteel establishment.

Ferries

Ferries, which are now falling into disuse, were many of them established as a regular service in the 13th century. There had also been Roman ferries, to judge by the line of some Roman roads. Ermine Street, north of Lincoln, comes to the Humber at Winteringham Haven, and from Brough on the other bank a continuation goes on to York. There was probably another Roman ferry over the Humber from South Ferriby to North Ferriby, the two villages which were known by their ferry names as early as the 11th century. Peddar's Way went to a ferry over the Wash. It goes straight across Norfolk to the Wash at Holme-next-the-Sea, a road continuing again on the Lincolnshire side. One of the ferries over the Severn, Arlingham

Passage (now disused), made the transit where a Roman ferry took the iron traffic from the mines of the Forest of Dean over the river to the Fosse Way; and lower down, where the awkward mediaeval ferry from Aust to Beachley has been superseded at last by the suspension bridge, Aust may preserve the name Trajectus Augustus, a ferry passage perhaps used by the Legio Augusta, which had its headquarters at Caerleon.

A regular ferry was sometimes piously established by a monastery, or piously maintained by hermits, with a riverside hermitage or chapel. The Benedictine monks of Sherborne Abbey, for instance, established and owned the Starcross Ferry from Exmouth across the Exe estuary in Devon. The Aust Passage was probably served by the hermits of St. Twrog's Chapel, built on a rock near the Beachley terminus. High up the Severn near Stourport the mediaeval hermits of Redstone Rock (*see* HERMITAGES) serviced a ferry alongside their scarlet cliff on what was an important route from Droitwich.

ST. CHRISTOPHER the ferryman may have been the inspiration of such ferry hermits, but ferries were also profitable. Each ferry was an exclusive privilege or 'liberty' granted by the Crown, and became a valuable property.

On the map ferry words include ferry itself, but this, originating in the Old Norse *ferja*, was used more often in the North Country, as in the two Ferriby villages on the Humber. More commonly a ferry was known as a pass or a passage, sometimes as a lode (e.g. Malpas, 'bad pass', where the ferry crosses the deep tidal water of the Truro river in Cornwall, and King Harry's Passage lower down; Malpas on the Usk near Newport; and the many Passages and Lodes up and down the Severn). Some ferry names contain hythe, meaning a landing-place, familiar in Bablock Hythe, outside Oxford, where cars are still ferried over the Thames on a wire-guided, willow-shaded punt, less obvious on the Trent above Gainsborough in the anciently named Walkerith (hythe of the walkers, i.e. fullers) and Stockwith (landing made of logs). Down-river there were ferries and landings at Burton Stather and Flixborough Stather, containing this time the Old Norse word for a landing or a wharf still familiar as 'staithe'.

Feudal place-names

Many villages have in their names what is technically known as a 'feudal affix', i.e. the added name of the family who held the manor in the centuries of feudal service. The families, descended from the followers of the Conqueror, whether Norman, Breton or Fleming, with names indicating their origin on the other side of the Channel, have long ago died out, estates have changed hands and been divided, but often that mediaeval family affix clings like a burr of the past, puzzling to those who wonder why a village should be Something Bagpuize or Something d'Abitot. The affixes, as one would expect, seldom became attached until a family had been in possession for some while. Most of them go back in use to the 13th and 14th centuries. Affixes, too, indicate not only family ownership of village and manor, but ownership by a religious house or by the Crown – manors kept as part of the king's own demesne.

To take one county, out of several hundred parishes in Gloucestershire, the names of twenty-eight are still combined with ownership affixes, most of them family ones: the families d'Abitot (Redmarly d'Abitot), le Bret (Westonbirt), de Kaynes (Poole Keynes, Somerford Keynes), de Pont de l'Arche (Stanley Pontlarge), de Valence (Moreton Valence), de Turville (Eastleach Turville), etc.

Hanham Abbots belonged, in the same way, to the Abbots of Keynsham, Bishop's Cleeve to the Bishops of Worcester, Clifford Chambers to the abbey of St. Peter's, Gloucester (the abbey of what is now the cathedral), for the support of its chamberer or chamberlain. Some affixes were attached to distinguish identically named villages from each other – Charlton Abbots was the Charlton of the Abbots of Winchcombe in distinction to the Charlton of the Crown, Charlton Kings. Guiting Power belonged to the feudal family of the le Poers, whereas the Knights Templar (*see* TEMPLE) owned Temple Guiting, two miles away up the Windrush valley.

Ffynnon

In Welsh place-names, Ffynnon is both source (or spring) and holy well (from the Latin *fontana*). In the mountains, it is sometimes attached to a lake or tarn, as the source of a stream, e.g. the tarn of Ffynnon Llugwy under Craig yr Ysfa in the Carneddau – source, spring or fountain of the Afon Llugwy. Ffynnon Gybi, at Llangybi in Gwynedd, is the celebrated holy well of St. Cybi, with its bath and beehive-shaped well-house. St. David has his Ffynnon Ddewi at Henfynyw (Dyfed), where he is supposed to have grown up.

Field names

Names to distinguish fields are an obvious necessity, and in past centuries the farmer named his fields no less than he named his cows or his children. The interest of the field names on a farm or in a parish will vary according to the past organization of the land. Names will be repetitive, tiresome and disappointing, as a rule, for the smaller fields which came into being when (*see* FIELDS) the huge open fields and meadows of a village were divided by the enclosures of the 18th and 19th centuries: they are likely to be more interesting where the enclosures were more ancient, as in much of Devon and Cornwall. Field names may give clues of every kind to the past – to hill-forts or barrows which have been ploughed away, to chapels, holy wells, pounds, mills, long ago destroyed, to places where sheep were washed or cattle rounded up, or where particular crops were grown such as hops, or saffron or woad, to corners which were felt to be frequented by demons or goblins. Its name may reveal that a field was once given as an endowment to provide bell-ropes for a church or candles to light the rood. Field names may preserve the names of owners or tenants, mediaeval or recent, may be coarse or satirical, may be bad jokes or good jokes, and may sometimes illuminate the character of the man who bestowed them; of which last the classic example is the new naming of his Dorset estates at Halstock and Corscombe by the 18th century republican and libertarian Thomas Hollis. Most of his fields (and farms) now bear the names of tyrannicides and regicides, of spiritual, philosophical, political and military heroes of freedom, from Harmodius and Aristogeiton to Brutus, Plutarch, Plato and Solon. Confucius on his Liberty Farm is a meadow and Socrates a pasture of thirteen acres.

Read the chapter on field names in P. H. Reaney's *Origin of English Place-Names* (1960), and read – if it has been published – what the volume for your county in the English Place-names Survey has to say of the field names in your parish and in the county at large, remembering meanwhile that field names like other place-names are subject to change and corruption (*see* PLACE-NAMES) and cannot always be taken to mean what they say.

Fields

The pattern of fields has much to say about the past life and organization of Britain, though in a language still incompletely understood. To begin with, groups of small, more or less rectangular, fields, of $\frac{1}{4}$ to $1\frac{1}{2}$ acres are faintly or sometimes clearly discernible on much upland country (particularly on the chalk downs of Wessex). They are best seen in the early evening or morning when low light picks them out in shadow. For some time such fields were lumped together as 'Celtic', as if they had all been measured out and then enclosed by British farmers of the Iron Age and the centuries of Roman occupation. Most of them are 'Celtic', or British; but some go back to the Bronze Age, Late or Middle, some possibly to the Early Bronze Age, so that the first fields – and farms – may have been laid out and turned over with the plough as much as 3,000 or 3,500 years ago.

Hedges. Where there is surface stone at hand, these little fields had often stone-built boundaries. In some areas one can still see the stone uprights in straight lines, which were infilled with smaller stones, as on Dartmoor and the Isles of Scilly (*see* DANES FENCES). In the far west of Cornwall, between Penzance and Land's End, some of the small primitive fields are still in use, with their granite hedges intact. Drystone walling around early fields has been found on the Cotswolds, grown over with turf. But the divisions usually consisted of earthen banks.

Lynchets. 'Celtic' fields may be on gentle or quite steep slopes, in which case the division which shows up most clearly may be a lynchet or ridge, sometimes overlying an original hedge. The soil, as it was turned over, slipped downhill, and tended along the downward boundary to build up in a lynchet – or 'positive lynchet' – higher than the natural slope. Along the top boundary of a field, the ploughing cut into the natural slope, with the downward creep of the soil, excavating a scarp of the kind known as a 'negative lynchet'.

Farmsteads and Sherds. Somewhere near was the ancient farmstead. Usually it is easier to recognize the fields than the dwellings or huts or farm space by which they were served. There may be little raised circles where huts stood, or enclosing ditches or banks, or hollows derived from storage pits, or quite sizeable banks – even a considerable hill-fort of the Iron Age – which surrounded and defended the dwellings and the farm space.

The ancient farmers used their household waste as manure. If there are plenty of moles working (or rabbits, but rabbits are less likely after myxomatosis), or if the old field areas have been newly ploughed and harrowed,

The effect of morning light on a strip lynchet in Dorset dramatically emphasizes one form of FIELD *division, created by the ploughing action, which tends to move soil down the slope from the boundary.*

scraps of pottery can often be picked up by the pocketful.

The Open Fields. The Anglo-Saxon settlers cleared more of the forests and the wooded valleys and either began or continued the marking of England with a different and far more extensive pattern of fields. The nucleus is the VILLAGE, the villagers living in the main off the produce of two or three great 'open fields'. Modern theory veers to the possibility that the system of open fields was not introduced by the Anglo-Saxons, but was taken over from the ROMAN VILLAS, or farm estates. From the Anglo-Saxon era the system developed through the centuries after the Conquest, and was broken down gradually by sub-division and enclosure of the great fields into more or less compact farms, a change which climbed to its maximum towards the end of the 18th century. As mediaeval population increased, the open fields grew, it might be, to 300 or 400 acres apiece. The fields were rested in turn, then ploughed and cultivated in long narrow strips (or 'lands', or 'selions'). According to size and the lie of the ground, so many parallel strips were grouped together inside the open field into 'furlongs' (which were not strictly furlongs by length). The strips and the furlongs lay along the fall of the land for good drainage. Each farmer's holding was made up of so many strips scattered through the various furlongs, mounting up to smaller or larger totals from a few acres to a hundred or more; and this divided 'farm' was worked from a farmstead in a group of farmsteads which made up much of the village (farmsteads are often grouped together still in the old way).

Enclosure. When this old system was broken up, mainly in the 18th century (though some enclosures were much earlier, and some later), more compact and convenient farms were created by dividing the open fields into smaller fields, often by throwing a hedge around one or more of the furlongs; and so many of these new closes were allotted to each farm (the fields making up a farm were often – and often remain – scattered; it was not always possible to make the new farm into a unit). The closes made in this way fit together like pieces in a jigsaw, but are more or less straightsided and rectangular. They were not always very distinctly hedged, so that even today an ancient open field outside its village may retain something of its boundless mediaeval look. (It may still keep its name 'Field' tacked on to the village name, or as North Field, South Field, etc.)

Ridge-and-Furrow. Also within the closes one can often detect the old plough-pattern. Moving up and down between the narrow confines of each strip, ploughs with fixed mould-boards threw the slices of mould or soil inwards, building up a pattern of parallel ridges divided by dips – the familiar ridge-and-furrow.

Strip Lynchets. When land on a pronounced slope was ploughed in long narrow strips, strip lynchets were also formed, which often gash a slope with bold parallels of light and shadow. These long, narrow, lynchetted strips are open at the ends, not square-ended and enclosed like the Romano-British or prehistoric fields.

Field areas, or the areas into which they were sub-divided, depended in the past on the amount of energy of oxen, horses – and men. The coming of tractors and other tireless farm machines made it possible and economic to work much larger units. So fields in the Second World War and since have often been enlarged by the grubbing up of hedges.

Some books to read: H. C. Bowen, *Ancient Fields*, 1962; H. P. R. Finberg, *Lucerna*, 1964 (for Roman Villas and Open Fields); E. C. Curwen, *Plough and Pasture*, 1946.

Firemarks

Firemarks attached high up on the corners of houses are the insurance signs of the various Fire Offices which came into being after the Great Fire of London in 1666 – and after the revolution in house-building in the 16th and 17th centuries, which made a house worth insuring. Frame-houses paid a higher premium than houses in stone or brick. Early marks are of lead, later ones of copper or iron, and the commonest include the phoenix rising from the flames, symbol of the Phoenix Fire Office, founded in 1682 and the first in the field (now the Phoenix Assurance Company), and the Sun in his Splendour, the sun with rays round his face – as if he was going to enjoy a good blaze – mark of the Sun Fire Office, founded in 1710. A number on the mark will be the number of the insurance policy. Firemarks arise from the fact that the early Fire Offices maintained firemen and fire-engines: the mark on the house told the particular brigade that the house was their responsibility. But affixing firemarks became general wherever the house was, in town or country, in or out of reach of a fire brigade. See *Specimens of British Firemarks*, by Bertram Williams, 1934.

Fishponds

Fishponds or stews alongside monastery or castle ruins or in a park were not made for ornament or the pleasures of fishing, but because a regular supply of fish was a necessity. To assure fresh food through the year the well-to-do in the Middle Ages provided themselves with every kind of living food store, DOVE-COTE, CONYGER for rabbits, PARK for deer, swannery (*see* SWANS), and fishpond. An extra reason for the fishpond was the observation through the year of 'fish-days', i.e. the many fast days when eating flesh, but not fish, was forbidden. Fasting or abstinence of this kind according to rule tended to the forgiveness of sins and the attainment of everlasting life, and was more strictly observed by the monastic population, so that even the tiniest priory could not do without its fishponds. Carp were the favourite fish, but the ponds or stews (from the Old French *estui*, something for storage) were also stocked with native fish from the rivers, fens, etc. – eels, pike, bream, perch, roach, tench.

Five Wounds of Christ

It was believed in the late Middle Ages that prayers in honour of the Five Wounds of Christ gave protection against the dangers and pains of dying suddenly unconfessed and unabsolved. Such prayers gained indulgences, and with epidemics of plague a cult of the Wounds became popular. So they were represented grouped in shields, on bench-ends, in stained glass windows, etc., sometimes as two wounded feet, two wounded hands, and a wounded heart, with or without a spear (Sutcombe, Devon; Cumnor, Oxon; North Cadbury, Somerset; all on bench-ends), sometimes as five disembodied wounds dripping blood. It was taught that 'Ihesus woundes so wide' were the wells of life (so interpreting Isaiah 12. 3). It was this cult which left behind it the expletive Wounds! or Zounds! (God's wounds).

-fleet

-fleet at the end of coastal place-names commonly means a sea inlet (Old English *flēot*). So also the 'fleets' around the Essex coast, Broad Fleet, Besom Fleet, Tollesbury Fleet, etc., and

Two specimens of FIREMARKS, *one from the Sun Fire Office (top) and the other (above) from the Farmers' Insurance Company.*

along the Dorset coast the brackish ten-mile lagoon of the Fleet (behind Chesil Beach – Old English *cesil*, gravel), once a low coastal tract which was 'drowned' by subsidence of the land in neolithic times. Transformed, the same word *flēot* occurs across the Channel in Harfleur and Honfleur.

Flint

Vital for prehistoric tools, weapons and strike-a-lights (the Anglo-Saxons also called it fire-stone), and for the development of civilization, important too as a building stone in many counties, flint owes its hardness to its content of silica. It is a rock which formed in nodules in the chalk when chalk surfaces began to feel the effect of heavy tropical rainfall. 'The percolating water, charged with ionized carbonic acid' – from the surface vegetation – 'attacked both the chalk and the contained opaline sponge spicules, so that it picked up both calcium bicarbonate and colloidal silica. The proportions of the two substances in solution maintained a delicate balance, upset by slight variations in the solubility of the chalk, with the deposition of either the one or the other constituent. In this way flint replaced chalk, particle by particle' (W. J. Arkell).

Flint-building in the chalk districts depends on having plenty of mortar to spare, whether the flints are rough as they come from the chalk or as they are found on the surface, or sea-worn into large pebbles. With their horns and hollows rough flints bind in very strongly and durably, and in building were first used by the Romans (e.g. in city walls, as at Silchester, near Reading, in the great lumpy FORTS OF THE SAXON SHORE, and the 4th century rectangular farmstead on Lowbury Hill, at Aston Upthorpe in Oxfordshire). The use of squared surface flints began late in the 13th century, developing (especially in churches in East Anglia) into 'flush work', panels of squared pieces of flint flush with surrounding borders of freestone. This highly decorative technique reached an extreme of rather ostentatious virtuosity in late Perpendicular buildings in the decades on either side of 1500.

Flint finds

Though the chances of picking up a shapely flint axe or dagger or sickle are not very great, chipped and shaped and edged flints were used for so long, over so wide an area, that anyone who keeps his eyes open may expect sooner or later to find something which has been held in a prehistoric hand. The first thing is to be familiar with shapes and methods of 'knapping', to be able to distinguish the real thing from the accidental approach to regularity, to recognize an artificially from a naturally chipped edge – which is a matter of handling (if possible) and books. The British Museum helps with *Flint Implements* (1950), an inexpensive handbook, illustrating flint tools from palaeolithic to mesolithic. See, too, Kenneth Oakley's *Man the Toolmaker* (1952), from the Natural History Museum; and from the Pitt-Rivers Museum, at Oxford, *Stone-Worker's Progress* (1953), by Sir Francis Knowles.

As for where to look, tools may have been dropped anywhere. But obviously they are going to be most abundant where prehistoric populations were least thin (e.g. chalk and limestone uplands). Flints were not only worked around FLINT MINES, and you may discover or learn of workshop areas (try the local museum or the publications of the local archaeological society). The plough helps. But it takes a very sharp eye to detect worked flints in ploughland where there is anyway an abundance of natural flint broken into all shapes and sizes. Implements are easiest to find, as a rule, in Bronze Age country, off the chalk, e.g. in ploughed fields near or around Bronze Age barrow cemeteries – flint having still been used in great quantities after the introduction of bronze, by a now considerable population of huntsmen, herders and farmers. In such surroundings an alien scrap of flint at once shows up among the ordinary stones. Try such fields in sun after rain, when the pieces of flint sparkle.

Flint mines

Some five thousand years old, flint mines are the first remains of organized industry in Great Britain; and two of them, two deep shafts with radiating galleries, are kept open as ancient monuments, at Grimes Graves, near Weeting, in Norfolk. Flint-mining seems to have been introduced from continental Europe. Thousands of years of making flint tools had taught European craftsmen much about the qualities of flint, especially that flints collected on the surface 'knapped' less well, making tools which soon broke, than flint picked out of a deep seam in the chalk – so much so that if naturally exposed seams were worked out, it was worth digging down to them elsewhere.

In England flint mines have been identified, not only in Norfolk, but in Oxfordshire on the Chilterns (Rotherfield Peppard, near Henley-on-Thames); in Hampshire (Martin's Clump, near Over Wallop, in the angle of A343 from Andover and B3084); in Wiltshire (Easton Down, Winterslow, north of A30, north-east of Salisbury, and two miles south-west of the Hampshire mines); and at several places along the South Downs in Sussex, near the neolithic cattle enclosures or CAUSEWAYED CAMPS of the same period (especially Blackpatch Hill and Harrow Hill to the west of Findon, just north of Worthing, and Cissbury, above Findon to the east). The signs, where a mining centre has not been smoothed down by ploughing, are broken ground over many acres dimpled into shallow, more or less round, depressions. In the undisturbed part of the Wiltshire mines on Easton Down some ninety shafts are clustered together. The depth of such filled-up shafts depended on the depth of the layer of fine flint nodules which the miners were after. Some go down only ten or twelve feet; at Grimes Graves one climbs down a thirty-foot ladder, as the miners must have done, into a darkness once lit by torches and lamps of animal fat (soot marks have been found). Miners cut steps into some of the shallower pits. They worked with flint axes, picks or levers of red deer antler, and the leg bones and shoulder-blades of oxen. Interspersed among the shafts are the real factory workshops, i.e. the flake-littered knapping floors where the nodules of black flint were rough-dressed into axes. These mining and knapping centres stayed busy for centuries, some of them well into the Bronze Age; and the axes they produced made the first inroads into the forest cover of Britain.

The thirty-four acres of Grimes Graves preserve a piece of the sandy aboriginal breckland of Norfolk, now rather hemmed in by black conifer plantations. This great concentration of depressions and rough ground suggested ancient burials: locally and correctly they are known as Grimmer's Graves, Grimr having been the god Woden, to whom the christianized Anglo-Saxons were inclined to ascribe anything artificial, prominent and inexplicable.

Flying buttresses

Flying buttresses outside the greater Gothic churches of the 14th and 15th centuries (the cathedrals, abbey churches such as Malmesbury in Wiltshire and Pershore in Hereford and Worcester, or such a great collegiate church as Fotheringhay, in Northants) are combinations of a flying arch and a buttress standing away from the church walls, the arch

A selection of FLINT FINDS *including, from top to bottom, an arrow head, a paleolithic axe head and a flint lance point.*

taking to the buttress the outward thrust of the walls and vaulting. When churches began to grow higher and roofs heavier, it became necessary to strengthen walls with buttresses built directly against them, regularly spaced, a buttress to the dividing point between each bay where the thrust was strongest. When architects pushed the church outwards with side aisles, such direct buttresses were impossible, and flying buttresses were built at first with the flyers hidden in the roofing of the aisle. Churches went still higher, the complex vaulting of the roofs added to the thrust, and clerestory windows were required in the walls to give light. So loftier flying buttresses had to be provided standing clear of the aisles – engineering necessities which were devised as one of the most exciting elements of design.

Fog

Fog – forgetting the smoke fogs of London and the great industrial areas – is cloud near the ground or sea, cloud at a low level, cooling of the air having caused its moisture to condense. The cooling or cold ground of autumn and winter nights cools the air above it, the air runs downhill and condenses its moisture into fog (more pleasantly known as mist) over the low meadows and in the valleys. The sun shining on fog may produce a white FOG-BOW or mist-bow. A glory is a different thing (though it may be surrounded by a mist-bow) – an aureole of colours seen round the shadow of one's own head thrown on to fog at a lower level by the sun, before the sun has risen very high. Coleridge and Wordsworth delighted in glories around their heads, which they saw on high walks in the Lake District. Since each person can see only the actual glory around his own head-shadow, Coleridge used the glory as an image to explain that one's joy in nature is personal and unique, projected from one's own person –

> Ah! from the Soul itself must issue forth
> A Light, a Glory, and a luminous Cloud
> Enveloping the Earth!
> "Dejection: an Ode"

He describes the glory very well as a phenomenon in another poem, 'Constancy to an Ideal Object'.

The Brocken Spectre is one's apparently elongated shadow on the mist, the head of which is encircled by the glory. It takes its name from the Brocken, the German mountain which provides good conditions for seeing Spectre and glory (though Coleridge climbed it twice for that purpose without success).

A typical FOOTPATH *with a stile erected to prevent the passage of beasts.*

Fog-bows

Fog-bows are wonderfully striking but not very frequently observed RAINBOWS, known also as 'white rainbows' or mist-bows. The very small size of the waterdrops making up the bank of fog or mist in front of the sun causes the colours of reflected light to overlap into a predominant whiteness, but the wide, colourless arch will have as borders the outer orange and the inner blue of the spectrum. In place of the sun, headlights of a car can produce a circular fog-bow of considerable beauty.

Font covers

Greatly elaborated and elongated in Gothic forms (especially in East Anglian churches), font covers had a plain and practical origin in the 13th century. In a reverent way they protected the sanctified water which the priest left in the font for the next christening. The water was liable to be stolen for medico-magical use, and orders went out that fonts should be fitted with lids which were to be locked and secured. They were fastened down as a rule with bars of iron fitting into staples (traces often remain) leaded into the font on either side. The magnificent canopied font covers of the 15th century are frequently topped (Ufford, in Suffolk; North Walsham, Norfolk) with a pelican. According to the Bestiary, the pelican was irritated into slaying its young, which it then brought to life after three days with blood pecked from its own breast. So God was the 'true pelican', and the pelican on the font cover aptly spoke of man redeemed by Christ's blood, and washed of his sins.

Fonts

Of the SEVEN SACRAMENTS of the Christian belief, the sacraments of the mass and of baptism have been pre-eminent, as the two instituted by Christ. So every church has a font, and from the 12th century fonts are often carved in a way that emphasizes the baptismal entry into the Christian life. Round the bowl of the 12th century font at Lullington in Somerset an inscription in large letters says HOC FONTIS SACRO PEREUNT DELICTA LAVACRO (sins perish in this holy font bowl) – washed away by the sanctified water. And fonts were placed symbolically at the entrance into the church.

Some of the earliest fonts are tubs of stone, scarcely raised above the floor, in which an adult could stand. Infant baptism became the rule, fonts grew more shallow and were raised on plinths, legs and pedestals, bringing the rim to the height of bent arms cradling a baby. The custom was to immerse the baby, which explains the lead lining of the font (and the FONT COVER). Rather than repeat the long ritual sanctification of the water every time a baby was to be christened, the water stood over in the font from one christening to the next, and, if the bowl had not been lined, would have soaked away through the often porous stone. Romanesque fonts of the 12th century, when many new churches were built, are often carved with major scenes or symbols of Christianity, e.g. the VINE which stands for Christ, the TREE OF LIFE, the AGNUS DEI, the Baptism of Christ, the Crucifixion, the HARROWING OF HELL, the Apostles, the signs of the Evangelists, the Magi, ST. MICHAEL slaying the dragon. Also the font may tread down or press down upon creatures which represent the Devil. New fonts for refashioned churches of the late 14th and the 15th centuries, often octagonal, are carved with greater sophistication and less force. Many of the old subjects are repeated. Saints proliferate, and the INSTRU-MENTS OF CHRIST'S PASSION. Late fonts carved with all of the Seven Sacraments abound in Norfolk and Suffolk, emphasizing the sacramentalism of the font and of baptism.

Footpaths

Footpaths are certainly some of the more ancient ways one can tread, some as old as the Anglo-Saxon settlements they link up or the church they led to, others older still in some of the Celtic parts of Britain, linking settlements perhaps of the 3rd or 4th century A.D. And one must suppose that there are also prehistoric paths still in use. The word path itself is a reminder of this antiquity or primitiveness. Connected with 'pad', it is a way padded or trodden into existence by the feet of man or beast.

Footpaths may or may not be highways for the passage of any of Her Majesty's subjects. If there is a right of way, it has accrued, in the main. The law says: 'When a path has been actually enjoyed by the public as of right and without interruption for a full period of twenty years it is deemed to have been dedicated as a highway.' The owner of a private path has a statutory guard against such an accrual: he must publicly exhibit a notice indicating that the path is private, and must give information to the same effect to the County Council.

It is county councils which are guardians of the public footpath, the Highways Act of 1959 laying down that it is their duty 'to assert and protect the rights of the public to the use and enjoyment of all highways in their district and to prevent as far as possible the stopping up or obstruction of these highways'. And by the National Parks and Access to the Country Act of 1949 footpaths are shown on the maps that county councils were then instructed to prepare.

A difference that those who trod out the original line of an ancient footpath would at once notice is the number of stiles along its course. For the most part their paths would have crossed open country, whereas the farmer's beast-proof stiles conduct path or man from one enclosure (*see* FIELDS) to the next. The law tells the farmer that such gates and stiles as he maintains are not to present trouble-some hindrances to passage. And if he wishes to plough over the path, he must – though he doesn't do so very often – give seven days' notice to the highway authority, and must restore the surface of the path as soon as practicable. It remains a highway although part of his crop grows on it; you can wade through his wheat.

Varying in shape and kind according to local fashion and materials, including everything from slab steps (around Dartmoor, etc.), stone steps set in a bank of earth and stones (Cornwall), flagstones set on edge, to wooden contraptions or pieces of old bedstead, a stile is by etymology something to be climbed (old English *stigel*, from *stigan*, to climb). Everything you pass through, such as a SQUEEZE-BELLY, is strictly a gate, the basic meaning of which is an opening or gap.

Force

A WATERFALL (Old Norse *fors*) in the Lake District and other parts of the north-west

The bowl of this squarish Norman FONT from Luppitt, Devon, depicts a scene of the most barbaric kind: a centaur carrying a spear fights two dragons; a group of dachshund-like beasts face each other with grinning jaws and two men (shown here) fight each other with long nail-shaped clubs.

*H*igh Force,
in Ullswater,
Cumbria, is a 'FORCE'
or fall on the Airy Beck.

settled by the Norwegians in the 10th century (Aira Force, Scale Force, High Force, etc.). Equivalent to the foss of Norway and Iceland, it is a sign word of the Norwegian settler, along with -BRECK and FELL and GILL.

Fords

Fords, where rivers or streams spread wide enough and shallow enough for a firm passage, have been points helping to determine our network of settlement and communication. Before there is a bridge, a track or a road must make for the point where a stream can be forded, preferably winter and summer alike; and names with 'ford', usually at the end, show the great number of such easy or tricky crossings before the bridge-building of the Middle Ages. (In Wales, ford is *rhyd*, at the beginning of place-names; in Cornwall, *rit*, *ret* or *red* – Cornish *rid*. With its innumerable streams, hilly Cornwall retains more than seventy *rit*, *ret* or *red* ford names.) Often one can still detect the approaches to the old ford above or below a bridge. Often, too, one sees a ford with nothing more than a narrow pack-horse bridge. Bridging a stream did not always dislodge the old ford names: Oxford remains Oxford, and in Wales the Welsh for bridge was often tacked on to the ford name, for instance in Dyfed, Pont-rhyd-y-groes, 'Bridge of the Ford of the Cross', or Pontrhydfendigaed across the Teifi close to the Cistercian abbey of Strata Florida, 'Bridge of the Blessed Ford'. Early Welsh poetry (see the translations in Kenneth Jackson's *Early Celtic Nature Poetry*, 1935) frequently talks of the pleasantness of fords in summer, the danger and the threat of them in winter or after a storm –

Slippery are the paths, violent is the shower
And deep is the ford. The heart concocts treason.

Some English ford names suggest the difficulties or dangers of passage. At Christian Malford, in Wiltshire, a bridge which crosses the Bristol Avon is often made useless by floods: before the bridge this difficult ford, where many drownings took place, was marked by a *cristelmael*, a Christ sign, or crucifix. Several of the Welsh *Stanzas of the Graves* (9th or 10th century) locate heroes' graves alongside fords, as if it was at fords that raiders were made to stand and fight, and die, when the fords were deep-flooded and impassable:

Above the ford of the rough stone
Is the grave of Rhun, Alun Dyfed's son.

Foreshore

The beach or the foreshore is legally that part of the shore subjected to the flux and reflux of the sea, stretching from medium low tide mark to medium high tide mark. Who owns it? If it has not been granted away (which is often the case) it belongs 'to the King by virtue of his prerogative'. To take away sand or shingle without permission, expressed or implied, is unlawful. It is also unlawful to take away goods cast upon the foreshore from a wreck. The law about the ownership of such goods was stated in the reign of Elizabeth I by Constable's Case, 'often argued at bar and bench', which still holds. The goods are taken by him that has the 'franchise of the wreck' (franchise, as defined by Blackstone, being a 'royal privilege, or branch of the king's prerogative, subsisting in the hands of a subject'). But 'when a dog or a cat escapes alive out of a ship, that said ship shall not be adjudged wreck; the goods shall be kept by the King's Bailiff, so that if any sue within a year and a day the goods shall be restored to him'. The King's Bailiff is now a Board of Trade officer, the Receiver of Wrecks, to whom wrecks must be reported. The queerly named case of 1886, *the King v. Forty-nine Casks of Brandy*, illustrates the extent of this franchise of wreck: the owner of the franchise got the two casks which were left on the foreshore, the other forty-seven, as derelict goods still found afloat, were 'droits of Admiralty' – rights of Admiralty.

Forests

The mediaeval areas of forest jurisdiction have left their mark all over England to such a degree that there is a common look and 'feel' about many of them, even though they were disafforested three or four hundred years ago.

In interpreting such a forest landscape, two things need to be realized. The first is that a 'forest' was an unenclosed extent in which the hunting and the game – above all the deer, red, fallow and roe – were reserved to the king: many different people might own the land which made up a forest territory, but their holdings and those who lived on them were subject to the severe and irksome Forest Laws, outside the common law of the kingdom. Secondly, the forests were not so much great extents of uninterrupted woodland as districts partly cultivated, partly waste, partly scrub and woodland interspersed with glades. William I introduced the Forest Laws, and the Norman kings greatly enlarged the extent of the royal forests until they existed in most English counties. According to soil (and terrain), some were more, some less, heavily wooded, or some (such as Exmoor or Dartmoor, each a royal forest left over from the vast forest extent which till 1204 covered the whole of Devon) hardly wooded at all.

The deer were paramount. Trees, underwood and thorn thickets (the 'green wood', or vert), the living leafy cover which gave food and shelter to the deer, might not be cut down or lopped. Your dogs, if you were a forest dweller, had to be 'humbled', i.e. their claws had to be cut, to prevent them damaging the deer; and during the midsummer breeding season your movements through the forest were curtailed. Deer had free exit and entrance to your land. Fences had to be low enough for the deer to leap in and out of your crops, from which they could be ejected only by the forest officers; or you had to provide your enclosed land with leap-gates (see LYPIATT) too high for cattle but not for these other lordly creatures. Rights of grazing cattle or running pigs through the forest were strictly controlled. If you wished to clear or 'assart' some of your own property in the forest (see ASSART), you could do so only by royal licence and the payment of dues. The forests were therefore valuable to the king for much more than the pleasures of hunting, as the court moved from place to place. Supplies of necessary meat were assured, especially in winter when meat was scarce (buck were hunted in summer and autumn, does after the breeding season, from early September to the beginning of February). Supplies of necessary revenue were also assured in dues and fines.

All the same, exploration of the old areas of forest law will show that many of them centred on poor land, such as clay or gravel, hardly worth clearing or cultivating for the yields of mediaeval farming.

Today an area 'disafforested' or excluded from the forest in the 16th or 17th century, or later, will have considerable patches of woodland, occasional old oaks in odd corners, often a poor road system, and that look of being neither the one thing nor the other which comes from late clearance and enclosure. Many place-names will recall the deer, and their privileged existence, the forest officers, Forest Laws and courts. Going back beyond the era of the Anglo-Saxons or the Romans, the actual name of the forest may be British. But there will be names containing not only such words as lypiatt and assart, but -leigh or -ley (Old English lēah) for a glade or a clearing, and purlieu, which meant land along the edge of a forest which had once been wrongfully included in the forest, and later excluded. There may be a Woodwards Farm, to recall the woodwards or forest keepers, who worked under the foresters, who in turn had above them the hereditary Warden of the forest. There are likely to remain houses called this or that Lodge, from the houses in which hunting parties were lodged and which were the homes of the foresters, each of whom controlled from his lodge his own 'walk' or division of the forest. Often the Crown made a grant or sale of the lodges when disafforestation came at last.

Chases, such as Cranborne Chase in Wiltshire and Dorset or Malvern Chase, were areas over which the hunting rights belonged to private persons, who had made these acquisitions usually by royal grant, the chase having been the whole or part of one of the king's many forests. To enclose a park inside the bounds of a chase, within the pales of which the deer could be fattened, still needed a licence from the Crown. It was the disafforestation of chases into more profitable farmland that had much to do with the rise of foxhunting in the 18th century. Having no more deer to hunt, the great landlords and squires took after the fox, which had been vermin; and many packs bear the name of the old chases where they were first formed.

Forest and chase were organized in much the same way (though on the chases you were not subject to the Forest Laws), and the huge extent of the two combined, and their long part in English life, have left common surnames behind – Woodwards, Foresters, Hunters, and the Parkers who looked after the imparked deer.

An aerial view
of one of the
ten FORTS OF THE
SAXON SHORE, at
Porchester (Portus
Adurni), Portsmouth,
Hampshire. Henry II
built his square,
bastioned castle within
the walls of one built by
the Romans to protect
the Saxon shore. Also
situated within the
Roman Walls is the
church, built in 1135.

Forts of the Saxon Shore

Roman forts round the coast from Norfolk to Hampshire. There were ten of them. Nothing remains of the fort of Walton Castle (Roman name unknown) near Felixstowe in Suffolk, the last of which vanished into the sea in 1933, or of the fort at Dover (Dubris); and there is little to be seen of the Brancaster fort (Branodunum) on the Wash or of Reculver (Regulbium) in Kent. Two more, Ythancaestir (Othona, across the fields from Bradwell in Essex, on a melancholy edge of the North Sea) and Stutfall Castle (Lemanis) at Lympne in Romney Marsh, in Kent, endure in fragments of grey wall. Brutally different are Burgh Castle (Gariannonum) in Suffolk, Richborough (Rutupiae) in Kent, Pevensey (Anterita) in Sussex, and Portchester Castle (Portus Adurni) now involved in the land and tidal pattern of the modern Portsmouth. These forts still show squat and massive walls, with wall-turrets and angle-turrets, enclosing rectangular spaces at Burgh, Richborough, and Portchester, and an oval space at Pevensey. Modern theory suggests that the forts (or most of them: Pevensey seems to be 4th century) were built in the 3rd century between 287 and 294 by the Roman usurper Carausius, to defend his British territory against Roman authority from overseas. Carausius was murdered in 294, legitimate Roman rule restored

in 296. The forts were retained as a chain of land and naval strong points against Saxon piracy. In the second half of the 4th century they were commanded by the *Comes Litoris Saxonici*, the 'Count of the Saxon Shore'. The forts were useful to the English and the Normans. The missionary St. Cedd built his church of St. Peter ad Murum (still to be seen) astride the Roman wall at Ythancaestir. Reculver keeps the 12th century towers of a church founded in the 7th century. There are remains of Norman castles inside the walls at Pevensey and Portchester, and the Norman earls of Norfolk had a castle inside the Walton walls of the 3rd century.

Fossil sea-urchins

Fossil sea-urchins or echinoids are to be found in and under chalk cliffs, in chalk quarries, in fields in chalk and limestone districts (Wiltshire, east Yorkshire, the Cotswolds, etc.). They are the commonest of fossils, and for their shape and markings have certainly appealed to mankind for thousands of years. More than two hundred were found in a Bronze Age barrow in Bedfordshire round the skeleton of a woman and child, and hundreds have been excavated around Romano-British dwellings in Cranborne Chase. They have been valued as charms, and given many names – Shepherd's Purses, Shepherd's Mitres,

Shepherd's Crowns, Fairy Hearts, Fairy Loaves, Sugarloaves. Sir Thomas Browne knew them as Fairy Stones. 'Of the Echinites, such as are found in Chalk-pits are white, glassie, and built upon a Chalky inside; some of an hard and flinty substance, are found in Stone-pits and elsewhere. Common opinion commendeth them for the Stone, but are most practically used against Films in Horses' eyes' (*Pseudodoxia Epidemica*, 1646).

Four Doctors of the Latin Church

These are St. Augustine or Austin of Hippo, St. Gregory, St. Ambrose and St. Jerome, and they were often figured in churches in the 15th century. They appear around fonts (e.g. Docking, and Walsingham, in Norfolk), in stained glass windows; and appropriately, as the most learned teachers and preachers of the Church, they are carved and painted on pulpits (e.g. Trull, Somerset), on panels of the screen shutting off the chancel, the centre of the mysteries and especially on the screen doors opening into the chancel. St. Ambrose, 'an honeycomb by sweet exposition of the scriptures', may be portrayed with a beehive, bees having settled on his mouth, in the cradle, and then flown up into the sky. St. Gregory may wear his papal tiara, St. Augustine may carry a book and a pen, St. Jerome may have the company of the lion from whose paw he extracted the thorn.

Fox

In church carvings (especially common in MISERICORDS), the fox represents the DEVIL. The 13th century Bestiary of Guillaume le Clerc tells how the fox steals fowls and capons and other birds by shamming dead and then snapping them up when they come to peck him –

> He is the evil one, who wars against us,
> Each day he comes to prey on us.

So fox images in church show him preaching, disguised as priest or friar. Or he is the false doctor or the alluring musician. Or – serve him right – the fox is in the stocks.

Frost hollows

You are unlucky if you live in what the climatologist calls a 'frost hollow'. Frost flows; that is to say, air which cools near the ground on still, cloudless nights, grows denser and will flow downhill like water, and then collect in dell or valley if the flow is obstructed. Given the right conditions, abnormally cold local temperatures may occur late in spring or early summer in such a frost hollow, making it a lethal place for fruit blossom.

Fuchsia

Naturalized from fuchsia hedges and one of the particular delights of some of the western sea areas, Cornwall, the west coast of Ireland, and the Isle of Man in particular, the fuchsia has been with us for less than two centuries. The first plant in England, ancestor of the scarlet hedges and the naturalized fuchsias, is said to have been brought back from Chile in the seventeen-eighties by a sailor, whose wife parted with it to a Hammersmith nurseryman. This would have been either *Fuchsia magellanica*, which grows from Peru down to Tierra del Fuego, or its variety *ricartonii*, to which all the naturalized plants belong (though *ricartonii* may be a nurseryman's variety raised in Scotland about 1830). Fuchsia has become a food plant of the Elephant Hawk Moth.

Furlong

Our measure of 220 yards. It originates in the Old English word *furlang*, i.e. a furrow long, or furrow length, the length of a furrow in the open field of the manor. So furlong came to be used for a division of the open field containing, each of them, so many strips or selions.

Galilees

Galilees, the west-end vestibules derived from the narthex of Byzantine churches which were built on to a few of the great cathedrals, were never a feature of the English parish church in the Middle Ages (entered, as a rule, through a porch on the south side). Reduced in size and function and better called narthex than galilee, or vestibule than narthex, they were reintroduced as part of the Stuart and Georgian churches of the 17th and 18th centuries, making a portion of the church in which the worshippers could leave their coats and their pattens, or give a last touch to hat or wig before entering the nave. Galilees (such as the one at Durham, where a line across the floor marks the limit beyond which women could not pass from the galilee into the rest of the cathedral) may be named from Matthew 4. 15, which speaks of Galilee, into which Jesus withdrew, as 'Galilee of the Gentiles'.

Galleting

Houses of roughish stone in south-east Norfolk and in parts of Kent, Surrey and Sussex have often been given a peculiar, rather

Two examples of GARGOYLES, *one from the church of St. Mary the Virgin, at Addebury, Oxfordshire (below) and the other, (bottom), a particularly grotesque creature from St. Peter's Church, Winchcombe, Gloucestershire.*

attractive, look by inserting gallets (French *galet*, a pebble) at regular intervals in the wet pointing. Gallets are more often chips than pebbles (though pebbles and even cinders may be used) – chips of Norfolk Carstone, Kentish rag, flint, red brick, red tile. Galleting is supposed to make the pointing more durable, and certainly it gives form and neatness to a surface of not exactly regular or smooth blocks.

Garden mounds

Now and then to be seen in old gardens, garden mounds were raised as far back as the Middle Ages for a combination of utility and pleasure. They were essential to the small enclosed garden or orchard without prospects. Climb to the top, and you could see over the walls or the high fence to the view; and you could see who was about. Often the mounds or mounts were planted with fruit trees and capped with an arbour or summer-house. In the Tudor garden they were popular. In the more extensive gardens or grounds of the 17th century, such as John Evelyn describes in his diary and helped to plan, the emphasis shifted to prospects contained in the garden itself. From the garden mound was evolved the GAZEBO.

Garden temples

Garden temples entered the English scene early in the 18th century, transferred, especially into the LANDSCAPE GARDENS pioneered by William Kent, from the paintings of Poussin and Claude Lorraine. Sir John Vanbrugh designed the large Belvedere Temple (1725–6), at Castle Howard, North Yorkshire, and some of the temples (though not the surviving ones) in Kent's famous gardens at Stowe, in Buckinghamshire, where one may see temples by Kent himself and by James Gibbs.

Such classical or pseudo-classical 'Grecian' temples reminded those who strolled in the landscape gardens, or entered the temple shade and coolness, of all the graces and virtues – temples of such deities as Venus and Diana, of Romulus and Remus, of Ancient Virtue or Friendship. Elements of the eye-guiding, eye-resting design of the gardens, along with water, grottoes and cascades, they stood specifically for beauty and dignity. Away from the 'Grecian' country house, in the wider landscape, the Gothic ruin might agree with the genius of the native scene. Nearer the Grecian house, in the contemplative garden, beauty and wholeness and dignity were appropriate in

emblems of polite culture – temples, that is to say, of the same or similar style. But before long Grecian temples were varied and accompanied by Gothic temples, even Chinese temples, and Turkish mosques, and models of dolmens and Stonehenge. Purists and champions of the natural did not approve; and by the turn of the century temples of all kinds were under attack by the connoisseurs. The temples, *c.* 1750–70, of the landscape garden at Stourhead, Wiltshire, now preserved by the National Trust, are the best matured assembly in existence.

'Garderobe'

'Garderobe', the privy in a mediaeval house or castle built in the thickness of the wall, sometimes a small room like a cell, at the end of a Z-shaped passage, with a shaft which drops down

inside the wall to a cesspit, sometimes a stone bench jettied out on corbels high over the moat, so that taking one's seat in the row was like sitting down on a cold pillar of draught. 'He's in the garderobe' would not have been understood, in a fundamental sense, in the Middle Ages, garderobe having been the word for clothes room or bedchamber (wardrobe). As we use it, garderobe is an antiquary's euphemism of that genteel order down the ages which includes the monks' REREDORTER or *necessarium*, privy, draught, siege, jakes, necessary house, lavatory and its shortened form latrine, w.c., loo, cloakroom and powder-room.

Gargoyles

These projecting gutterstones, which church masons so often carved into fantastic demons and dragons, were due to the 14th century development of ornamental traceried parapets as a way of finishing off a wall. With no eaves to carry off the rain, it was necessary to build long lead bow-gutters behind the parapet, with a gargoyle every so often to drop the rainwater well clear of the masonry. The name and the notion were borrowed from France, *gargouille* in Old French having meant a throat, and so a stone spout or gullet through which water guggles, gurgles, or gargles.

Garth

In the north and in Lincolnshire, garth (which comes from the Old Norse): elsewhere, yard. In modern usage a yard is generally an enclosed space with a hard surface: it has taken over the sense conveyed in courtyard. But yard and garth alike meant originally a small

The remains of the GATEHOUSE *and external walls of the 12th century Queen Mary's castle, Framlingham, Suffolk.*

enclosed space of any kind, hard or soft. Yard keeps the simpler meaning of enclosure in churchyard, vineyard, farmyard, stackyard, poultry-yard. So also there are churchgarths and willowgarths (willow-gardens) and applegarths (apple orchards: in mediaeval times men spoke of apple yards). A fishgarth was an enclosed space on seashore or in river shallows for taking fish.

Gatehouses

Gatehouses of Tudor and Jacobean mansions, colleges, palaces, etc., developed from the fortified gate-tower of the castle. The entrance into the fortified space of the castle was obviously a weak spot. Gateways through the bailey palisade of the MOTTE-AND-BAILEY castles were defended with wooden towers. Later stone castles were entered through a great tower or between flanking towers by a gateway secured (*see* CASTLES) with a portcullis, gate and towers combining into an extra strong, formidable and prominent feature of

castle design. When the castle weakened into the semi-fortified mansion or COUNTRY HOUSE at the end of the 15th century, there were both practical and ostentatious reasons for retaining and developing the towered gatehouse. It was the port of entry into the enclosed area, the point where the visitor stopped, the place (as in the courtyard colleges at Cambridge and Oxford) for the interrogating porter, the *portarius* or gatekeeper. The pomp of a gatehouse was the introduction to wealth and power, a fact magnificently exemplified in the great gatehouses of red brick in East Anglia (Oxburgh Hall, Norfolk, *c.* 1482; Deanery Tower, Hadleigh, Suffolk, 1495; Layer Marney, Essex, *c.* 1520–30; Kirtling Tower, Cambridgeshire, 1530). When the Puritan lawyer and merchant Lord Robartes built his granite mansion at Lanhydrock, near Bodmin in Cornwall, more than a hundred years later, he still felt that he must have the grandeur of a gatehouse. The gateways into the high-walled monastery precincts followed the same development, from the single gate-tower to the Tudor gatehouse.

When the mansion developed into the country house surrounded by its landscaped park and approached by long winding drives, the gatehouse dwindled into the lodge, classical or neo-Gothic or rustically picturesque.

Gazebo

This mock Latin word of the 18th century, with its future ending, seems to have been coined as our synonym for the Italian-named BELVEDERE (pleasant view) on top of a house. Sometimes it was used of garden belvederes or PROSPECT-TOWERS, but gazebo, for a gazing place, is now commonly applied to one of those small fancy buildings or rooms perched at the corner of a garden wall to give a view of the road or the country on the other side. Such gazebos developed from GARDEN MOUNDS or mounts or toots, which were topped with arbours. By no means rare, and some of them earlier than the 18th century, gazebos were pleasant places for idling, watching the passing of public or private coaches, or waiting for a first glimpse of arriving relations or friends. They belong to the quieter horse-drawn age when traffic was an event, and for that reason are now often neglected or half in ruins.

Geo

A ragged, steep and narrow cleft or gully in the sea-cliffs of Shetland and Orkney (a 'goe' in Caithness), from the Old Norse *gja*.

Gill

In the north-western landscape and speech, a narrow rocky valley or ravine threaded by a stream (Old Norse *gil*); one of the words used by the Norwegians who crossed from Ireland to settle much of north-western England in the 10th century.

Gipseys

Gipseys are streams in the chalk country of Yorkshire which only break out and flow in winter or periods of exceptional rainfall. The word – with a hard g – has nothing to do with the caravan GYPSIES, which it long antedates.

Glasshouse

As a name in an old forest or woodland district, glasshouse will indicate where glass was once made (and where slag ought to be found) – probably window-glass and bottle-glass. From about 1570 glass-making spread through England, as more and more yeomen built themselves better houses with the luxury of glazed windows; about 1630 glasshouses began to turn out bottles, especially for wine (*see* BOTTLE SEALS). The glassmakers needed a local supply of their three basic ingredients, sand (or crushed flint for bottles), lime and potash. So to the woods they went for the potash (and the charcoal for the furnaces). The window-glass of these woodland glasshouses was of poor quality to begin with. Of glass made in the Weald of Sussex, William Camden wrote in his *Britannia* (1586) that 'by reason of the matter or making I know not which' the glass was 'not so transparent and clear' and was therefore used only 'by the ordinary sort of people', i.e. the people who were then so busy rebuilding their farmhouses.

Glebe

In a country parish, glebe is the land (*glæba* is Latin for soil, earth – so land which can be cultivated) anciently set aside for the maintenance of the parish priest. Nowadays the glebe, if it has not been sold, will be let and farmed by someone else. But when men lived by the produce of the lands around them, the priest needed land as much as any other parishioner to provide him with a basic livelihood, in addition to his tithes, funeral fees and Easter offering. Often the clergyman's glebe is among the best of the parish lands, close to village and parsonage, and equivalent in acreage to the run of other small farms or holdings; and parsonage buildings may still include barn, cow-sheds, pigsties, etc., with a stackyard.

Glebe lands were also known by the Latin term *sanctuarium* (often surviving as 'sentry'), a fact which sometimes misleads people into believing that their parish church had special rights of sanctuary.

Glen

Glen for a valley is a word the Anglo-Saxons borrowed from their British neighbours. In Welsh and Welsh valley names it is *glyn*. The glens of Scotland, Man and Ireland are from the Gaelic *gleann*.

Gloop

A hole that makes a throaty, glooping, gulping noise – i.e. a blow-hole coming up from a sea-cave to the cliff-top. Waves at high tide sway in and compress the air, and the gloop spouts air and water. Gloops are specially notable in the cliffs of Shetland (around Papa Stour, etc.).

Goblin and demon names

These are still to be found up and down the country from days more haunted than our own, usually minor names of nooks and corners on a farm, in valleys or among the fells. BARROWS, CAVES, MERES and FORDS might be the home of a large and dangerous *thyrs* (called by Norse speakers a *thurs*), later somewhat tamed and diminished into the hobthrust or hobthrush of folklore stories. *Thurs* names are not uncommon for caves and other limestone features in the northern limestone districts, Thirst House, Hobhurst House, etc. Thor's Cave, which opens like a black ear in Thor's Cliff above the Manifold river in Staffordshire, owes its name to the demon, not the god. The demon known as *scucca* or *sceocca* has left names with Shuck- or Shock- or Shack- on hills, streams and barrows. The commonest south-country goblin was the *pūca*, the later Puck or Pook of folklore, who has an abundance of Puck-names for pools, .pits, ponds, streams, holes, lanes, paths, fields.

Gold

Gold was one of the worthwhile things which the Romans hoped to find in Britain. They were disappointed, though for perhaps a hundred years they worked the gold mine at Dolaucothi in Dyfed. (There is little to see, though the mine is in a fine National Trust valley. Adits remain; water for washing the ore, after it had been milled in querns, was brought to the mine by an eight-mile leat from the Cothi.) The Romans would probably have

done better if they could have crossed the Irish Sea and taken possession of Co. Wicklow and the Wicklow Mountains. Much of the gold recovered from Bronze Age barrows, beaten into beads, sun-discs, ear-rings, cups, torques, etc., probably came from this part of Ireland, panned out of the streams running off the small mountain of Crochan Kinshela, where there was something of a gold rush at the end of the 18th century, particularly after the finding of a $21\frac{1}{2}$-oz nugget in 1795. The Ovoca, which runs into the sea at Arklow, has also yielded gold dust and nuggets. Scottish alluvial gold has been found in Sutherland near Kildonan in six or more tributaries of the Ullie, on the river and rivulet system of the Blackwater and in the Gordon Diggings by Loch Brora. The modest gold rush to Sutherland in 1869 produced more for the Duke of Sutherland in licence fees at £1 per month per head than for the prospectors. A small amount of alluvial gold has been found in Cornwall in the tin-streaming works and occasional nuggets are found along Welsh streams.

Gospel Oak

A place-name often to be found (if no longer with its reverend oak tree) on parish boundaries, a fossil from the mediaeval festival observed on the Rogation Days, or Cross Days, immediately before Ascension Day. A procession was formed. Crosses and green boughs and flowers were carried around the parish, the boundaries of the parish land were noted and confirmed, crosses were traced on the ground, and at recognized stopping-places, such as an oak, the priest read the scriptures and invoked divine blessings on the land and the crops. There are many more boundary names of the same origin, such as Gospel

Thorn, Amen Corner, or St. Paul's Epistle (name of a mound on the boundaries of a Gloucestershire parish). Much dancing and fun went into this spring festival of the community, which had been introduced into England as early as the 8th century. At the Reformation the processions were banned, and the festivity declined to the 'beating of the bounds' on Ascension Day, a useful and necessary proceeding before there were maps.

Gossamer

The spider threads which fly through the air in late September, October and November, and fall to the ground where dew condenses on them, making a glistening net of gossamer as far as the eye can see; on this net one sometimes observes a hyperbola-shaped dew-bow, caused by the drops catching and refracting the early sunlight (*see* RAINBOWS). Gossamer, unexpectedly, appears to be named from the time of year: it comes in the 'goose summer', i.e. the late spells of sunshine and summer-like weather which make up St. Luke's Summer around 18 October and Allhallow's Summer around 1 November, the time when the goose is in season after the Michaelmas goose-fairs. In Germany one name for gossamer has an equivalent origin: it is *Altweibersommer*, i.e. (the stuff which appears at) 'Old Wives' Summer' around Martinmas (11 November). Gossamer is manufactured by the small, dark, shiny spiders of the *Linyphiinae* family as a means of dispersal, the young standing head to wind as they exude the liquid silk which the wind draws out into several feet of thread. The same spiders weave the untidy sheet webs which one finds, for example, on gorse bushes.

Granite

Granite, rough, tough and crystalline, sparkling among its lichen and growth with little facets of mica, is a rock which was formed underground. Magma welled from inside the earth, mineralizing the veins of the surrounding rocks which had been laid down overhead (as in the mining districts of Devon and Cornwall). It cooled and crystallized into bosses of granite (Italian *granito*, something grained), which protruded, as the covering rocks wore away, and were themselves exposed to weathering, producing the granite landscape of TORS and shapes as fantastic as the tiered Cheesewring on the granite upland of East Cornwall. Deep underground, much granite was chemically decomposed by the rise of steam and carbon dioxide, one of its crystalline components, the white feldspar, breaking down into the china clay which is watered out of huge pits on the edges of Dartmoor and the Cornish moors, leaving behind it snowy mountains of sand above celadon-coloured pools.

Gravestones

Gravestones for the farmers and small tradesmen and craftsmen of the country parish first became common in the late years of the 17th century and early years of the 18th. The gentry were commemorated – and frequently buried still – inside the church. In the CHURCHYARD were laid members of a commonalty increasingly prosperous, literate and individually self-conscious, many of them the new farmers who profited by the Enclosure Acts (*see* FIELDS): like their landlords, they were interested in a commemorative exhibition of their status and in giving a posthumously correct display of the emblems of piety or confidence or repentance or triumph over death. With a time lag, their headstones outside imitated the various grander, sophisticated types of memorial inside: and in the freestone and slate districts 18th century stonemasons executed graveyard slabs for them with an extraordinary virtuosity of detail and craft, from the earlier rococo to the later neo-classic. As if it stood for an entrance into another, deserved, existence, the 18th century headstone frequently reproduces in basic design the 18th century doorway with pilasters (flat pillars) holding up a pediment. On the headstone the pediment has room for a conventional cherub with wings outspread.

Along the limestone belt, across the Cotswolds and the Midlands, the battalion or regiment of headstones in churchyard after churchyard often achieves in tone, lichen, moss and weathering a harmony with the materials of the church which can never be repeated, now that most of the quarries are abandoned.

How such headstones developed is ably illustrated and analysed, with a care for the religious and social causes, in Frederick Burgess's *English Churchyard Memorials* (1963), which explains the imagery and emblems and their sources (Death's-head, Hourglass, Death and Time, Scythe, Reaping-hook, Angels, Urn, Tree of Life, etc.), and discovers four successive trends between the 17th century and the Victorian age. In the late 17th and early 18th century, the designs emphasize mortality and corruption (an inheritance from late mediaeval and Tudor morbidity, the age of the CADAVER and the grave-worm). This mor-

bidity gives way to an 18th century predominance of the symbols of Resurrection. Under the influence of Methodism and a concern for the means of salvation, allegorical figures of Faith, Hope, Charity, etc., and carved scenes from the Bible were preferred. Nineteenth century graveyard memorials, within an eventual welter of style, imagery and sentiment, changed to a concentration on the direct symbol of the Cross – 'Hold Thou thy cross before my closing eyes' – which had previously been considered popish.

Great Bear

Looking up into the night sky, what ought we to call this most famous of the constellations, always visible, circling round the celestial pole, with its Pointers toward the Pole Star? Great Bear? Wagon? Plough? or Dipper? The names in fact identify the seven stars with items of different stages of Near Eastern or European culture. Bear has priority. Surviving from huntsmen's cultures before the breaking of the soil, this group of stars was still the Bear (symbol of a bear god or myth?) to the civilizations of Mesopotamia; from which the name descended to the Greeks, who called it the *Arktos* or She-bear (hence Arctic for the North Polar regions) or the *Megale Arktos*, the Great She-bear, to distinguish it from the bear cub, the neighbouring Little Bear (which includes the Pole Star). From the Greeks the name descended to the Romans, who made the two constellations *Ursa Major* and *Ursa Minor*; and from the Romans to ourselves, who find it hard to see bear or bear cub in either set of seven stars.

Names with Wain or Plough have a later origin. Four-wheeled wagons with a pole attached to paired animals go back in Mesopotamia to the 4th millennium B.C. They had reached Europe by *c.* 2000–1600 B.C., and to the Greeks this Bear constellation was also the *Hamaxa*, to the Romans the *Plaustrum*, both words meaning wagon or carriage. Applied to the constellation, this would be less a goods vehicle than a vehicle of ceremony; and wain, which was our oldest term for the constellation, would have indicated a ceremonial wagon of one of the gods (Woden for the English and Germans?) carrying death and rebirth. This fits in with our name Charles's Wain, *Carles Wægn* in Old English, the Charles being Charlemagne: it was the wain of this great 9th century Emperor of the West, who was connected mythically with Woden.

In English the name Plough is more or less

*K*aolin is a fine
white clay used
in the manufacture of
porcelain. Formed deep
underground by the
decomposition of
GRANITE *when steam
and carbon dioxide rise
and cause one of its
crystalline components,
felspar, to break down
into the china clay. This
is then watered out of
huge pits on the edges of
Dartmoor and the
Cornish moors leaving
behind it snowy
mountains of sand above
celadon coloured pools.*

A GREEN MAN – *or Jack-in-the-Green, as he was called in Worcestershire – represented on a cloister boss in Norwich Cathedral, Norfolk.*

modern, not cited by the *Oxford Dictionary* before 1513. But it is ancient in source, and is the most fascinating name of all. The Greeks made the nearby Arktouros, the Bear Guard, or rather his constellation, into Boötes, the driver of the oxen, the Ploughman, whose ploughs (Ursa Major and Minor) he guided for ever round the pole. The Romans also called these two constellations the *Triones*, the ploughing oxen, as an alternative to Ursa Major, or Plaustrum, and Ursa Minor. In fact the shape presented by the two constellations is the shape of a wheel-less wooden plough used in the Bronze Age and Iron Age and later, and in use still in some parts of Greece and the Alps: first the huntsman's Bear, then the farmer's Plough, on which life depended in turn. Boötes as ploughman stands in the sky at the business end of a plough 'team', which is indicated (though there are no stars for the share) by the first four of the seven stars; and this beam (usually made in two pieces, as shown by the bend in the star line) extends to the two ploughing oxen, seen in the box shape at the other end of the constellation. Bronze Age and Iron Age rock pictures in the Alps and in Sweden show just such two-ox ploughs in action, with a ploughman.

The Dipper is modern. This name was invented by American farmers in the last century: the ancient plough beam became the handle of a metal dipper for taking up water, the box or ox shape became its bowl.

Green lane

A term of pleasant summery emotion rather than a distinct category of ancient ways: it implies hedges on either side, and it implies grass underfoot – a grass-grown length edged with blackthorn or may or trees, which may be historic or prehistoric, part of a RIDGEWAY or a ROMAN ROAD or a mediaeval market road or even a main road which has fallen out of general use through changes of trade or circumstance. Kept open now by occasional farm traffic, green lanes may have been convenient for mediaeval salt merchants (*see* SALT WAYS) and other travellers from market to market, or for the cattle drovers of the 18th century (*see* DROVE-ROADS). It will be seen from a map that such green lanes, which will be public highways, are or were through routes, often continuing as metalled lengths of road, as footpaths, or as long cross-country lines of hedge. Not always so easily explicable on map or ground, other green lanes may be fragments between fields. The answer is sometimes to be

found in the lost layout of the open fields and open pastures as they existed (*see* FIELDS) before enclosure, the now enclosed green lane having been a length of common baulk, which was left unploughed to give access to the strips; or – if longer, but still without obvious sense – having been a 'mere' or 'meare' (Old English *gemære*, a boundary), a wide grass strip which divided the open lands of two villages.

Green men

Heads of men wreathed in foliage, which usually grows out of their mouths (sometimes out of eyes, ears and nostrils), are very commonly found among church carvings of the 13th to the 15th centuries, on bosses, misericords, responds, capitals, corbels, shrines, etc. The foliage is frequently recognizable as oak or hawthorn (may tree), and the face is often, indeed generally, made to wear an expression of pain and sadness, and a decided frown. Though mediaevalists incline to dismiss these heads as pure ornament, there can be little doubt that they represent (as an image of Easter and resurrection?) the Green Man, the Man-in-the-Oak, or Jack-in-the-Green – i.e. the May King of the common May Day ceremonies, who wreathed himself in green leaves and flowers, acted a death, and then came to life, jumping up and comforting his disconsolate May Queen, and dancing with her. He is the Green Man who has given his name to innumerable inns.

Green ray

The last curve of the sun glimpsed as it dips under the sea may show a brilliant emerald for a very brief while, or (but rarely) a very brief green ray, or green flash, may seem to stand over the vanishing or vanished sun. The density of atmosphere between the setting sun and the lucky observer absorbs the yellow and orange light, much of the violet light is scattered, and the dense atmosphere bends the blue-green rays so that the red rays are invisible. The green flash may be seen from the low oceanic platforms of the Isles of Scilly.

Greensand

Greensand is not always or generally green. Belonging to the Cretaceous System, the greensands (Upper Greensand and Lower Greensand, separated by the gault) are beds of sands, clays and sandstones underlying the chalk. In vales under a chalk escarpment (e.g. the Vale of Pewsey, in Wiltshire) the Upper Greensand comes to the surface, making farmlands of great fertility, very expensive to rent or buy. Greensands may be greenish or greenish grey from the mineral glauconite, but the commoner tints, due to staining with iron, are reddish, purple, brown, and yellow. Building stones of the Lower Greensand include the grey or greeny-grey Kentish rag and the brown Carstone or 'gingerbread' of Norfolk.

Griffin

Inherited from the Greeks, the griffin of remote India, with the cruel beak and claws and wings of an eagle united to the back portions of a lion, symbolized for the Gothic carver the power and savagery of the Devil. In churches, he appears on bench-ends, misericords, fonts, etc., sometimes solitary, sometimes clawing and tearing at his prey (man, rabbit, lamb), and sometimes fighting with a knight (carnal passions valiantly withstood). Anciently the griffin was sacred to Apollo and Bacchus, and was a creature of good against evil, in which guise he seems to appear on some of the earlier church carvings.

Grim

The 'Grim' in the names of various running earthworks (Grim's Ditch, Grim's Dyke, in Wiltshire, Oxfordshire, Berkshire; Grimspound, the walled Bronze Age settlement on Dartmoor; the Grimsbury hill-fort near Newbury, etc.) is held to derive from Grim, the Masked One, one of the names of Woden, the high god of the Anglo-Saxons before their conversion to the Christian god in the 7th century. Woden appears to have been the god of victory, death and magic power, and most of the Anglo-Saxon royal families claimed him as their ancestor. The Long Man of Wilmington (see HILL-FIGURES) may be a likeness of Grim or Woden, and his name seems to have been attached to otherwise inexplicable earthworks as a folklore explanation of their building, presumably after the conversion of the Anglo-Saxons, who did not remember that many of these works of Grim had in fact been the handiwork of their own ancestors. In much the same way giants and the Devil were invoked in later times. Under his proper name, Woden was also credited with building Wansdyke (*Wodnes dic*), the running boundary fence or defence which crosses the Marlborough Downs between Avebury and Devizes. This and some other Woden names, e.g. Wensley (*lēah*, grave, or glade, of Woden) in the Peak District, and Woodnesborough ('Woden's Hill') in Kent, may point to actual

worship when he was an accepted god in the sixth century. Grimes Graves in Norfolk (see FLINT MINES) are known locally as Grimmers Graves, which suggests that they were anciently attributed to the Scandinavian Odin, whom the Scandinavians also called Grímr.

Grisaille

In church windows of the 13th and 14th centuries, grisaille is clear glass painted in silvery grey, often with stem and leaf patterns on a background of delicate cross-hatching, and with interlacing bands of strapwork. Not shutting out too much light, such glass gives an 'abstract' effect of coolness and quiet. A careful look at grisaille windows with field-glasses will often reveal a delicately charming sinuosity of stems and leafage.

Grottoes

Derived from the formal grottoes of the Renaissance gardens of Italy, the grottoes of 18th and early 19th century England were essential elements of the LANDSCAPE GARDEN. Gradually they lost their more formal plan, their rococo decoration of shells, spars, minerals, etc., and their classical association with nymphs (cf. the 'nymph of the grot', round whom the waters flow in the grotto of the seventeen-forties at Stourhead, in Wiltshire), and approximated to the natural cave, becoming improved versions of the water-caves of the English limestone districts. They are less a feature of the countryside than an occasional tumbling relic of great gardens dismantled or in decay. Such an example will be found opening off the lake at Fonthill, Wiltshire, part of the huge romantic complex of Beckford's Fonthill Abbey (where the lawns or glades of the landscape garden were scythed by night, by the light of torches, so that by day the natural illusion was maintained).

Gulls

Where gritstone or limestone presses heavy on a softer formation, along an edge, or the side of a valley, blocks have sometimes slipped downwards out of place, leaving a 'gull' or cave-like fissure, e.g. Kinderlow Cave, at 1,800 feet in the millstone grit of Kinder Scout in Derbyshire, or the various 'windy pits' along Ryedale (the dale of Rievaulx Abbey) in the North Yorkshire Moors.

Gypsies

Gypsies reached England very early in the 16th century, and were first known as Egyptians,

A GRIFFIN *is a fabulous beast, with the beak, wings and talons of an eagle and the body and back legs of a lion.*

Gypcians or Gipsons, as if they had come from Egypt, an idea encouraged by the Gypsies themselves, who inherited no recollection that India was their real country of origin. Eventually it was shown that Romany, the Gypsy language, was basically Indian, a Hindi dialect which had picked up Persian, Slavonic and Byzantine Greek words as the Gypsies moved across Europe from the south-east, during the late Middle Ages. They had been, it seems, an Indian nomad people of low caste living by dancing, singing and metal-working.

Persisting awkwardly and half-secretly in the seams of English, Scottish and Welsh life (Ireland was never overrun), the Gypsies were soon regarded with feelings of attraction and repulsion. They might be in rags, but they were dark, had gold or silver rings in their ears, and spoke a strange speech. They might steal, but they told fortunes, and had 'powers'. Justices of the Peace moved them on (one of the earliest recorded uses of 'Egyptian' meaning Gypsy is in a handbook for magistrates in 1514). Further immigration was forbidden. But these people intrigued a Tudor and Jacobean England which after the Reformation was somewhat starved of the colours of superstition and fancy. This effect of allure comes out in Ben Jonson's masques and poems –

> Knacks we have that will delight you,
> Sleights of hand that will invite you
> To indure our tawny faces
> And not cause you quit your places –

The feelings revived in a new way when 19th century romantic writers made the Gypsies an image of freedom and escape which might be hiding the secret of life. In between the autobiographical fictions of *Lavengro* (1851) and *The Romany Rye* (1857), in which the raffish George Borrow wrote of his wanderings with the Gypsies, the respectable and intellectual school inspector Matthew Arnold published his poem 'The Scholar Gypsy' (1853), in which the seeker, the *Romano rai*, the Gypsy gentleman, the scholar among the Gypsies, searches in their company for the secret, in quintessential English scenery, wood anemones, dark bluebells, purple orchises, Thames meadows, the abandoned Lasher, etc., free of contact with 'this strange disease of modern life'.

While these attitudes were being built into the gentile in his contemplation of the Gypsies (but not into the farmers who detest them, and village people who despise them), the Gypsies themselves continued, as John Clare called them, 'A quiet, pilfering, unprotected race',

intermarrying more and more, smoothing out many of their characteristics, and losing the Hindi language they brought with them from the Indian plains.

By 1894, when John Sampson the gypsiologist was surprised and delighted to discover a vigorous and authentic Romany still spoken in Wales by a clan of 'harpers, fiddlers, fishermen, horse-dealers, knife-grinders, basket-makers, wood cutters, fortune-tellers and hawkers' descended from an 18th century Gypsy 'king', Abram Wood, Romany among the English Gypsies had become more or less a jargon, spoken without grammar, inflections, or most of its vocabulary. In *The Dialect of the Gypsies of Wales* (1926) Sampson recorded a language of structure, dignity and lively metaphor, which is no longer spoken in Wales, England or Scotland. But whatever gypsiologists plead, their researches have shown nothing more than an unlettered race of quiet, rather mildly cuckooish independence, which is culturally dependent on its unwilling hosts for folk-tales, folk-rhymes, religion, etc., 'mysterious' rather by its conservatism than by a specifically Romany inheritance (for instance, Gypsy knowledge of medicinal plants has been simply a preservation of the home medicine derived from the herbals and once familiar to every housewife). Allowing for the lag of their conservatism, the Gypsies change with the rest of us. When hard roads came in, they changed largely from tent and cart to the coloured caravans they began using late in the prosperous 19th century; they have changed again from horses to cars, horse caravans to motor-drawn holiday-maker's caravans; as salesmen, they change from hawking to wholesaling.

Some Gypsy words –

Romano, adj.: Gypsy, from *rom*, a man. Romany is from the plural *romane*. Gypsies also called themselves *Kale* (pronounced korlay), 'black ones'.

Petelengero: a smith (familiar in George Borrow's Jasper Petulengro), from *petali*, a horseshoe, which is one of the words the Gypsies borrowed on their way through Europe, Greek *petalon*. Another borrowing from Greek is *kakaracha*, a magpie.

Pokonyos: a magistrate or Justice of the Peace, borrowed from a Slavonic word. But it also means a turkey-cock – J.P.s having so often gobbled at Gypsies from the bench?

O Bero: "The Ship", i.e. the constellation of the Plough or Great Bear.

I Bari Raniaki Fuzhara: 'The Great Lady Fern', i.e. the Pleiades, or Seven Sisters.

O Trin Mienge Bara: 'The Three Mile Stones',
  i.e. the belt in the constellation of ORION.
Urchengo munthos: 'Month of the Urchins
  (Hedgehogs)', i.e. October.

Hafod

Welsh families drove their cows and goats for
the summer from their permanent valley
home, the *hendref*, or 'old farm', up to higher
grazing around the *hafod* or *hafoddy*, the
'summer house', alongside a spring, a long,
low, very simple hut, of temporary construction, refurbished every year and fitted up with
new beds of heather. Here the family milked
the animals and made their butter and cheese.
Life in a *hafod*, in June, with the sound of
cuckoos floating up through the morning air
from the valleys, could be idyllic, the family
living more or less of a holiday life, as in the
Irish BOOLEY HOUSE, or the Scottish SHIELING
or *airidh*.

Ha-ha

Whether bordering a vicarage garden or a
landscape garden, a ha-ha, or sunk fence,
epitomizes more than a century of English
feeling about gardening and nature. The ha-ha
combines a wall and an outward-sloping ditch
in such a way that from inside there appears to
be no break between the garden and the
prospect of 'nature': garden and nature are
united (eyes cross, cows can't). 'What adds to
the beauty of this garden,' wrote a visitor to
Stowe in 1724, 'is, that it is not bounded by
walls, but by a Ha-hah, which leaves you the
sight of a bewtifull woody country.' Then
some twelve years old, that ha-ha, one of the
first in England, still exists, and was the work
of Charles Bridgeman, who laid out the
gardens, and seems to have adapted the ha-ha
from its use in French baroque gardening to
border a terrace without breaking the view.
By mid-century everyone was building ha-
ha's.

  Skeat the etymologist long ago explained
the word (in *A Student's Pastime*, 1896), though
the wrong explanation goes on being repeated.
Borrowed from the French in 1712, in an

A family of GYPSIES *foregather on the outskirts of Appleby, Cumbria, for the traditional June Horse Fair.*

Empshott HANGER, *Hampshire, south-east of Gilbert White's village of Selborne.*

architect's translation of a French gardening manual, the word is certainly the interjection ha! ha!; but it is the sunk fence which cries ha! ha! Stop!, not the visitor to the garden surprised by the sudden possibility of a broken leg (in which case mightn't one expect it to have been called a goodgod or a *mondieu*?). In French *haha* was an ejaculatory warning to stop or take care, which came to be applied, *inter alia*, to a break in the ground.

-ham

At the end of place-names, -ham may be either a word for an enclosure or a water-meadow, or else one of the basic words of English life, in Old English the *hām*, the village, the settlement, which was home, where you were safe and sound and all things were familiar. It is companioned with particularizing words of very many kinds; and when there is a personal name in -ing affixed to it, -ham belongs to early years of settlement, the home or village of such and such a man's family or tribe, e.g. Winteringham, home of Wintra's people, the Wintringas, or Wintrings; Rockingham, the home of the Hrocings, Hroc's people. *See*

-TON, -STED.

The other ham (in Old English *hamm* or *homm*), sometimes standing by itself as Ham, sometimes introduced by a particularizing word, means variously an enclosure (e.g. Dyrham, on the Cotswold escarpment in Avon, 'deer enclosure': it still has a deer park) or an enclosed place by a stream or river, a waterside meadow (e.g. Otterham, 'otter meadow', Lackham, 'stream meadow', Bremilham, 'bramble meadow').

Hammer-beam

Devised as a roof support in the 14th century and brought to structural and decorative perfection in the 15th century churches of Suffolk and Norfolk, the hammer-beam is a roof timber which projects at right angles from the wall, and is supported at the free end by a brace or bracket incurving to the wall, while itself it supports a brace curving upward and outward towards the apex of the roof. Hammer-beams make for an open-spaced roof, marking the length of a nave with regular accents. In the great East Anglian roofs angels with outspread wings, a row of them on each side, look down into the nave from the free end of the hammer-beams.

Hampton or -hampton

Hampton or -hampton in place-names can have several meanings. It may have been the home village or chief village or farmstead (*hām tūn*) of a neighbourhood. It may have been the village or farmstead of some particular *hæme* or home-folk or inhabitants (Ditchhampton in Wiltshire is the *tūn* of the *dic hæme*, the dwellers by the dyke known as Grim's Ditch). Or it may mean the 'high farmstead' or village – in Old English, *heān tūn*.

Hand of God

The *Dextera Dei* or Right Hand of God coming down from heaven, often out of a cloud, is a way of representing the first person of the Trinity in the act of blessing, which goes back to the early centuries of Christianity. In this country the *Dextera Dei* occurs in Anglo-Saxon and Romanesque carvings. In the late Anglo-Saxon carving in the little Wiltshire church of Inglesham the Hand blesses the Virgin and Child. It hangs from a curly cloud over Christ in the 11th century rood outside Romsey Abbey in Hampshire. On the Romanesque tympanum at Elkstone on the Cotswolds, it depends over a Christ throned between the symbols of the Four Evangelists.

Hangers

Hangers, as Cobbett said in his *Rural Rides*, when he rode to the steep Hawkley Hanger, north of Petersfield in Hampshire, which he described with great enthusiasm, are woods which hang on a steep hillside. And it is the Hampshire, Sussex and Wiltshire hangers, beech trees on precipices of chalk, that the word brings to mind, dark eyebrows in winter, billows or runners of waving green in the summer – above all, the famous hanger, north again of Hawkley, which shelters Gilbert White's village of Selborne from west winds. But *hangr* in Old English was used for steep slopes, bare or wooded. It is not always immediately recognizable in place-names, e.g. in Clehonger (Hereford and Worcester), 'clay hanger', or Hartanger (Barfreston, near Dover), 'hart hanger'.

Hanging valley

A side-valley which hangs over a main valley, i.e. which opens into it at a higher level. Hanging valleys are frequent in the mountainy parts of Britain which were subjected to the glaciers of the Ice Age. The tributary glacier of a side-valley could cut the valley floor only down to the top surface of the glacier in the main valley. This glacier-in-chief was all the while gouging the main valley deeper and deeper into the U-shape of glaciated valleys: the side-valley was left hanging, joining the main valley higher up on one slope of the U.

Harrowing of Hell

How Christ harrowed Hell is told in church carvings and paintings. The apocryphal *Acts of Pilate*, of about the 5th century, says that Christ when he descended into Hell brought back two of the inmates, Karinus and Leucius, who wrote down what had happened in Hell when he arrived. First there shone in the black depths a 'golden heat of the sun'. Then a thunderous voice ordered the gates and doors to be opened, echoed by the saints, and by David crying 'O thou most foul and stinking Hell, open thy gates that the King of Glory may come in.' Christ entered, caught Satan and handed him to the powers of his own darkness, and set up the cross of his victory in Hell. Then he took Adam by his right hand and led him out of Hell, followed by the saints. Hell is harrowed on Romanesque TYMPANA and FONTS, in more and less detail.

Hart

In church imagery the hart or stag is sometimes carved in his legendary fight with snake or dragon, a piece of pseudo natural history which goes back to classical sources. According to the Bestiary, in the early 13th century rhyming version by Guillaume le Clerc, the hart when grown old seeks out the serpent, which it hates, spews water into its hole, entices it out, eats it, and is restored to health and vigour. So the hart is Christ, who broke the gates of Hell and destroyed the Devil.

Harvest moon

This orange or reddish full moon hangs low and large over the horizon, and gives light enough to continue harvesting, at the time of the autumnal equinox in September, when the moon's orbit is nearly parallel with the horizon, and the moon rises only a few minutes later each night. The harvest moon keeps its colour longer than a full moon rising high above the horizon at a steeper angle, because its light has to continue to traverse the greater extent of atmosphere between ourselves and the horizon; this depth of atmosphere scatters the violet and blue rays of the light, but not the orange or red rays. The same phenomenon explains the hunter's moon of October (when men had time for hunting after bringing in the harvest).

Hatchments

Hatchments, on a church wall, heraldic shields of the dead in a black frame either square or lozenge (diamond) shaped, are relics of a genteel concern for status, even in death. Until fairly late in the 19th century, it was usual to display a hatchment on the house of a dead man or woman, fixed at second-floor level, over the porch or doorway. It hung there for six months or as much as a year after death, and was then transferred to the parish church, via which the landed interest went to heaven. Hatchment is from 'achievement', the heraldic term for a shield of arms with its crest, supporters, and motto; and this funeral custom appears to have begun in Jacobean times, when new armigers on the make and old armigers on the defensive were particularly concerned about ancestry and the arms they bore, the College of Arms having been reorganized and reincorporated to this end in 1555. Funerals with an heraldic show of banners and escutcheons, under control of the heralds, were *de rigueur* for a long while.

A hatchment indicates by special treatment if the dead person was bachelor or spinster, married man or widower, wife or widow. If the left half of the ground is black, and the other half white, the hatchment was for a wife; if the reverse, it was for a married man. Hatchments for a widow, widower, spinster and bachelor have the whole ground black, with various distinctions for each. The ecclesiologist J. Charles Cox, who died in 1919 at the age of 76, remembered hatchments hung out on houses in Bath and Cheltenham and the West End when he was a boy. Sometimes on a hatchment the motto is *ad hoc* in place of the family motto, which might not have been at all appropriate to death and eternity. *Resurgam* (I will arise) is common, if hopeful.

Hawthorn

Hawthorn, the *haga* thorn, the thorn bush which produces the red haws or hags (Old English *haga*), has in England been the tree or shrub most evocative, through the centuries, of the coming of the summer. Whereas in Ireland the May Flower is the marsh marigold, the hawthorn for the French and the English provided the flower which was 'brought in' on May Day: the 'May', the white, sexy-scented

flower of this tree which blossomed in the month between spring and summer. For the English the link between hawthorn blossom and May Day was weakened by the change of the calendar in 1732, when May Day was brought forward by thirteen days into the colder season of the spring. On the average, hawthorn flowers now come out on 10 May south of London, and in the Midlands on 13 May. Originally the May was hung about doors and windows and cow byres to avert evil beings at a dangerous moment in the year when the young growth was under way. It was one of the plants of magical power. It then became associated less with protection, more with the pleasures of being young.

Heart burial

A frequent practice in the Middle Ages, especially in the 13th and 14th centuries when an eminent person might direct that his heart, the portion of him which was held to be the seat of piety and love, should be separately interred in a particular church, especially a monastic church. The New Abbey or Sweetheart Abbey (Dulce Cor) of the Cistercians in Dumfries and Galloway, south of Dumfries, owes its name to the burial there of the heart of John Baliol, husband of Devorguilla Baliol, who founded the abbey *c.* 1269. Effigies in miniature appear to have been set over heart burials in the 13th century. There are examples of miniature knights in armour in the churches of Bottesford, Leicestershire; Mappowder, Dorset; Halesowen Abbey in the West Midlands; Little Easton, Essex; and Horsted Keynes in West Sussex. The church of the Cistercian Abbey Dore, in Hereford and Worcester, has a miniature effigy of a 13th century Bishop of Hereford. At Tenbury Wells in Hereford and Worcester a half-sized effigy of a knight holds a heart in his two hands.

Hedgehog

Occasionally carved in churches (misericords, etc.), sometimes with fruit on his spines, as a symbol of the wiles of the Devil. This was the mediaeval interpretation of the report in Pliny's *Natural History* that hedgehogs roll on fruit, and so collect it for the winter. The Bestiary speaks of hedgehogs rolling on grapes. Guillaume le Clerc's rhymed version of the early 13th century says that the hedgehog shakes down grapes and apples, and takes them off in this way, so corresponding to the Devil who wastes the spiritual fruit of mankind.

Just as the Devil robs men of their souls, the HEDGEHOG *was shown in church carvings stealing grapes from the vine. This example is from a misericord in Cartmel Priory, Lancashire.*

Hell mouth

In DOOM PAINTINGS and other representations in church of the Last Judgement, carved or in glass, the wide open mouth of a gigantic fish which has teeth, emits flame, and swallows the souls of the condemned forked in by demons, is Leviathan, the great whale of the Book of Job: 'Who can open the doors of his face? his teeth are terrible round about. His scales are his pride . . . By his neesings [sneezings] a light doth shine, and his eyes are like the eyelids of the morning . . . his breath kindleth coals, and a flame goeth out of his mouth . . . He beholdeth all things: he is a king over all the children of pride' (Job 41. 14–34). This great whale of the Book of Job was equated in the Middle Ages with the Devil himself. As a rule, only his mouth is depicted. But the 15th century window of the Last Judgement in Fairford Church, Gloucestershire, includes in purple-red glass the scaly whole of this Satan-Leviathan, with legs and arms and fish eyes, gaping his mouth to swallow terrified men and women.

Sometimes a fish mouth is carved swallowing down figures in the act of sin. Rather than Leviathan-Satan, this is Satan as the mythical Sea Tortoise or Aspido Chelone, who opens his mouth when hungry, according to the Bestiaries, and emits a sweet scent which entices the wicked into his mouth. When they are well hooked, he swallows them. The Aspido Chelone in this way sucks down a wicked man and the girl he is embracing on a bench-end in Wiggenhall St. German church in Norfolk.

Henges and stone circles

When remains of a more or less round structure of which the uprights had been timbers and not stones were found not far from Stonehenge in 1926, the site by analogy was named 'Woodhenge'. Before long 'henge' was given currency as a special word for a class of circles, in spite of the fact that in Stonehenge it was part of a name meaning 'stone gallows' (Old English *hencgen*), i.e. the trilithons of two uprights and a hangman's lintel. Henges by origin are enclosures of *c.* 2500 B.C. with one or two entrances, ringed with a rampart and a ditch (the ditch inside as a rule), sometimes several hundred feet in diameter (e.g. in Cornwall, Castlewich, near Callington; in Dorset, Maumbury Rings at Dorchester, afterwards adapted as a Roman amphitheatre, and Knowlton Rings near Cranborne; in Somerset, Gorsey Bigbury near Charterhouse, on the Mendips; in North Yorkshire, the huge Thornborough Circles, at West Tanfield, near Ripon; in Cumbria, Mayburgh, near Penrith). They were sometimes built, or equipped later, with circles of stone uprights inside the rampart and ditch (e.g. in Cornwall, the Stipple Stones, on Bodmin Moor; in Wiltshire,

Avebury and Stonehenge; in Derbyshire, Arbor Low, near Bakewell; in Lothian, Cairnpapple, near Torphichen; in Orkney the great Ring of Brodgar).

But what were henges used for? We do not know. And guessing has sometimes lacked common sense. Archaeologists repeat that they are 'sacred sites' or 'ritual centres', 'ritual' seeming to have boiled down in part from older convictions that Stonehenge and Avebury – and all stone circles in the land, of whatever kind – were temples which had been served by the Druids. They forget a warning Gordon Childe uttered about cup-and-ring carvings, which applies as piquantly to henges: 'As we have no insight into their inner function and significance, we mask our ignorance by calling them religious.' Intermediately it was insisted that the major stone circles must have been astronomical observatories for determining the calendar. Gordon Childe ridi-

culed this idea as well when he wrote how fantastic it was to imagine 'the ill-clad inhabitants of these boreal isles' shivering in the nights and 'peering through the driving mists to note eclipses and planetary movements in our oft-veiled skies'; and it is scarcely less fantastic to imagine that these not very advanced inhabitants of Britain differed from other peoples in a low cultural stage by providing themselves with so many large temples up and down the country. It is true that cremation burials have been found inside henges, and pits or holes in which it is supposed that offerings were made; but a castle is not called a 'ritual monument' or a 'sacred site', and its towers and curtains are not called 'sacred architecture', because it happens to contain a chapel.

Common sense explanations are called for, and the clue seems to be in the earlier CAUSEWAYED CAMPS: henges can reasonably be

One of the most famous of HENGES AND STONE CIRCLES, *at Stonehenge, Wiltshire. Stonehenge represents an amazing feat of engineering and is a beacon of the prehistoric landscape.*

explained as more elaborate and more convenient places of periodic assembly than the old 'causewayed camps', which larger and more prosperous communities had outgrown. The spaced-out monoliths or stone circles added to henges, where stone was available, may be no more than grandiose fencing, the spaces between the stones having been filled with thorn, or hurdles or loose stones. Henges are generally on low ground not far from water; and avenues bounded with bank and ditch (Stonehenge) or with standing stones (Avebury; Stanton Drew, in Avon) leading from the circle to the nearby river, also indicate that something which needed water – cattle, that is to say – were driven back and forth, or could graze back and forth, between the enclosing sides. Cattle may have become more important in the 'fairs' or assemblies. But all of this is not to deny that henges no doubt served the same mixed purposes, economic

and religious and social, probably served by the old causewayed camps; becoming centres of increasing authority and power. If they were set out as calendrical indicators of the rising and setting of sun and moon at the solstices, that would have been no more than an item in their social evolution and function.

The technique of walling or fencing between uprights of stone seems repeated in the very numerous free-standing stone circles of every kind which lack the ditch and rampart of a henge. These are also susceptible of common-sense explanation, in spite of the Druidic and sacrificial mists which have collected round them, as around Stonehenge and Avebury. Some of these Bronze Age circles may be all that is left of circular cattle pens or stockades surrounding a homestead. Some small stone circles are known to remain from the kerbs which were set close around barrows of loose stone (cairns) to keep the stones in place. Others, larger in diameter and of larger monoliths, are known to have been set around, and some distance away from, burial cists and cairns, which makes them no more 'sacred' or 'ritual' or more extraordinary in themselves than a fence around a cemetery or around an object. Other circles could be the remaining uprights of a roofed building. See Colin Renfrew's *Before Civilization* (1973).

Hermitages

Hermitages are of two kinds, genuine, of the Middle Ages, and affected (if that is the right word), as a property of the 18th century LANDSCAPE GARDEN. Many islands and out-of-the-way places were resorted to by Irish and British holy men in the 6th and 7th centuries, and later; but these were often coenobites, rather than solitary hermits, members of small communities observing the rule of St. Pachomius in desert places, withdrawn from the world. (The Atlantic rock of Skellig Michael off the Kerry coast, and St. Helen's, in the Isles of Scilly, both preserve remains of such small coenobite communities.) Holy men were also given to retreat in the Anglo-Saxon centuries (e.g. St. Aidan, and St. Cuthbert in the Farne Islands; St. Chad according to legend at Armitage – 'hermitage' – in Staffordshire), and various hermitages were maintained in the Middle Ages. These were not always remote. Anchorite or anchoress might inhabit an endowed cell in church or in churchyard. The Black Prince helped to maintain a hermit in the park of Restormel Castle, outside Lostwithiel, in Cornwall, above the Fowey river,

Two famous HILL FIGURES of the south of England are the White Horse (right) and the Long Man of Wilmington, Sussex (below). The horse was cut (or recut) in 1778 on the side of Bratton Castle, near Westbury in Wiltshire. This castle is a rampart farmstead of the 2nd or 1st century BC and encloses a long barrow. The Long Man, which may perhaps be an Anglo-Saxon image of the god Woden, was first recorded in 1764, although his age is uncertain.

who said masses for the souls of the Prince's ancestors. In old forest or wilderness country, various rock-hermitages can be seen. These include the (now inaccessible) remains of a hermitage and chapel dedicated to St. John the Baptist in the travertine mass of Southstone Rock, Stanford-on-Teme; a hermitage of several chambers cut into the red sandstone face of Blackstone Rock, near Bewdley, immediately above the Severn; and on the west bank downstream, the extraordinary (and shockingly neglected) remains of chapel, cells, etc., cut into the flaring red sandstone of Redstone Rock, where the Brethren of Redstone lived from the 12th century. Northumberland has the most perfect mediaeval hermitage (the remains are 14th century) cut into the bright yellow sandstone of a small, now tree-lined, cliff above the Coquet at Warkworth. This hermitage of the Holy Trinity, on two floors, is part excavated, part erected: in the rock a sacristy and small chapel, in masonry, a hall, a kitchen and a solar. Up above, the hermit, or chaplain, had a small farm and an orchard. A cosy withdrawal. The Peak in Derbyshire was also a suitable wilderness for hermits. Deepdale near Dale Abbey has remains of a hermitage gouged in the sandstone cliff. A small chamber in the gritstone of Cratcliffe Tor, near Birchover, is carved with a crucifix, and appears to have housed a hermit in the 13th century. The knights in Sir Thomas Malory's *Morte Darthur* (late 15th century) frequently visit such rock hermitages as Redstone, Dale Abbey and Warkworth; for instance the hermitage 'under a wood, and a great cliff on the other side, and a fair water running under it', to which Sir Lancelot comes (Book XVIII, Chapter XII) to be healed of his wound.

For the 18th or early 19th century proprietor, intrigued by nature and the 'gothic' past, the hermit was a cult-figure, and the hermitage a construction or excavation in keeping with the spirit of his landscape garden. William Beckford contrived a hermit's cave above the lake at Fonthill, Wiltshire (which can still be seen, though minus most of its adornments), in conjunction with a long top-lighted cavern at a deeper level, opening into a grove of 'druidical' yew trees. There is a Hermitage or Hermits Sanctuary in the woods at Burley House, Burley-on-the-hill, Leicestershire, round, and thatched, and habitable. It was indeed inhabited, a hermit having been hired for the delectation of the Earl of Nottingham's guests.

Hill figures

Soil creep and weathering on a chalk escarpment often leave bare white patches suggestive of man or animal. This probably led to the ancient cutting of hill figures: what was indicated by natural accident was improved or completed by man (a process often to be seen in palaeolithic painting, engraving and carving in the caves of Spain and France), or imitated by man. The earliest hill figures are the stylized white horse of Uffington, in Oxfordshire, above the Vale of the White Horse, thought to be a cult figure made by Britons of the 1st century B.C., and the Giant of Cerne Abbas in Dorset, the only ithyphallic possession of the National Trust, likely to have been a figure of a British god corresponding to Hercules, which may have been excised in the 1st century A.D. British figures (others no doubt existed) seem to have been imitated by the Anglo-Saxons. The Long Man of Wilmington with a staff (or spear?) in either hand, on a steep face of the South Downs in East Sussex, has been identified by his likeness to a similar figure on an Anglo-Saxon buckle found in 1964, with Woden, the war god, who as the Odin of the Scandinavians was God of the Spear, and also lord of the *Skjálf*, or steep slope, from which he looked out over the world; and above Warwickshire's Vale of the Red Horse at Tysoe there was until the 18th century a gigantic red horse cut down to the ironstone of the Edgehill scarp, probably an emblem of Tiw, the war god we commemorate in *Tues*day, Tysoe meaning the hill or spur — see HOE — of Tiw. The Whiteleaf Cross on the Chiltern scarp above the Vale of Aylesbury may have been cut in the Middle Ages, a two-dimensional counterpart to the wayside cross, intended to impress travellers along the Icknield Way immediately below.

So far the hill figures have all been religious. In the 18th century a combination of causes, antiquarian interest in the Uffington white horse, landscaping, coach travel along the new turnpikes (*see* TOLL-HOUSES) and the popularity of horse-portraits and engravings, produced an outbreak of hillside horse-making of a very different kind, which continued into the Victorian age. The horse on Waughton Hill near Strichen, in Grampian (filled in with white quartz), has been ascribed to 1775, but it was probably imitated from the new white horses of the south, which began with Wiltshire's Westbury white horse, cut on the scarp of Salisbury Plain in 1778 (or recut: it replaced an older horse of uncertain date or kind). Of the others which followed, Wiltshire horses were cut at Cherhill, near Calne, in 1780; Marlborough, in 1804; and Alton Barnes, above the Vale of Pewsey (designed by an itinerant portrait painter afterwards hanged for forgery) in 1812. The Osmington horse in Dorset (with George III in the saddle) was cut in 1815; the horse on Hackpen Hill, Wiltshire (above the turnpike road from Wootton Bassett to Marlborough) in 1838; the horse on the Hambleton Hills, at Kilburn in North Yorkshire in 1857; and the horse at Broad Town, Wiltshire, in 1863, again along the Wootton Basset—Marlborough road. One or two more have disappeared, including a third horse on the last mentioned road.

Hoe

Hoe as in Plymouth Hoe and a number of Ho and -hoe place-names – is a spur or ridge, from the Old English *hōh*. It may be over a plain or valley (Buckinghamshire's Ivinghoe). It may, like Plymouth Hoe, be over the sea. It may be a high ridge, as at Martinhoe and the neighbouring Trentishoe in north Devon, where the land breaks to the sea in hogsback cliffs. It may be quite a low spit such as the spit of sand on which Hugh Town ('hoe town'), the Scillonian capital, is built.

Hollow ways

Hollow ways are lengths of track on sloping ground, worn down through soft rock (chalk, sandstone) by the passage of cattle and traffic of one kind and another and by the rainwater of centuries. Always with a personality and sometimes a coloured beauty of their own, they may be historic, cut fairly rapidly and recently by carts, wagons, farm sleds, etc., and latterly by tractors, or they may be prehistoric. There are Bronze Age hollow ways associated with downland settlements and fields, and a hollow way can often be detected running down from a hill-fort or camp to a stream, cattle having been driven along it to be watered and back again to the safety of earthen rampart and palisade. O. G. S. Crawford maintained (*Archaeology in the Field*, Chapter 7) that the oldest visible road in Great Britain is a short length of hollow way leading to the neolithic FLINT MINES on Harrow Hill, near Findon, in West Sussex.

Holly

As a woodland tree disliking heavy wet soil, and none too tolerant of lime, holly is by no means universal in the landscape, or in gardens. On top of which, the holly you have may be a male-flowering tree with no female tree nearby for fertilization: it will produce no berries. Red is a colour of power in European belief. That explains the protective virtue ascribed to the red-berried holly, no less than the dark-red berries of the HAWTHORN and the orange-red berries of the ROWAN, an ascription which is no doubt older than the conversion of our English or British ancestors. Pliny, in his *Natural History* of the 1st century A.D., credits holly planted by the house with power to avert witchcraft; and the holly decorations of Christmas, useless without the berries of a good holly year, originate in this old belief coupled with a mediaeval christianization of the holly: images of Christ and the Passion of Christ were read into a plant which shows leaves of the healthiest shining green in the dead of winter, has milk-white, if not very conspicuous, blossom, and bitter bark (taken in medicine, so men knew the taste); which is armed with spines, and produces berries as red as any blood. But holly seldom (if ever?) appears in church carving of the Middle Ages.

–holt

A midland and south country place-name ending which means a wood, often coupled with names of trees, including oak, ash, alder, and beech. First on record in the 10th century, Sparsholt in Hampshire and Sparsholt in Oxfordshire ('spears wood') were probably named after ash woods where men went to cut spear shafts.

Holy wells

Basic to the holy well – not a well in the modern sense, but water which flows, bubbles or wells from rock or ground (Old English *wella, wiella*) – is the fascination exerted by springs, the birth of water, a necessity of life which itself seems alive. The ways in which this fascination has been expressed have changed with changes in religious belief. It was natural to identify a spring with a deity, who lived in the waters which were so clear and sparkling. Properly treated or entreated, she would give health or healing or happiness or a glimpse into the future. So offerings were put in the water, as they were by Roman soldiery in the well of the goddess Coventina at Carrawbrough, along the Roman Wall. An extraordinary medley of objects was recovered from the well when it was excavated in 1875, *ex voto* carvings (one with a relief of Coventina), pearls, vases, bronze safety pins, shoes, and more than 16,000 coins. When pagan religions gave way to the Christian religion the church authorities understood that there were fundamental impulses better re-directed than repressed. The worship of springs was repeatedly forbidden, but people still wanted the supposed benefit of drinking the water or bathing in it; and the tutelage of wells was transferred to saints, whose virtue explained the virtue of the water, and whose intercession might be valuable against illness. The offering to the deity of the well became the thankoffering acknowledging a cure or a feeling of betterment, the pilgrim having soaked himself in the water, bathed his eyes in it, or drunk it, according to his disease.

Mediaeval holy wells were often fitted out as curative centres, with well-houses and stone-lined tanks and chapels – Struell Wells, for instance, in Co. Down, near Downpatrick, now preserved as an ancient monument. Here there are ruins of a chapel, and mediaeval buildings covering a Drinking Well, an Eye Well and tanks for men and for women. Pilgrims still resort to Struell Wells on the night of 23 June; and it is St. Patrick, who died a mile away at Saul Abbey, who is supposed to have sanctified the waters. One of the most remarkable of these small establishments to survive in England is St. Winifred's Well at Woolston in Shropshire, south-east of Oswestry, said to have broken out after St. Winifred's body had rested there for the night when it was translated in 1138 from Gwytherin in the Vale of Clwyd to Shrewsbury. A Tudor well-house stands over the first of a descending series of stone tanks, with a niche in the wall which once housed a statue of this supposed virgin martyr, who has her more

"PREPARE YE THE WAY OF THE LORD."

ST. MICHAEL AND ALL ANGELS

HATHERSAGE

There are two distinct schools of HOLY WELL*-dressing. Some, like this splendid Well Dressing Tableau at Tideswell, Derbyshire, are designed entirely with petals, others with mosses, flowers, bark, dried peas and beans, shells and stones.*

famous healing centre and chapel at Holywell in Clwyd.

With the Reformation saints lost their already diminishing hold. But springs or wells remained no less fascinating and no one wished to forgo their supposed virtues. At first people disregarded the saints and went on taking the waters. For instance the Holy Well at Malvern was still popular in the time of James I:

> A thousand bottles there,
> Were filled weekly,
> And many costrils rare,
> For stomachs sickly;

> Some of them into Kent,
> Some were to London sent,
> Others to Berwick went,
> O praise the Lord.

John Evelyn went to Malvern in 1654 and remarked on the 'holy wells' before he climbed to the heights: 'They are said to heale many Infirmities, as Kingsevil, Leaprosie etc: sore Eyes.' But the shift towards sceptical enquiry in Evelyn's day made it common form to analyse spring waters and ascribe the good they were supposed to do to their mineral content, an attempt to square inclination and tradition and reason which justified resort to old wells, and led to the discovery in the 17th, 18th and 19th centuries of new wells – or spas, to use the conveniently neutral term uncontaminated by saints or superstition which became current in the late 17th century, a derivation from Spa near Liège, famous for its sulphur springs.

The German or Batavian soldier who left his *ex voto* in Coventina's well, the mediaeval pilgrim who left his crutch at St. Anne's Well at Buxton (once Aquae Arnemetiae, or the Springs of Arnemetia, a British Goddess of the Sacred Wood), Elizabeth I's Robert Cecil, Earl of Salisbury, dying of the pox on his way to the hot waters of Bath (which had belonged to the god Sulis; the Aquae Sulis, or Waters of Sulis), and Dr. John Wall who analysed the Malvern Waters in 1743, all took part in the same basic, fascinating, but not exactly rational drama of the waters of life. And they are joined by every National Health Service patient who pickles himself in the brine at Droitwich.

Dressing the wells in Derbyshire in midsummer is a modern revival and extension of the old habit of making offerings to the deity of the waters. The mode is to dress the well with coloured designs made by pressing petals, moss, and other natural bits and pieces, into large flat panels of clay. Hymns are sung, prayers are said, and the wells – or taps in some cases – are blessed by the parson. Five wells at Tissington have been dressed since at any rate the 18th century, and the revived custom seems to have spread from this village to Youlgreave, Ashford in the Water, Wirksworth, etc., and even to Arnemetia's Buxton.

Horse Chestnut

This native of the Balkan mountains (no relation of the Sweet Chestnut, which belongs to the family of oak and beech) was introduced into England about 1629. It was some while before it became a popular tree. John Evelyn in his *Sylva* (1664) wrote of it as common in France, in AVENUES; and it was for avenues and walks that it was much planted in the next half century. But many people disliked the shape of the Horse Chestnut, which reminded them of the pyramidically grown evergreens of the old formal or artificial gardening, which were 'now very justly despised by all curious Persons' (Philip Miller, *Gardeners Dictionary*, 1741). Fifty years later, William Gilpin, the lawgiver of the 'picturesque' in trees and natural scenery, was still writing against the

Though self-sown HORSE CHESTNUT *trees are common, it is an ornamental rather than a woodland tree, and is usually found as a magnificent spreading park and avenue tree. The horse chestnut may be easily recognized by their divided leaves and inedible fruit, known colloquially as 'conkers'.*

Horse Chestnut as a lump devoid of picturesque virtues – all of which was forgotten or disregarded in the High Victorian era when flowers meant more than shape, and the Horse Chestnut became one of the favourite trees of Great Britain, for its cliffs of blossom and its green fan-leaves (and its autumn conkers). Goethe discovered, or at any rate put on record, the pleasant fact that light passed through a glass of water in which the bark of Horse Chestnut twigs has been soaked produces a pretty sky-blue fluorescence.

Horse steps

Horse steps are a form of paved and stepped causey or CAUSEWAY, mediaeval in date, by which packhorse trains climbed steep and difficult terrain, particularly to a pass. There are several such horse steps in Wales (Welsh *sarn*, a causeway; also used of Roman roads), of which the best known and most striking are the (decidedly non-Roman) 'Roman Steps' in Gwynedd over the Rhinogs by the pass of Bwlch Tyddiad, part of a packhorse way from and to Harlech (which had a port in the Middle Ages, under the castle, now long silted up) by way of Bala. The 'steps' are long slabs of moss-grown stone.

Hundred meeting places

Hundred meeting places are worth searching out in one's county for an insight into the past. The hundred, called the WAPENTAKE in the old Danish-settled areas of the Midlands and north Midlands, and the ward in Cumbria, Durham, Northumberland (and the south of Scotland), was the unit of administration between SHIRE and VILLAGE, going back to the 11th century. Nominally a hundred is supposed to have been made up of a hundred hides, each hide of 120 acres being the amount of land required to maintain a free family and its dependents, but hundreds varied in size from small to large. The free men of each hundred came once a month to a moot or assembly in the open air, to deal with crime, lawsuits and taxes, under a hundred reeve, the bailiff of the sheriff (or reeve of the shire) who presided over the shire moot, to which one could appeal from the hundred moot. The meeting place was often distinguished by some feature, natural or artificial, a tree, a stone, an earthwork, a barrow; or it might be an upstanding hill, a cross-roads, a copse. Hundred names and boundaries are listed in the larger county histories (including the Victoria County Histories) and in the county volumes of the

English Place-name Survey (which identify the actual meeting place wherever possible). To visit such a meeting place, which may be lonely and isolated, yet central to the hundred, is to go back in time to one of the most ancient of English institutions. Sometimes footpaths still converge on the meeting place; sometimes it gives a wide view over the hundred. Sometimes it will have an evocative name, not simply Moot Hill (which is common), or some other name beginning Moat-, Mot-, Mut-, Mod-, but a name such as Swanborough Tump, where the free men of one of the Wiltshire hundreds foregathered, which is a tump or barrow, and means (*swana beorh*) the Barrow of the Peasants.

The hundred moots were not held only in Anglo-Saxon times. Through the Middle Ages men trudged or rode to the old windy centres, every month, or every three weeks; and after 1217 there were two additional meetings every year, the Sheriff's Turn, with the sheriff or his deputy presiding and judging, one at Easter, the other at Michaelmas. The records of a Sheriff's Turn for the Wiltshire hundreds round about Easter 1439 show fines inflicted on millers in every hundred for taking too much toll of the flour they ground, and fines for letting the king's highway fall into disrepair, for selling beer in false measures, selling bad meat, brawling, and thieving. The hundred system decayed at the end of the Middle Ages.

-hurst

-hurst is one of the common place-name words (Old English *hyrst*) the meaning of which cannot be exactly defined. Interpretation wavers between a rise, or hillock, and a wood. The two combined fit many of the -hurst names, a rise, hillock, bank, with trees on top. So there are Hawkhursts, Crowhursts, Ravenshursts, where hawks, crows and ravens nested, Ashhursts and Nuthursts and Ewhursts (yew hursts), Fernhursts (where bracken grew), Deerhursts, Brockhursts (badger hursts), and Buckinghamshire's Fingest, the slope not at any rate too thick with trees to be the place where the men of the hundred came for the *thing* or moot (*see* HUNDRED MEETING PLACES).

Hut circles

These remain from the collapse of stone-walled prehistoric huts, which were typically round-shaped in the Bronze Age and Iron Age, and even later. Early or late, hard turf-grown or heather-grown rings, or rings of mossed and lichened stones, they may be recognized by their diameter, which ranges from nine to twenty-five feet, or as much as thirty feet. In England these little circles of a crude existence abound most of all on Dartmoor and Bodmin Moor, where Bronze Age people lived for about 1,000 years from *c.* 1400 B.C. in small communities, herding sheep and cattle and growing barley in small, more or less rectangular, fields turned with the plough. The circles are frequently grouped inside oval enclosures or cattle pounds, and are all that is left of huts which were walled with moorstone (surface granite) to about five feet, and low-roofed with a cone of thatch or turf upheld on wooden branches and forked uprights. (The pounds were walled round with moorstone to six or seven feet, enclosing several acres, often with a spring or stream – e.g. Grimspound, near Moretonhampstead, four acres and twenty-four huts; the two Riders Rings, near Buckfastleigh, seven acres and three acres, each with some twenty huts.) Inside the huts, which gave good head-room, there were sleeping platforms and hearths, from which the smoke rose to a hole in the apex of the cone. Not very luxurious quarters, but the surrounding moors in the Bronze Age were drier and warmer than they are today. More often of Iron Age or later date, there are hut circles to be seen in other stony districts, in Lancashire, Cumbria, Northumberland; in Dyfed and Gwynedd; in Scotland (*see* ROUND-HOUSES), and in Ireland. Irish clocháns have also collapsed into a circular shape.

Hypocaust

The ROMAN VILLA proprietor of the 3rd and 4th centuries (when the richer Britons had taken more completely to a Roman style of life) liked to be warm in the winter months, and liked to be able to relax in a suite or wing of private baths. In the excavated villa one often sees the flues and vents of the under-floor heating system, and in particular the small forest of rectangular brick pillars which raised the solid floors of concrete and brick above a hollow air-space. Through this space and through hollow bricks in the wall the hot air flowed from an outside furnace, which burnt wood. A hypocaust or 'under-heat' system of the kind might bring the warm air under living rooms or under the warm and hot rooms of the bath wing, the warm *tepidarium* and the hot *caldarium* with its hot plunge bath, preliminaries to the bracing plunge bath of cold water in the *frigidarium*. This graded plan developed from the simple sweating-chamber introduced from Greece, which the Romans called a *laconicum* (i.e. *balneum laconicum*, 'Spartan bath', thought to have originated in Sparta).

Ice-houses

Ice-houses, the French *glacières*, were introduced from France in the 17th century. Charles II had one in St. James's Park (described in Waller's poem, 1661, 'On St. James's Park, as Lately Improved by his Majesty') and they spread rapidly to the great country mansions to provide for ice-cream, iced drinks, and ice-puddings. Often surviving the mansion itself (as at Hafod, near Aberystwyth, or Weston Park, Long Compton, Warwickshire), ice-houses will be found on top of slopes, in open, sunny positions, where the necessary mound on top did not interfere with the look of park or garden. The slope allowed for drainage, the open position avoided damp, which was the worst enemy of the stored ice or snow. A door into the mound may lead right and then about turn to a second and third door arranged to check the flow of warm air from the outside. Then comes the ice-well, egg-shaped, narrow end down, with thick walls and ceiling of stone, or brick. A drain leads off the bottom, with an air-stop in its course (on the principle of the lavatory S-bend). The drain was covered with a wooden grille or a cart-wheel, covered again with faggots topped with reeds or straw. The mound above was clay capped with earth. Labourers filled the well with ice powdered from thin sheets or with snow, which was then pounded with a heavy wooden rammer into a solid mass. Vegetables were sometimes stored in niches in the wall.

Ice-scratches

The 'glacial striae' of the geographer and geologist, ice-scratches run parallel across exposures of the ice-polished rock flooring a valley or along the rocky sides of a valley, in the glacier districts of the British Isles. The scratches were engraved by sharp points of stone held in the under-side of the glaciers and drawn slowly along under the vast tonnage and pressure of the ice. Look for them e.g. in the Pass of Llanberis or the Nant Ffrancon valley in north Wales.

Inauguration stone

A stone carved with a pair of footprints, in which an Irish chieftain or king stood during his inauguration. There are two famous inauguration stones (both National Monuments) in Co. Derry: St. Adamnan's Footprints, a block of basalt at Gortnamoyan, near Garvagh; and outside Derry itself, in the garden of Belmont House, St. Colum's Stone or St. Patrick's Stone, supposed to have been transported there from the hill-fort of the kingdom of Ailech or Greenan Mountain, and to be the stone which was blessed on Greenan Mountain by St. Patrick (see Whitley Stokes, *The Tripartite Life of St. Patrick*, 1887).

Inclined planes

On smaller canals through very up-and-down country, especially in the west of England, inclined planes were substituted for LOCKS or flights of locks, which would have been too expensive to build. The small tub-boats used on such canals, of only a few tons' burden, were lifted or lowered from one level to another inside a timber frame or cage which ran up and down the incline on two sets of grooved lines. The inclines were powered hydraulically or by steam. A dramatic inclined plane can be seen joining the end of the disused Tavistock Canal (opened in 1817 for copper ore) to Morwhellam Quay on the Tamar 240 feet below. The Bude Canal (1826), which wound along the northern reaches of the Tamar, climbed the hills by no fewer than five inclined planes, most of them worked by waterwheels. The gradients were between one in four and one in seven. On this canal the tub-boats, which carried fertilizing sea-sand to the inland farms, were fitted with wheels, obviating the need for cages.

Ing

In midland and northern counties where they spoke Danish or Norse, an ing is a meadow (Old Norse *eng*). There are many Ing(s), -ing(s) place-names, not to be confused with the various -ing place-names in English, for some of which see -TON and -HAM.

Inn names

There should be a critical dictionary of inn names as of place-names or surnames, to block the flow of whimsical and usually wrong interpretation. In the Middle Ages the law insisted that inns should have distinctive signs (it was an age of illiteracy, and symbols). So it was then – and later – necessary to choose obvious names which could be translated into obvious signs. Inn names and signs have therefore been drawn as a rule from the stock of

This INN SIGN *appears outside a public house, The Trusty Servant, in the village of Minstead, Hampshire. The emblematic figure, personifying all the virtues of a good man-servant – as listed below – originated in Western Europe during the Middle Ages. The emblem spread and by the 17th century similar figures could be observed as far east as Poland. His attire was updated in the early 19th century when the original painting, of which this is a copy, was commissioned to celebrate a visit by George III to Winchester College, where it still hangs.*

A Trusty Servants portrait would you see
This Emblamatic Figure well survey
The Porkers Snout not nice in diet shows
The Padlock shut no secrets he'll disclose
Patient the Ass his Masters Wrath will bear
Swiftness in errand the Staggs Feet declare
Loaded his Left Hand apt to labour saith
The Vest his neatness Open Hand his faith
Girt with his Sword his Shield upon his arm
Himself and master he'll protect from harm

Two examples of relatively latter-day INN SIGNS *which nevertheless portray the characteristics originally demanded of them by law.*

A peasant with a ewer exclaims: 'What — Wansford in England' on the sign for the Haycock (above), and The Cat and Fiddle (below).

symbols and concepts commonly understood at any one time – and as commonly misunderstood a hundred years later.

Heraldry provided such a stock, when inns proliferated at the close of the Middle Ages – a ready-made miscellany of badges, crests, charges, particularly of the family on whose estates the inn was built. The heraldic 'monsters' which found their way on to inn signs or carved devices above the door in this basic layer include, plain or qualified, the Dragon, Wyvern, Lion, Eagle, Griffin, Unicorn, Hart, Antelope and Dolphin. Heraldic crests and badges have also provided Falcon, Feathers, Swan, Swan's Head, Fleur-de-Lis, Rose, Blue Boar (badge of the Veres, Earls of Oxford), Eagle and Child (badge of the Stanleys, Earls of Derby), Bear and Ragged Staff (badge of the Beauchamps, Earls

of Warwick), as well as Talbot (after the breed of hound named talbot), Mitre, Mermaid, Saracen's Head, Stag, Horseshoe, Star, Sun. Many inn names and signs descend through heraldry from religious symbols, which in turn may descend from the Bestiary of the Middle Ages. Some have been mentioned (Lion, Eagle, Unicorn, Dragon, Mermaid). Others are Pelican, Lamb and Flag (*see* AGNUS DEI), (St.) George and Dragon, Three Crowns (of the Three Kings or Magi). Many more sources came to supply names for an increasing multitude of inns – proverbs, puns, catchphrases, popular kings and queens, generals, admirals, victories, modes of transport which an inn served, from 18th century turnpike roads (Black Horses, White Horses, Flying Horses), canals and railways to airways (the Air Hostess, outside London Airport). Heraldry was still invoked in the 18th and 19th centuries, setting complex achievements on the board of the So-and-So Arms – crest, motto, supporters and all – a fashion which led to Masons Arms, Miners Arms, and the like.

Though many inn names derive from local circumstances in one way and another, allowance has to be made for fashion and repetition, and for the fact that an emblem may have been drained of its original significance long before it was painted on the board. Not every Catherine Wheel or Cat and Wheel derives from a local cult of St. CATHERINE – or from a fireworks factory. A full explanation of many inn names would require knowledge, not only of heraldry, but of when the inn was built, and why, and by whom, and on whose property.

Instruments of Christ's Passion

These were often represented in mediaeval churches for the worshipper to contemplate. They include the thirty pieces of silver, the lantern which guided Judas and the others into Gethsemane, the sword and staff, the cock which crowed thrice, the crown of thorns, the spitting Jew, the rods, the ladder, the nails, the hammer and pincers, the sponge and reed, the spear, the wound touched by the unbelieving hand of Thomas, the dice, the feet ascending into heaven.

Ironstones

Ironstones are rocks, sandstones and limestones alike, coloured with oxide of iron. Celebrated limestones of the kind include the shelly Ham Hill stone, long quarried out of Hamdon Hill, west of Yeovil, in Somerset, responsible for the warm colour of many Somerset villages, churches, manor-houses, and mansions (including the National Trust's Montacute House, a mile or two from the quarries), and the soft Hornton stone, named after Hornton near Banbury and still worked along the top of the Edgehill escarpment, where it is sawn into large slabs, brown, green and even blue. Ironstone-built villages of this opencast iron-mining country of north Oxfordshire and Northamptonshire have extraordinary tints of rusty orange and brown, under caps of thatch.

Jacks of the clock

The carved and coloured men who strike the bell of a clock, as on the clock-tower (1496–9) at Venice. The oldest English clock-jacks are the ones of 1390 or thereabouts, who perform their office for the clock at Wells Cathedral – inside, the seated 'Jack Blandifer'; outside, the two quarter-jacks, striking the quarter hours. Jacks survive in the great Suffolk churches of Southwold (a 'Jack in Armour' of the late 15th century, with sword and battle-axe) and Blythburgh. Such clockwork animations appealed so much to the fancy that they are often mentioned in Elizabethan plays and poetry. King Richard, for instance, at the end of Shakespeare's *Richard II*, bitterly describes himself before his death as the Jack o' th' Clock which idles and strikes the happy hours for Bolingbroke.

Jet

Jet, as washed out of the Jet Bed on the Cleveland coast of Yorkshire and carried along the beaches to Flamborough Head, and then south along Norfolk and Suffolk (e.g. at Felixstowe), is to be picked up in the shape of dark pebbles with the outside rolled and worn to a dullness belying its brilliance when cut and polished. This strange stuff is fossilized wood, the fossilized timber of monkey-puzzle-like conifers which drifted on an ancient Jurassic sea, sank waterlogged to the bottom and into the mud, decomposed and slowly carbonized. Making objects out of jet is very ancient. One Neolithic use was for belt-slides, found in barrows. Neolithic and Bronze Age buttons and necklaces, also from barrows, anticipated the jet jewellery of the Middle Ages and Tudor times, the jet rosaries of the Black Monks of Whitby Abbey, and the ear-rings, necklaces, bracelets and brooches so much produced at Whitby in the mid Victorian era. Prehistoric people, one may suppose, found enough jet along the beaches near Whitby and along Runswick Bay. In the 19th century it was necessary to pick and dig into the top ten feet of what is known as the Jet Rock, which sometimes runs high along the cliff and sometimes comes down to foreshore level, as at Port Mulgrave, north of Runswick Bay. Victorian miners picked and pecked for jet inland as well as along the sea, leaving spoil heaps behind them in the dales of the Cleveland – Eskdale behind Whitby, Scugdale, Bilsdale, and along the northern slopes of the Cleveland dales. If you rub jet, it will attract small pieces of paper, etc., like AMBER. The more drastic test for a jet pebble is to set it alight. Jet burns like coal with a strong coal-fire smell.

Jupiter

Jupiter is a necessary planet to recognize on walks in the evening as the largest and, after Venus, the most brilliant, of the wandering stars, deserving the name of the Roman sky god. Consult the almanack – e.g. Whitaker's, in the monthly Astronomical Notes – for its position, visibility, and relative magnitude through the year as evening or morning star. It glitters with particular solemnity in the winter night of Dorothy Wordsworth's *Journals*, in sentences which are an invitation to 'learn Jupiter' for oneself. From the Quantocks in Somerset –

> January 23rd 1798. The sun gone down. The crescent moon, Jupiter, and Venus. The sound of the sea distinctly heard on the top of the hills –

or in the Lakes, above the fells –

> November 10th 1800. Jupiter over the Hilltops, the only star, like a sun, flashed out at intervals from behind a black cloud.

Keeils

Keeils in the Isle of Man are – or were – small rectangular churches or oratories of stone which were built from the 7th century into the Middle Ages. Many of the keeil sites have been excavated, giving evidence of a very simple undivided structure, often near a *chibbyr* or holy well. Their function must have been rather that of a chancel without a church, or without a nave for the people, who did their praying, or were preached to, outside. Every Manx treen or family estate seems to have had its keeil; and the keeil usually bore the name of an Irish saint, presumably its founder, such as the great missionary saint, Colum Cille.

Kelds

In the limestone areas of Yorkshire which the Norwegians occupied, kelds are springs (Old

Montacute House and village, Somerset, are built almost entirely of the locally quarried Ham Hill IRONSTONE. *Ironstone is a limestone coloured by iron oxide.*

This JACK OF THE CLOCK *at Abinger Hammer, Surrey, is an extension of the use of such clocks from church to domestic architecture. The village was once a centre of the iron industry which gave it its name, hence the portrayal of a blacksmith, seen here in the act of striking.*

Norse *kelda*), but often springs of a special kind – RESURGENCES, where a stream wells up after its underground passage; such a deep dark spring as Keld Head under the road in Kingsdale, near Ingleton, in North Yorkshire. The Ebbing and Flowing Well at Giggleswick in Ribblesdale is a keld which has produced a saint, the mythical St. Akelda, said to have been martyred by the Danes – i.e. St. *hālig keld*: St. 'Holy Well'.

Kelp kilns

Kelp kilns may be found above high-water mark along beaches on the western seaboard, a relic of the production of alkali or soda from the broad-bladed seaweeds variously known as kelp, tangle, slack marrow and oarweed (species of *Laminaria*). In the Isles of Scilly (where kelp burning was introduced in 1684) the kiln was a round basin with a low wall of moorstone (the stone-lined base of such a kiln is sometimes mistaken for the foundation of a prehistoric hut). Along the Irish beaches the preferred shape was a long narrow rectangle of stones, open at either end. In the Outer Hebrides (where kelping continued well into this century, in a small way), the seaweed was calcined in long trenches. Drying walls were also built (in Scilly as in Ireland). The low-grade soda produced in the kilns went from the wild coasts to the cities, e.g. to London, Bristol and Gloucester, for making glass and soap, and from late in the 18th century as a constituent of bleaching powder. This poor man's industry lasted in general from the 17th century to the 19th. It flourished, with a good price per ton, when the Napoleonic Wars cut off foreign supplies, and died out when potash from the clearing of Canadian forests was imported in the eighteen-twenties and thirties, and when soda began to be synthesized from salt.

Kingdom districts

Areas of England, Wales, Scotland and Ireland continue to be known by the names of the small kingdoms they once formed in the Dark Ages and later.

Wessex, the land of the West Seaxe, the West Saxons, a name repopularized by Thomas Hardy's novels, stretched across the south, comprising Hampshire, Berkshire and Wiltshire, Dorset, Somerset and Devon. The heart land of Wessex was not Dorset, but the first three of these six counties. East Anglia comprised in the main the Anglian territory of Norfolk and Suffolk – the land of the East Angles, west of whom lived the Middle Angles across the Nene (Essex, the land of the East Saxons, had affinities with Kent rather than the East Anglia to the north). Mercia, the midland country of the *Mierce*, the boundary people (*see* MARCH), is a scholar's name, not an ancient kingdom name. Elmet in north Yorkshire was a small British kingdom conquered by King Edwin of Northumbria at the beginning of the 7th century. (Northumberland, the modern county, is only a part of the considerable kingdom of Northumbria, which extended from the Humber to the Firth of Forth across the border.) In Lincolnshire the Parts of Lindsey was the kingdom of Lindissi swallowed up by the Mercians at the end of the 8th century.

In Wales, people commonly speak of four districts which were kingdoms founded in the 5th century: Gwynedd, or North Wales; Powys, from the Dee, across the upper Severn, west of Offa's Dyke; Gwent, in the south-east; and Dyfed in the south-west. At the beginning of the 7th century the English drove to the western sea, and divided the Britons of Powys and Gwynedd from the North Britons of Cumberland ('land of the Cymry') and the old kingdom of Strathclyde, across the Border, the capital of which was Dumbarton.

In Ireland, the provinces of Ulster, Connacht, Leinster and Munster descend from the chief ancient kingdoms, four of the Fifths of Ireland; the other one was Meath, of which kingdom the counties of Meath and Westmeath were a part.

Knock

In Irish and Scottish place-names, and some in England, knock is a knoll or distinct hill (Irish and Gaelic *cnoc*), as in the Knock of Crieff in Tayside, Knockninny (St. Ninnidh's knock) in Co. Fermanagh, or Knock in Cumbria. Along the Lincolnshire coast and the Thames shores of Essex and Kent a knock is a sandbank, e.g. the Kentish Knock, the Knock off Shoebury Ness.

Knocking stones

An abandoned knocking stone is often to be seen lying around in Ireland, the Highlands and the Western Isles of Scotland. It is a large stone mortar which was used for various purposes, especially pounding barley meal and preparing green whin or furze for cattle fodder. The spines of the furze needed to be broken up with a wooden maul. Feeding broken furze to cattle was common practice in

Ireland, the Highlands, the Isle of Man, Wales, Cornwall, and Brittany. Every Cornish farm had its furze brake, to provide not only food for the stock, but firing for bread ovens.

Kyle

Kyle, around the Highlands and Islands, as in the Kyles of Bute, the Kyle of Tongue, etc., means sound or strait, or narrows (Gaelic *caol*, narrow).

Labours of the Months

Surviving here and there in the imagery of churches, the Labours of the Months, one scene for each of the twelve, sometimes with the corresponding sign of the zodiac, recalled the curse laid on Adam, and so on mankind, in Genesis – 'Cursed is the ground for thy sake; in sorrow shalt thou eat of it all the days of thy life ... and thou shalt eat of the herb of the field; in the sweat of thy face shalt thou eat bread, till thou return unto the ground; for out of it wast thou taken: for dust thou art, and unto dust shalt thou return.' But the scenes also promised redemption: they showed the congregation not only the lot of the Children of Man, but the dignity and holiness of labour, through the Christian year, as a way to salvation and the undoing of the Fall. There are English examples around 12th century fonts, in Romanesque doorways, in wall painting, and on misericords. The twelve labours are not always identical, though February is usually a man or man and woman by a fire, March sowing, May a figure with flowers, June a man scything, August sickling the corn, October feeding acorns to pigs, and November or December pig-killing.

Lady chapels

Chapels of Our Lady, of the Virgin Mary, were commonly added to churches, the larger ones giving the lead, in and after the 13th century, in response to the increasing cult of the Virgin, who was believed to have been taken up from earth by Christ (the Assumption, observed on 15 August, when the Sun enters the sign of Virgo, the Virgin) and crowned by him Queen of Heaven. She was the patroness of the great Cistercian order and of each of the abbeys they founded in the 12th century. Her cult was advanced by the special devotion of the Dominican and Franciscan friars in the 13th century, a time which specially emphasized the Five Joys of Mary, which were the Annunciation, the Nativity, the Epiphany, the Resurrection of her son,

and her own Assumption to Heaven. For the laity, love of the Virgin became the spiritual counterpart of the ideal *amour courtois*, the ideal chivalrous love of the troubadour poets: she seemed everywhere, in life and after life, the Mother of God, Queen of Heaven, Chaste Tamer of the UNICORN, Lily among Thorns, Rose without a Thorn, Woman clothed with the Sun, Shield against the Devil, Star of the Sea.

> The odour of hir mouthe aromatike
> Did comfourd the world universall.

So as an expression and place of this devotion, the Lady Chapels were added to churches, especially in the great rebuilding of the late 14th and 15th centuries – small chapels which seem involved in the fabric and large ones more or less separate, like the Lady Chapel added at the east end of Long Melford church in Suffolk in 1496 by rich clothiers.

Lakes

The best analysis of lakes in general, and the lakes of the Lake District in particular, was written in William Wordsworth's *Guide to the Lakes*, first published in 1810. The form of a lake – here the lakes of the Lake District scored highly – is said to be best when it least resembles the form of a river, when it is indented, given variety by islands and enlivened by streams; and when with all these qualities it is small, so that the opposite shore can be seen. (If it cannot be seen, the traveller 'has the blankness of a sea-prospect without the grandeur and the accompanying sense of power'.) And the sense that lakes, which are so peculiar and exceptional in the landscape, are numinous and excellently rather than cruelly haunted, was most felt by Wordsworth when a still lake reflected the sky in autumn. Two things then happen: the sky is 'brought down into the bosom of the earth', and the earth 'is mainly looked at, and thought of, through the medium of a purer element', so that the imagination 'is carried into recesses of feeling otherwise impenetrable'. A visit to a diffcrent kind of lake, Llyn Fawr, grandly and wildly situated under the precipices of Graig-y-Llyn in Mid Glamorgan, will link this civilized expression of the haunted quality of lakes to a more savage expression of it in the Iron Age. This lake was drained in 1911, revealing offerings – bronze sickles, bronze axes, a cauldron, a sword, a spear-head, etc. – reckoned to have been made to a lake deity *c.* 200 B.C. Offerings of about 600 B.C. – including cauldrons again, part of a war trumpet, slave chains, chariot harness and swords – were found in the peat of a small Anglesey lake, when it was swept away in making an aerodrome in the Second World War. (Finds from both lakes in the National Museum, Cardiff.)

Landscape gardens and landscaping

Few landscape gardens remain, owing very largely to a revulsion of taste in the early decades of the 19th century, when the basic 18th century idea of 'improving' nature seemed blasphemous and artificial. The carefully composed features of such a garden, uniting water and reflection, vistas, garden temples, bridges, touches of the classical, mediaeval, the Chinese and the pastoral, and relying on foliage effects, can still be enjoyed at Stourhead, in Wiltshire, a banker's elysium, developed between 1740 and the seventeen-seventies, and now cherished with historical cunning by the National Trust. Elsewhere features survive in ruin or neglect, piecemeal.

The creation of landscape, in the wake of Lord Burlington and his circle, did not stop at the confines of the landscape garden. A countryside which had been bare and open in the 17th century was altered with aesthetic determination and deliberateness during the 18th century. Trees were planted to destroy monotony and to accent and improve prospects or views, of which landlords became highly conscious; monuments and towers were sited for effect – all of this *pari passu* with agricultural enclosure, until England began to have that parklike look which is one of its chief attractions from Northumberland to Cornwall. In 1805, in a letter on the laying out of grounds, Wordsworth spoke against putting 'a whole country into a nobleman's livery', and hoped that the landscaping of England was on the decline, and that no more violation would be done to 'the holiness of Nature', probably not realizing how much of the 'nature' he enjoyed, even in the Lake District, had been 'unnaturally' and profanely improved. Without understanding how it had come about, others after Wordsworth accepted the landscaped look of England, with Scotch Pines exactly at the just place, trees beautifully setting off a church or a village, etc., and concentrated their venom on particular elements of landscaping and the landscape garden – the GROTTO, the PROSPECT-TOWER, the EYE-CATCHER, the SHAM RUIN – making posthumous fun as well of the landscaping

practitioners and theoreticians of the previous century or decades, Kent, Capability Brown, Repton, Gilpin, Uvedale Price, and Richard Payne Knight.

Lasher

Where there was a mill or lock on the Thames or one of its tributaries, a bypass or backstream was devised to carry off flood water, which lashes and foams down an opening, a 'lasher', to rejoin the river. Lashers are part of the undergraduate idyll of the Thames, Cherwell, etc., above and below Oxford among the willows, as in Matthew Arnold's 'Scholar Gypsy'. The wandering scholar is seen by

– Men who through those wide fields of breezy grass
Where black-wing'd swallows haunt the glittering Thames,
To bathe in the abandon'd lasher pass.

Latin place-name words

Latin place-name words, especially the prepositions *juxta* (by or alongside), *sub* (under), *cum* (with), *super* (on), *in* (in or among), survive from the Latinized forms used in the Latin deeds and other law documents of the Middle Ages. Sometimes a name is linked by the preposition to an additional Latin term, sometimes the preposition is stuck in between two native words. Aston Subedge in Gloucestershire lies (like Wotton-under-Edge) under the edge or escarpment of the Cotswolds, Stratton-sub-Castle in Wiltshire is a little village around church and church tower tucked below the castle hill of Old Sarum. Essex had its Bradwell-juxta-Mare, 'by the sea', just as Avon has its Weston-super-Mare, 'on the sea'. Nottinghamshire has a Barton-in-Fabis, 'among the beans'. Villages with identical names may be distinguished as Magna and Parva, big and little. A parish made up of two parishes or villages which had the same name may have *ambo*, 'both', tacked on, e.g. Huttons Ambo, 'the two Huttons', 'both Huttons', near New Malton in Yorkshire, combining High Hutton and Low Hutton. Or a village may still be distinguished by a Latin indication of its former owners – e.g. it may be Monachorum, 'of the monks', if it belonged to a monastery, Canonicorum, if it belonged to a community of mediaeval canons, Sororum, 'of the sisters', if the owners were a nunnery, Episcopi, 'of the bishop', if it belonged to a see, Regis, 'of the king', if it was royal property, or Ducis, 'of the duke', if it was once ducal property and so on.

An ethereal view of Ullswater, one of the LAKES, *photographed very early in the morning, looking east near Waterford. Ullswater consists of three reaches which increase in grandeur to the north. It is bordered by Gowbarrow Park (property of the National Trust) which Wordsworth immortalized in his poem 'I Wandered Lonely as a Cloud'.*

Laver

A laver, or lavatorium, in MONASTERIES was the washing-place of the monks. At hand level a stone trough with running water was set in an arcaded recess in the wall along the cloister alley, by the door into the refectory (the monk's dining-hall). Here the monks washed hands and face when they rose and before their meal (examples at Hexham Priory, Fountains Abbey, Chester, Worcester and Gloucester cathedrals).

Lecterns

Ancient and modern, wood, latten or brass, lecterns are commonly in the shape of an EAGLE, because this bird symbolized St. John the Evangelist, and renewed itself, according to the Bestiary, by looking into the sun, i.e. it soared up into the presence of Christ. So an eagle's wings were a proper support for the gospels. This was the function of the mediaeval lectern, such as the fine eagles in latten of Bovey Tracey in south Devon, Cropredy in Oxfordshire, or Wiggenhall St. Mary in Norfolk (all examples of eagle lecterns made in East Anglia in the 15th and early 16th century, and exported widely through Europe: there is an East Anglian lectern in St. Mark's at Venice). The lectern was placed on the north side of the altar holding up the gospels when they were read at High Mass (some churches have stone lecterns or book-rests for this purpose, north of the altar, e.g. Ottringham in Humberside, Crich in Derbyshire). In their modern position in the nave lecterns belong to the congregational worship which came in with the Reformation, though until the eighteen-forties the congregation heard the lessons read from the reading pew, which was combined so often with the PULPIT and the parish clerk's seat in a 'three-decker'. When these were done away with, the fashion for the lectern in the nave was introduced from the cathedrals.

Ledgers

Ledgers are the (usually black marble) slabs laid over interments in the floor of a church, especially in the chancel. A modest speciality of the 17th and 18th centuries, they are carved as a rule with the dead man's coat of arms and the briefest details of name, dates and dwelling. East Anglian churches often show them at their best, beautifully proportioned and with exquisite lettering. Materials vary. Touch, the black marble imported from Tournai, was the standard. Various local stones were used, including slate; and there are cast-iron ledgers in the iron-working districts of East Sussex (e.g. at Wadhurst, Mayfield, Chailey, Salehurst) and Shropshire (e.g. Leighton, Onibury).

Limekilns

Scattered around the coast above picnic beaches and in creeks and up tidal rivers, limekilns were mostly built in the years on either side of 1800. Farmers were anxious to improve their land, and an extra large acreage was under corn owing to the wars with France and the high prices which were ruling. The lime was spread to sweeten soil which was acid from an underlying absence of chalk or limestone; which meant that the raw material for feeding into kilns had to be fetched, very often, from a long distance. Water was the cheapest and most reliable form of transport in the absence of good roads. Barges were loaded, wherever possible, at cliff quarries, and then unloaded at kilns adjacent to the farms. The barges also transported the necessary culm, or low-quality coal, for the limeburning. Horse and donkey back were used to carry the raw linestone and the culm from the beach or riverside up a ramp to the kiln platform, where labourers cracked the chunks to size, and then charged the crucibles or 'bodies', one, two or more to every kiln. The culm and stone were laid in alternate layers on top of brushwood, which was then lit from kindling holes inside the often Gothic-seeming and now ivy-hung archways. Once alight, the kilns filled the air with rolling grey volumes of unpleasant smoke. Farmers took their lime away to the fields in bags laid across their own packhorses, which explains why these now ruinating kilns are sometimes in a position which no wheeled vehicles could have reached. From the emptied kilns lime-ash was bought by the poor for making a hard flooring to their cottages and hovels. Note how above many lonely beaches a limekiln of the Napoleonic wars and a concrete pillbox of the Second World War decay side by side.

Limestones

Limestones are rocks of which the chief constituent is lime, or more exactly carbonate of lime (calcium carbonate), consolidated from the ooze which floored ancient seas; and though in ordinary speech one uses 'limestone' only of the hard rocks such as limestones of the Peak or of Craven or the building limestones which cross England in a belt from Dorset via the Cotswolds to Yorkshire, the younger and softer chalk of the cliffs and the downs is no less a limestone, and is practically pure calcium carbonate. The limestones are exceedingly various. In colour they may lack the frequent brilliance of the SANDSTONES, and the limestone which makes the most exciting scenery, the old tough carboniferous limestone, does tend to a slightly dismal greyish black. But this is the rock of the finest natural architecture in Britain, brought about by weathering and solution. It creates its special felicity of CAVES, POTS, gorges, CLINTS (limestone pavements), streams which appear and disappear, rounded river pools with lips immaculately polished by running or falling water, and reflecting surfaces which cause peculiar lighting effects (as in Courbet's landscapes of the Jura limestone), in districts which seem especially healthy and clean, and are coloured with unusually vivid grass and an unusually brilliant flora.

Among the areas of Carboniferous Limestone to visit are the Peak, in Derbyshire and Staffordshire, for caves, gorges, streams and pillars of limestone; Craven, in North Yorkshire (for the Ingleborough clints, Gordale Scar, etc.); the limestone of Yorkshire along the border with Durham (for the Greta, High Force, etc.); the limestone of the Wye precipices in Gwent; the compact gorge, cave and waterfall area of the upper Vale of Neath in south Wales; the Mendips (for their gorges and caves); and, most peculiar of all, the pavement limestones of Burren, in Co. Clare, one of the great natural rock-gardens of Europe, reaching down to a blue Atlantic, in view of the Aran Islands – a district of which one of Cromwell's soldiers is said to have brought back the news that it yielded neither water enough to drown a man, nor wood enough to burn a man, nor soil enough to bury a man. For the limestones of the British Isles, read F. J. North's *Limestones*, 1930.

Lime trees

Lime trees, as we plant them along streets and in avenues, are a fairly recent addition to the English scene. They were much imported from the Low Countries to make arbours in the 17th century, and then the new-fashioned AVENUES, leading up to country houses, in the 17th century, with John Evelyn as their great advocate. The tree employed – it is still much planted, in spite of leaves made sticky by aphids – was the Common Lime (*Tilia × europaea*), a hybrid between the Large-leaved Lime and the Small-leaved Lime. In his *Sylva* (1664) Evelyn speaks of it as if it was

not at that time so very much embedded in the English tradition, though he mentions that it was much carved by his friend Grinling Gibbons, and that bass-ropes were being twisted from the bass of the inner bark.

Lions

In church imagery, lions are usually creatures of power and virtue, signifying Christ, especially Christ risen from the dead, since the Bestiary told that lion cubs were born dead and given life only on the third day when licked by the father lion. The good lion fights the dragon who is the Devil, as on the 14th century Percy tomb in Beverley Minster. Contrariwise the lion could be evil, and when you see him trodden under foot like the dragon, he gives form to the declaration in the Psalms (*see* DEVIL) that lion, adder and dragon should be trampled upon. The lion with wings images St. Mark, as one of the Evangelists, one of the four beasts around the throne (Revelation 4. 6–9), which rested not day and night, 'saying Holy, holy, holy, Lord God Almighty, which was, and is, and is to come'. Each of them had six wings – 'And the first beast was like unto a lion.' *See* WODEWOSE for lions (especially on fonts) in combat or company with wild hairy men.

Litany desks

A desk or stool in the nave of a parish church at which the priest kneels for the reciting of the Litany, at the head of the congregation, though not unknown in the 17th and 18th centuries, was something introduced as a rule in the early years of the Victorian era, along with the LECTERN in the nave. Before that the litany was recited from a reading pew often built in with the PULPIT.

Llan- or Lan-

Welsh Llan- in Welsh names, Cornish Lan- in Cornish ones, means a church, followed usually by the name of the saint or holy man

*T*he Cheddar
Gorge, Somerset,
is composed of carboni-
ferous LIMESTONE. A
favourite haunt of pot-
holers, it is best known
for its caves and
underground rivers.

The LOCK relies for its operation on gravity, water pressure and manpower. The gates point uphill, the water pressure forcing them together and water is flooded in through underground tunnels, called culverts, which are closed and opened by paddles attached to the gates. When the lock is full, the top gates (on the left of the drawing) can be opened. The boat on the left may then enter, and the gates and paddles close afterwards. The paddles on the right are then opened and water in the full lock drains out into the canal to the right of the picture at a lower level, bringing the boat in the lock down to that level. The gates can then be opened and the boat proceed.

who founded it. In most of Europe churches were built and then dedicated to favourite saints. In the Celtic countries a saint's name attached to the word for church is generally that of the saint who founded it between the 5th and 7th centuries. The church word in place-names is Kil- in Scotland and Ireland, *keil* in the Isle of Man (from Latin *cella*).

Llyn

In Welsh place-names, a lake. The same word unexpectedly survives (for 'lake' at high tide) in Norfolk's King's Lynn. It means really no more than 'water', in the same way that 'water' is used in the lake names, Ullswater, etc., of the Lake District.

Llys-

Llys- in Welsh place-names, Lis- or Les- in Cornish names, Lis- or Liss- in Irish and Highland names (Irish *lios*), means the court or place from which a chieftain or a king ruled over his territory – as in the Lizard ('high court') or Liskeard in Cornwall, or Liscard in Cheshire, and Liss in Hampshire. To begin with, it seems to have meant the space in which the buildings stood, inside the surrounding oval or circular ramparts of earth or stone.

Locks

River locks preceded the canal lock. Originally 'lock', a word going back to the Middle Ages, meant a river barrier from bank to bank, a weir (also known as a 'stanch', 'staunch', or 'stank', or 'pen') holding the water back to work mills and allow the passage of boats. A portion of the lock or weir could be opened, and a boat dragged through. When the river was too low for traffic, the weir would be opened to let down a sufficient 'flash' of water, which gave these primitive river barriers the name of 'flash-lock'. Traffic up and down rivers was simplified and long canals were made possible when locks in a modern sense, allowing a boat to rise or drop on their imprisoned or impounded water, were developed in Holland, Germany and Italy in the Middle Ages. These 'pound-locks' were at first rather clumsily fitted with a single vertically opening gate at either end. Leonardo da Vinci improved them by inventing the familiar double gates which close to a mitred fit, and are swung open or shut with long balance beams. Leonardo's pound-lock was first used in Britain on the Exeter Ship Canal (1563–6).

Logans

Logans ('logging-stones', 'rocking-stones', which 'log' or rock when touched) are natural, and of two kinds: large pieces of rock which have weathered along the joints to such a degree as to be separated from the underlying rock, on which they balance in delicate poise, or (in glaciated districts) perched blocks which have been shifted by ice and have come to rest in equilibrium on a rock of another kind. Logans on the granite moors of Devon and Cornwall, the millstone grit moors of the Peak, in Wales, Ireland, Scotland, etc., were made much of by 18th century antiquaries. They maintained that logans had been set in place by Druids, were idols, were used in divination, or were used to demonstrate the magic power of the Druids and so frighten criminals to confession, as 'Stones of Trial'. Less credulous people have amused themselves by using logans to crack nuts. The crass have upset them.

Lombardy Poplars

Lombardy Poplars did not become part of the English scene until the end of the 18th century. When a new edition of John Evelyn's *Sylva* was published in 1776 the editor remarked that the specimens planted were still too young to judge of the excellence of the tree; which had been introduced from Lombardy in 1758 by the Earl of Rochford, ambassador at Turin, and planted in his landscape garden at St. Osyth Priory in Essex. But this Lombardy Poplar, Italian Poplar, or Po Poplar, as it was called, soon became a favourite. As it spired above the lower wide-spreading native foliage, it reminded the English of their Italian journeys across the Po plain to Venice, Mantua, Bologna, etc. The shape was compared with the cypress, and in sentiment the Lombardy Poplar fitted the neat neo-classic villa of the Regency period – to the disgust of champions of the picturesque such as Humphry Repton who wrote in 1816 of 'spruce villas, surrounded by spruce firs, attended by Lombardy Poplars, profusely scattered over the face of the country'. He was disgusted, too, when houses in the Gothic style were also surrounded by firs and Lombardy Poplars instead of by trees with a rounded outline. But the Lombardy Poplar triumphed. By origin the Lombardy Poplar belongs to Afghanistan and Russian Central Asia.

Long houses

It was an old custom for peasants whose livelihood depended more on their cattle than on cereals to house themselves and their cattle in one building. Cows and calves and parents and children shared the comfort of the hearth; and to tend the cattle there was no need to go out of doors into rain or snow. In Britain the commonest way of combining living quarters with byre or shippen was a 'long house', under a single thatched roof, cattle at one end, the family at the other – an arrangement going back to prehistoric times in the Iron Age. Originally (as on the Isle of Lewis) there may have been no more than a row of stones between them. But in the developed long house man and beast were separated by a wall

or wooden screen at the back of the hearth, and a cross passage from side to side of the house. Alongside the hearth a door opened into the passage, and from the passage another door opened into the byre, with its breathing cattle and mounting piles of dung. The byre was at a lower level, and the cattle went in and out by the cross passage. Long houses may have been common in many parts of England until the end of the Middle Ages, but by the 16th century they seem to have been left only on the uplands. Today, transformed long houses, which no longer house the family and the cows side by side, are to be seen in some of the moorland parishes of Wales (several of them are built on CRUCKS), and on Dartmoor. The common line of roof has sometimes been broken by adding a second storey above the living room; sometimes a porch has been added at one end of the cross passage, and the byre or shippen has been translated into a parlour. The Welsh long houses are well described in *The Welsh House* (1940) by Iorwerth Peate, and the Dartmoor long houses of moorstone, many of which are mediaeval, in R. H. Worth's classic *Dartmoor* (1953), and in the National Park Guide to Dartmoor (1969).

Lost lands

Lost lands – several of them – are supposed to have been suddenly overwhelmed by the sea off the Kentish, Welsh, Cornish (and Breton) coasts. Off the Kentish coast the story is that the Goodwin Sands were the island of Lomea, which belonged to Godwine, Earl of the West Saxons, and was overwhelmed by a great storm in 1099, an abbot of Canterbury having used materials and money intended for the sea-defence of Lomea to build the steeple of Tenterden church. Between Cornwall and the Isles of Scilly the land of Lyonesse or Lethowstow was overwhelmed at a blow with all its towns and churches. Only a certain Trevilian escaped on a horse fast enough to outpace the waves. In Brittany the city of Kaer a Iz, 'lowland city', in the Bay of Douarnenez, was drowned, a proper punishment for its profligates and drunks, when enemies opened the sluices. Off the Welsh coast three areas of pebble reef have been accounted lost lands, destroyed at a blow: the Cantre'r Gwaelod or 'Lowland Hundred', also called Maes Gwyddno, 'Gwyddno's Plain', in Cardigan Bay off the west coast of Wales; Caer Aranrhod, supposedly a 'druidic' circle, off Gwynedd in Caernarfon Bay; and Llys Helig, the palace of

Helig ap Glannawg in Conwy Bay, off the north Gwynedd coast. The story of the Cantre'r Gwaelod is that the sluices of the sea-wall defending a lowland plain forty miles long and twenty miles deep were left open when Seithennin, keeper of the wall, was drunk after a banquet.

All the Welsh legends have been brilliantly investigated by the geologist F. J. North (*Sunken Cities*, 1957). He has shown that the detailed story of the Cantre'r Gwaelod is mostly a composite fiction of the 18th and 19th centuries, with their taste for the falsification and inflation of folklore, which grew out of unembroidered 13th century references to a Maes Gwyddno overrun by the sea. In the 17th century the Cantre'r Gwaelod was first connected with the pebble reef in Cardigan Bay, supposed to be the remains of 'a stone wall made as a fence against the sea'. In the same century the Cardigan Bay legend was first used to explain the pebble area of Conwy Bay. The name Caer Aranrhod, a castle in the legendary *Mabinogion*, was imposed on the geography of Caernarfon Bay in the 16th century to account for the pebble reef. However, the Welsh coast has suffered prehistoric loss of land. The reefs in the three bays remain from the erosion of boulder-clay lands; evidence of a slow and intermittent (not sudden) process of prehistoric submergence lasting from the end of the Ice Age to about 2,000 years ago (see F. J. North, *Evolution of the Bristol Channel*, 1955). The mediaeval statements about lost land, from which the modern stories have been elaborated, may descend from a prehistoric abandonment of sea-logged coastal areas. F. J. North calculated that a single catastrophic overwhelming of the supposed Cantre'r Gwaelod would have required a sudden rising of the sea or a sinking of the land to the extent of about 120 feet', a disaster which would have affected all of the coasts of Britain, and probably the coasts of continental Europe.

In the Isles of Scilly there is evidence that a single island has been divided into several islands by submergence since the Bronze Age. This may be the seedling of the story of Lyonesse, which goes back to the 12th–13th century *Chronicon ex Chronicis* begun by the Benedictine monk Florence of Worcester.

The story of Lomea may be largely a nonsensical fabrication. It is not certain that the Goodwins were formerly an island, and Goodwin (see the *Oxford Dictionary of English Place-names*) is more likely to mean 'good friend', a flattering or propitiatory name given to a dangerous shoal, than to derive from the Earl Godwine. But at the back of the story may be the gradual loss of the North Sea lands from *c.* 7000 B.C., and continued coastal submergence, as well as the steady erosion of lands along the east coast, responsible for the historical loss of upwards of thirty Humberside villages between Flamborough Head and Spurn Head (a two and a half mile width of land between the headlands has vanished since Roman times) and for the nearly total loss of Dunwich in Suffolk between the 14th century and the 20th.

Lough

Lough, in Ireland, a lake. The loch of Scotland (with 'lochan' for a little lake) preserves the original Irish word. *Loch* passed from Irish into Cornish: it is to be found, for instance, in Looe, in east Cornwall, where the high tide forms a wide, still lake at the junction of two valleys.

Luminescence

Herrings glowing on a plate in a dark larder (from luminous bacteria) are probably our commonest introduction to natural luminescence, the emission of 'cold light' produced by chemical interaction. A by-product of physiological processes, the light has become useful to some creatures, including our glow-worm.

This luminescent beetle ('worm', not because our ancestors had failed to take a B.Sc. in zoology, but because worm, which now suggests only creatures of one particular shape, was the word they used for anything which crept or crawled, glow-worm, slow-worm, silkworm, earthworm, etc., anything from larva to dragon) has a wide but patchy distribution from Scotland to Cornwall. It is the larva-like female which emits the blue-green light, from the underside of two tail-segments. 'The females . . . will, when needing attention, climb up a grass stalk and wave their flashing tails with the impatience of an Isolde' – upon which the males, which have matured into correct beetle-shape, with only two small spots of luminosity, fly towards them, and they mate. These creatures of the damp September night excited Sir Thomas Browne (as well as Shakespeare), Browne denying that a luminous water could be distilled from them, but saying that science might enquire if their light 'be of kin unto the light of Heaven . . . whether also it may not have some original in the seed and spirit analogous unto the Element of Stars'

(1646). Coleridge and Wordsworth (and his sister, they glow in her *Journals*) were particularly excited by them. Late in the year, after listening to autumnal robins, Wordsworth wrote of seeing one clear shining under bracken:

> . . . The Child
> Of Summer, lingering, shining, by herself,
> The voiceless Worm on the unfrequented hills.
> *Prelude*, VII, 44–45

The poetry of glow-worm light is so strong – or more exactly our eyes are so responsive to its spectrum, which is devoid of infra-red or ultra-violet – that it shows up distinctly in the prosy glare of the headlights of a car.

Sea-sparkle, of autumn or late summer, visible in breaking waves or wavelets, in water disturbed by oars (crossing a ferry at night), in the water disturbed by the passage of nets, producing a waving wall of luminescence, occurs when a sufficient population has built up in the sea of the luminous protozoan *Noctiluca miliaris*. When the water is agitated, the light-chemical in these little one-celled flagellates combines with oxygen, and the sparkle is produced. West Country children, at any rate Cornish ones, are brought up to know this sea luminescence as 'briming' (i.e. burning – also known as 'burning of the sea'). Richard Carew, of Shakespeare's at times outward-looking generation, described it with wonder and precision in his *Survey of Cornwall* (1602): 'If the sea-water bee flashed with a sticke or oare, the same casteth a bright shining colour, and the drops thereof resemble sparckles of fire, as if the waves were turned into flames.' With luck one may also see the small luminescent globes of the jellyfish *Pelagia noctiluca*, which sometimes reaches south-western coasts.

Damp rotten wood which glows, in timber, logs, tree stumps, roots of old rose bushes, etc., does so with light of the same nature emitted by the far-ranging threads or mycelium of the honey tuft (*Armillaria mellea*), the browny-yellow toadstool which tufts trees and stumps in huge colonies (and can be eaten).

If you go into a damp leaf-floored wood on a late summer or autumn evening, and find the whole floor faintly milky and eerie with luminescence, this again will be due to fungal threads, from the little bell-shaped toadstools of the genus *Mycena*.

Lychgates

Lychgates are 'corpse gates' (lich, a corpse – in the north 'lyke' or 'like', as in the Lykewake Dirge, which was sung in the watch over the dead). Mostly framing the main entrance into churchyards with a gabled roof, lychgates – with the word – came into fashion in the Victorian era, when ecclesiologists were bent on tidying up church and churchyard and restoring what they believed to be mediaeval practice. Timber or stone lychgates may have existed here and there in the Middle Ages. A number were certainly built in the 16th, 17th and 18th centuries. But it is to the point that in Edward VI's Prayer Book of 1529 the Order for the Burial of the Dead begins with the priest 'metyng the Corps at the Churche style'. There at the stile he says the introductory sentences, 'I am the resurrection and the life,' etc., before the corpse is carried to the grave and 'made readie to be layed into the earth'. (Always the 'corpse', since coffins, except for the well-to-do, came into use only in the 18th

A LYCHGATE *was a covered gateway, usually wooden, placed at the entrance to a churchyard and where, during a funeral, the coffin could be set down until the clergyman arrived. This Victorian lychgate is from All Saints church, North Cerney in Gloucestershire.*

century.) The shrouded corpse was carried along the road or along one of the paths from outlying farms and hamlets, which led, and still often lead, into the churchyard by a stile. Shelter, at this point, where the service began, and where the corpse was transferred to the parish bier, brought out from the church, was obviously desirable. Sometimes old stile and new 17th or 18th century lychgate can be seen side by side (e.g. in north Wales, Caerhun, lychgate of 1728, and Llanfaglan, lychgate of 1722), the stile steps ending in a stone gap through the wall, on which the corpse was once placed.

Lypiatt

Lypiatt, Lipgate, Lippet, is a name to notice on the map as an indication of past ways and privileges. It means a leapgate – a gate too high for cattle, but low enough for deer to leap. Deer were privileged animals. They belonged to the Crown, and were free to go in and out of woods, commons, etc., as they pleased. So leapgates had to be maintained. Leapgate names occur frequently in the old forest counties of Hereford and Worcester and Wiltshire.

Maps

Maps are more than schemata for finding one's way about. They can be used comparatively for finding one's way into the past, for which reason it is worth collecting and comparing every edition of the 1 : 50 000 Ordnance Survey maps for one's own district. Publication of the first edition of these maps began (with Kent) in 1801. The third edition was published by the beginning of this century, the seventh by 1961; and on the ground the changes of more than a century have been considerable. Also it is possible (though not for all districts) to supplement the first edition of these O.S. maps with a photostat of the original drawing made by the surveyors, which is often on the larger scale of two miles to an inch, showing details omitted when the maps were engraved. Photostats are obtainable from the Map Room at the British Museum. For older maps, whether published or drawn from private surveys (estate maps) or made for such particular purposes as parliamentary enclosure or commutation of tithes, or the construction of turnpike roads, consult the Record Office of the county you live in.

March

March, as in the Welsh Marches or the northern marches, means border or boundary (Old English *mearc*, from which many place-names beginning with Mark- are derived), and so border land. The Mercians, the pushing Anglian people of the Midlands, were the *Mierce*, the Border People, next door to the Welsh – though the border which gave them their name was not the dyke that their King Offa was to build about A.D. 790 between Wales and a larger Mercian kingdom, but (see Stenton's *Anglo-Saxon England*) a line not so far west of the Trent, running some thirty miles south-east from Cannock Chase to the Warwickshire forest country north of Stratford-upon-Avon.

Market crosses

When a newly founded town or borough of the 13th or 14th century acquired under its charter the right to hold weekly markets, it needed a space for the market, and then a market cross as its focal point. The characteristic market cross was for a long while little different from a CHURCHYARD CROSS, having a stepped base around a tall shaft. The cross or lantern at the head of the shaft emphasized the Christian nature of just dealing, the steps provided seats for the market women and shelf room for the produce they brought in to sell (one needs to remember that the markets were small, serving only a small population). In the 15th century people began to think more of comfort. It was no pleasure to sit or stand around selling eggs and butter, etc., in the rain. Towns that could afford it or were left money for the purpose built more elaborate market centres in the shape of an octagonal or hexagonal stone tent supported on open arches, with a cross or lantern overhead. There are good examples of the late 15th century at Chichester in West Sussex, and Malmesbury in Wiltshire. Of the Malmesbury market cross, occupying the centre of a market space outside the abbey precinct, John Leland wrote that it had been built by the men of the town – 'a right fair and costely peace of worke in the market place made al of stone & curiously voultid for poore market folkes to stande dry when rayne cummith'. A town that could not afford such a new vaulted cross would set a shelter around the old crosses, steps and all, as at Castle Combe, in Wiltshire, or Cheddar, in Somerset. When a town grew, the next innovation, in and after Elizabethan times, was to have a covered market under a market house supported on pillars, which again was often replaced in the 19th century by a larger covered market with classical façades.

A village MARKET CROSS *will often testify to a period of mediaeval importance, although many ambitious market enterprises sank without trace within a few years of their foundation. They functioned both as billboards and to promote the trading site. This one can be seen at Alfriston, Sussex.*

Marl-pits and dene-holes

Marl, as farmers understood it, ranged from chalk to chalky clay, and was spread as a fertilizer or sweetener over sour land, along with dung. The Romans found that it was used in that way in Britain, and in his *Natural History* (A.D. *c.* 60–70) Pliny described how the marl was brought up from underground, through narrow shafts a hundred feet deep, which opened out into galleries at the bottom. He was describing what antiquaries of the last century knew as 'dene-holes' (i.e. Dane-holes – holes attributed, like much else, to the Danes), which it was necessary to sink where the required chalk was overlaid by deposits of sand or gravel. Pliny's informant may have known of dene-holes in Kent, one or two containing rubbish of the Roman period.

Fields here and there are still marled with chalk, if not from dene-holes, though O. G. S. Crawford stated in 1953 in his *Archaeology in the Field* that dene-holes had been sunk within living memory, by specialists (so he was told in Hampshire) who travelled round with a donkey and a windlass; they were also being made in Berkshire, where they were known as chalk-wells, in the eighteen-eighties. In Surrey they were called 'draw-pits'. When dene-holes have collapsed they form wide dimples on the surface. Usually they occur in clusters.

It was not always necessary to sink a shaft. Marl was dug from shallow surface pits around chalk hills, leaving – as one can often see in Wiltshire and elsewhere – a mess of bumpy hollows often approached by a length of sunken lane, grass-grown and long ago disused. 'Marl' was borrowed in the Middle Ages – perhaps with a renewal of marling – from France, from the Old French word *marle*, which goes back to Pliny's word *marga* (in modern French *marle* has become *marne*, and marling is *marnage*); and in chalk counties you find such minor place-names, some of them originating in the Middle Ages, as Marlpit, or Marlingpit (Marlengpytte, 1348). Before marl became the usual word, the farmers talked of their fertilizer simply as chalk. Some chalk names, Chalkhills, Chalkways, etc., probably point to pits frequented for marl. In 826 Broad Chalke in Wiltshire was called *Cealc*, 'chalk (place)', the place you went to for chalk-marl for your fields. More than 800 years later John Aubrey wrote of 'pitts called the Mearn-pitts' (i.e. marl-pitts, French *marne*, as above) on a hillside at Broad Chalke, though he did not know the meaning of 'mearn', or understand the purpose of the pits.

Mars

The sky objects likely to be mistaken for the red Mars, the war planet, and our neighbour, are red Arcturus in the spring and summer constellation of Boötes, the Herdsman; and red Antares (Greek *anti Ares*, i.e. contra Mars, the red rival of the red planet of Ares or Mars, the god of war) in the summer constellation of the Scorpion. But we do not see so much of Antares. He appears low above the south-east horizon in the evenings of May, reaches his greatest altitude, which is not so very lofty (it is below the ecliptic), in June and July, and then vanishes again below the horizon. Arcturus is a truer rival in the matter of identity. But he soars above the zodiac, where no planet can be. He can easily be fixed by his relationship to the GREAT BEAR or Plough (his Greek name means 'Bear-keeper': he keeps watch on the Great Bear); and by May he has risen high towards the zenith. It is when he is high in the west on summer nights, and when he drops north-west in the autumn, that Arcturus is confused with Mars: he is then the first star to show in the evening sky. As a star, he twinkles, and so does Antares. But for the whereabouts of untwinkling Mars at any time, consult the almanack, as for the EVENING STAR (Venus, consort of Mars) and JUPITER.

Martello towers

From Sussex to Suffolk, Martello towers were built against the threat of invasion in the French Wars, successors to the FORTS OF THE SAXON SHORE and the TUDOR COASTAL FORTS, and predecessors to the concrete pillboxes of the Second World War. The name comes from the Torre della Mortella (Tower of the Myrtle) commanding the anchorage of the Gulf of San Fiorenzo in the north of Corsica. When attacked by an English naval and military force, this tower with its small garrison and three guns proved so difficult to take that the design was adapted for English coastal defence. Between 1804 and 1812 the Royal Engineers built 103 Martello towers between Seaford and Aldeburgh, small round forts sturdily made in brick, with garrison quarters reached by a ladder through a door twenty feet above ground (cf. the ROUND TOWERS of the mediaeval Irish monastery), and a gun platform on top. Most of them have been pulled down, but there are still concentrations between Dymchurch and Folkestone, along the Essex coast from Seawick Sands to Walton-on-the-Naze, and along the Suffolk coast from Felixstowe to Shingle Street.

Masons' marks

Masons' marks are to be seen on blocks of worked freestone in churches, castles, etc., from the 12th century down to the 19th century. Masons travelled round the country from job to job, and each mason signed the blocks he had carved with his personal mark. Any mistake or misfit could then be traced back to its author. These craftsmen's marks, shallowly incised, usually between an inch and three quarters and two inches high, are of many kinds, from letters to circles and straight-sided figures, arrows, double or single triangles, crosses, swastikas, etc. On the inside walls of Edington Priory church in Wiltshire forty different masons' marks have been recognized, which suggests the size of the team of craftsmen employed on building the church in the eight years between 1352 and 1360. Several of these Edington marks have been found on stones in Winchester cathedral, in the west end, the rebuilding of which began (under the same ecclesiastic, William of Edington, Bishop of Winchester) in the thirteen-sixties – as if the masons had moved on from Edington to Winchester.

Mausoleum

The mausoleum designed by Hawksmoor at Castle Howard in Yorkshire (it took more than ten years to build, from 1731) was the first and grandest death-house to be added to the grounds of an English country house. Others followed, and some were built even in the first decades of the 19th century. The architects who designed them and the grandees who paid for them had at the back of their minds the original Mausoleum, the long-vanished tomb built in the 4th century for Mausolus, satrap of Caria, which had been graded among the Seven Wonders of the World, and the great tombs of Augustus and Hadrian in Rome. And although some of the park mausoleums are memorial rather than sepulchral, the idea was to withdraw the family dead, if not from death, then from the common, overcrowded soil of churchyard (or church), and from the plebeian gaze, into the rational calm and dignity and beauty of a private tomb, which would also be an adornment to the devised landscape: the aristocratic dead left their cool classical mansion for their cool classical resting-place. So demanding size, marble, statuary, urns, sarcophagi and a good design, a proper mausoleum was beyond the ordinary purse, or the normal conceit. After Castle Howard ('a mausoleum that would tempt one to be buried alive' – Horace Walpole), notable examples are Gibside, Co. Durham, by James Paine, c. 1760 (turned into a church); the Dashwood Mausoleum, on the hilltop at West Wycombe in Buckinghamshire, open and hexagonal, 1762; Bowood House, near Calne, Wiltshire, by Robert Adam, 1764; Seaton Delaval, Northumberland, 1766; Brocklesby Park, Lincolnshire, very splendid, appropriately built on what was believed to be a Roman tumulus, by James Wyatt, c. 1787–92 (Wyatt also built the mausoleum at Cobham Hall, in Kent); Wentworth Woodhouse, South Yorkshire, with a statue of Lord Rockingham and busts of his friends, by James Carr, 1788; Halsham,

*O*f the 103 MARTELLO TOWERS *built in anticipation of a Napoleonic invasion, only 45 survive. Two of them can be seen at Hythe, in Kent, one of the original Cinque Ports. Purely defensive, these stubby, cylindrical buildings have no great aesthetic appeal, but were used to garrison troops. The entrance, which was more than 20 feet (6 metres) above the ground, was reached by a ladder, and there was a gun platform on the top.*

A superb *example of a* MAUSOLEUM, *to be seen in Brocklesby Park, Brocklesby, Lincolnshire. It was built in about 1787–92 in the Neo-classical style by James Wyatt. The fine park lands, landscaped by Capability Brown, in which it is set, show it off to advantage.*

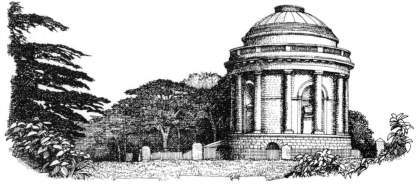

Humberside, by Thomas Atkinson, 1792–1802; Blickling Hall, Norfolk (National Trust), by Joseph Bonami, 1794; Trentham, Staffordshire, by William Blake's friend, C. H. Tatham, 1807–8.

Mazes

Mazes are less mysterious than they are sometimes made out to be. Probably, before the Reformation and the Commonwealth, there were plenty of them up and down the country on fair grounds, PLAYSTOWS, village greens, etc., cut in the turf in traditional patterns and kept up for the simple open air game of treading as fast as possible to the centre without overstepping the narrow, usually circular paths, especially at dead ends where one had to do an about-turn. This was an ancient game, and Pliny in his *Natural History* wrote of 'mazes made in the fields to entertain children'. It seems to have been introduced into England, or popularized, late in the Middle Ages; and it was about up to the mental level of many of the games of a modern fair or village fête (egg and spoon race; sack race).

> . . . the quaint mazes in the wanton green
> For lack of tread are indistinguishable

says Titania in *A Midsummer Night's Dream* (published 1600): that just about expresses the matter. Country games and sports which had centred on religious festivals, patron feasts, days of resort to holy wells, etc., were frowned upon by magistrates in and after the 16th century. The mazes were untrodden, until actual mazes became fewer than place-names which indicate where they existed. The names are various, Troy or Troy Town (because the game or a similar game had once been known as the Game of Troy, or *Lusus Troiae*), Julian's Bower (Julian's chamber: ? because the classical game was played in Virgil's *Aeneid* by Iulus, son of Aeneas the Trojan), Maiden's Bower (the girl's bed-chamber), Shepherd's Race, Robin Hood's Race and, plainly, mismaze or maze (i.e. a place where you are mazed or bewildered). Often the meeting place for games was a hilltop inside the convenient enclosure of a prehistoric hill-fort. Several recorded mazes had such a site. Some existing mazes: Hilton, Cambs (dated 1660, as if recut in the year of Charles II's restoration, after the Commonwealth); Wing, Leicestershire; Saffron Walden Common, Essex (recut in 1699); St. Catherine's Hill, Winchester (formerly the playstow of the boys of Winchester College); Breamore, Hants (in a copse, on a knoll on the edge of the downs); Alkborough, Humberside (a Julian's Bower); Agnes, Isles of Scilly, at Troy Town (fashioned of sea pebbles). In various continental churches, especially in Italy and in France (St. Quentin, Bayeux and Chartres cathedrals), the maze pattern or maze game was adapted to Christian symbolism, and laid down in the paving.

Formal mazes or labyrinths with walls of evergreen, as at Hampton Court, derive from Renaissance gardens in which the same basic game was elaborated, the designs recalling the Cretan maze of the Minotaur.

Mediaeval tiles

On the floor of a parish church mediaeval tiles are usually confined to the CHANCEL, which was the holy of holies, where in front of the high altar they contrasted with the rush-strewn earth or rush-strewn paving stones in the nave. With an inlaid pattern, as a rule, under a yellow glaze, these dark tiles are of a kind made from the 13th century to the Reformation. A design was carved in relief on a wood-block. The block was pressed into the dark clay of the tile, leaving a shape which was filled with a white pipeclay. The tile was then glazed and fired. (Sometimes, the other way round, a dark pattern was laid into a light-coloured tile.) Designs are mostly religious and heraldic. The pelican, the fleur-de-lis, the INSTRUMENTS OF CHRIST'S PASSION, the three-letter monogram for Christ, are common. So are heraldic shields and beasts and REBUSES, these often indicating the donor. Four tiles usually go to a unit in the floor pattern. The occurrence of identical tiles in churches miles apart suggests that the tilers travelled from job to job very often, setting up kilns as they went, and taking their wood-blocks with them. Monasteries were their chief customers, and tiles are often to be seen in the floor of a parish church which was appropriated to a monastery (e.g. Launcells, in Cornwall; Seagry, in Wiltshire; Abbots Bickington, in Devon) – left-overs, it has been suggested, from a monastic job.

Merchants' marks

Perhaps better called identification marks, since they were not confined to merchants, merchants' marks frequently occur on early houses and in churches. A merchant would inscribe his mark on the bales, casks, etc., in which he sent off his goods. If he built himself a house his mark might be added as an ornament inside or out. If he paid for some addition to a church his mark might be cut on bosses, capitals, the spandrels above the shoulders of a doorway, on corbels or bench-ends, or might enter into the stained glass of a window. Sometimes the mark is enclosed in a shield (which may be held by an angel), in a roundel, or within a quatrefoil. His mark would often be incised on a dead man's brass or ledger stone, sometimes over his head, sometimes between his feet. On brasses in Cotswold churches the mark of one of the wealthy wool merchants is often incised between his feet on a woolsack. Of various forms, frequently combining initials, marks are characteristically based on a vertical stem with added arms, cross-lines, circles, etc., and it is thought that such stem marks remotely originate in runic lettering. Marks of the 15th and 16th centuries are commonest, though they occur both earlier and later. Many are illustrated and identified by E. M. Elmhirst in *Merchants' Marks*, Harleian Society CVIII, 1959, and by F. A. Girling, *English Merchants' Marks*, 1964.

Meres

The Old English word *mere* meant a pool, often an artificial pool or pond, and many place-names ending in -mere or -more derive (O. G. S. Crawford, *Archaeology in the Field*, 1953) from existing ponds as much as a thousand years old. In Essex, Wiltshire and Staffordshire, there are ponds which were anciently called Grendelsmere after the black mere or pool in *Beowulf*, which was the home of the man-eating demon Grendel, and which reddened with his blood when Beowulf dived down and killed him.

These encaustic MEDIAEVAL TILES, *which can be found on the floor of the Henry VII's Chapel, Westminster Abbey, are of 13th century glazed and decorated earthenware.*

Mermaids

Mermaids are common in church carvings and paintings as warning of the snares and deceits which await the Christian in his voyage through the wickedness of this world. They derive from the man-eating, sweetly singing sirens of Greek myth, whose song Odysseus heard, bound to the mast of his ship, as it passed near their island. The sirens were bird-bodied, developing later in classical times into fish-bodied mermaids. The classical account of mermaids (and mermen) became a commonplace of mediaeval encyclopedias and the Bestiary in its many versions. Their breasts naked, the mermaids sing and attract the voyagers, who fall asleep, whereupon the mermaids climb aboard and kill them.

> We who through the world do pass
> Are deceived by such a sound,
> By the glamour, by the lusts
> Of this world, which kill us.
> (Guillaume le Clerc's *Bestiary*, 1210–11)

The mermaid on bosses, bench-ends, misericords, capitals, in wall-paintings, etc., combs her long hair, looks at herself in a mirror, sometimes represented with a double instead of a single tail. She is standard in wall-paintings of St. Christopher in the sea around his legs, and occasionally mermaid or merman holds a fish (misericords in Exeter Cathedral and Beverley Minster), signifying the capture of a soul. At Long Stow, Huntingdonshire, a mermaid is the central figure of a Romanesque Tympanum.

Milky Way

Trailing across the night sky our galaxy seemed to the mediaeval mind like a horde of pilgrims making their way to a shrine. Or they regarded it as a sign of pilgrimage placed by God in the sky. The English knew it variously as Watling Street, because the Roman road led across England to the shrine of St. Thomas at Canterbury; Walsingham Way, or Our Lady's Way, as if it indicated the pilgrim route to Walsingham Priory in Norfolk, where the monks displayed the supposed house from Nazareth in which the angel of the Annunciation had visited Mary; and the Way of St. James, as if it was the route to the shrine of the apostle St. James at Santiago de Compostela in Spain. The Welsh, much given to the Compostela journey, called it by the same name in Welsh, *Hynt Siam*. The Spaniards still say that the Milky Way ends at Santiago. The Italians knew it as the *Strada di Roma*, the pilgrims' way to the sacred places of Rome.

Millstone Grit

Gritty coarse Sandstones, often brownish-yellow like a bruise, and weathering to black, laid down over carboniferous limestone. Millstone Grit along the Pennines makes some of the strangest, and glummest, of English scenery, black pinnacles and crags, such as the Roches, backbone of a mediaeval hunting ground, in Staffordshire, west of the Leek–Buxton road, A53; the abrupt Edges along the Derwent Valley in the Peak District; the grim Kinder Scout (2,088 feet), summit of the Peak; the glum black moors between Manchester and Sheffield (including that celebrated image of literary gloom, the moorlands around the home of the Brontës, at Haworth). It has been quarried for buildings, for paving stones, roof tiles, querns, grindstones, and – millstones. Along the Millstone Grit 'edges' of the eastern side of the Derwent (Curbar Edge, Froggatt Edge, Burbage and Stanage) one can see abandoned quarries with unfinished millstones lying about at odd angles, like the half-completed idols in the mountain quarry of Easter Island.

Minsters

Minsters were the parent churches of the countryside conversion of the English. Preceding the smaller parish churches, a minster (Latin *monasterium*) was a church serving a considerable district or estate or tribal area, whose clergy, collectively known as a *familia*, acted as missionaries. Later the area would split up in Parishes, each around its Parish church. The minster settlements which began to be founded in the 7th century consisted of church, thatched huts and halls, the whole 'surrounded by a wooden stockade or thorn hedge or a wall of turf and stone ... In outward appearance the simple type of minster would have looked like a native village in Africa' (G. W. O. Addleshaw). Several places have in their names the word minster, by itself or compounded, recalling the old minster status of the church, e.g. Minster in Thanet and Minster in the Isle of Sheppey, Kidderminster in Hereford and Worcester ('Cydda's minster'), Sturminster in Dorset (minster by the Stour), Axminster in Devon (minster by the river Axe). Some of the surviving Anglo-Saxon churches were minsters, for instance Corbridge in Northumberland with its Anglo-Saxon nave (8th century), and Brixworth in Northamptonshire (7th century) – two churches built partly of Roman material. Later, 'minster' became used simply of a large church or cathedral.

Misericords

If there are hinged oaken seats to the choir stalls of a church, turn them up and see if there are carvings on the underside. The seats are misericords – mercy seats (Latin *misericordia*, compassion, mercy) – devised so that the projection on the underside gave merciful support to clerics standing through the long services: with the misericord tipped up, they sat without sitting. Misericords indicate more clerics than the one parish priest. Away from cathedrals, a set of misericords is most likely to be found in a church in which there were CHANTRY CHAPELS served by their own clergy (chantries explain the misericords, for instance, in Ludlow parish church, in Shropshire, and in the country church of Ripple, in Hereford and Worcester, where two chantries were endowed in 1320, and where the 14th century misericords are carved with the LABOURS OF THE MONTHS). Or misericords may remain in churches (e.g. the priory churches of Cartmel, in Lancashire, and Great Malvern, in Hereford and Worcester) which were part of a monastery. The plain projection of solid oak called out for decoration, allowing room and depth for some of the liveliest mediaeval carving, moral, hortatory, fanciful, ornamental, sometimes an aphoristical scene out of daily life, or an admonitory creature from the Bestiary, or an episode from the Bible or the lives of saints. Read G. L. Remnant's *Misericords in Great Britain*, 1969.

Mistletoe

In the British Isles, mistletoe is commonest in the border lands of the Severn, especially in Gwent, Hereford and Worcester and Gloucestershire. There is evident 'magic' in the

Two fine examples of MISERICORDS. *The top one portrays a redress in the balance of justice and can be seen in the Priory Church of St. Mary and St. Michael, Great Malvern (c. 1480): three mice are hanging a cat, by pulling a rope over a crossbar fixed on two rough staves. The supporters on either side are barn owls. The scene on the lower example (c. 1520) seems to be some sort of domestic quarrel between husband and wife and is from Bristol Cathedral.*

way it grows on a tree, but with us its magical tradition comes mostly from literature – from Norse mythology, from the classical record that it was revered by the Druids, and from the 'Druid mania' of the 18th and early 19th centuries. In the Severn counties, all the same, decorated mistletoe boughs were hung up either on New Year's Day or on Christmas Day and left for a year, to keep evil away from the house. Women should be careful about being kissed under the mistletoe: the original motive was to induce fertility, partly because this peculiar winter-green plant was powerful, partly because its berries and their arrangement suggested the male apparatus.

Moated sites

Moated sites, consisting of a wide moat filled with black water around a level, more or less rectangular, platform, are common in the Midlands and East Anglia, and frequent elsewhere. Often the moat is too deep even now (and too dirty) to cross except in a very dry summer; and when at last one succeeds in treading over the smelly mud to the platform, the most careful search among the brambles and under the oak trees reveals nothing, no trace any more of house or occupation. Yet from the late 12th century or the 13th century till the 15th or 16th century the site is likely to have been occupied by a timber-built manor-house, the moat having been copied from the water defences of the castle.

Abandoned perhaps in the 15th century for

a larger house on a drier and more extensive site more in keeping with fashion and increased wealth, the old wooden house and its outbuildings would soon rot to the ground. In the Middle Ages a moat around one's manor-house (or around a substantial yeoman's house) may have come to appear as socially necessary and distinctive as lawns and a long drive in the 19th century. But in the first instance, in low-lying country without good building stone, the moat and the timber house must have been a cheap and satisfactory solution. It was cheaper to dig and surround yourself with water and live in a wooden house than to have stone quarried and transported over a great distance. Backed with a palisade around the platform, and crossed by a bridge which could be drawn up or interrupted at night or at need, a moat was defence enough against men who might break into your house and against beasts (including red deer and fallow deer and autumn-running herds of swine from neigh-

bouring woodland) which might break into your garden. The moat could be stocked with carp and other fish for the meatless days of the mediaeval week. The content of privies could conveniently be emptied from sight and stench under water. And moat and palisade ensured separation from the commonalty.

Model villages

The most celebrated of model villages, at Milton Abbas in Dorset, inclines one to look at these products of the landscaping era with some suspicion. It was built late in the 18th century by Joseph Dormer, Earl of Dorchester, who housed himself in a new mansion flanking the noble church of Milton Abbey and found the company of the lower orders in a small if decayed market town alongside distasteful. He demolished the town, and resettled a remnant of its people out of sight in a rural street of model cottages of greatly overrated charm. The picturesque

The most celebrated of MODEL VILLAGES, Milton Abbas in Dorset was built in the 18th century by the first Earl of Dorchester to replace other dwellings which marred the privacy of his own home. Although the cottages are large and attractive, many in cob and thatch style, the internal arrangements were designed to cram four large families into each cottage unit.

theorizer, Sir Uvedale Price, put Milton Abbas and its creator in their place when he condemned the rebuilding of a village in two parallel lines of identical houses, identically spaced, as 'formal and insipid' (1798). He insisted that the 'characteristic beauties of a village ... are intricacy, variety and play of outline', and his warning, which had not reached Rural District Councils by the nineteen-sixties, went home to other landlords when they built model villages. The motives in making such villages were multiple, as a rule, adding up to a more or less enlightened self-interest. The landlords and their designers attempted to square landscape attraction, suitability of approach to mansion, abbey or castle, and the welfare of their tenants. They read Goldsmith's *Deserted Village*, which had been published in 1770 (and which fits Milton Abbey and Abbas, and Wimpole Park, southwest of Cambridge, where the Earl of Hardwicke (d. 1764) had also pulled down the old village and built a model village outside his new park):

> The man of wealth and pride
> Takes up a space that many poor supplied;
> Space for his lake, his park's extended bounds,
> Space for his horses, equipage & hounds . . .
> His seat, where solitary sports are seen,
> Indignant spurns the cottage from the green.

Avoiding such insolence, they produced their paternally controlled villages, picturesquely intricate, every cottage of which often bears the family crest. Picturesque model villages include the National Trust's Blaise Castle Hamlet, outside Bristol, designed by John Nash (1809); and Erlestoke, near Devizes, in Wiltshire, which, as he rode through it in 1826, delighted Cobbett, who noticed that every white cottage was covered in jasmine, roses or clematis. In Northumberland there are late 18th century model villages at Blanchland, designed to fit the abbey ruins, and at Bamburgh, designed to fit the castle, both of them built from the estate which Lord Crewe, Bishop of Durham, left as a charitable trust.

Moel, foel

Moel, foel, in Welsh mountain and hill names means a mountain or hill which is bald, naked of vegetation (from the adjective *moel*, which mutates to *foel* after the definite article expressed or implied, the Welsh *f* having the sound of English *v*). Thus Moel Hebog, 'Hawk Hill' (2,566 feet), with its precipices above Beddgelert for nesting hawks, has for neighbours Moel Lefn, 'Smooth Hill' (2,094 feet), Moel Ddu, 'Black Hill', and *Moel yr Ogof*, 'Hill of the Cave' (2,020 feet). The adjective *moel* survives in an earlier form in the name of the bald blue range of the Malverns (Malvern = 'bald hill').

Monasteries

Various entries in this book explain some of the peculiarities met with in exploring monastery ruins, where monks lived inside their world-excluding walls, around the church and the cloister. But it needs more than a ruined monastery, however beautiful, to suggest the scope and the scale of convent life through the Middle Ages. In number of abbeys and priories, and of monks, nuns, canons, canonesses and friars, convent life was at its maximum between A.D. 1300 and 1350. There were at that time in England and Wales – excluding the Scottish and Irish houses – some 17,000 men and women in about 1,000 monasteries and monastic dependencies; and many felt that the spread of monasteries through the whole country was proof that mankind had entered a third and last age in history (*see* TREE OF JESSE) in which the religious life was becoming universal and was preparing for Christ's imminent return to the earth and for the end of the world, and the Last Judgement and the life-without-end. In a single monastery there might be what was called a 'full convent', i.e. an abbot, or prior, and twelve brethren (on the analogy of Christ and his Twelve Apostles), or fewer still, compared to the 100 or 150 monks of one of the major abbeys endowed with great wealth. Abbeys ranked higher than the more numerous priories. The abbot was a high dignitary of the Church. Sometimes, if his abbey was rich enough and important enough, he was equivalent in church rank to a bishop – a 'mitred abbot', entitled like a bishop to wear a mitre and carry a crosier or pastoral staff. And he might also be summoned to Parliament.

Each under its prior (prior was also the title of the second-in-command of an abbey), the priories were generally much smaller, though organized in the same way, and served by fewer inmates. Usually they were founded from abbeys (which might be overseas in France or Normandy), often remaining dependent on their mother houses; or they could become rich and independent, sometimes developing into abbeys. Abbeys and priories might also maintain distant 'cells', from which two or three monks would administer one of

Little remains of the church attached to the MONASTERY *of Dryburgh Abbey, Borders, except the transepts, visible here. The cloisters, however, still remain.*

their more distant estates. Dryburgh Abbey, one of a group of border abbeys, was founded by Hugh de Morville in about 1152 for monks from Alnwick in Northumberland.

Though abbeys and priories of one order and another proliferated in the hundred and fifty years after the Norman Conquest, the first Benedictine monasteries had been founded long before, after St. Augustine's mission to the English, starting with a house at Canterbury. In Ireland, Scotland, Wales, and some of the northern and western parts of England, monasteries of this more elaborate kind had been preceded by small communities of hermits, praying in the wilderness on the model of the earliest monastic communities of the Egyptian desert, and housing themselves in drystone huts within an enclosing wall. Remains of a few such primitive monasteries can be seen, e.g. on the high Atlantic rock of Skellig Michael off the Kerry coast; St. Laisrén's monastery on Inishmurray, Co. Sligo; the monastery on Mahee Island in Strangford Lough, Co. Down; the monastery on St. Helen's in the Isles of Scilly (see BEEHIVE HUTS, CASHEL, CELTIC SAINTS, ROUND TOWERS). The great Benedictine abbeys of Glastonbury and Malmesbury had a remote origin in such Celtic communities. So too the priory on St. Michael's Mount in Cornwall, which began as a Celtic monastery, and in the 11th century became first a cell, then a priory dependent on the Benedictine abbey of Mont-St-Michel, across the Channel.

Monastic place-names

Names with Abbot, Abbas (Latin for Abbot), Prior, Monk, Monachorum (genitive plural of the Latin for monk), Friar (from *frater*, brother), Canon, Sisters, Sororum (genitive plural of the Latin for sister), Nun, Maiden, White Ladies (Cistercian nuns or Premonstratensian Canonesses in white habits), or Black Ladies (Benedictine nuns in black habits), indicate estates which were once given to religious houses by grandees, royal or aristocratic, concerned, after a sinful life, for the transit and destiny of their souls. (Canons in a place-name may indicate ownership either by canons – priests, in canonical orders – living in monastic communities, or the secular canons of a cathedral.) The huge number of these monastic names from end to end of the British Isles shows the grip which monks and nuns had on the countryside before a Dissolution which was sooner or later inevitable; after which arose the smaller of the estates of the 'landed interest', often made up of monastic lands and centring on a country house adapted from the buildings of a monastery – supreme, in turn, along with the larger aristocratic estates, until the inevitable, if less complete, dissolution again which followed from the application of death duties to land in 1894, and the Budget increasing those duties introduced in 1909 by Lloyd George, who declared that the landlord 'was no more necessary to agriculture than a gold chain to a watch'.

Monkey-puzzles

Recovering from a recent charge that they look 'artificial' or 'unnatural' or Victorian, monkey-puzzle trees were introduced from Chile in 1795. The tree (*Araucaria araucana*) was first known as the Chile pine, or Sir Joseph Banks' Tree, Sir Joseph (who was President of the Royal Society) having given Kew Gardens five of the first six seedlings to reach England. The familiar name is said to have arisen from the exclamation of a once well-known parliamentary lawyer, Charles Austin, when one of the new Chile pines was being ceremoniously planted in the young Sir William Molesworth's grounds at Pencarrow in Cornwall, in 1834. He caught hold of it, pricked himself on the leaves, and cried out that 'it would be a puzzle to a monkey'. Most Victorian specimens descended from a batch of seed sent home later, in 1844, by the Cornish plant-collector, William Lobb. By the sixties the Chile pine was commonly called monkey-puzzle pine, or monkey-puzzle for short. And for a while there were purists or literalists who insisted on calling it a puzzle-monkey. Mid Victorian gardeners thought of it as harmonizing with the architecture of the villa and the COTTAGE ORNÉ, and by 1861 it was already common to find a single monkey-puzzle planted on a villa lawn, still a favourite position. The seeds, thrown down from the large female cones at the rounded summit of the monkey-puzzle, are edible, raw or boiled, but they are not very good eating.

Moon-bow

In the right conditions the moon produces a RAINBOW no less than the sun. The bow may be seen, always with a shock of surprise, in showery night weather, only when the moon rises full or nearly full, a grey or whitish arch across the dark sky of the opposite horizon. The light causing the lunar rainbow (in exactly the same way as the diurnal rainbow) is not strong enough to make the colours visible.

Moon-glade

The 'path' of moonlight across the sea, broken and catching the motion of the waves, between the moon and the observer. In Tudor speech 'moonshine in the water' was a common phrase for empty notions or visions.

Motte-and-bailey

Motte-and-bailey was the type of castle or fort introduced by the Normans which preceded the true mediaeval CASTLE fashioned in stone. Many of these motte-and-bailey fortresses remain, and are recognizable by the earth rampart and ditch surrounding an oval forecourt (the bailey) and by the grass-grown or tree-grown mound (the motte) to one side, twenty to forty feet high, in the shape of a cone with the top sliced off. The lord and his family lived in a wooden tower-house or keep on top of the motte, out of range of spear or arrow; the soldiers and retainers occupied a wooden hall in the bailey, where there were also timber-built storehouses and stables. The rampart around the bailey was capped with a palisade, which continued around the base of the motte. In England, motte-and-bailey fortresses may belong to the times of conquest and consolidation after 1066, or to the terrible anarchy of Stephen's reign from 1135 to 1154 when 'every great man built him castles' – by forced labour – 'and held them against the king', and men were tortured, and villages were charged protection money, or else plundered and burnt. The motte-and-bailey conditions of the time are fiercely described in the *Anglo-Saxon Chronicle*. In Wales and along the Marches, where they are particularly abundant (and known as tomens or tumps), they belong mostly to the period between 1069 and 1121,

Pleshey Castle, Essex, is a Norman MOTTE AND BAILEY fortress of the 12th century. The summit would have been ringed by a timber palisade of vertical logs which enclosed a timber tower-house. The base was surrounded by a ditch which, depending on local drainage, might hold water.

The long MYNDD, *Shropshire, is a heather-covered plateau of grit and shale. The bleak wild central area is shared by wild ponies, sheep and grouse, and to the west the hill falls suddenly away so that the prevailing winds provide a constant surge of eddies and upcurrents which account for its popularity as a centre for gliding.*

in which they were built by the Welsh against the Normans as well as by the invading Normans against the Welsh. These earthen and wooden strongholds reached Ireland with the Anglo-Norman invaders under Strongbow and then Henry II. They began to go up about 1169; they were still going up and still being occupied, in the ebb of attack and counter-attack, a hundred years later.

Moutons

Moutons are cloudlets of altocumulus covering the sky not in bands, but like a flock of sheep (French *mouton*), 'gros moutons' or 'petits moutons' according to size. Alto-cumulus cloud floats at between 6,500 and 20,000 feet, well below the level of CIRRUS.

Mynydd

In Welsh, a mountain, e.g. Mynydd Moel ('bald mountain') of 2,804 feet, alongside Cader Idris, or Mynydd Perfedd ('middle mountain') of 2,664 feet, north of Snowdon. The word has been left behind in the English scene, for instance in the wild Shropshire ridge of the Long Mynd.

Nant

Nant, in Welsh place-names, nant or nans in Cornish place-names, a valley, occurs in very many Welsh and Cornish place-names.

National parks

National parks in England and Wales are the result of an international movement which

*S*ome of the most breathtaking views in Britain are to be found at Brecon Beacons NATIONAL PARK, *Powys. Here is the highest ground in all South Wales: a mountain range whose two chief peaks are Pen y Fan and Corn Du.*

began over a hundred years ago when the Yellowstone Park in the United States was designated in 1872 'as a pleasuring ground for the benefit and enjoyment of the people'. Parks of the kind were thought of as proper to countries with great areas of more or less virgin wilderness; and it was not until 1929 that the idea and the need of national parks in our own crowded country began to be considered seriously. More and more people in and out of authority appreciated G. M. Trevelyan's aphoristical warning of 1931: 'Two things are characteristic of this age, and more particularly of this island. The conscious appreciation of natural beauty, and the rapidity with which natural beauty is being destroyed.' A year later the Irish government took over 10,000 acres at Killarney as the first national park in the British Isles.

Report followed report in England, the Dower Report of 1945 defining a national park as 'an extensive area of beautiful and relatively wild country in which for the nation's benefit and by appropriate national decision and action (*a*) the characteristic landscape beauty is strictly preserved, (*b*) access and facilities for public open-air enjoyment are amply provided, (*c*) wild life and buildings and places of architectural and historic interest are suitably protected, while (*d*) established farming use is effectively maintained.' At last in 1949 time was found by the Labour government for the Act which established a National Parks Commission, and one by one the parks were specified, beginning with the Peak District, Lake District, Snowdonia, Dartmoor, Dyfed Coast, North York Moors, Yorkshire Dales, Exmoor, Northumberland and Brecon Beacons.

In more ways than one the national parks recall the royal FORESTS of the Middle Ages. Some of them cover more or less identical areas of semi-wilderness (Dartmoor, Exmoor and the Peak were 'forest'); and just as forest law extended over lands which were not the actual property of the king, so such supervisory and protective duties as are exercised by the Commission and the local planning boards and committees, extend over parks which do not belong to the public. The forests were 'privileged for wild beasts and fowls of forest, chase and warren to rest and abide there in the safe protection of the king, for his delight and pleasure' (John Manwood's *Treatise of the Laws of the Forest*). In the national parks wild life and scenery are – to some extent – privileged for the delight and pleasure of the people.

The park authorities have the double job of preserving natural beauty and giving help in its enjoyment; and the Commission publish guides which introduce with unusual authority the works of nature and man within each park. As guardians who control and plan, the Commission also have an eye on specially designated 'areas of outstanding beauty'.

Nature reserves

Nature reserves are extensively maintained by the Nature Conservancy, a research council and public corporation set up in 1949, to some extent as a result of the thinking by which the NATIONAL PARKS were engendered. An enjoyable environment cannot be secured by scolding, litter baskets and a country code; and the national nature reserves established by the Conservancy form open-air laboratories in which the scientific naturalist discovers how the countryside works and produces its effects. In the reserve the naturalist investigates the exceedingly complex interlocking patterns of life and environment, to make it possible to sustain a balanced variety of fauna and flora and keep the landscape from being impoverished more and more by human pressure. Conservation, which is his guiding light, and the scientific charter of the public body which employs him, has been defined as 'a wise principle of co-existence between man and nature, even if it has to be a modified kind of man and a modified kind of nature' (Charles Elton, in *The Ecology of Invasions by Animals and Plants*). Its study is our insurance against denaturing Britain.

Nave

That main part of a church given over to the parishioners: in this hall-like space (frequently enlarged by opening it left and right into aisles) the people assembled to hear the sermon, and from the nave they could faintly discern the priests performing the offices of the church in the screened-off chapels and before the high altar on the other side of the rood-screen. The nave was the place for helpful or edifying paintings such as the ST. CHRISTOPHER usually set on the wall opposite the south door or the encounter of the THREE LIVING AND THE THREE DEAD, or CHRIST OF THE TRADES. or the DOOM which spread across the chancel arch. In the nave parishioners watched plays and processions, they used it for parish assemblies of one kind or another – even (*see* CHURCH HOUSES) for the festive church-ales which the early Puritans regarded with disgust.

Ness

Ness (headland), in promontory names around the coast may be English (from *næss*), as in the Essex protrusions of The Naze or Foulness, '(sea)fowls' ness', or the similar Old Norse word *nes*, which the Viking seamen would have used, as in Shetland's Sandness, or down the west coast Cumbria's Bowness, 'bowl-(shaped) ness', or Furness, 'arse ness'.

Newel stairs

Newel stairs made of stone and spiralling up around a newel, a central pillar or post, are the commonest form of mediaeval staircase, built (so that they can be illuminated by small lancet windows) in round, or (later) octagonal, turrets, or inside the enlarged corner angle of a building. Notice as you climb a newel stair in church tower or castle how through the centuries the newel itself has been smoothed by the touch of hands. Newel stairs are supposed to be of Byzantine origin.

Oak

One of the natural forest trees of Great Britain, the oak was prehistorically and historically preferred above most timbers for its strength and durability. It was a basic material of life (and of death, used for burning the dead, and for coffin burial in the Bronze Age), always ready to hand, before extensive felling in recent centuries, for house-building, ship- and boat-building, furniture-making and smelting ores of one kind and another. In the west of England oak was commonly grown in coppice to provide oak-bark, rich in tannic acid, for the tan-pits. The rinding took place in the spring, when the sap was rising.

The oak invited worship, or an association with divine power. It was linked with powerful sky-gods, Zeus of the Greeks, Jupiter of the Romans, Thor of the Scandinavians, Thunor of the Germans and Anglo-Saxons – partly because it was observed to be struck and split by the lightning they wielded more often than other forest trees. The fact that oaks are so commonly damaged by lightning has been explained by their furrowed bark. Smooth-barked trees have a stream of water running down the branches and trunk in a storm, affording an uninterrupted channel for the lightning, which as a rule causes only surface damage to such trees. The deeply furrowed bark of the oak precludes conduction: the lightning takes an internal path, turns the sap to steam and explodes the trunk.

Most OAST-HOUSES *are circular and have a cowl over the vent which is adjustable to the wind. This particular example is a double cylindrical oast-house built in Kent in the 19th century.*

Oast-houses

Oast-houses, their ventilation cowls adding an unusual outline to farmsteads in the hopping areas of Kent, Sussex and Hampshire, Hereford and Worcester, are buildings which house the oasts or kilns for drying the newly picked hops, oast having once been the word for a kiln of any kind. (London's Limehouse was *les lymeostes*, 'the limekilns'.) The techniques of hop culture and hop drying on a farm scale were introduced from Flanders, chief source of imported hops, early in the 16th century. Peacocks, hops and heresy (the Reformation) were said to have arrived in one ship. By the fifteen-seventies there was need for a textbook of Kentish experience in hop growing, and it was provided by the Kentish squire, Reginald Scot, of Smeeth near Ashford, who described all the complexities of growing, poling, picking and drying over the 'oste', in his *Perfite platforme of a Hoppe Garden*, 1574. Colonies of wild hops, though the hop plant is native, must often be a relic of the much smaller hop gardens which were planted all over the country from the 15th century to provide hops enough for home brewing. The revolving cowls of the oast-house adjust the draught to the wind, helping to draw the heat up from the oasts through and around the hops, which are laid on finely woven horse-hair cloths.

Obelisks

The Greeks gave these tapering, four-sided Egyptian pillars capped with a pyramidion the name *obeliskos*, a little spit. The pharaohs set them up in front of temples, as a formalization of the rough standing stone. They belonged to the sun god; the pyramidion on top was covered with copper, and caught the first and last rays of the sun. Succeeding civilizations fastened on obelisks as trophies of pomp and pride. Many Egyptian specimens were carried off to Rome, where many home-designed obelisks were also erected. From paintings, engravings and recollections of travel, they were imitated in turn by English architects and garden designers of the 18th century, and set up in LANDSCAPE GARDENS or on hills to give a focal point to the landscape, in deference to the classical spirit expressed in the Palladian mansion, or the other way round.

Opinion split on the appropriateness of classical ornament to English landscape, and on the better claim of Gothic ornament such as ruined 'abbey', hermitage, or tower – differences which were reconciled by allowing that Gothic ruins, which had a prescriptive

right to existence in a land with a Gothic past, were appropriate to a Gothic mansion, and 'the Temple, the Obelisk, the Column, or triumphal Arch' to the classical mansion, with the proviso that these classical addenda must always be made to appear 'modern contemporaries' with the mansion, 'the idea of a Greek ruin in England being a contradiction both to history and experience' (Burgh's Commentary, 1783, to William Mason's poem *The English Garden*).

Obelisks were raised as memorials more often than not, and were meant to suggest, or induce, like the urn and the GARDEN TEMPLE, a melancholic mood of reverie and reflection. William Kent was on one occasion so affected by melancholy while he sat under the obelisk still to be seen in the garden of Chiswick House, our first Palladian mansion, 'that he remained all night, as if enchanted, in that spot until released by the morning sun'.

Having outlived 18th century taste to become a standardized type of public memorial, with associations to match and a shape sometimes suggesting the elderly Queen Victoria, obelisks have lost their magic. Perhaps they should have been capped with copper, like their Egyptian prototypes. But 18th century landlords were less mindful of deity and eternity than the pharaohs, and more mindful of cash: the copper-tipped Egyptian obelisk was a single piece of granite, the landlord's obelisk of melancholy was too often a cheap core of brick with a freestone facing. Many of them are soon likely to fall.

This 18th-century OBELISK appears above a folly at Castletown, Celbridge, Kildare. It was built by Mrs. Connolly of Castletown to relieve the famine in the winter of 1739–40 and was probably designed by Richard Castle.

Ogham stones

Ogham stones, standing stones with a memorial inscription in ogham script, exist in Kerry, Waterford and Cork, in Wales, especially the south-west, Cornwall, the Isle of Man and Scotland. The script seems to have been invented in south-west Ireland in the 4th century, traditionally by a certain Ogma to provide secret signs for the learned. It represents twenty letters of the Latin alphabet by notches (the vowels), and strokes (the consonants). The vowels are notched along the line like beads; the consonantal strokes, single, double, treble, quadruple and quintuple, are cut either across the line or to one or other side of it. The edge of the standing stone usually serves for the line. After the break-up of Roman power in Britain, Irish from the south-west were able to cross St. George's Channel and found little principalities or kingdoms in Wales and Cornwall and elsewhere. Ogham stones commemorate their chieftains. The up-and-down inscriptions in Irish and Ogham, sometimes repeated in Latin and Latin script as well, give as a rule no more than the dead man's name, in the genitive (before which stone, memorial or body needs to be understood), followed by the word for son, and then the father's name. Plenty of ogham stones, especially Irish ones, of which there are more than 300, are still *in situ* (e.g. in Co. Kerry on the Dingle peninsula – Minard, Ballinlarrig, etc.; or the Maen Madoc, beside the Roman road Sarn Helen, near Ystradfellte in Powys); some are in churchyards or churches (e.g. Nevern and St. Dogmael's in Dyfed; Lewannick in Cornwall), some in museums.

Organs

Organs were not usual in country churches until the Victorian era, when they were introduced, often bulky and ugly, and ill-fitted into an aisle or side-chapel, alongside pitchpine choir-stalls and a surpliced choir. Now and again an old organ – or organ-case – is to be seen, as in Old Radnor church in Wales (a panelled case of *c.* 1500), or Stanford-on-Avon, Northants (*c.* 1649). But before the Victorian innovations music was provided as a rule by musicians who occupied part of a singing loft or WEST GALLERY.

Orientation

The idea that our mediaeval churches were orientated (i.e. built on an east-west line, with the chancel towards the east) for symbolical reasons, since Jerusalem is in the east, and the rising sun symbolizes the Christian deity, Christ being the Sun of Righteousness, appears to be an *ex post facto* explanation of the usual, but in the Christian countries of western Europe not inevitable, axis of churches. The idea was reinforced by the romanticism of Victorian ecclesiologists determined to discover symbolism in every feature of a church. The origin of the east-west line, with chancel and high altar and CHANTRY CHAPELS at the eastern end, was more practical – the need, in a northern country where the light is poor, especially in the winter, to have as much morning light as possible for the celebration of the mass. This need to take advantage of daylight also explains the increase of size in mediaeval windows. As J. H. Dickinson has pointed out in his *Monastic Life in Mediæval England* (1961), candles, or oil for CRESSETS, were expensive, and 'in Italy where the light is strong, mediaeval folk put few windows in their churches and paid little attention to orientation'.

Orion

Best known of the winter constellations, Orion images a gigantic and lustful hunter, whom the Greeks believed to have been a child of Earth, created when three of the gods urinated or dropped their seed on an ox-hide, which was then buried in the ground. Eos, the dawn goddess, took him for a lover, for which upset to the other deities he was killed – according to one account – by the arrows of Artemis, the goddess of the chase. According to another story, which fits him better in the sky, Orion tried to rape Artemis, for which she had him stung in the heel by a scorpion – the summer constellation of Scorpio. The stars in Orion which at once take the eye are Betelgeuse, the brilliant reddish star above the Belt, to the left; Rigel, the brilliant knee star below the Belt to the right; and the three stars of the Belt itself, which from left to right have three more Arabic names, Alnitak, Alnilam ('the String of Pearls') and Mintak. These belt stars have also been called the Three Kings, on their way to Bethlehem. In the sky Orion chases the SEVEN SISTERS, and is followed by his hounds, the great star Sirius to the south-east twinkling blue and red in the constellation Canis Major ('Greater Dog'), and the yellow star Procyon, east of Orion in Canis Minor ('Lesser Dog'). Orion drops out of the western sky on April evenings.

See GYPSIES for another name for the stars of Orion's belt.

Ossuaries

Ossuaries, or charnels, belonged to town churches, where the graveyards soon became chock-a-block. It was thought impious not to protect the bones which their owners would require at the Resurrection, and with some charnels there went an endowed charnel-chapel in which prayers were offered for the disjointed dead (as at Abingdon, Oxfordshire, outside the great abbey church). Charnels (e.g. in the crypts under Ripon cathedral and St. Mary-le-Crypt, Gloucester) were hygienically swept away in the last century. But the bones can still be seen in the crypt of St. Leonard's, Hythe, in Kent. In the church at Micheldean, Gloucestershire, the rood loft stairs continue downward to a vaulted charnel equipped with a shoot for the bones. The charnel, with its charnel chapel, in St. Paul's churchyard, was famous in the Middle Ages as a lesson in mortality.

Ovens

Ovens visible on the outside of small houses and cottages as a bulging half-cylinder of masonry with a sloping roof, tiled or slated, came into common use only in the 17th century, when oven baking (except in the baker's oven, to which the housewife sometimes took her pies) began to supersede baking in a flat-lidded iron or earthenware baking-pot on the open hearth, with ashes heaped round it. With a door to one side of the open hearth (on which much of the cooking continued to be done until the insertion of a coal range in the 19th century) the built-in oven was pre-heated with a quick internal fire of dry faggot wood or furze. The fire died down, the ash was quickly swept out, and the door was shut on the pies, bread, dough cakes, etc., which were gently baked in a diminishing heat. Inside, the domed oven of this kind is lined with closely fitted stones or bricks, covered sometimes with clay. In Devon and Cornwall, the ovens set partly in and partly out of the softness of a COB wall were prefabricated in earthenware, with an earthenware door – 'cloam' ovens.

Owls

In the past, owls were birds of evil, whether in common belief or church symbolism. Guillaume le Clerc's versified Bestiary of 1210–11 indicates the general feeling –

> This bird is foul and stinking.
> Daylight and sunlight alike it hates

– and goes on to declare that the owl stands for the Jews, since they preferred darkness to the light of God, the true sun. Carved frequently on BENCH-ENDS and MISERICORDS, sometimes mobbed by small birds, the owl is at any rate a creature of sin and darkness, if in a generalized way.

Oyster shells

Found in digging the garden of any house or cottage two centuries or more old, oyster shells are witness that for hundreds of years till the mid 19th century oysters were one of the cheapest of foods. Supplies, English, Welsh, Irish, Scottish, seemed inexhaustible. No market could be more than fifty miles from the sea, and in damp packing the oysters travelled well in cool weather; and were a welcome supplement to reliance on salt herring (especially when three fish days a week were enjoined in the Middle Ages). They were eaten not only raw, but stewed, fried, roast, grilled, in pies (with sweetbreads) and in soup and in steak-and-kidney pudding. Markets and shops were also supplied with pickled oysters, especially from the Glamorgan area. Oysters became scarce – and a luxury food – in the sixties of the 19th century, owing to the increased population and the demand for them in the industrial cities.

Pandy

Pandy, in Welsh place-names, is a 'fulling place', i.e. a fulling mill or tucking mill. *Pân* in Welsh is fulled cloth, *pannwr* a fuller.

Paramoudras

Tubes of flint standing up like round pulpits on the chalk reefs below cliffs near Seaford (Sussex) and Sheringham (Norfolk). Paramoudras were produced by the percolation of silica-charged water down the sides of infilled sink-holes. Their odd name is said to have been invented by an Irish labourer working on the beach at Sheringham.

Pargetting

To parget or purge a façade or a gable of a timber-framed house is to *pour jeter* it – to throw (plaster) over it; as the plaster was often ornamented, pargetting is now the term for such ornamentation, which was a favourite technique for smaller town houses and cottages in Essex and Suffolk in the 16th and 17th centuries, extending into Kent, Hertfordshire and Cambridgeshire. Some pargetting is incised, but the most effective is plaster with panels of ornament in relief – foliage, flowers, birds, etc. – which the plasterers made by pressing moulds on to the wet plaster or else shaped by hand. It is a technique for more humble outside work which they derived from the plaster ceilings of the Elizabethan mansion or manor-house.

Parhelia

Under certain conditions parhelia ('suns alongside'), sun-dogs, or mock suns, appear on the Small Halo of 22° around the sun, which is caused by ice-crystal clouds. The parhelia appear left and right of the sun at the sun's altitude: they show in prismatic colours, bluish-white, yellow, and then red nearest to the sun itself. The Large Halo of 46° may appear around the Small Halo; and touching both there may be tangential arcs. Cotman saw a wonderful parhelion display over the Wash from the cliffs at Hunstanton in Norfolk one July evening in 1815, and made a drawing of it – large halo, small halo, mock suns and tangential arcs. Like COMETS, parhelia and haloes were taken as portents of storm and fortune. Not always bad fortune: the Duke of York (Edward IV) saw the three suns on the February morning of the battle of Mortimer's Cross, in 1461 – according to Hall's Chronicle – and was encouraged to the rapid defeat of the Lancastrians. Parhelia are admirably explained in Minnaert's *Light and Colour in the Open Air* (1959).

Parish churches

Parish churches are the most persistent items of continuity and cultural expression in the villages. But we forget their original purpose, which is best explained in a sentence from G. H. Cook's *English Mediaeval Parish Churches*: 'The *raison d'être* of a church was the celebration of the Mass': it was an altar-house, and it was this fact which 'shaped the form of the parish church from its earliest days'. Once this is realized everything fits into place – above all the division of the church into the screen-guarded CHANCEL of the priest, where he offered the sacrifice of the body of Christ at the high altar, and the NAVE, where the parishioners came and went. The church, nave included, was holy, the chancel extra holy; with differences in imagery, etc., to match. Thus above the rood-screen (*see* ROOD *and* ROOD LOFTS) which separated them from the chancel, the parishioners were warned by the DOOM PAINTING of the necessity of the mysteries performed on their behalf on the other

side of the screen: they saw the red fate demons might push them into, if their evil living outweighed the effect of the mass. ANGELS hovered in the chancel; which was the place for relics. The nearer one contrived to be buried to the high altar and the influence of the relics, the better one's chances of unending existence of the right kind.

Realizing that the church was built as this kind of altar-house which emphasized the mass and not the congregation, also explains the changes which took place after the Reformation: removing distractions which were felt to be idolatrous and superstitious, whitewashing the wall-pictures, smashing the stained glass, and opening up the church and altar for a new congregational worship – a process with its counterpart in opening up ritual with an English prayerbook and the Bible by translation, but a process with its continuing tug between post-Reformation and pre-Reformation, between innovation, or clarification, and tradition (recovering, replacing, restoring, etc.).

The position of the church in law seems to reflect ancient distinctions between the priest in the chancel and the parishioners in the nave. The parish priest, the incumbent as he is called, owns the church, the parochial church council having possession jointly with him for the fulfilling of their functions. The incumbent keeps the key. The churchwardens own the movables, bells and books and candles. In *Jackson v. Adams* (1835) a churchwarden sought damages for slander, the defendant having said 'Who stole the parish bell-ropes, you scamping rascal?' But the judge said 'No slander is here; for he could not steal what he owned, and no one attaches weight to vulgar abuse'. The churchwarden, though, had no right to appropriate the ropes to his own use; and to remove chattels from a church requires a faculty – a permission, that is – from the bishop. In the church, 'faculty-pews' – pews appropriated by a faculty from the bishop – may be reserved for owners of property in the parish. Memorials inside the church (as in the CHURCHYARD) belong to those who erect them and their successors, and action can be taken for removing them or damaging them.

Parishes

Parishes began as church districts. Between the 9th and 11th centuries more and more local lords built their own estate churches. Having built his church, the lord chose a priest to serve it. The area this priest served, the inhabitants of

The PARISH
CHURCH *of*
Stanton Lacy, near
Ludlow, Shropshire.

which paid him the usual tithe and other dues for his ministrations, became his 'parish', by origin a Greek word for an area occupied by neighbours. The parish usually coincided with the estate, i.e. with the village and its manorial lands. But to make sure that the extent was not forgotten or diminished (and that his tithes were not diminished), the priest once a year customarily 'beat the bounds' in the Rogation-tide ceremonies. In principle, the priestly in-cumbent of the parish was God's priest. The lord might choose him, but the bishop insisted on controlling him, and the bishop alone had power to remove him. In the same way the church, the nucleus of the parish, once it was built, became God's house, controlled not by the builder, but by the parish priest, and maintained by his parishioners. Many more 'estate churches' were built in this way, and many more parishes were formed around them, after the Norman Conquest. These priestly units which made up the bishop's dioceses, outlasted the mediaeval organization of life and became in the 16th century the units of local administration.

Parks

Attached to greater or lesser mansions, parks were an early mark of status, not so much for seclusion and landscape (considerations which changed the look of parks in the 18th century) as for the deer they enclosed for fattening and hunting. Great mediaeval landowners, abbots and bishops included, wanted deer parks to ensure a supply of fresh venison in the difficult winter months, and, deer being royal crea-tures, with free right of coming and going, landowners could impark them only if granted a (costly) royal licence. The enclosing barrier was customarily an earthen bank capped with a pale or fence too high for leaping, shutting off at least thirty acres. Often the banks can be traced where all other signs of the park have disappeared (clues to ancient deer parks are summarized in chapter 18 of O. G. S. Craw-ford's *Archaeology in the Field*, 1953). Later the wooden pales were replaced with high deer-proof walls.

Parks were enclosed – with roe deer, fallow deer and red deer, hunted with solemn cere-mony inside the confines of the park – mainly in the 13th and 14th centuries; some were enclosed in the 12th, and a few as late as the 16th century. There are older parks; for in-stance, at Dyrham in Avon, alongside the mansion which belongs now to the National Trust, there must have been an Anglo-Saxon deer park (*dēor hamm*, deer enclosure), which lapsed. Then in 1511 the owner was licensed by Henry VIII to enclose the 500 acres of deer park to be seen up and down the Cotswold escarpment (with all the Tudor oaks now dying or dead).

When parks were landscaped in the 18th century, the deer, though still cherished as a sign of standing and privilege (and still pro-viding haunches when required), were chiefly looked upon as ornaments appropriate to the now aesthetically arranged vistas and glades. In recent times owners have been unable to afford to repair gaps in the park walls, so deer have escaped, forming the various feral populations which are described in F. J. T. Page's *Field Guide to British Deer*, 1959.

Peat bogs

Peat bogs are relatively modern. They began to be laid down about 7000 B.C. owing to changes in climate; and from neolithic times into our own cool wet phase they greatly thickened, killing forests, burying tree stumps, and rising here and there above neolithic circles and DOLMENS. 'Walking over the up-land bogs I have stepped on to the roofing slabs of a great stone monument which once stood seven feet clear of the ground' (Estyn Evans, in *Irish Folk Ways*). The peat formed on water-logged soil when evaporation failed to keep pace with the supply of water, and when summers became cool enough to stop the bog-land growth of the soil bacteria which break dead plants up into humus. Season by season through the centuries the tardily decomposing and altering vegetable remains – sphagnum mosses, sedges, sundews, etc. – built up into the dark spongy substance of the bogs.

As woodland and scrub vanished or were cleared, a substitute fuel or additional fuel was found in this more or less newly deposited stuff. Techniques of cutting and drying devel-oped; which is how the two words for it came into use. In Scotland and the north they talk of 'peats', i.e. the separate pieces cut out of the peat-moss or bog. Peat (apparently deriving from a British word for 'piece') became the collective word for all the peats or pieces. In the Midlands and the south and in Ireland (except in the Scottish-settled area of the north-east, where they talk of peat), 'turf' is the commoner word, a collective again for all the turves or sods. Commoners exercised – and still do sometimes – the right of cutting peats or turves from any turbary (from *turba*, law-yer's latinization of 'turf') that might exist on the common land (*see* COMMONS); and one of the surprising discoveries of recent years is that the Norfolk Broads developed in the Middle Ages out of very extensive and deep-dug turbaries along the valleys of the Yare, Waveney, Bure, Thurne and Ant. Shifts occurred in the relative levels of land and sea along the east Norfolk coast. At the beginning of the 10th century the land level had risen, and extraction of turf began and, since east Norfolk had next to no trees and was becoming one of the most populous areas of mediaeval England, increased rapidly (turf may also have been required by the salters who evaporated salt from brine along the Norfolk coast). At the end of the 13th century and in the 14th century storms coupled with a relative sinking of the land brought the North Sea into the turbaries, and within two centuries the 'broad waters' or 'brodings' were formed.

Pen-

Pen- at the start of Welsh and Cornish – and a good many English – place-names, may be taken as a rule to mean head, top, hill, end (Welsh and Cornish *pen*), e.g. Hereford's lofty Penyard is *pen ardd*, 'high hill'; Cornwall's Penzance is 'holy headland', Penquite is 'wood end', etc. But *pen-* isn't to be found in the *Pen*nines, which is a name invented by the 18th century forger Charles Bertram, for his concocted chronicle of Richard of Cirencester. Pentre at the beginning of Welsh names is *pentref*, a village.

The PARK *at Knole, Sevenoaks, Kent, with the house itself visible in the background. The park lands, grazed by fallow deer, provide the perfect setting for this splendid building.*

A PICTISH SYMBOL STONE (7th–9th century AD) from Dunnichen House, Dunnichen, Angus. This great decorated boulder stands a few miles from Forfar. The decoration belongs to the earliest class of Pictish symbols.

Pictish symbol stones

Like the Picts themselves (probably a fusion of Celtic and Bronze Age people), Pictish stones have long been regarded as one of the mysteries of Scotland. They are to be found mostly in eastern and north-eastern Scotland, standing stones of granite and sandstone incised or carved with the symbols of a picture 'language'. Some are rougher and less rectangular in outline, and pre-Christian, probably carved from the 5th to the 8th century A.D. Later ones, trimly faced and shaped, retain some of the old symbols in conjunction with the Cross and Christian scenes. All told, the symbols, some of objects, some of animals, add up to nearly fifty. The stones were probably set up as memorials to the dead (some have uninterpreted inscriptions in ogham – *see* OGHAM STONES), and the animals probably relate to the animal cults of the tribes to which the dead men belonged. They include wild boar, bull, horse, raven, eagle, goose, trout or salmon, otter (or seal), dog, wolf, adder; also a peculiar 'elephant', which seems to be a formalized or debased horse with an elongated muzzle, and an equally peculiar S-dragon or sea-horse, which seems to have been derived from a stag. It has been argued convincingly that the art of the symbol stones has its origin in the La Tène art of the British of southern and eastern Britain, which was taken north and then developed in the Pictish kingdom. The animal shapes of this La Tène art, in turn, derive from the art of the Russian and Asiatic steppes. The 'sea-horse' of the symbol stones thus descends, in a roundabout way, from pairs of confronted stags often depicted in Luristan bronzes. Some of the Pictish stones still stand in the open, from Fife to Ross and Cromarty, such as 'King Malcolm's Gravestone', the Christian stone outside the manse at Glamis, in Tayside, carved and incised with the Cross, fish, mirror and adder symbols, or the tall Boar Stone, decorated with wild boar and mirror, near Inverness, or the Maiden Stone ten feet high in the local red granite, five miles from Inverurie in Highlands, half a mile from the church of Chapel of Garioch. In Tayside there is a splendid little museum of these stones at Meigle, between Coupar Angus and Glamis.

Pikes

Pikes are pointed mountains or hills, as so often in the Lake District (Scafell Pike, 3,210 feet, Grisedale Pike, 2,593 feet, Red Pike, 2,470 feet, etc.). Probably a Norse word, pike also gives our commoner word, 'peak'.

Pill

A pill in the south-west is a tidal creek, a word often used to describe creeks opening off the DROWNED VALLEYS, such as Pont Pill, off the Fowey estuary in Cornwall, or Westfield Pill and Garron Pill opening off the main tidal valley of the Milford Haven complex in Dyfed. At low tide the pills empty, at high tide they fill like a winding pool between the hills;

The Pike of Stickle and Harrison Stickle viewed rising above the Langdale Valley in Cumbria.

and pill (*pyll* in Old English) may derive from a British word for pool. There are also pills of less distinction along the Severn estuary, Oldbury Pill, Littleton Pill, and others.

Pineapples

Pineapples as late 17th century or 18th century gatepost finials or as ornaments setting off the corners of an 18th century house, derive not from the fruit we eat, the ananas of Central and South America, which was first grown in English hothouses about 1712–19, but from the pine-cone, which came into ancient classical ornament as a symbol of fertility. Pineapple, the ordinary name for a fir-cone, was transferred to the cone-like inflorescence of the ananas, when it was introduced, and in need of a name to match its great popularity;

169

and occasionally one does discover a finial or series of finials in which the old pine-cone shape couched in conventional foliage has taken on characteristics of the ananas, including its tuft as well as its sharp, serrated leaves.

Piscina

Usually south of the altar in the wall of chancel or chapel in a mediaeval church, the piscina, with its arched opening, its shallow ornamental basin and drain, was used after mass by the priest to rinse the chalice and the paten and his hands. He had been in contact with the Elements, the Host and the wine, transubstantiated, as he believed, into the body and blood of Christ, and with the sacred vessels which contained them. A holiness imparted itself from the Elements to the hands and the vessels, and so to the rinsing water, which therefore needed to be disposed of with reverence and care. The drain took the water down through the wall of the church into the consecrated ground of the churchyard. Early piscinas are frequently basins on a shaft or pillar which contains the drain. Late 13th and early 14th century piscinas are often double, with one basin for the vessels, one for the hands.

Place-names

The rule about them is don't guess; they do not usually explain themselves; which is true particularly of English place-names, the English language having developed and changed so strikingly since the early Middle Ages. A name may have been given 1,300 or 1,400 years ago,

This PISCINA, (c. 1275), is from St. Mary's church, Long Wittenham, Oxfordshire. It has a dual purpose, combining a practical function (that is, as a piscina) with its role as a memorial to a knight, a small carving of whom forms its base. Above the recess two small angels fly upward, bearing in a napkin the soul of the departed knight.

earlier still if it was a British name taken over by the English (and of still greater antiquity if it was a name – some RIVER NAMES seem to be of this kind – taken over by the British when they arrived at the end of the Bronze Age). The word or words that make the place-name may lie concealed in changes of spelling and pronunciation. They may be words that have dropped out of use, they may have changed their meaning; or in its present guise the place-name may look as if it derived from quite different words of current speech, suggesting in that way a wrong explanation. To find the true meaning, the place-name scholar (who requires a knowledge of Old and Middle English, of Old Norse and Old Danish, Old Welsh, Old Cornish, Old French, etc.) needs to know the early forms of each name, the earlier the better.

So the rule is never guess; and look up, which is easy for a great many English place-names, thanks to the work of English and Swedish scholars in the last seventy years. Eilert Ekwall's great *Concise Oxford Dictionary of English Place-names* (latest edition, 1960) interprets the more important names, of towns, counties, districts, parishes, major natural features such as hills, rivers and headlands; and if you are lucky the names in your county will have been dealt with in one of the volumes which are being published by the English Place-Name Society, founded in 1924. These go down the scale to farm names and field names.

The ordinary reader will find these technical place-name surveys much easier to follow if he can consult another publication by the society, A. H. Smith's *English Place-Name Elements* (1956), which is also an extraordinary compendium of clues to Dark Age and mediaeval and more recent ways and facts of life in rural England. The rivers of England have their own famous volume, Eilert Ekwall's *English River-names* (1928).

Beginning to think more of the ordinary man's interest in place-names and the past, scholars have now provided one or two general books. Kenneth Cameron's *English Place-Names* (1961) and P. H. Reaney's *Origin of English Place-Names* (1960) give much information. Unfortunately, Wales, Scotland and Ireland are not served yet by an up-to-date, scholarly and dependable place-name literature.

In spite of the injunction 'Thou shalt not guess', some of the commoner and more interesting place-name words have entries in this book. If a name which intrigues you seems to contain one of these words, don't be too hasty. Check in the *Concise Oxford Dictionary of English Place-names*, or one of the Survey volumes.

Playstows

Playstows, open spaces, sometimes VILLAGE GREENS, where games were played in and after the Middle Ages (including often the game of treading the MAZE) have left their memory behind in place-names, most commonly the name Plaistow. At Selbourne in Hampshire the playstow has become the Plestor, the open place which Gilbert White described: the '*locus ludorum*, or play-place . . . a level area near the church of about forty-four yards by thirty-six', in the midst of which there stood until 1703 'a vast oak, with a short squat body, and huge horizontal arms extending almost to the extremity of the area . . . surrounded with stone steps, and seats above them . . . the delight of old and young, and a place of much resort in summer evenings'. The Plestor was also used for the Selborne markets. In Cornwall a playstow was a *plan-an-guare* (literally 'place of play'), a name which led antiquaries of the 19th century to suppose – and the myth is still current – that they were all for the performance of miracle plays in Cornish. Such are the celebrated round playstows at St. Just-in-Penwith, near Penzance, and Perran-zabuloe, the Perran Round, the latter an Iron Age earthwork, the rampart of which is terraced, or stepped and seated, in a way that recalls the steps around the Plestor oak.

The Plestor – or PLAYSTOW – at Selborne, Hampshire, was once a market place.

Sea-cliffs of PORTLAND STONE *(oolitic limestone) on the Dorset coast, at Durdle Door.*

Polissoirs

Polissoirs, i.e. boulders grooved and hollowed by the polishing and sharpening of neolithic stone axes, are something to search for, rare – perhaps because they have been overlooked and unthought of – in Great Britain, yet very common in some parts of France (e.g. to the south-west of Chartres and between Montargis and Fontainebleau), where the village people know them by such names as La Pierre Cochée, 'Nicked Stone', or La Griffe du Diable (though they are also credited to St. Martin). Two polissoirs have been found on the Marlborough Downs in Wiltshire, blocks of SARSEN (sarsen and PUDDINGSTONE are the usual material of the French polissoirs), one of them marked in a way which conforms exactly to the French type, with straight and more or less parallel grooves, and a 'cuvette' or shallow basin. On a polissoir the grooves and the oval or circular basins retain a high gloss quite different even to the smoothest areas of the natural surface (though sometimes all or part of the gloss along a groove has weathered away). At Avebury one of the stones forming the Avenue between the circle and the Kennet has small grooves and some gloss near the ground, which suggests some use as a polissoir before the stone was set upright; and one of the stones in the chambered barrow of Wayland's Smithy in Oxfordshire, above the Vale of the White Horse, and another in the West Kennet Long Barrow have glossy patches (in France a polissoir block has often been built into a chambered tomb). This makes a meagre total, and it seems likely that there are polissoirs of the more complex kind waiting to be recognized. Look for them wherever there are tough-grained boulders about, remembering not only the unnatural and rather uncanny gloss, but the shape of the grooves, which may be few or many, usually parallel in groups. They are what one would expect from men kneeling on the boulder (so that their legs didn't get in the way) and rubbing axes forwards and backwards with one hand, and perhaps treating the groove with fat and a fine abrasive. If the polissoir was in use for a long while, the grooves are likely to be sixteen to eighteen inches long, up to an inch or more deep, and two to three inches wide, narrowing at the ends; they have a very well defined and sharp V section, curving up slightly to each end along the valley, like a bow.

In north Wales there are grooved boulders known as *cerrig saethau* or arrowstones (described in W. B. Lowe's *Heart of North Wales*, vol. 2, 1927), many of them on the moorland no great distance from Penmaen-Mawr Mountain, where (under Graig Llwyd) neolithic craftsmen roughed out axes from the igneous stones of the scree. One long smooth arrow-stone at Camarnaint near Llanfairfechan, less than two miles from this axe factory (which has now been quarried away), has more than 120 grooves. But on arrowstones the grooves as a rule are not as long, as wide or as deep as on the polissoirs, and they were perhaps used to give the igneous stone axes no more than a cutting edge. An arrowstone with seventy grooves on Lazonby Fell in Cumbria, near Kirkoswald, is less than thirty miles north-east of the axe factories discovered above Great Langdale.

Pont

Pont in many Welsh place-names, pont or pons in Cornish names, means a bridge, a word which the British borrowed from the Latin *pons*. The word would have been familiar from the many bridges on the course of the Roman roads, such as the Pons Aelius across the Tyne at Newcastle.

Portland stone

The best known of all English building stones, Portland stone takes its name from the bleak Isle of Portland jutting from the Dorset coast, which is built up on the Portland beds. Three of the beds, under forty to fifty feet of 'overburden', provide the Portland stone, an oolitic limestone brown (in the middle bed) when quarried and becoming white on exposure. It was too hard to be used much in the Middle Ages. Inigo Jones introduced it to London in 1619 as the material for the king's Banqueting House in Whitehall, and Sir Christopher Wren ensured its celebrity half a century later, after the Fire of London, by choosing it for his new St. Paul's and his new City churches. At Portland he found quantities of the stone exposed by a landslide. So there was no difficulty in quarrying huge blocks and trolleying them down short slipways into barges for transport to London. There are still blocks with his wineglass mark on them lying on the east side of the island. Portland stone is not confined to Portland. Eastward along the Dorset coast it makes the sea-arch of Durdle Door and much of the great Gad Cliff, and then between St. Alban's Head and Durlston Head it makes sheer sea-slapped cliffs. The Tilly Whim Caves along the cliffs near Durlston (a 'whim' is a stone miner's windlass) are

Portland stone quarries. The stone formerly quarried at Chilmark in Wiltshire and used for Salisbury cathedral belongs to the Portland series.

Port ways

Often to be found on the map, port ways are ways, tracks, roads, leading not to a port meaning harbour (from the Latin *portus*) but to a port meaning market town (from the Latin *porta*, a gate), originally a town with a gateway. There are roads named Port Way in many counties, e.g. Gloucestershire, Devon, Dorset, Derbyshire, Berkshire, Wiltshire, Hereford and Worcester; some of them ROMAN ROADS, such as the Port Way running from Silchester to Andover and Old Sarum, or the Port Way running to the village of Aynho in Northamptonshire, which was a market town in the Middle Ages.

Pots

Pots (a better word than the modern tautological 'pot-hole') are caves on end, or vertical holes into the limestone. The Craven, in North Yorkshire, is the great pot country, and it is from Craven speech, probably from Old Norse, that 'pot' for a deep hole is derived (in Lowland English 'pot' was used for the bottomless pit of hell). Where they have a wide gullet, pots are some of the most surprising and fearsome of natural features. Two in this rank belong to Ingleborough mountain in Craven, Gaping Gill on one flank, 450 feet deep, first descended by the French caver E. A. Martel in 1895, and at the back of the mountain, on Simon Fell, Alum Pot, 292 feet deep, first descended in 1848 by the alpinist John Birkbeck, the pioneer of caving as a sport. Alum Pot has been described as going down into the rock like a black arum lily. Others to visit are Hull Pot and Hunt Pot on Pen-y-ghent, and especially Rowten Pot, above Kingsdale and the road from Ingleton in North Yorkshire to Dent in Cumbria. All told, Craven has upwards of two hundred pots, of which the deepest, also one of the deepest in the British Isles, is Meregill Hole in Chapel-le-Dale. The Derbyshire limestone is less potted with sudden entrances into hell, having Eldon Hole near Castleton as its showpiece, opening with a direct drop of 186 feet in a long narrow chasm. Only small pots descend into the limestone of Gloucestershire, the Mendips and south Wales. Pots abound in the Irish limestone, their names usually beginning with Poll-, i.e. pit, the Irish equivalent of Pot. The deepest known is Noon's Hole, 250 feet, in the cavaceously and archaeologically exciting district around Boho, Co. Fermanagh. Pots are spoken of in terms of depth, difficulty and sport. But they can be exceedingly attractive to the (superficial) eye, with bird cherries overhanging their gullet, a white thread of a stream dropping into blackness past wood anemones, bluebells, water avens and pink campion, and sometimes with one or more ash trees rooted far enough down for their tops to show just above or just below the level of the opening, this last being a pleasant accent on pots in Ireland – Pollnagollum under Slieve Elva in Burren, Co. Clare, for instance – and pots in North Yorkshire.

Prospect-towers

Prospect-towers, 'observatories', or 'pavilions', exist from end to end of the country in high places, especially on landscaped estates, and are relics of that movement of the spirit in the 18th and 19th centuries which flowered in an appreciation of nature and scenery, in the pictures of the English landscape school, and in the poems of Wordsworth, and led to our own sense of refreshment in the country.

Such towers, in many shapes, round, triangular, octagonal, etc., were set up where they 'commanded the prospect', or distant view.

Heav'ns, what a goodly prospect spreads around,
Of hills, and dales, and woods, and lawns, and
    spires!
And glittering towns, and gilded streams, till all
The stretching landskip into smoke decays.

From *The Seasons* of James Thomson (1700–1748), those lines were the inspiration of the tower-builders, whose towers raised the hilltop, extended the prospect (preferably, as the concern for pure nature increased, a prospect uninterrupted by Thomson's glittering towns), and recalled the primitive virtues by their mediaeval look.

Builders were also inspired by the 'lantskip' passage in Milton's *L'Allegro*, on the pleasures of the eye:

Towers and Battlements it sees
Boosom'd high in tufted Trees.

On one of the upper floors would frequently be a well-appointed room, now given over to jackdaws, where the ladies and gentlemen of the great house would dine or take tea, read the poets, and meditate on the landscape, which looked still more ravishing from the castellated top. Prospect-glasses (telescopes)

This late 18th-century PROSPECT TOWER *is situated at Kimmeridge, Dorset. It comprises a circular tower three storeys high and is beautifully positioned on the clifftop.*

PUDDINGSTONES

Luttrell's Tower (c. 1780), Eaglehurst, is a PROSPECT TOWER *situated on the edge of the Solent, Hampshire.*

added to the pleasure. The towers might combine piety with aesthetics, commemorating king, hero, or battle (e.g. King Alfred's Tower (1772) at Stourhead, Wiltshire). The towers were designed to be looked from, also to be looked at. They were embellishments of the landscape. 'The prospect-tower', Loudon wrote in his *Encyclopaedia of Gardening* (1828), 'is a noble object to look at, and a gratifying and instructive position to look from. It should be placed on the highest grounds of a residence, in order to command as wide a prospect as possible, to serve as a fixed recognised point to strangers, in making a tour of the grounds'. Loudon said the rooms of a prospect-tower were 'resting places' – 'absolutely necessary, where ease and enjoyment are studied, and where some attention is had to the delicacy of women, and the frailties of old age'.

Great landlords and nabobs no doubt made too much of their towers, which came to seem a joke to the new middle-class Victorians, who lumped them with SHAM RUINS, landscape temples, etc., as 'follies' (though 'folly' was used of such towers before the 18th century was out). All the same, prospect-towers are true and valuable, and now venerable, antiquities, which should be preserved.

Puddingstones

Weathered lumps or boulders of sometimes very tough conglomerate, puddingstones are familiar in one variety in the Home Counties and especially in Hertfordshire. They look like something left behind by builders, conglomerations of large and small pebbles of flint, water-worn and rounded and held together by a silicaceous cement, the result of water charged with silica (cf. SARSEN STONES) percolating among the pebble beds of which they are remnants. In Buckinghamshire there is a notable collection of sarsens and puddingstones alongside the village green of The Lee, between Great Missenden and Tring. Hertfordshire people have had several names for these curiously artificial-looking objects, these 'plum-pudding stones', arising from a belief that each lump or boulder was breeding and growing smaller lumps round itself – motherstones, breeding-stones, growing-stones. Now and again puddingstones have been used in buildings, churches included. Harder puddingstone was sometimes made into QUERNS; and it is possible that some tough boulders of puddingstone in the Home Counties and elsewhere may be found, as in France, to be scored with neolithic axe-sharpening grooves (*see* POLISSOIRS).

Pulpit

Pulpit (Latin *pulpitum*), a platform or a stage. Preaching in the parish churches spread in the 14th century under the influence of the Franciscan friars, making the church rather less an exclusive shrine for the celebration of the mass. No pulpit in an English parish church is earlier than about 1340, and most of the pre-Reformation pulpits up and down the country, sometimes in oak, sometimes in stone, with traceried panels, set against the wall of the nave or against a pier, are late additions of the 15th century or early 16th century. Since the pulpit was for preaching and teaching, it was not infrequently carved with likenesses of the greatest preachers and teachers, i.e. the FOUR DOCTORS OF THE LATIN CHURCH (examples are the 15th century pulpits of Castle Acre in Norfolk and Trull in Somerset), often in company with the Four Evangelists. With the Reformation and the change to a liturgical worship embracing congregation and priest, the pulpit acquired a new importance and centrality. In the 17th and 18th centuries the pulpit, the newfangled reading desk or reading pew, from which the priest read the prayers, lessons and litany, and the desk or pew occupied by his parish clerk, were frequently combined in the triple-tiered 'three-decker'. The pulpit lifted the preacher well above the tallest BOX PEWS, and there was separate access to each tier. The clerk, from his tier, the lowest of the three, led the responses and the singing. Victorian ritualists and ecclesiologists liked to disencumber churches of box pews, galleries and three-decker, all of which survive, for example, in Old Dilton church, near Westbury in Wiltshire. In Suffolk, Kedington church has an exceptionally fine three-decker of the early 17th century, complete with accessories – the tester or sounding-board overhead, to send the preacher's voice round the nave, the iron stand for the hour-glass by which he timed his discourse for an impatient congregation with colds and chilblains, and even a stand for his wig.

Purbeck marble

A favourite material in English churches of the 13th century, Purbeck marble is a hard, dark, fossiliferous limestone (not a true marble) made up of freshwater snails. Occurring in two bands, usually about a foot thick, in the Isle of Purbeck in Dorset, it was mined along the hills between Swanage and Kingston and shipped all over England and across the Channel to Normandy. On the spot the Purbeck marblers carved this polishable stone into effigies of abbots and bishops and nobles and knights and their ladies, into fonts, capitals, and slender shafts to be used in conjunction with bulkier freestone. Purbeck marble has been found in Romano-British towns. Its mediaeval use began after the Norman Conquest, in the 12th century, when it was employed in tomb-slabs and effigies as a substitute for the touch or true black marble imported from Tournai. It was in common use until the 14th century. There is much Purbeck marble in Salisbury cathedral, in tall pipe-like shafts, carvings and effigies. Durham cathedral exhibits both Purbeck (in the Galilee) and its northern substitute, Frosterley marble (in the Chapel of the Nine Altars).

Querns

It is not uncommon to find the lower part of a mediaeval quern preserved in a church in the belief that it was a font. Invented in the eastern Mediterranean world between 500 and 200 B.C. (and still used by women in the Greek countryside), the quern is a hand-mill for grinding corn, or anything else which needs to be ground, and was among the first of the world's rotary devices. In one form it had reached Britain by the late Iron Age, superseding the old saddle-quern, a primitive affair with which meal or flour was ground between two stones, the upper of which was pushed backwards and forwards. Earlier rotary querns, of types used till this century in the Highlands and Islands, consisted of two round stones of similar diameter, the upper one (turned by a wooden handle) with a more, or less, concave under-surface. The round base to which it was pivoted, had a grinding-surface more or less convex, or even flat.

The kind of mediaeval quern the base of which is so often mistaken for a small font, was perhaps, by origin, a cross between a quern and a mortar. A thin round upper stone revolved on an iron spindle *inside* the base, in a circular trough, flat-bottomed, and three to four inches deep, nine to fifteen inches across. Outside, this base-stone is sometimes round, frequently octagonal. A small tunnel slopes down from inside to outside to convey the meal or flour. Sometimes a man's face is carved on the outside, like one of the human faces carved on a 15th century boss, the tunnel opening in his mouth. These home mills were turned by somebody standing upright, grasping a long stick, the top end of which pivoted

into a beam while the bottom end fitted loosely into a shallow hole near the circumference of the millstone.

From the Old English *cweorn*, there are quite a few quern place-names, some of them indicating where the querns were quarried – especially from the MILLSTONE GRIT of Yorkshire and Lancashire. Wharncliffe (the wild Wharncliffe Chase and Wharncliffe Crags, near Sheffield) is one quern site. Whernside (the mountain on the Cumbria and North Yorkshire border) means 'quern side'.

Rainbows

Caused by sunlight on raindrops up to about a mile and a half away, rainbows show best against a blackness of wood, hill, cloudage, etc., the colours (though all of them will not be present in every bow) merging from red outside through orange, yellow, green, blue and indigo to violet inside. It may not be discernible, but there is always a fainter outside bow ('double rainbow'), the colours of which are in reverse order.

Each raindrop acts as a prism, refracting the sunlight. The light enters the drop, is reflected from the back and emerges at the angle of the primary bow. Some of the light entering the raindrop is reflected twice before emerging at the wider angle of the outer bow. So the colour-order of the two bows is reversed, the reds in either one coming next to each other.

These outer bows – 'water-galls' – are supposed to presage storms. Stumps of a rainbow rising above the ground, also a traditional presage of more rain, are 'weather-galls'.

Raised beaches

Raised beaches round the coasts of Great Britain are relics mostly of the glacial period and its aftermath, which brought about the most complex shifts in the relative levels of the sea and the land, the sea level falling or rising as ice formed or melted, the land level falling or rising as the weight of ice increased or lessened, or disappeared. In many places an old sloping offshore platform of rock once washed and planed by the waves has been left high and dry above today's sea level. Sometimes this old beach-platform will be backed, at more or less distance from the sea, by its ancient line of cliffs; and here and there the platform may still show some of its beach – the actual material of the beach, if it has not been obscured or removed long ago, the actual sand and shingle and marine shells, now uplifted it may be 10, it may be 100, or 150, feet above the sea.

Rampart farmsteads and villages

Rampart farmsteads and villages (the camps and hill-forts of archaeological handbooks, but both 'camp' and 'fort' suggest a wrong kind of military significance) are far and away the most conspicuous prehistoric antiquities of the British Isles, the peculiar memorial, from the 6th century B.C., of the quarrelsomeness of the Celtic peoples. By contrast, the CAUSEWAYED CAMPS and HENGES of the neolithic and Bronze Age past are relics of a more or less peaceful era of pastoralists and small farmers unpressed by competition and land hunger. Then came the peoples with Celtic speech crossing from a disturbed continent, introducing iron weapons, and soon finding themselves, wave after wave, in competition for a scarcity of land for their herds and their crops. They attacked each other, and they had to defend themselves: they took to sheltering behind tall ramparts, of earth or stone according to situation, and deep ditches, enclosing a hilltop or cutting off a headland, with a space inside the ramparts varying from an acre or two to twenty acres or more, family size to tribal size, farmstead size, or small village size, to large village size.

Earlier comers built wooden stockades first of all, then enclosures with a single ditch and rampart, which might be altered and strengthened as the Iron Age centuries went by. Extra ramparts with ditches became the fashion (putting the inside out of range of slingstones), entrances were cunningly turned and dog-legged to strengthen what was the weakest point. Wooden stockades might cap the ramparts, which might be faced with timber, entrance gates might be strengthened with wooden towers, and the gap through the ramparts spanned for easier defence by a wooden bridge. Some enclosure builders liked to augment the defences by setting chevaux-de-frise in the ground, in the shape of stone spikes. There are examples in Wales, at Pen-y-gaer, Llanbedrycennin, Gwynedd, and Craig Gwrtheyrn, above the Teifi, between Llanfihangel-ar-arth and Llandyssul, in Dyfed; and in Ireland there are very prickly chevaux-de-frise of limestone outside the ring-fort of Ballykinvarga, near Kilfenora, in Co. Clare, and around Dun Aonghus, on the Aran Islands.

The community of a rampart farmstead or rampart village occupied round thatched huts set close under the inner rampart. They lived by herding and farming – and fighting, or raiding. Inside an enclosure one may be able to detect hut platforms, the round dimplings of

An aerial view of the RAMPART FARMSTEAD AND VILLAGE *on Hambledon Hill, near Iwerne Minster, Dorset. Recent excavations of this iron age hill fort show that many human bones were buried in the ditches.*

pits in which grain was stored, and, if it is ploughed, scraps of rusty slag (*see* BLOOMERIES) from iron-working; and as well as ditch and rampart there may be a SOUTERRAIN. From Irish sagas and classical descriptions of Gaul, Kenneth Jackson (in *The Oldest Irish Tradition: A Window on the Iron Age*, 1964) has drawn up a very unflattering portrait of the life of warrior aristocrats and cattle-raiders who would have controlled the major fortified villages: they took their enemies' heads, removed the brains and moulded them with lime into hard brain-balls, and would fight each other for the 'hero's portion' of roast pig, a self-dramatizing, boastful, exaggerating, tetchy crew, with a liking to hear themselves praised by their bards or poets. As far as England and Wales were concerned, this hilltop life was largely brought to an end in the 1st century A.D. by the authority of Rome; and many of the major rampart villages or small towns were slighted by the legionaries. The people moved, or were moved, downhill to new Roman towns, e.g. from Dorset's Maiden Castle, stormed by the 2nd Legion under Vespasian, *c.* A.D. 43, into Durnovaria or Dorchester, capital of a tribal canton or *civitas*.

In Ireland and Scotland the life of the rampart farmsteads and villages continued; and in Ireland it is known that the neatly circular ringforts or raths, of which there are upwards of 30,000 still to be seen, continued to be built and occupied as late as A.D. 1000. There are counterparts to these in Cornwall.

Scotland has its peculiar 'vitrified forts', more than sixty of them. In the technique of the *murus gallicus*, which Caesar described in his *De Bello Gallico*, the ramparts were fashioned of stones, interlaced, in their thickness, with horizontally laid timbers. Sometimes the huts inside would catch fire, the fire would spread to the timbers in the wall, and the heat inside them would rise to a furnace temperature of 950 to 1,200 degrees Centigrade, enough to melt the silica and other mineral content of the stones and fuse them together (some famous examples: Craig Phadraig, near Inverness; the magnificently perched Tap o'Noth, near Rhynie, in Grampian; Knock Farril, near Strathpeffer, in Highland). Sometimes vitrification seems to have followed an attack on the camp.

Rapes and lathes

Rapes in Sussex and lathes in Kent, each comprising several hundreds, are the very ancient divisions of either county, which may go back to early days of settlement before England was divided into SHIRES: they are thought to represent tribal provinces or regions. After the Conquest, William I organized the six Rapes of Sussex as castleries, castle districts, to maintain, each of them, one of the castles built to defend the southern approaches

179

(and the river-gaps through the South Downs). Of the Rapes, naming them from west to east, of Chichester, Arundel, Bramber, Lewes, Pevensey, and Hastings, only the Rape of Chichester has lost its castle. Kent was likewise divided into six Lathes, reorganized in the Middle Ages as the Lathes of Sutton-at-Hone, Sheppey, Scray, Aylesford, St. Augustine and Hedeling, and then reduced to five when Hedeling and St. Augustine were joined.

Lathe is from an Old English word meaning estate or territory; Rape may derive from the word for a roped-off place of assembly.

Rebus

Tombs and windows towards the end of the Middle Ages are often decorated repeatedly with the rebus of the dead man or the donor, i.e. with an emblematic representation of the name by the things (*rebus*) which can be read

The REFECTORY *of Cleeve Abbey, near Old Cleeve, Watchet, in Somerset, was built in the early 12th century.*

into it – a visual form of a bad pun. The antiquary William Camden in his *Remaines concerning Britaine* (1605) wrote an acid note on rebuses or 'name devices' and those who hammered out of their names 'an invention by this witcraft', instancing William Chaundler, Warden of New College, Oxford, who 'playing with his own name' (i.e. candle-maker or candle-seller), 'so filled the Hall-windows with candles, and these words Fiat lux, that he

darkned the Hall'. Names ending in -ton were a particular temptation, suggesting combinations of a tun or barrel with everything from a lute (Luton) to a thistle (Thistleton); as in Edington Priory, Wiltshire, where one of the 15th century brethren whose initials were I.B., and whose name was probably Baynton, has a tomb liberally supplied with sprigs growing out of tuns – Bay in tun.

Red hills

A speciality of the east coast, each red hill is the remains of a platform on which salt was evaporated from sea-water in British and Roman times. Essex alone has more than two hundred red hills, to be found on farm land often some distance now from creek or salt-marsh. Tide-water was trapped, and the salters poured the brine into earthenware cauldrons or pans set on a layered pile of porous earthenware bars separated by earthenware 'pedestals', which were splayed out top and bottom. A fierce fire of brushwood or straw heated the bars, the pedestals, and the brine; and the salt effloresced on the bars as the brine dripped over the sides of the pan. The red hills are made up of wasted pans, fire-bars and pedestals, which could only be used a few times; and one frequently comes across a chunk of reddish earthenware or briquetage glazed by heat and salt to an exquisite and now rain-washed green. Since the red hill soil grows excellent crops, the hills or platforms are often fenced round into small fields at their slightly different level – or they may be marked by a growth of blackthorn, brambles and teazles. In Essex a number of red hills are concentrated between Maldon (where sea-salt is still made) and Brightlingsea, along the Blackwater and the Pyefleet Channel. Some of them are shown (but not named) on the 1 : 25 000 map as irregular mounds. One parish along this stretch is Salcott ('salt cottage'), suggesting that here as elsewhere the salt industry continued into the Dark Ages and Middle Ages. Salt was necessary not only for salting down winter supplies of fish, meat, etc., but for correcting a cereal diet. *See also* SALT WAYS.

Refectory

Refectory (or 'frater' for short). In MONAS-TERIES the great hall, the place of refection, or refreshment (on the south side of the CLOIS-TER), where the monks had their daily meal, in silence, listening to a homiletic reading from the pulpit projecting high up from the walls. Cleeve Abbey in Somerset preserves a very

The REREDOS *carving of the last supper (c. 1400) at Somerton church, Oxfordshire. The figures of Christ and the Apostles are each carved into a separate niche.*

fine 16th century frater. At Beaulieu, in the New Forest, today's parish church is the 13th century frater of the Cistercian abbey.

Reredorter

In monastery ruins the foundations can sometimes be seen of the reredorter, privy, *necessarium* or necessary house, or house of easement, which was attached at right angles to the monks' dormitory or DORTER, both of them on the first floor. Long and narrow, the reredorter was often comfortably and discreetly fitted with wooden seats and divisions. Water flowed along the large drain below. Excavations at the great Benedictine abbey of St. Albans recovered small squares of cloth used by the monks and seeds from the buckthorn berries they had taken against constipation.

Reredos

The bright reredos at the back of an altar painted or carved with images of saints, the Passion, the TREE OF JESSE, etc., seldom survived the Reformation, except now and again in one of the cathedrals or great churches. The Lady Chapel at Christchurch Priory in Hampshire, for instance, retains above the altar part of an elaborate 14th century reredos with figures in stone of Jesse, the Virgin and Child,

and the Three Kings offering their gifts. A humbler reredos might consist of a band or row of little figures each in a compartment or niche – as at Bampton (Christ and the Twelve Apostles) and Somerton (The Last Supper), both in Oxfordshire. From the 14th century onwards the reredos was often made up of little panels or 'tables' of Nottingham ALABASTER carved in relief with bright colouring and gilding. These were set together in a wooden frame. Drayton church in Oxfordshire fortunately has such a reredos of the 15th century, which was dug up in the churchyard (and there are many of them in the Victoria and Albert Museum). Sometimes all that remains of a reredos is a wooden frame set back into the wall, or canopied niches and recesses, minus their figures, as at Theddelthorpe All Saints and Theddelthorpe St. Helen in Lincolnshire. After the Reformation reredoses of the old kind were replaced with more sober emblems painted on boards and often enclosed in a classical frame with pilasters. The accepted scheme was to paint the boards with the TEN COMMANDMENTS, the Creed and the Lord's Prayer, adding IHS for Jesus or the four Hebrew letters (the Tetragrammaton) which stand for Jehovah, with cherubim nestling in their wings and flanking representations of

Rhododendrons

Rhododendrons became a familiar flash of brilliance in the scenery of the British Isles during the Victorian era, first of all in the shape of one of the few European species, *Rhododendron ponticum*, which had been introduced in 1763 from the south of Spain. This is the only rhododendron which has established itself extensively as a wild shrub. Where conditions allow (it needs a soil without lime, preferably sandy or peaty), it spreads and becomes dominant, sometimes as the undercover of a wood, and is exceedingly hard to get rid of. Like the HORSE CHESTNUT, this rhododendron with its purple flowers chimed with the Pre-Raphaelite feeling of the eighteen-fifties that the English scene needed brilliance of colour – local colour, as in Pre-Raphaelite landscapes and subject-pieces.

Ricks, stacks, mows

Ricks, stacks, mows into which corn or hay (also peas and beans) are built after harvesting, either in the farmyard or the field, belong to very ancient farming practice. Mow and rick derive from the words the Anglo-Saxon farmer used, stack derives from the word used by the Norse-speaking settlers. But it seems that the varieties of shape, round, oval, rectangular, cannot be precisely traced to particular origins or districts. In Midland and southern counties and elsewhere ricks will often be built round and rectangular on the same farm, though it is true that the small round stacks are commoner in the rainier areas of north and west, and that round 'pikes' (i.e. tall pointed stacks built around a pole, as in other countries) now belong to the north rather than to the south. With their straw finials or dozzles and thatched roofs (now superseded by sheets of black plastic) ricks as a rule were given a house shape. The small circular stacks are perhaps remotely related to the round huts of prehistoric centuries, surviving in the damper and less fertile (and more conservative) areas, where the smaller size and the shape were ruled by the lower yields of hay and corn and were better fitted to the conditions of wind and weather. Even in the good corn and hay counties the landscape was probably not very extensively marked by ricks until the eighteenth century, when yields were increased by larger holdings and better farming until they were too much for the old storage space of the thatched barns. Storage in barns went with the flail, thumping on the threshing floor in the centre of each barn.

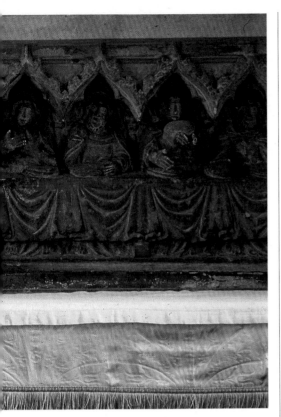

Moses, who brought the Tables of the Law down from Sinai, and Aaron. A reredos of the kind (though Moses and Aaron have usually been removed) is often to be seen in a Stuart or Georgian church. Nicholas Farrar's famous church at Little Gidding has such a reredos with the Commandments, the Lord's Prayer and the Creed engraved on tablets of brass.

Resurgence

In limestone areas the upwelling of an underground river or stream (one of the particular delights of Craven in North Yorkshire or the dales of the Peak District) is a 'resurgence', the stream bubbling up 'like human life from darkness'.

Rhaeadr

The commonest Welsh word for a waterfall – e.g. in north Wales near Capel Curig the famous Rhaeadr Ewynnol (Rhaiadr y Wennol), the 'Fall of the Swallow', and Rhaeadr Ddu or Black Fall, near Tyn-y-groes. Other waterfall words are *pistyll*, a spout (e.g. in Gwynedd, Pistyll Gwyn, 'White Spout', near Llanymawddwy, and Pistyll Cain, 'Spout of the Cain', on the Cain river), and *sgwd*, a flow, used for several of the exquisite falls in the upper part of Glyn Neath in south Wales.

Ridgeway

Ridgeway, for an ancient track, is not a word coined by antiquaries looking wistfully but a little mistily back to the past, but a term descending to us from Old English and meaning exactly what it says, a *hrycg weg*, a way or road along a ridge; and since ridges – especially long ridges of chalk or limestone athwart England from south-west to north-east – were likely to be clear of timber as well as dry and firm, and part of a landscape nibbled down by the sheep and goats and cattle of the early pastoralists, in contrast to the vales and plains likely to be wet, heavy, and dark with oak forest and thorn scrub, early man travelled by the ridges where possible; and ridgeways became, and remained, by custom, long or short ways of communication. The best introduction to the exploration and understanding of ancient ridgeways and tracks will be found in two chapters of O. G. S. Crawford's *Archaeology in the Field* (1953) which begin by defining the track as 'not made or designed' but something which has grown 'in response to the need of going from one place to another', and stating that with a few exceptions all mediaeval roads (other than Roman roads still in mediaeval use) were 'natural tracks, unmetalled and wide'. He gives an account of four main prehistoric trackways or ridgeways which took the path of forest-free hill belts: (1) The Icknield Way, from near the Wash past Stonehenge to the Channel coast. (2) The ridgeway of the South Downs from the neighbourhood of Beachy Head to Stonehenge and beyond. (3) The North Downs ridgeway from the Canterbury neighbourhood, part of it the so-called Pilgrims' Way, then the Harrow Way to Stonehenge (*?hearg weg*, Old English for 'temple way'), then south-west, perhaps skirting Dartmoor and along the spine of Cornwall. (4) The 'Jurassic Way', recognized in modern times as running south and south-west from the Humber, crossing the Cotswolds to Bath and continuing possibly along the Mendips. Partly modern roads or lanes, including GREEN LANES, partly adapted as modern roads, partly discernible as boundary lines of parish or estate, these are to be regarded as ancient trading thoroughfares, much trodden in the Iron Age (passing Iron Age hill-forts), but probably used in the Bronze Age and earlier, Stonehenge being on the route of the first three. The 'Jurassic Way' (a way across the limestone formation) crosses the surface iron deposits of Northamptonshire and north Oxfordshire. The other three skirt known groups of neolithic FLINT MINES. Other minor ridgeways, many of them still in use, can also be traced throughout the country.

Riding

A riding is a third (Old Norse *thrithjung*), and the three ridings of the great county of Yorkshire, each with its modern county council, were thirds of the shire, under the old administration of the Danes. The Parts of Lindsey, northern and largest district of Lincolnshire, were also divided into North, West, and South Ridings. Till the early Middle Ages the riding had its courts or assemblies, intermediate between those of WAPENTAKE and SHIRE.

River

Like the wind, the flowing water of a river has no owner. The riparian owner may abstract water for his own concerns, domestic and agricultural, and the other owners of riverside land downstream have to reconcile themselves to a lessened flow. The water impounded is owned, and can be stolen: till impounded, it is for whoever takes it. And when passage over the surface is possible, the public has a right of passage, by ship, boat, barge, skiff, punt, canoe, etc., and no one, whether or not he owns the adjoining land, or has an exquisite garden to the water's edge, and likes his privacy, and indulges his love of fly-fishing during the evening rise, is entitled to block the way. The right of taking fish along your bank (above the reach of the tide) is your own; but if you were to set stakes across a river bed or stretch a chain from bank to bank you would expose yourself to a civil suit by a frustrated punter; and you would be liable to prosecution under Section 31 of the Malicious Damage Act, 1861, which created the offence of 'doing any injury or mischief so as unlawfully to obstruct the navigation of any navigable river or canal'. Only a river authority has the requisite power to control navigation, as on the Thames, when a way is kept clear for the boats and launches in the Oxford and Cambridge university boat race.

Tidal waters, too, are for public navigation and enjoyment, and private rights exist only above the point to which the tide comes twice a day. Above that point no acquiescence by a riparian owner in a trepass upon his fishing can alter things. This is so however long the trespass has been tolerated, and however many the trespassers have been. The owner's right remains unimpaired, and trespassers must go when he requires their going.

The river Avon, Warwickshire, as it flows through Stratford-upon-Avon, Shakespeare's birthplace: the playwright is in fact buried at the Holy Trinity church, the spire of which can be seen in the distance.

River names

River names include some of the more ancient names on the map, many of them British, some of them perhaps older still. When settlers come to a country and live among the inhabitants already there, they learn the native names of the more momentous features of the landscape, especially the ones which impinge on day-to-day life, which interrupt a journey or make it necessary to take a way round – names of forests, ranges of hills, and especially rivers, which have to be waded where a ford can be found, or crossed by boat. British river-names learnt in this way by the English and preserved in English speech often have the simplest basic meaning, such as 'water' (a word which has often been used in exactly the same way by the English in their own names of river, lake, ford, inlet, etc.). The British *isca*, 'water', explains the Axe, the Usk, the Esk, the Exe. The various Avons preserve simply the British word for 'river'. Rivers may look black or dark, the explanation of the British-named Dove, in the Derbyshire limestone; another British word for dark explains Thames, Thame, Teme, Tavy and Tamar. Occasionally a name has a more exalted origin such as Dee. The Dee was worshipped, and the name means 'goddess'. Any name that was not English (e.g. one of the many river-names to which the Old English *ēa*, a river, had been added, so ending in -y, -ye, -ey, -ea) was thought till lately to be British. But no Old British root can be found to explain quite a number of these names, for which confident interpretations had been given – among them Tyne, Tees, Till, Test, Tweed, Ouse, Kennet, Wye, Wey Nene, Stour. British settlers or invaders in their earlier time must have acted precisely as the English were to act later on: they asked the people already in the land, they took over the pre-British names, from languages of which we know nothing. Broadly it can be said – but this is no more than one would expect, in spite of the Dee's divinity (she was a goddess of war) – that obvious rivery qualities have given rivers their names: they are made of water, they simply flow, they wind, run, creep, shine, are dark, quiet, noisy, forceful, gentle, stony, or muddy, or they nourish fish or otters, and were named accordingly.

Roads

Roads, as they are today, other than the new motorways or the old main roads which have been so altered in the last sixty years, possess many interpretable and peculiar features. In logic a road should no doubt follow the shortest and straightest possible line from one place to another. But in historic times that unfettered logic, in these islands, has been possible only to Roman military engineers, who had the advantage of a more or less empty country unencumbered by towns, villages and estates. Of our road network some portion is prehistoric, following the dry RIDGEWAY tracks of Iron Age and even Bronze Age. Much of the net of lowland roads and lanes dates back to the new villages of the Anglo-Saxon settlement and the extended clearances and colonization from the 12th to the 14th century. The roads linking village and village, village and hamlet, grew by custom before becoming stabilized in law as highways of the king. Left to ourselves, we neither walk nor ride straight: we have no ruler inside us. Obstacles have to be avoided, such as bog or marsh or boulders. Roads have to turn aside to a ford. Clearance of vast areas of forest made for a legacy of roads with an exceptional amount of still uncorrected twisting and bending, owing to ancient avoidance of soft leaf-mouldy hollows and patches and of individual wide-spreading trees such as the oak, which had not been felled (*vide* the intricately winding road-system in the old up-and-down forest lands of Warwickshire or Hereford and Worcester).

Abruptly zigzagging by-roads and lanes with many apparently senseless right-angled turns are explicable according to district by colonization and enclosure of previously open farmland. Lanes are apt to zigzag between small fields which were taken in piecemeal from the waste and then walled or hedged with stone off the new-won arable, as mediaeval colonization proceeded. Enclosure of open fields produced both zigzagging roads and more or less straight wide roads according to date. Earlier enclosure often led to a fossilization of old linkages and lines of access which had wiggled along the sides and ends of the furlongs of the open field (*see* FIELDS). Enclosure commissions in the 18th century, and the early 19th century when many of the COMMONS were enclosed, inclined to disregard the past, more ruthlessly laying out new, straight, wide ENCLOSURE ROADS irrespective of old divisions. Abrupt turns in a road when it comes to park gates and walls are due to 17th and 18th century landlords enlarging park or grounds and brashly sending the road and the commonalty around boundaries of the park or pleasure grounds to ensure their privacy.

Often the line of the road will be picked up again on the other side of the park.

Basically our net of by-roads came as a response to horse-traffic – hoof traffic and not wheel traffic, to horses as beasts of burden carrying on their backs everything from passenger to dung or lime. This long era of hoof traffic which began to weaken, though it was by no means finished, late in the 17th century, has its relics in the packhorse bridges, the UPPING-STOCKS, and stretches of deserted hollow road (see HOLLOW WAYS) often too steep and narrow for wheeled traffic and supplanted later by lengths of new road which make a sideways ascent of hills by an easier gradient. From 1700, carriage, cart and wagon traffic increased and dug into the soft road surfaces. Every parish was responsible for road repair inside its own boundaries, and most parishes fell down on this responsibility; which led to the ingenious establishment by law of turnpike trusts (see TOLL-HOUSES), by which 22,000 miles of road were built or repaired between 1700 and 1840, and to the road engineering of Thomas Telford (1757–1834) and J. L. McAdam (1756–1836), the one by temperament a builder of new roads, the other an ingenious repairer of old roads who worked out his method for the dry and hard surfacing of roads with broken stones of the same size which bound together under the pressure of traffic.

Dust then became the bugbear of summer travel, and was greatly increased after 1896 when pneumatic-tyred cars were made free to use the roads; and since the improvements of Telford and McAdam the one basic invention has been the smooth, dust-free road surface following the first experiment in May 1907 with a crust of tar macadam. Some remaining antiquities of the era of horse-drawn vehicles are roadside ponds and charitably built hillside watering-troughs, fords still unbridged (water having been little obstacle to the high-wheeled horse vehicles), high-doored and wide-doored coach-houses, and an occasional fossilized length of old highway which splayed out into innumerable ruts and tracks as it descended a hill.

Roches moutonnées

Roches moutonnées or sheep-backs – like the ICE-SCRATCHES which mark them, if they have not been weathered away – are evidence of the glaciers which pushed down the mountain valleys of the British Isles: they are hummocks or mounds of bed-rock ice-smoothed and rounded end on to the flow of the glacier, and left rough or abruptly stepped at the other end, where loosely jointed fragments were torn away by the ice.

Rock basins

Scooped by weathering in various surface rocks, granite, sarsen, gritstone, limestone, etc., rock basins were supposed to have been hollowed out by Druids for various ritual purposes. At the time of the mania for seeing the finger of the Druids in every peculiar outcrop of stone, antiquaries such as Cornwall's William Borlase (1695–1772), and Devonshire's Edward Bray (1778–1857), vicar of Tavistock, were convinced that Druids made the rock basins to collect pure snow-water or rainwater for ritual lustrations and divination. Tourists were shown Druidical basins on the granite of Dartmoor and Cornwall, and on the gritstone of the Derbyshire uplands (the inn at Birchover near the curious gritstones of Rowtor and Robin Hood's Stride, on which there are rock basins, is still called the Druid's Inn). Sometimes connecting, sometimes with an edge weathered away into a gutter, rock basins can look remarkably regular, and have no doubt fascinated people for centuries (cf. the Irish BULLAUNS). R. H. Worth in his *Dartmoor* (1953) showed that the granite rock basins were the result of weathering mainly in a much colder phase than the present. Water action and abrasion by pebbles swirled round by water also makes very fine basins in carboniferous limestone, known to the caver as 'rock mills'.

Rock scribings

Rock scribings are among the most tantalizing enigmas of the Bronze Age. The most frequent and characteristic are cup-and-ring marks, cup shapes encircled with rings, often with a line cutting across the rings from the cup. Why were they made? No one sat to punching and pecking designs into hard stone for the fun of it; they had a meaning, a purpose and an importance, probably to do with ensuring life and fertility. Possibly the cup-and-ring marks are schematized representations of a mother goddess, derived from the eastern Mediterranean. At any rate, they are to be seen on chambered tombs in Ireland (e.g. stones of the great Newgrange tomb near Slane, Co. Meath; of tombs in the barrow cemetery of Slieve na Caillighe, near Old Castle, Co. Meath; tomb uprights in Co. Tyrone, at Sess Kilgreen, near Ballygawley, and on Knock-

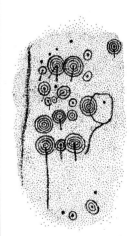

Cup-and-ring ROCK SCRIBINGS *from Cairnbaan, near Lochgilphead, Argyllshire. These Bronze Age carvings were only recognized as archaeologically significant in 1860, although their existence has long been known.*

187

many, near Augher), and on isolated boulders or outcrops in Ireland, Scotland, Northumberland. Ireland has a fine group of cup-and-rings in the Killarney district, in Kerry (e.g. Ardcanaght, west of Castlemaine; Coolnakarragile Upper, south-west of Glenbeigh; and Gortboy, ten miles from Killarney and south-west of Beaufort Bridge); Scotland a particularly fine group on ice-polished rocks in Strathclyde, north-west of Lochgilphead, especially those at Achnabreck and Cairnbaan (see Richard Feachem's *Guide to Prehistoric Scotland*, 1963). In Northumberland, on the low, smoothly curving moors between the Cheviots and the North Sea, the most easily found and rewarding are east of the hill-fort above Old Bewick; on a huge boulder at Roughtinglinn, near Wooler; and high up on Dod Law, within a few yards of the Shepherd's House above Doddington village.

Roman forts and camps

Roman forts and camps, many of them in the frontier districts, north and west, are less imposing than they were efficient; and are very distinct from the RAMPART FARMSTEADS AND VILLAGES in which the British lived and defended themselves. The Romans were measurers, with an object in view, the British inside their ditches and ramparts were approximators. The site dictated the shape of a British enclosure on any scale, the Romans imposed a shape; and the shape of their forts and campaigning camps is as a rule rectangular with rounded corners, a shape particularly unpleasing, if efficient for the purpose. The Roman camp is likely to be defined by a ditch and a low rampart, which was crowned with palisades (sometimes the rampart will have been rebuilt in stone); and there is likely to be an entrance in each side. The contrast between the outlook of the conquered and conqueror is very curiously emphasized on Hod Hill, at Stourpaine, north-west of Blandford in Dorset, where the fifty-acre British ramparted enclosure was captured about A.D. 45. In one corner the legionaries built a small auxiliary fort of about three acres with the usual rounded angles. Often the site of the Roman border fortresses is as striking as the fortresses are plain and practical. Visit in Northumberland the Roman camps at Chew Green, on the moors above the Coquet at more than 1,400 feet, alongside the Roman road known as Dere Street. Road and camps, including two auxiliary camps and a camp for his labour force, were built by Agricola, *c.* A.D. 80, in his

campaign to secure the north of Roman Britain against the Selgovae. Or visit the camps of Y Pigwn, enclosing a moorland triangulation point (1,353 feet) above A40, from Brecon to Llandovery, on the roof top of south Wales (easily enough reached by a firm unfenced Roman road) – these were camps and road built against the Silures of South Wales.

Roman roads

According to Ivan Margary (whose *Roman Roads of Britain*, in two volumes, 1955, 1957, is the necessary book for exploring them), Roman roads are the earliest man-made objects that we are still using. They were made to keep the British in order, for the quick movement of troops and supplies, and for the Imperial Post, which was a government service for governmental needs, complete (on the main roads) with official inns and posting stations where fresh horses were available. The labour for maintaining the roads had to be supplied by the native population of each *civitas* or tribal division. Used or unused or little used, the Roman road has its obvious features. Straightness is one, though it is not absolute. The military engineers laid the roads out in sections from one sighting point to another. A road will go straight to such a point, change direction abruptly, and go on straight again to the next sighting point. The route would roughly have been decided upon by riding over the ground, after which the exact sectional alignments would have been worked out with the aid of portable beacons on hilltop sighting points, which were visible above the intervening forest, and could be moved one way or the other in answer to signals. Now and then the lie of the land dictated an indirect course. A road, for instance, may tackle a hill by zigzags, or descend to a river crossing by a terrace cut into the side of a valley (the crossing might be by stone and timber bridge or by a paved ford). A second feature, often visible after nearly 2,000 years, is the agger, the platform of the road thrown up from a ditch on either side. Crossing a meadow, it often looks like a flat ridge or a raised green ribbon, clearly marked by shadow in the evening light. Agger and ditches took care of good drainage; and on the agger, which may be as much as fifteen yards across, was laid the road metal, of fair-sized stones bonded and surfaced with gravel or small stones, which turned a *via*, a way, into a *via strata*, or *strata* for short, a way which was *laid*. To the Anglo-

Saxons *strata* became *strēt*, or *strǣt*, a 'street' (*see* STRAT-). Another distinction of a Roman road, at any rate of such a main road as the Fosse Way through the Midlands (the way marked by its fosses or ditches on either side), is its frequent loneliness: it will go on for mile after mile its own way, divorced from villages, i.e. from the later Anglo-Saxon organization of the countryside. For this there may be two reasons. The 'streets' prefer high ground; for their farms and villages the Anglo-Saxons preferred low ground in the valleys. Also, living too near a 'street' might have been dangerous. The Anglo-Saxons may have let the streets and their bridges fall into decay, but they still used them when they were on the warpath. Notice too that a Roman road or the line of a Roman road will often be a PARISH

A view looking down from the top of Hod Hill, Dorset, to the north-west. The rampart of this ROMAN FORT *can be seen in the foreground.*

boundary, i.e. it was taken as a recognizable dividing line between the Anglo-Saxon estates from which the parish developed.

No Roman road in Britain has a name which was given to it by the Romans. Some were named from the people whose territory they passed through – Ermine Street, the road of the Earnings, who lived around Arrington, the Earnings' *tūn*, in Cambridgeshire; and Watling Street, the road of the Wæclings, in Hertfordshire. Others were named, like the Fosse Way once more, or like Stane Street (stone street) or Stangate (Old Norse *gata*, a road), from their Roman characteristic, others after the people who used them, e.g. Peddars Way, in Norfolk, pedlars' road. A great many minor Roman roads have still to be traced.

Roman villas

Roman villas appear to have been the 'manor-houses', Roman-style, of British territorial lords, who took the conqueror's way of life. By contrast, their retainers or tenants continued to live in little British-style farmsteads.

Occasionally it has been possible to trace under villa foundations the postholes of a timber house on the native plan, which was then replaced in stone, or stone and wood, by the long, single-storeyed rectangular villa, divided into rectangular rooms, with glass in the windows, and a tidy roof of red earthenware tiles or stone tiles overhead instead of thatch. If the chieftain lived in this new kind of house on his old dues or rents, he was also an agriculturalist. Like the mediaeval lord in later

Just off the Fosse Way, near Fosse Bridge, Gloucestershire, is the Chedworth ROMAN VILLA, *now owned by the National Trust. The comprehensive remains, which include mosaic pavements, date from between AD 180 and 380. The hypercaust system of central heating employed in this villa and clearly displayed in this photograph, consisted of pillars under the floor, around which hot air circulated from an outside furnace. Concealed flues would have channelled the heat up the walls.*

centuries, he no doubt had his DEMESNE, he certainly had his barns and cowsheds, his well, his granary and threshing floor, and his slave or servant labour, living alongside his villa in a native 'barn' divided into living quarters.

If he could afford it, the British villa lord became less British and still more Roman, or continental. He added or rebuilt. Wings were tacked on, and exterior stone corridors which gave access to the rooms. Roman style decorations were painted on the plaster walls, floors were smoothed with TESSELLATED PAVEMENTS, patterned in classical style, or telling the myths of Greece and Rome. Cold was driven out by underfloor heating, baths were added (*see* HYPOCAUST), Graeco-Roman sculpture was imported. Villas were then extended or rebuilt round courtyards, and were given large central dining-rooms. *Civis Romanus sum.* Latin was no doubt spoken in the richer villas (much as the country noblemen of 19th century Russia spoke French in the drawing-room, and Russian to the serfs). After the withdrawal of Roman troops early in the 5th century, the villa life decayed, the Romanism weakened. The villas were deserted, the roofs fell in, and British or Romano-British ways and speech were overlaid by English ways and speech.

Rood

The Great Rood (Old English *rod*, a cross) in a mediaeval church was the carved and painted figure of the crucified Christ high up on the rood beam above the ROOD LOFT and the rood screen which shut the CHANCEL from the NAVE. Dominating the nave, it at once caught the spectator's eye. Christ was flanked on one side by a figure of his mother, on the other side by a figure of St. John. At the Reformation the coloured figures of the Rood were among the first images to be taken down and burnt.

Rood lofts and screens

Steps inside the wall which turn inwards into the church and end abruptly in nothing, are all that remains in most churches to speak of the rood loft. This projecting loft or gallery ran the length of the rood screen, below the ROOD. Reached by the steps (now so convenient for brooms, dusters and vases), it allowed for lighting and snuffing the many candles which twinkled under the rood, along the rood beam or 'candle-beam' – also for reaching up to cover the crucified Christ with a cloth during Lent. The rood loft was used as well by singers and musicians.

In structure the rood beam was often a part

of the loft, which itself was structurally combined with the screen; and both loft and screen were made rich with carving, gilding and colouring. Panels below the tracery of the screen were often painted with figures of the saints. The screens cut the CHANCEL from the NAVE. Emphasizing the special character of the chancel in this way, they survived the Reformation (minus the lofts), only to be torn down, very often, in Victorian times.

Rose-

Rose- in place-names is a good example of their deceptiveness, suggesting wild roses or a land of roses, as in the Melrose of the Borders – *If thou wouldst view fair Melrose aright* – or Cornwall's Roseland (St. Just-in-Roseland). In Cornish names, 'rose' or 'ros' generally means a ridge or headland (like 'ross' in many Gaelic and Irish names). In Welsh names (*rhos*) and some names in old British territory, it means a moor or a mountain meadow. Melrose is 'naked' moor'.

Round-houses

Variously called Blind Houses (because they have no windows to speak of), Cages, and Lob's Pounds, round-houses served the same purpose of parochial restraint and punishment

A ROUND TOWER, or 'bell-house' built in the late 12th century at Ardmore, Co. Waterford.

as the STOCKS under control of the parish constable and the local magistrates. Such lock-ups were first built of timber, and were then classically refashioned in the 18th century, as a rule, into circular or octagonal buildings with thick walls and a domed roof and an iron-studded door. It cost more to make such a neat little building than to make a pair of oaken stocks, so they are most often to be seen in small towns or large market villages, coolers for those who broke the peace of the fair or the market alongside.

Round towers

Round towers in Ireland, slim and tall, tapering to a conical top sometimes a hundred feet or more above the ground, with few windows and a doorway which could be reached only with a ladder, were common form in MONASTERIES before the Cistercians arrived in Ireland at the end of the 12th century with European forms of convent architecture. They were Irish versions of the campanile, or bell-tower, developed in northern Italy in the 9th century. Irish monks of the 10th century brought the idea back, and Irish masons interpreted it in their own way. The round tower or *cloigtheach* ('bell-house') has been compared to a minaret. The muezzin's part was taken by a monk who climbed ladder by ladder to the top storey, where he rang, not a mounted bell, but a hand bell. The secondary function of the round tower was safeguarding monastic treasures. Viking attacks were common in the 10th century, when the first towers were built; and with the success of a raid depending on a quick getaway, the raiders had no time to go searching for ladders or for breaking into the bell-house, which was proof also against destruction by fire. When the new architecture was introduced in mediaeval Ireland, the round tower was sometimes supplanted by a mediaeval square tower, but left standing, as at Colum Cille's monastery of Kells in Co. Meath.

Rowan

Growing at a higher altitude than any other British tree, the rowan (*Sorbus aucuparia*), or mountain ash, is the characteristic small tree of the acid uplands of the British Isles. In Celtic and Norse areas it has always been regarded, perhaps on account of its brilliant orange-red berries, as a tree of supreme protective power, the proper material, leaf or wand or berry, for repelling the threats and assaults of goblins, evil spirits, witches, etc. As a protector, in

Cornwall, the Marches, Wales, the Lakes, Yorkshire, Ireland and the Highlands, the rowan does duty for the HAWTHORN, which belongs more to lowland country. It has been associated in particular with the god Thor. In Iceland – and perhaps this was once current in the Norse districts of Britain – they had a proverb that the 'Rowan is the salvation of Thor' (and so of mortals), which recalled the legend of Thor's visit to the Land of the Giants. To reach the giant's world from the world of men, he had to cross the river Vimur, which flowed between them. It was hugely swollen by the menstrual blood and urine of the giantesses, and Thor pulled himself to safety on the far bank only by catching hold of a rowan.

Royal Arms

From Henry VIII's time it became the practice to set up the Royal Arms on the wooden tympana which filled the chancel arch, or else above the arch itself. Where the laity had stared at the great ROOD and at paintings of Christ presiding over the universal DOOM, with devils torturing the guilty and thrusting them into a lurid hell, they now saw the arms of the Sovereign, to remind them of their Christian duty towards him. This prominent display of the Royal Arms seemed less peculiar to our ancestors; they thought more earnestly than we do of the divine right of kings, who were the Lord's anointed. 'The arms were not those of a purely secular person; because the sovereign is the centre of a society which is both a Church and a State, he is himself what 17th century lawyers called a spiritual person, capable of jurisdiction in spiritual things, though not, of course, of exercising pastoral and priestly powers' (Addleshaw and Etchells, *The Architectural Setting of Anglican Worship*). The Royal Arms were sometimes painted or fixed elsewhere in the nave or were moved elsewhere when the tympana across the chancel archway were demolished by Victorian restorers.

Runes

Runes, the letters of magical alphabets used by our English and Scandinavian ancestors and other Germanic peoples, are most frequently to be encountered on crosses or fragments of crosses, notably the magnificently carved Bewcastle Cross (in Bewcastle churchyard, Cumbria, near the border) and the Ruthwell Cross (in the church at Ruthwell, Dumfries and Galloway). There was an original or basic alphabet of twenty-four runes, most of which were derived, it seems, from an ancient alphabet employed for inscriptions in the Italian Alps, which in turn derived from the alphabet of the Etruscans. Extra runes were added from the prehistoric symbols carved on rocks; and the basic alphabet so combined was in use in the north by the 3rd century A.D. Tall, narrow and angular, and characteristically made up of straight lines so that they could easily be carved, runes were not a script for ordinary communication. The word 'rune' meant something obscurely uttered, a mystery, a secret. Spells and the like were cut in runes on weapons, amulets, rings, etc., and their function was 'to invoke higher powers, to affect and influence the lives and fortunes of men' (R. W. V. Elliot in *Runes*, 1963, the best introduction to these strange symbols). Each rune had its own peculiar and suggestive name, and objects were inscribed with runic sentences, or single runes, or even the whole runic alphabet. The Y letter we still use for 'th' in 'Ye' (and insist on mispronouncing as if it were an ordinary Y) developed from a rune named originally after the Germanic word for a giant and suggestive of the power of giants.

The English increased the basic alphabet by four, commonly using twenty-eight of these letters of power and mystery. The Norsemen reduced the alphabet to sixteen; and in time both English and Norsemen came to cutting runic inscriptions on memorial stones, pagan and then Christian. The tall Ruthwell and Bewcastle crosses (early 8th century) are both inscribed in English with English runes, the Bewcastle Cross commemorating a King Alcfrith, the Ruthwell Cross commemorating or celebrating the cruxifixion of Christ with runically cut passages from the Old English poem, *The Dream of the Rood* (the cross of Christ). In Hackness church, near Scarborough in North Yorkshire, fragments of another cross of the early 8th century, which commemorates an abbess, are carved with runes in a cryptogram which has not been decoded. The Isle of Man is the place for runic crosses of Norse origin of the 10th to the 12th century (e.g. Gaut's Cross, under the lychgate of Michael parish church, and the Juan Stone in Maughold churchyard). In the north-western counties the font at Bridekirk, Cumbria, carries an English sentence in Norse runes naming the sculptor Rikarth, who pictures himself on the font holding his mallet and chisel. The most extraordinary and most moving collection of Norse runes is to be seen

The lock-up or ROUND HOUSE *at Castle Cary, Somerset. Such stone cylinders with fancy domed tops, were popular in the West Country. They can be easily identified by their tiny barred windows and the heavy ironwork on the door.*

on the stones of the great Maeshowe chambered tomb on Mainland, Orkney, carved by the rune-master of a party of Norse crusaders on their way to Jerusalem in 1152, a memento as evocative as the Norse runes carved at the Piraeus on the marble of an archaic Greek lion which was taken off to Venice, where it now stands at the gateway of the Arsenal.

Saffron

Saffron has left its name here and there from the cultivation of the saffron crocus (*Crocus sativus*, from Asia Minor), which began in the 14th century, perhaps spreading from monastery demesnes. (At Maiden Bradley in Wiltshire a piece of land on the site of an Augustinian priory is still called Saffron Garden.) Particular areas came to specialize in the crop: the country round Stratton in Cornwall (saffron – imported – is still much used in Cornish cakes and buns), Norfolk (around Walsingham), Cambridgeshire and Essex, between Cambridge and Saffron Walden. The Walden saffron was reckoned superior to any from overseas. The corms needed a light soil and were set in the Walden neighbourhood in saffron-grounds of one to three acres, in open country. But the grounds had to be hurdled off to keep out not only cattle, but hares which ate down the crocus leaves in winter. Camden wrote of the country round Saffron Walden 'looking merrily with most lovely saffron', i.e. with the pale purple flowers, which were picked on autumn mornings. The stigmas were then removed, and were at once dried over little kilns, into cakes formed between sheets of paper. It took 4,320 flowers to make an ounce of dried saffron, but it was a profitable crop till well into the 18th century. Saffron was used in medicine (it was regarded as a cheerful medicine) as well as cooking, and for 'saffroning' under-linen and bed-linen against fleas.

St. Barbara

St. Barbara who frequently appears in church windows and carving, though very few churches are dedicated to her, carries the tower in which she was shut up, according to her legend, by a heathen father. Also a palm of victory. The tower is likely to exhibit three windows, Barbara having contrived that a third window should be added to the two ordained by her father, to show forth the power of the Trinity. Learned, beautiful, devoted to Christ, her legend says that she was beaten with bull's sinews, that her flesh was rubbed with salt, that she was hanged between forked trees, and her breasts were cut off, before she was at last beheaded by her choleric father, at Nicomedia, in Asia Minor, in the 3rd century A.D.

St. Catherine

The saint whose catherine wheels revolve and flame on Bonfire Night, twenty days before her own festival on 25 November, St. Catherine is frequently depicted in churches with her wheel. She was one of the favourite saints of mediaeval England and more than fifty churches were dedicated to her. According to her legend, she was a learned young queen of Egypt and bride of Christ, broken and torn, by order of the Emperor Maxentius, between the two pairs of iron wheels which turned against each other, 'and were environed with sharp razors, cutting so that she might be horribly all detrenched and cut in that torment' (*The Golden Legend*). An angel broke the wheels, but St. Catherine was beheaded. Angels transported her body from Alexandria to Mount Sinai, where it was discovered in the 9th century.

St. Christopher

According to his life as it was told in *The Golden Legend*, the great 13th century collection of the legends and lives of saints by Jacob de Voragine, St. Christopher was a Canaanitish giant who repented of his ways and, under the teaching of a hermit, took to ferrying passengers across a dangerous river, where he found himself one night carrying a child whose weight was almost too heavy for him. The child revealed himself as Christ – 'Marvel thee nothing, for thou hast not only borne all the world upon thee, but thou hast borne him that created and made all the world, upon thy shoulders.' Huge St. Christophers carrying the child through the perilous waters of life past MERMAIDS and monsters were customarily painted in churches directly opposite the south door: they had only to be seen on the way to work in the morning to guarantee a day's immunity from harm. So St. Christopher was – and remains – the patron saint of travellers. WALL-PAINTINGS usually show not only the dangerous mermaid, but the ferryman's house, and the staff St. Christopher leant upon, Christ in the legend having told him to set the staff in the earth: in the morning he would find it bearing fruit and flowers as a token of the truth of Christ's words.

St. Cuthbert's beads

The fossilized segments of the stem of 'sea lilies', or crinoids (animals, not plants), St. Cuthbert's beads are so called from their occurrence on the beaches of Holy Island, off the Northumberland coast, where St. Cuthbert was prior from 664 to 676. The description – they are the beads which St. Cuthbert told in his rosary – is at least as old as the 17th century, and was given extra currency by Sir Walter Scott in his best-selling *Marmion*.

St. Laurence

One of the most popular of all saints in the Middle Ages, with more than 200 English churches dedicated to him, St. Laurence is the saint who carries or lays his hand on a gridiron, large or small. His legend says that he was martyred by roasting in 258, in Rome. 'And then said Decius: Bring hither a bed of iron, that Laurence contumax may lie thereon. And the ministers despoiled him, and laid him stretched out upon a gridiron of iron, and laid burning coals under, and held him with forks of iron' (*The Golden Legend*). But he was sustained by three refroidours or coldnesses, desire of heavenly glory, remembrance of the law of God, and cleanness of conscience, which prevented him from feeling the torments of fire in his entrails. His whole story is told in the east window in Ludlow church.

St. Michael's churches

St. Michael's churches are by ancient tradition on hilltops, the sharper and more nakedly upstanding the better – such as Glastonbury Tor, in Somerset, and volcanic Brent Tor, on the edge of Dartmoor. The association between hill, or crag, and archangel arose partly because this Prince of Heaven and Captain of the Heavenly Host, who overcame Satan so that he dropped from Heaven to Hell, was held to have manifested himself by alighting on Monte Gargano in Italy in the 4th century, partly because the Coptic anchorites of 4th century Egypt endowed him with qualities of Osiris, the Light of the Sun in Egyptian religion, and built chapels to him on top of their monasteries to catch the sunrise. The hermit monasteries of Upper Egypt much influenced the Celtic Christianity of Ireland, Cornwall, Wales and Brittany, all of which have their Michael's mounts (most startling of them the 700-foot crag of Skellig Michael in the Atlantic off the coast of Kerry, to which there cling the BEEHIVE HUTS and church of an early monastery). St. Michael is said to have made several appearances to St. Aubert at Avranches in Normandy instructing him to build in his honour on Mont-Saint-Michel, the saint refusing the injunction until an exasperated St. Michael pushed a finger into his forehead (St. Aubert's indented skull is preserved in Avranches). A duty of Osiris taken over by St. Michael was the weighing of souls at the Last Judgement, in which role mediaeval churches depict him frequently. Whether weighing souls or subduing the dragon (=Satan), St. Michael is winged: he may be in armour, robed, or feathered down his body. He appears in windows, carvings, WALL-PAINTINGS and DOOM PAINTINGS.

St. Swithun's Day

St. Swithun's Day, 15 July, on which if it rains it will go on raining for forty days. It seems this is more to do with the calendar than the saint (who died in 862 and was bishop of Winchester), i.e. a common European prognostic that forty days' rain will fall if it rains on a particular day – in England 15 July – fixed itself to Swithun simply because 15 July was the day of the translation of his remains in 970 from the graveyard into the cathedral at Winchester. He was a popular saint and more than fifty English churches were dedicated to him. The only rainy element in his legend is that in his humility St. Swithun had asked to be buried outside his cathedral, under the rain-

An early 14th-century stained-glass window portraying ST. CATHERINE *with her wheel, to be found at Deerhurst church, Gloucestershire.*

drops and the feet of passers-by. A story more or less modern and no doubt an *ex post facto* explanation of the forty days' rain, also says that he objected to his translation and prevented it for some time by miraculously producing a heavy downpour. The French rain-day foretelling forty days' rain is 8 June – *la sainte-Médard* – feast of St. Médard, Bishop of Noyon, whose *ex post facto* rain legend is that he was once sheltered from a storm soaking everyone else by the wings of an eagle which flew down and hovered over his head. In Wales the rain saint was St. Cewydd, whose day was also 15 July, the day, according to the Welsh and Irish, on which Noah's flood began.

Salamander

Common in church carvings, the lizard-like salamander, inherited from the Greeks and described by Aristotle, had two legendary attributes. With a skin of the pure amianth, or asbestos, it was untouched by any fire, which it immediately put out (an emperor of India was supposed to wear a battle coat stitched of a thousand salamander skins); and it infected apples on apple trees and water in wells with a venom so powerful that no one could eat the apples or drink the water and survive. So the salamander symbolized the virtuous Christian who extinguished the flames of lust and the heat of vices, resembling one of the three Hebrew Children in the burning fiery furnace. In carvings the salamander has a long knotted tail (or a tail dividing in two), wings, and two feet. It is often to be seen on fonts, to which its virtues are appropriate – particularly on Romanesque fonts of the 12th century.

Salt ways

Roads or lanes so named are worth tracing and exploring. They were the routes regularly taken by salters, or salt-merchants, and their pack-horse trains travelling from the seaside salt-pans (*see* Red hills) or the inland salt-boiling centres of Hereford and Worcester and Cheshire. In the north Midlands and the north a salt route is likely to have the name Saltergate (Scandinavian *gata*, way or road) instead of Salt Way. Salt was needed in great quantities in every household when life in the winter depended on salt meat or salt fish, and when cattle were heavily slaughtered in the autumn for lack of winter feed to keep them all in good condition. Many Salt Ways radiate from Droitwich, where boiling salt from brine collected in brine-pits goes back to the time of the Romans (whose name for Droitwich was

Salinae, 'Salt Springs'). In Henry VIII's time John Leland recorded that 360 furnaces were busy at Droitwich, and noticed how "ill coloured" the salt-workers were made by their peculiar pursuit. The brine, soaking into the pits from underground deposits of salt, was boiled in leaden pans, drained in wicker baskets, then dried in an oven into salt loaves. The Salt Ways and the Saltergates and other salt names round the countryside such as Salters

Bridge, Salters Hill, Saltford, will be understood if one thinks of the periodical arrival of the salter or salt-merchant at certain recognized places along the route. An open space by a bridge or a ford would be a good pull-in or temporary headquarters for the salter and his animals, as at Saltford between Bath and Bristol, where there was a passage over the Avon. Though the names of some places where brine was boiled end in -wich, the word (Old English *wīc*) meant no more than sheds or buildings, collectively – in those instances, sheds for salt: Droitwich, 'dirty sheds'; Northwich, 'north sheds'; etc.

Sandstones

Sandstones are rocks re-made from fragmented rocks, i.e. from sand (small grains of quartz, for the most part) to which ancient rocks were reduced. The sand was deposited in

An aerial photograph of the ruins of the 13th-century Beeston Castle, Nottinghamshire. This border castle was modelled on a Saracen fortress and stands on an outcrop of red SANDSTONE, *giving a remarkable view of the surrounding country. Note the curtain wall around the bailey, and the twin-towered gatehouse.*

seas or freshwater lakes, and then cemented into rock by one substance or another such as silica, calcium carbonate, or clay. In crags, sea-cliffs and river-cliffs and buildings the sand-stones help to colour the countryside. Some of the most familiar are the sandstones reddened by iron oxide – whether the very old rocks of the Devonian system (Old Red Sandstone, which all the same is not always red), charac-teristic of Hereford and Worcester and Gwent, where they form, for instance, the red preci-pices above the Honddu valley between Cwmyoy and Llanthony, or the less ancient New Red Sandstone (again not always red) familiar in the west Midlands, along the Severn, and in Devonshire's anchovy sauce cliffs at Dawlish. The Red Rock hermitage on the Severn (*see* HERMITAGES) is carved out of a New Red Sandstone cliff of an entirely start-ling cherry red. The MILLSTONE GRIT along the Pennines, which makes by contrast for black moors and EDGES and sombre farms, villages and towns, is a specially hard sandstone of coarser, sharper grains of sand cemented by silica. Sandstones of the Carboniferous System can be much gayer, e.g. along the golden and brown sea-cliffs of Northumberland. The

sandstones in Kent, deeply cut by lanes (as in some of Samuel Palmer's Kentish landscapes) belong to the much younger GREENSANDS (which are not usually green). The SARSENS of Wiltshire are another sandstone hardened and cemented by silica. Most of the stone buildings of the English countryside are made either from sandstones or LIMESTONES, with the sand-stones predominating north of a line from the Wash to the Severn estuary.

Sarsen stones

Sarsen stones, which have their greatest con-centration on the Marlborough Downs in Wiltshire (though thousands of tons have been split up and removed for building and paving), seemed out of place on the softness and the smoothness of the downs, so in the 17th century, if not before, they were known as 'Saracen stones' – 'Saracen', soon contracted to 'sarsen', having come to be a convenient adjective for something unusual or outlandish.

Sarsens are the relics of a layer of sand, of Eocene age, deposited above the Upper Chalk, and cemented to a considerable hardness by silica (the mineral familiar as quartz). Palm trees growing in silt overhead sent their lower

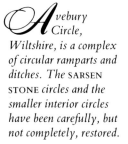

*A*vebury *Circle, Wiltshire, is a complex of circular ramparts and ditches. The* SARSEN STONE *circles and the smaller interior circles have been carefully, but not completely, restored.*

roots down into the sand before its transformation to a sandstone, making the root holes which are conspicuous in sarsen boulders (and leaving in them the occasional scraps of fossilized root). The silicified sandstone itself is supposed to have lain on a softer foundation of sands which were washed out, leaving the sandstone layer to break up into the separate pieces which have been water-rounded and weathered into today's boulders. The name 'grey wethers', i.e. grey sheep, for sarsens lying about on the surface (and in a mist they certainly can be mistaken for sheep) suggests a stone which is always a dull grey. But apart from attracting moss and lichen, sarsens vary in surface tint from grey to browns and reds or pinks caused by a superficial staining with oxide of iron. Inside they are sparkling white. In England sarsens occur in other counties as well as Wiltshire and the neighbouring Berkshire – sparsely in Somerset, Hants, Sussex, Oxfordshire, Herts, Essex and Bucks, a little less sparsely in Surrey, Kent, and Suffolk.

Neolithic people were the first to exploit sarsen, transporting huge boulders for stone circles and chamber tombs. Most of Stonehenge and all of the Avebury circles are sarsen, the material also of many chamber tombs. Mediaeval builders used large blocks of undressed sarsen as a foundation for church towers and buttresses. Since the 17th century Wiltshire people, especially the farmers, have built it dressed as well as raw (sarsen is dangerous rather than difficult to cut, the chips flying off sharp as arrowheads) into sheds and barns, paving, garden walls, stiles, gateposts, bridges, signposts, stone floors and house-footings. Sarsen houses, or houses with sarsen floors, incline to be damp, owing to condensation on the hard surface of this strange stone.

Scallop shells

Scallop shells carved in church (except in an obviously heraldic context) are symbolic either of St. James the Apostle, who is patron of more than three hundred mediaeval churches in England, or of a pilgrimage to his shrine at Santiago de Compostela in the north-west of Spain. The Spaniards maintained that they had his remains at Compostela, which by the 12th century had become, after Rome and Jerusalem, the third most important centre of Christian pilgrimage. For no obvious reason, the scallop shell (*coquille de St Jacques*) was the badge which showed one had made the journey to Compostela, and so the badge of the apostle himself. Scallops were sewn to the pilgrim's clothing or to the scrip or shoulder bag he carried (as on two 15th century effigies of men who had been to Compostela, one in the church of Haverfordwest in Dyfed, one in the church of Ashby-de-la-Zouch in Leicestershire). St. James is usually shown with a scallop shell on his hat. Pilgrims from Great Britain made the long journey in great numbers, from southern and western ports, Weymouth, Sandwich, Winchelsea, Southampton, Bristol, Plymouth, Dartmouth, Fowey, Saltash, etc., sometimes sailing direct to Corunna, more often to Bordeaux, from which they travelled on by land. They came back not only with the shells, which were sometimes buried with them, but with little figures of St. James carved in Spanish jet.

Scar

Looking upward in the limestone dales of West and North Yorkshire, the grey rocks one sees projecting like reefs above the talus are 'scars', from the Old Norse *sker*, rock or crag or reef, the word used by the Norsemen who settled western Yorkshire in the 10th century. The Norsemen of Shetland and Orkney used the word *sker* (in Gaelic *sgeir*) for a sea reef, or sea rock, or 'skerry', as in Sule Skerry, the Atlantic reef of the seal-man in the Shetland ballad.

Scotch pine

Scotch pine in many parts of Britain is a tree reintroduced when picturesque planting spread in the 18th century. In prehistoric times it was largely, but not altogether, wiped out by climatic changes and the formation of peat (*see* BOG TREES), surviving in ancient Scottish forests, such as Rothiemurchus below the Cairngorms, and here and there in dry situations in England and Wales. As an embellishment of landscape it is said to have been popularized after his Culloden campaign of 1746 by the Duke of Cumberland, who as Ranger of Windsor Great Park had Scotch pines planted in clumps through the park in a less reprehensible landscaping campaign. Landowners frequently used Scotch pines to mark or accent a particular feature of a landscape such as a hill-top or a barrow. In North Yorkshire around Ribblehead particular limestone caves are marked with a pine or pines growing near them or above them.

Scowles

In the Forest of Dean, scowles are old ore-pits or iron-workings which have fallen in –

'scowl' being a local word for rubbish or debris. The Scowles of Bream or the Scowles at Deans Pool, Clearwell, are of a fantastic and formidable attraction. Ancient miners – the scowles are probably mediaeval – followed the iron ore along a narrow band of 'crease' limestone which is stained by the iron to a deep red. Little chasms, shafts, black holes leading underground, broken red rock, sometimes velvety with very green moss, form a litter of desolation repossessed by yew trees, beeches, rosebay willowherb, ferns, and strings and curtains of ivy. There is no proof that the scowles are Roman, as guidebooks maintain, although the Romans worked the Forest ore at Lydney Park above the Severn and smelted ore on the other side of the Forest at what may have been the Roman town of Ariconium.

Sea-cliffs

Cut back by the action of waves and boulders, and fretted into stacks, caves, and natural arches, sea-cliffs exerted little appeal until the Romantic era at the beginning of the 19th century, when in their height, their resistance to storm, and their perpetual contest with the sea, they attracted painters, writers and tourists as embodiments of the 'horrid' and the 'sublime'. The cliff scenery we admire, from Scotland to Land's End, was 'discovered' in particular by the artist William Daniell (1769–1837), a minor master of broad panoramic effects, who travelled the coasts and produced the 308 aquatints, many of them noble ones of cliff scenery, which make the eight folio volumes of *A Voyage Around Great Britain* (1814–25) into one of the great works of British topography. Turner on the whole preferred mountain to sea-cliff. In Scotland John Thomson of Duddingstone (1778–1840) specialized during the eighteen-twenties and after in wild seas lashing and butting at cliffs, especially castle-crowned cliffs, which turned his pictures into double images of the sublime (cliffs with Tantallon Castle, East Lothian; Dunluce Castle, on the Antrim coast; Fast Castle, Borders, etc.). He shared this cliff and castle taste with his friend Sir Walter Scott –

> ...Tantallon's dizzy steep
> Hung o'er the margin of the deep
> *Marmion*

– who shared it with other Romantic novelists. The tall adamantine cliffs of the Cornish peninsula helped to establish Cornwall's reputation for romantic holidays; and for a

hundred years from the eighteen-fifties most summer exhibitions of the Royal Academy exhibited badly painted Atlantic waves bashing the badly painted granite ramparts of Land's End. Our now established taste for the loftiest and most ragged and sheer and bird-whitened sea-cliffs (St. Kilda, etc.) ought not to blind us to the charm of low cliffs along the North Sea – for instance, the brown and golden sandstone cliffs which indent Northumberland and are scenery of the most exquisite, if not most powerful or grandiose, kind.

The best introduction to the formation of cliffs and their different types and features is J. A. Steer's *The Coastline of England and Wales*, 1946.

Seaweed lanes

In coastal areas seaweed was long used as a fertilizer, and is still so used, for instance in the Isles of Scilly and in Ireland. In Ireland lanes zigzagging between the tiny stone-walled fields to the shore were 'seaweed lanes', or 'wrack roads', along which the wrack thrown up by the storms was brought back at the wrack harvest in and after the New Year (see Estyn Evans, *Irish Folk Ways*, 1957). Seaweed for fertilizer has even been cultivated in Northern Ireland (e.g. in Carlingford Lough, Co. Down) in submarine wrack-beds set with boulders from which the wrack was sickled between March and June. English farmers also spread seaweed and sea-sand on their fields, which is the explanation of the frequent and now often overgrown lanes running direct to a beach. Now and again intervening rocks have been cut through (as on Lansallos beach, in east Cornwall) to allow passage for carts and packhorses.

Sedilia

Sedilia (Latin for seats), built usually into the fabric of the church, south-west of the altar, were provided for the priest celebrating mass, and for the deacon and sub-deacon who assisted him. They occupied their stone sedilia during part of the singing of the mass, the celebrant nearest the altar (on the highest of the seats when they are stepped), the deacon next to him, then the sub-deacon. So as a rule there are three sedilia. They are frequently built as an architectural unit together with the PISCINA, under four arches, elaborated in some 14th century sedilia with crockets and cusps and finials and figures of saints and angels. Often there appears to have been no leg room below

A SEDILIA *and* piscina *(c. 1330) with a rich canopy, installed during the dedication of Blackawton Church, Devon.*

the sedilia, as if the celebrant and deacons sat there in peculiar discomfort. This is due to raising the chancel floor in the 19th century, so as to distinguish chancel from nave and bring the altar into dominant view.

Seven Deadly Sins

Mediaeval religious and moral teaching often went in sevens: Seven Deadly Sins, Seven Virtues, SEVEN WORKS OF MERCY, SEVEN SACRAMENTS, Seven Ages of Man, etc. The Sins – normally Pride, Avarice, Lechery, Envy, Gluttony, Anger and Sloth – lent themselves to carving, as in the great Suffolk church of Blythburgh, where 15th century BENCH-ENDS are capped with Sloth sitting up in bed, Gluttony with arms round a big belly, etc., instead of poppy-heads.

Seven Sacraments

The instructive imagery in a parish church may include in stained glass or in carving scenes which stand for the Seven Sacraments, the seven rites which imparted super-natural grace – Baptism, Confirmation, Mass, Penance, Extreme Unction, Ordination, and Matrimony. Norfolk and Suffolk have a famous series of eight-sided fonts of the 15th century carved on seven sides with a Sacrament and on the eighth usually with a crucial event in the life of Christ – either his baptism or his crucifixion (see M. D. Anderson's *Imagery of British Churches*, 1955).

Seven Sisters

There are in fact hundreds of stars, not seven, in this famous cluster, which appears in our latitude in the winter sky. Most people detect six of the Seven Sisters; Pleiades, and are uncertain of a seventh or an eighth (but try looking at the cluster with the eyes turned slightly away, so that you are making fuller use of the night-vision cells of the retina). As usual with the constellations and clusters, we have inherited the Greek names for the sisterhood. The Seven were the daughters of Atlas and Pleione, desirable nymphs who had children, most of them, by the gods – Electra, Taygete and Maia, all loved by Zeus; Alcyone and Celaeno, loved by Poseidon; Sterope or Aster-ope, loved by Ares; and Merope, who disgraced herself by taking a mortal lover, Sisyphus. Pleione was desired by ORION the wild hunter, and ran from him with her seven daughters. Orion strides after them across the sky, to the east of the group. Like ourselves the ancients were certain of only six stars in the group, and they supposed that the invisible sister was Merope, who hid herself out of shame for her mortal misalliance. Modern astronomy names nine stars in the cluster, seven after the sisters, two after their parents. The brightest star, more or less in the middle, is Alcyone.

Seven Works of Mercy

Parishioners in the 15th century were urged not to forget the Seven Works of Mercy, which were often illustrated in church in bench-end carvings, wall-paintings and windows. Six of the Mercies were feeding the hungry, giving drink to the thirsty, hospitality to the stranger, and clothes to the naked, visiting the sick, and those in prison. These derived from the words of Christ on the Mount of Olives (Matthew, 25. 35–6) describing how at the Last Judgement God would set the sheep on his right hand and the goats on his left, and would tell those on the right that they would now inherit the kingdom, because they had done these mercies to him, in doing them to others. From Tobit's words in the Apocrypha (Tobit, 1. 15–18) listing the mercies he performed, a seventh Mercy was added, which was burying the dead. ('If I saw any of my nation dead, or cast about the walls of Nineve, I buried him.')

Sgòrr

In Gaelic, a craggy summit or sharp peak, common in mountain names, e.g. Sgùrr na Lapaich, 3,775 feet, in the Highland.

Sham ruins

Better called artificial ruins, sham ruins were much built in the 18th century, to give a mediaeval or Gothic accent to improved landscape, and to direct the eye to a scenically desirable point, and hold it there. They are not to be despised as 'sham', having now themselves joined the realm of genuine antiquity. These ornamental or suggestive ruins had overtones of chivalry – the ruined castle; or of religion – the ruined piece of church, abbey, priory, or hermitage; and were regarded as historically appropriate to their English environment. The ruin induced moral reflection on the transience of earthly things. In building an imitation ruin, vagueness of effect was held to be wrong. The fancy had to be engaged at once by knowing what the ruin represented. 'The mind must not be allowed to hesitate; it must be hurried away from examining into the reality, by the exactness and the

The remains of an old engine house — a relic of Cornwall's industrial past — is perched on granite SEA-CLIFFS *near Botallock, Land's End, Cornwall. The Levant Mine nearby produced more tin and copper than any other in the Land's End peninsula.*

Hedsor Priory, Bourne End in Buckinghamshire, is a SHAM RUIN *of the late eighteenth century. This large flint folly consists of three towers, circular, hexagonal and square, connected by curtain walls.*

force of the resemblance.' Ivy and shrubs helped with such picturesque ruins: 'An inter-mixture of a vigorous vegetation, intimates a settled despair of their restoration'. (Both quotations from Whately's *Observations on Modern Gardening*, 1770.)

Such ruins work – on children, at any rate. The compiler of this book had his first intimation of antiquity from visiting Mount Edgcumbe, on Plymouth Sound, and seeing (at five years old) the Gothic ruin, with 'a flight of stone steps leading to a shattered window . . .

which enables the spectator to glance over the numerous attractions of the neighbourhood'.

-shaw

Commonest in north country place-names, -shaw means a thicket, a scrap of woodland (Old English *scaga*). It could be a shaw where you might expect to see a red squirrel (*ikorni* in Old Norse), Ikornshaw; or where a badger had an earth, Bagshaw; or where otters laid up, Ottershaw; or where the trees were alders, Aldershaw, or birches, Birkenshaw, etc.

esque sculptors as part of the instructive decoration of churches. The sheilas—there is a particularly brazen one outside Kilpeck church, in Hereford and Worcester, whose likeness used to be on sale in the village shop— are grotesque little females, usually squatting, with legs apart and hands thrust in under their thighs, holding their privates open. Antiquaries have argued romantically but implausibly that they represented the survival of a pre-Christian fertility cult. More likely they were a warning against Lechery, the third of the SEVEN DEADLY SINS. A number of sheila-na-gigs suffered indignities. One has been chipped from the stonework of St. Michael's, in the Cornmarket at Oxford, and another mutilated, in Ampney St. Peter church, near Cirencester (though a neighbouring sheila survives intact—which may not be the *mot juste*— high up on the outside wall of Oaksey church, across the Wiltshire border). South Tawton, in Devon, sports a late sheila on a 15th century boss. Sheilas in Ireland include one on the outside of the ruined Romanesque church of Killinaboy, in Co. Clare, and one on the chancel arch of the 12th century Nuns' Church (also a ruin) at Clonmacnoise, in Offaly. Some churches also exhibit male figures ithyphallically indicative of the same deadly sin, e.g. Abson in Avon. Sopley church in Hampshire has both a male figure and a female one.

Shieling

To explore green sites of shielings (shiel: a hut) in the mountain glens is to establish contact with an ancient summer happiness of the Highlands and Islands. Something of what went on at shielings is described, in Irish and Welsh terms, under BOOLEY HOUSES and HAFOD. Gaelic and English-writing poets of the 18th century speak of the singing and sense of freedom among the women and girls and herdsmen at these summer dairying places. Robert Tannahill in his 'Braes o'Balquhither' celebrates the long summer days, the smell of thyme, the sound of waterfalls in the night, the singing, and summer storms as well—

> So merrily we'll sing,
> As the storm rattles o'er us
> Till the dear shieling ring
> Wi' the light lilting chorus.

The Gaelic-writing Duncan Bàn MacIntyre has stanzas in his *Song to the Summer* about the songs of the girls, the foaming milk-pails, the cattle-pairing and the young heifers, and the calves in the fold (*Gaelic Songs of Duncan*

Sheading

One of the six ancient districts into which the Isle of Man is 'shed' or divided. The word is supposed to have arrived with the Englishman, Sir John Stanley, when he became king of Man in 1405. The sheadings are now the Manx electoral divisions.

Sheila-na-gig

Sheila-na-gig (Irish for 'Sheila of the paps'). A name invented by antiquaries to describe a peculiar subject carved sometimes by Roman-

MacIntyre, ed. G. Calder, 1912); and the lilting of girls at the ewe-milking before dawn in Jean Elliot's famous 'Flowers of the Forest' belongs to the summer shieling, where sheep were milked (for cheese), as well as cows. Transhumance survived into this century on the Outer Hebrides; on Lewis one can still see BEEHIVE HUTS built for shielings, which were in use up to 1859. The Gaelic for shieling, *airidh* or *airigh*, appears in place-names (sometimes as *airy*).

Shire

Shire, in Old English *scīr*, first of all meant the charge of something, then the something in one's charge, a province, then one of the particular provinces or districts through which England was governed (and afterwards Wales, Scotland and Ireland), each one made up of a number of smaller units of government, the now almost forgotten hundreds and wapentakes. By Alfred the Great's time, at the end of the 9th century, Wessex was administered in shires. Within a hundred years or so the Midlands and East Anglia had been divided into shires; and the Normans eventually created the northernmost shires of England between the Tees and Scotland. Some of the shires were old lands of particular people, and kept the old names, such as Sussex, (land of the) South Saxons, or Cumberland, Land of the Cymry or Welsh, or Dorset, (land of the) Dorchester settlers. Most were distinguished by the name of the shire's chief fortified town or stronghold, *York*shire, *Hereford*shire, *Wilt*shire, shire of the town of Wilton, *Wiltunscir*,

etc. (the derivation of all the English county names will be found in the *Concise Oxford Dictionary of English Place-Names*). The chief officer of the shire was first of all the alderman, afterwards the sheriff, the *scīr-gerefa* or reeve of the shire, the chief officer appointed by the king, who presided over the shire-moot, the open-air assembly of the shire held twice a month, part administrative, part judicial – the *comitatus* or court of the shire, in Englishman's French the *counté*, which, part for whole, came, as 'county', to supplant the word shire in the late Middle Ages.

Shooting stars

However capricious and sudden the individual meteor or shooting star may be, it is pleasant that some meteors come with a collective regularity, caught by the earth's pull when the orbit of the earth intersects the orbit round the sun of a particular stream of these celestial fragments of ore or rock. Familiar showers from stream to earth (named after the constellations in the background of their fall) are the Lyrids, from the direction of the Lyre, 20–22 April; the Perseids, from the direction of Perseus, 1–20 August, maximum about 12 August; and the Geminids, from the direction of Gemini, 9–14 December. At maximum, Geminids and Perseids fall fifty to sixty an hour. But particular showers do not always parade the same abundance every year. If you wish, when you see a shooting star, the wish, so it is said, will not come true unless you have completed it while the trail of incandescence is still visible. So it is as well that some meteors (e.g. the rather scarce Taurids – direction of Taurus, 26 October–16 November, maximum 17 November) trail in a leisurely way across the sky. Showers differ in luminosity as well as brightness. The Geminids, for example, are brighter, as well as faster, than the Perseids, which are still pretty fast. One common – and rather attractive – theory of shooting stars has been that they are wicked souls shooting rapidly from the Last Judgement to hell. Check on meteor showers each year with the current almanac.

Signal stations

Sending warning over a distance by the smoke or light of a fire is a method about as old as belligerency, if not as old as the hills on which the fires were lit. Roman legionaries refined on long-distance signalling by building signal stations with towers from point to point along some of their roads and along threatened

Two early MILESTONES, *one, at Trumpington, painted black and white, directing travellers to Cambridge, the other (right), in Sussex, in stone and cast iron, marking the distance from London.*

stretches of coast. Signals were sent up and down Hadrian's Wall, and stations have been found along roads in the north and in disturbed country in Scotland beyond the Antonine Wall. On the north Devon coast stations gave warning of raiders from Ireland, on the East Anglian and Yorkshire coast warning of Saxon raiders from across the North Sea.

The station was sometimes a rectangular earthen platform inside an oblong of ditch and dyke; sometimes a wooden tower on timber legs on a round platform of earth, inside a ditch; sometimes a small stone tower by itself (or built out from Hadrian's Wall); sometimes a tall square stone tower enclosed in a square curtain-wall which had corner towers, which in turn was enclosed within a rectangular ditch with rounded corners. This last was the plan of the signal stations along the Yorkshire coast, built about A.D. 370, after disastrous raids.

The sites are less something to see than to think about. But they take one into excellent country, inland or on the coast. For a road signal station, drive along A66, the Roman road across the wild, lofty moors of Durham and Cumbria, between the Roman forts at Rokeby and Brough. The road goes through a temporary Roman fort at 1,468 feet above the sea-level at Rey Cross, then continues into Cumbria. South of the road, south-west of the camp, at a slightly higher level across the railway, stands the signal station of Round Table or Roper Castle. Or on the burly north Devon coast, visit the little round signal station 850 feet above the sea at Martinhoe, west of Lynton and Lynmouth (called the Beacon, it was presumably used to give warning by fire in more recent times), and afterwards, east of Lynton and Lynmouth, visit the signal station of ditch and dyke, round and rectangular, at Countisbury, on Old Barrow Hill, with the sea more than 1,000 feet below. Those would have been part of a warning system for the Romanized country revolving around Bath. The great towers once on the Yorkshire coast, at Filey, Scarborough, Ravenscar, Goldsborough and Huntcliff, flashed or semaphored warning (what system the Romans used no one knows) for the defence of the rich Romanized country whose centre was York.

Signposts and milestones

Signposts telling the way at cross roads and known first as 'direction posts' or 'direction stones' were an innovation of the late 17th century, when travel was increasing through England. The first stones were set up by individuals, such as the Nathan Izod whose stone on Broadway Hill descending from the Cotswolds into Hereford and Worcester bears the date 1669. In 1697 direction posts or stones at 'cross highways' were enjoined by law, and in 1698 the inquisitive and energetic Celia Fiennes riding across Lancashire to the Lake District was delighted to find 'one good thing in most parts of this principality . . . that at all cross wayes there are Posts with Hands pointing to each road with the names of the great town or market towns that it leads to'. But they were not put up everywhere as they should have been, and the General Turnpike Acts of 1766 and 1773 made direction posts compulsory at turnpike cross roads. The same acts and earlier acts establishing individual Turnpike Trusts (see TOLL-HOUSES) insisted that mileposts as well should be set up along the turnpike roads. Many of these mileposts are still in place, some of them stone, some of them iron, some flat-faced, some triangular with town and mileage lettered on each of the two projecting faces. Milestones from ROMAN ROADS, of which more than sixty have been found in England, Wales, and Scotland, may give the distance from a town, but more often have nothing inscribed on them but the name of the ruling emperor. They were apparently set up when the road was made, enlarged or repaired. Most of them are now gathered into museums. The uninscribed milestone at Chesterholm in Northumberland still stands where it was erected by the Romans alongside Stangate, the Roman road which runs parallel with Hadrian's Wall from Corbridge to Carlisle.

Sike

Sike, in the north, is a small stream (Old English sīc, or Old Norse sik), a runnel or trickle of water, often the head waters of a burn. In the south the corresponding word is a 'sitch'.

Singing sand

Dry blown sand around the coast may emit an unexpected musical sound, slight or pronounced, when you walk over it or drag a stick across it. Off the dunes and below the high-tide mark, water is drawn in and held between the grains of sand by capillary action. The grains do not touch. Without this water cushion dry grains rub together when they are moved, and if they are of the same shape and size they jerk against or across each other as they do so, vibrating and 'singing'.

Slate

Slate used to be applied to any kind of stone which could be cleft into thin or less thin slats for roofing (Old French *esclate*, something split), or flags for flooring, gravestones, etc. It is now generally applied to rocks which can be split in a particular way, the variously coloured slates of Cornwall, Wales, Leicestershire, the Lake District, etc., which divide much more finely and regularly owing to changes which they have undergone. Most slates are basically a deposit of mud (the Lake District slates were formed of volcanic ash) subjected to immense pressures with movements of the earth's crust, which produced in their substance microscopic plates of mica arranged in vertical parallels at right angles to the pressure. So slate cleaves neatly and smoothly along these induced planes, whereas the 'stone slates' of limestone and sandstone cleave with less precision and more thickly and roughly only along the plane of their original bedding. Though slate in this sense has been used here and there for roofing slats since the early Middle Ages, it became popular only in the 19th century, when it began its career of ousting the immemorial THATCH and sandstone and limestone roofing as well. Since they could be trimmed into identical rectangles, slate from the Welsh mountain quarries fitted the new steam era of exact mensuration, which enthroned neatness and smoothness as moral necessities. Slate lasted, thatch decayed and became squalid, and caught fire. Slate weighed less and required slighter timbering than the sandstones and limestones, which made even the heaviest timbers sag sooner or later. But slate fashioned roofs by the million which were – and are – monotonous and dull, agreeing only with the exact rectangularity and smoothness of Victorian brick and stone.

Snowhill

A not infrequent country name for a hill or escarpment facing in a northerly direction, so that snow lies there long after it has melted elsewhere. At sunset such snowhills, when they live up to their name, and are snow-covered, turn as pink as an Alpine slope.

Souterrains

Souterrains are long, underground, stone-walled, slab-roofed, usually curving chambers much built by Celtic peoples during the Iron Age in connection with their hill-forts, raths and homesteads in western Cornwall, in Ireland, and in Scotland and the northern and

*B*laenau
Ffestiniog,
Gwnedd, Wales,
famous for its SLATE
quarrying. As railways
became available to
distribute the products of
the quarries, the use of
slate tiles for roofing,
(such as you can see
here) became a standard
feature.

209

western isles. In Scotland a souterrain is an 'earthhouse' or weem, in Cornwall a fogou (weem and fogou both mean cave). Today, a souterrain, which may be entered through a hole hidden by furze or brambles and explored by the twinklings of candlelight, suggests ancient secrecy or secretiveness; and secrecy suggests hiding things away in face of danger or attack, as if the souterrain had been a kind of safe or strong-room. In fact, the souterrain was perhaps intermediate between safe and cellar, strong-room and store-room, the place to store anything which would not be damaged by dark, cool and rather damp conditions (? grain, salted meat, salted butter, cheese, of which not so much would be required at a time); the place for a temporary storage of valuable goods (or children or women) in times of danger or the likelihood of attack – fireproof, unlike the thatched huts inside a rampart. There is an Icelandic account of a Viking raider of the early Middle Ages who discovered the way into an Irish souterrain, where an Irishman sat in the dark with his sword guarding his wealth. A glint of light on the sword gave him away, and the Icelander killed him. In Ireland it is thought that souterrains were made as early as the Late Bronze Age and were in use down to the Middle Ages. For the disputed whys and wherefores of the souterrain, and for examples to visit, read the souterrain chapter in Seán Ó Ríordáin's *Antiquities of the Irish Countryside* (1953), *Souterrains of Southern Pictland* by F. T. Wainwright (1963), and *Cornish Fogous* by Evelyn Clark (1961).

Spital

Spital, spittle, in a place-name usually indicates the mediaeval presence of a hospital or hospice of some kind (*see* ALMSHOUSES). Yspytty Ifan, in north Wales, is the site of a *hospitium* founded in the twelfth century.

Springs

Springs well out under scarps and hills along definite lines. The slope may cut across the level at which rocks holding water from the clouds meet underlying formations, such as clay, which prevent the water soaking down any further, so springs emerge. Or water may be thrown out in springs along the edge of a fault; or the 'water-table', the height to which the water-holding formations are saturated, may come to the surface along the valley. However they are formed, the springs are points of life and settlement very often. Farms,

and farms which have grown into villages, and villages which have grown into towns, may be due to the presence of a spring. Or a notable spring may have become a holy well, pagan and then Christian, and then a spa. A town, a village or a farm may owe its name, as well as its existence, to a spring – for instance, names in -well (Old English *wella*, *wielle*, water which wells up or out). These may describe the spring, or even tell who took possession of it or settled by it; Loxwell Farm, the farm of the spring which belonged to a Saxon named Locc. Or names with -font (in Old English *funta*, which the Anglo-Saxons borrowed from the British, who had borrowed it from Latin, *fontana*, a fountain or spring): Teffont, boundary spring; Mottisfont in Hants, the spring of the moot, the HUNDRED MEETING PLACE. In Wiltshire the two Fonthills, famous for their association with William Beckford, preserve a British name, 'spring of the fertile ground', and in either Fonthill there is a spring coming from the greensand under the chalk and above the gault clay, pouring out many thousands of gallons every day. In the north, springs are indicated by names ending in -*keld*, from the Old Norse. Your county and its springs may have the benefit of one of the Geological Survey's memoirs on underground water supply (*The Water Supply of Lincolnshire, Oxfordshire, Norfolk, Sussex, Worcestershire,* and others), full of facts about springs, wells, mineral springs, etc.

Squeeze-belly and kissing gate

A squeeze-belly is a footpath stile made of two pieces of timber set close together in the ground and curving outwards. If you are fat, you need to squeeze through sideways.

A kissing-gate is a small gate which swings in a U- or V-shaped enclosure, and allows only one person to pass at a time.

Squint

From some parts of a church – from CHANTRY CHAPELS in a side-aisle or from the space to left and right of a wall separating the nave from the chancel – it was impossible to see when mass began at the high altar, or the stage that had been reached in the celebration. So openings, or squints as Victorian ecclesiologists named them, were cut slantwise through the intervening masonry (and often given decorative treatment at either end), affording a limited view of the high altar. The usual purpose of a squint was to enable a chantry-priest chanting masses for the eminent dead at his subsidiary altar to see when the parish priest was about to begin High Mass, at which point it was his duty to stop for a while or assist.

Stacks

From the Old Norse *stakkr*, stack is the word the Vikings used for isolated cliff-columns off Caithness, Orkney, Shetland, etc. Stacks are last remnants of the endless battle of cliff erosion. A projection of cliff is attacked on both sides by the waves (and the sand and stones that the waves bring with them). Where the rock is softest or weakest along the joints and bedding planes, the projection is holed, and gradually enlarged by waves and weathering to a cliff-arch or cliff-door, such as Durdle Door (in Portland stone) on the Dorset coast, near Lulworth Cove, or the Green Bridge of Wales (in carboniferous limestone), near Bosherston on the coast of Dyfed, or the Needle Eye (in red sandstone) near Duncansby Head, in Highland. Some cliff doors are cut through a projection where the rock folds over. The sea eats through the vertically bedded rock, the lintel, which remains, consisting of horizontal beds. But the lintel weathers, weakens, and falls, leaving a stack at last, free of its parent cliff. Stacks differ in shape ac-

A KISSING-GATE in the grounds of Gilbert White's house, The Wakes, Selborne, Hampshire.

This vivid STAINED-GLASS window, depicting St. Francis and the birds, commemorates the author of 'The Natural History of Selborne', Gilbert White.

cording to the hardness and softness of the rock, the thickness or thinness of the beds, and whether the beds are horizontal or tilted or vertical. Family groups of stack and arch naturally occur, as at Flamborough Head or, most fantastically, at Marsden Bay, Tyne and Wear, where cows used to graze on top of the main stack. Place-names show how cliffs change. Durlston Head, on the Dorset coast by Swanage, to the east of Lulworth and Durdle Door, once no doubt had a cliff door, a *thyrel stān*, or stone with a hole in it, just as Thurle-stone, in south Devon, near Salcombe, still has its red sandstone sea-door in Bigbury Bay (mentioned in a land charter of A.D. 845).

Staddle-stones

Staddle-stones (or stack-stools), the round stones set on pillars like the cap of a mushroom which uphold a granary or the criss-cross platform for a stack of corn, were meant to bar the ascent of rats and mice – though even a moderately athletic rat could climb round them. The staddle is the platform of timbers (from the Old English word for base or support). In *The Chace* (1735) William Somerville writes

> Inwardly smiling, the proud Farmer views
> The rising Pyramids that grace his Yard,
> And counts his large Increase; his Barns are stor'd,
> And groaning Staddles bend beneath their Load.

– and the farmer goes off for a day's hunting.

Stained glass

Stained glass is left in sufficient quantity to give a hint of the mediaeval appetite for jewelled colour. When the feeling against images began to clear churches and cathedrals after the Reformation, WALL-PAINTINGS could be conveniently hidden under whitewash. It was another thing to put a ladder up and smash the lights of window after window, which meant an unusually cold church during service, also – and worse – that the parish had to buy new plain glass. Still, they tried. The celebrated purger of art as well as idolatry, instructed by Parliament to clean up Canterbury cathedral wrote of himself, 'on the top of the citie ladder, near sixty steps high, with a whole pike in his hand, rattling down proud Becket's glassy bones' – a splendid sentence – 'from the great idolatrous window' (Richard Culmer, *Cathedrall Newes from Canterburie*, 1644).

'Stained' in stained glass means no more than coloured; and the mediaeval principle – the original Gothic principle – in coloured windows was to fill them with a realm of divine or saintly imagery which seemed to create its own life between earth and heaven. In England the mediaeval glass-workers obtained their coloured glass, and much of their white glass (windows needing both), from the Rhineland and from Normandy. But this was no more than buying one's pigments or materials from elsewhere. They combined the colours into their own splendid designs, laying the raw glass of various tints over a cartoon of the window light, cutting it into the corresponding shapes, and then drawing or painting as required on the pieces with a pigment of iron oxide or copper oxide mixed with powdered glass which melted at a low temperature. The pieces were then fired in a kiln until the glass and oxide pigment coalesced with the glass; after which the pieces were joined up into the window design within an armature of lead. When the window was in place, the drawing incorporated on the glass in this way faced inwards, away from the weather. The 'tracers' (who did the drawing on to the glass from the cartoon) learnt two additional tricks, apparent in windows of the 14th century and after. It was discovered that glass acquired a yellow tint if it was coated with a silver salt and then fired. This gave them a means of colour drawing; and enabled them to have red and yellow and white on one piece of glass, since 'ruby' glass, unlike the imported glass in other colours, was ruby only on the surface, not all through, and where required this red surface could be cut away and the glass stained yellow.

The most brilliant and jewel-like windows, depending particularly upon a combination of ruby and blue, belong to the 12th and 13th centuries. Windows of the 14th century incline more to green and yellow; and seem to hold less light in suspension. Windows of the 15th century, in the wide window-spaces of the Perpendicular church, more emphatically present the message of the design, in more naturalistic forms, at the expense of radiance. In the early Gothic times of its greatest virtuosity the stained glass window was a 'homogeneous fabric of light' (Erwin Panofsky) which induced mystical contemplation, rather less instructing the worshipper in the story of the forms than raising him from earth by its unearthly glow, a full effect it is hard for us to experience from fragments of glass, however wonderful they may be, in a parish church, or from fragments of an original scheme, or from complete windows of the 15th century. It needs a visit to Chartres.

Standing stones

Standing stones are not always ancient. They may be scratching posts set up for cattle. They may be boundary stones, recent or mediaeval. They may be memorial stones inscribed to British or Irish chieftains of the Dark Ages, before crosses were erected and when it was still usual to be buried, not in a churchyard, but beside a road or a track. (In south Wales at the Margan Museum, the 6th century stone inscribed to Pumpeius, son of Carantorius, stood by a road. So did the 6th century Buduoc Stone, commemorating Buduoc, son of Cattegern, great-grandson of Eternalis Vedomarus. Both were Romanized Britons, of a time, a hundred years or so after the Romans had left, when Latin was still spoken or understood.) Uninscribed, they may mark still older burials, old as the Bronze Age. Or a standing stone *may* be something which was worshipped in pre-Christian times, Iron Age, Bronze Age, or neolithic. The rough St. Levan's Stone, in St. Levan churchyard in Cornwall, may have been a British idol; the stone at Turoe, near Loughrea in Co. Galway, covered with Early Iron Age abstract designs, must have been an idol – perhaps a phallic idol. (Ireland has two more of these strange decorated stones, the Castlestrange Stone near Athleague, in Co. Roscommon, and the stone at Killycluggin, near Ballyconnell, in Co. Cavan.) St. Gobnat's Stone at Ballyvourney in Co. Cork, which has crosses cut in each side (one of them topped by a figure of a bishop with a crozier) seems to have been an idol which was christianized.

Going back further to the Bronze Age and neolithic times, a standing stone may be a surviving upright of a Late Bronze Age fieldfence, or it may be the only stone left from the verticals of a neolithic DOLMEN.

-sted

-sted, -stead, in names of places, means just a place, a site (*stede* in Old English), and it is very much a name word of the home counties and East Anglia. In the north it is often used of (farm) places. Stead indicates a place where living went on, where some activity was

*S*TEPPING-STONES *across the River Wharfe in front of Bolton Abbey in North Yorks. Most of the priory buildings, founded in the 12th century for black canons of the Augustinian order, have been razed to the ground. But the beautiful ruins are open to the public and the nave of the church is still used for services.*

pursued, which might be distinguished in the rest of the name by its look, its position, its trees, its animals. If your -sted or -stead is a plant one, it is worth looking to see if it is still marked to any special degree by the same plants or trees – Ashstead, Nurstead (nut stead), Elmstead, Brumstead (broom stead), Maplestead, Plumstead, etc. The many Hampsteads or home steads (*see* -HAM) are home sites, home places, of a locally prominent or important kind – manors, manor villages.

Stepping-stones

Stepping-stones, or steps (in the North 'hippings' or 'hipping-stones' on which you hip or hop across a stream) are likely, if they are large and permanent and well worn, to be as old as the 13th or 12th century, or older still. On Dartmoor the dead were carried miles to burial in Lydford churchyard along the Lickway ('corpse way') which crosses a ford over the Tavy by granite stepping-stones laid end-on to the stream and each long enough to allow the bearers to pass with their corpse two by two. Tennyson – to balance this mortuary offering – exactly catches the summer feeling of stepping-stones in the first version of *The Miller's Daughter* (1832):

> The tall flag-flower that springs
> Beside the noisy stepping-stones.

These would have been Lincolnshire stepping-stones across a stream off the wolds. One may solemnly prefer Wordsworth on the Duddon stepping-stones, as if chosen for ornament:

> stone matched with stone
> In studied symmetry, with interspace
> For the clear waters to pursue their race
> Without restraint.

Stocks

Stocks, as we see them preserved on village greens and by market crosses, sometimes with a whipping post attached, are relics of the time when the parish had more control over its own affairs. They were instruments both of restraint and of punishment. Every parish inherited from the manorial organization of the Middle Ages its own Petty Constable, unpaid and serving as a rule for a year, who kept the peace, and was answerable to the magistrates, the Justices of the Peace, whose warrants he executed. The Constable could arrest an ill-doer or someone likely to cause a breach of the peace, and restrain him in the stocks, until he could bring him in front of a Justice; and a Justice, on his own say-so, could award a four-

hour stretch in the stocks for such petty offences as drunkenness, or the encouraging of drunkenness, blasphemy, or indulging in sports on Sunday; he could order male or female beggars or vagrants to be set in the stocks, or whipped with bare back at the whipping-post, before being sent back to their place of origin. Though never expressly forbidden by law, stocks had fallen into disuse by the eighteen-thirties. It was realized that they degraded spectators and offenders alike, and in any case justice and administration were rapidly becoming less parochial and more centralized. By that time the stocks had had a long run, as a cheap instrument easily made by village carpenter and smith and well within the means of a poor community. They had been in familiar use in the 14th century, and an act of 1405 had laid down that stocks should be provided in every town and village.

Stone roofs

'Flat-stone' roofs, not made of what we now understand by SLATE, are a speciality of houses of the limestone belt running across country north-east from the Cotswolds, weathering to pleasant colours, yellows, browns, tones of buff and grey, uneven, not trimmed with geometric regularity, collecting lichens and moss. These stone tiles are – or, one must generally say, were – split and trimmed from various fissile sandy limestones, which divide along the bedding plane (the plane of the original layers of marine ooze which bedded down and hardened into rock), in contrast to the very compact anciently pressurized slates of Wales, Cornwall, etc., which cleave in much thinner and more finical sheets. The Cotswolds, Oxfordshire (Stonefield Slates), and Northants (Collyweston Slates) have all produced stone tiles from open 'slat quarrs' or

A combination of stocks and whipping post such as would have been used in the first part of the last century. Examples are easily spotted and can be seen throughout the country.

STONE ROOFS

'tile quarrs' or shallow mines. Some of the stones can be split only if they are exposed to a sharp frost. W. J. Arkell, in *Oxford Stone* (1947), describes the methods used at Stonesfield, which is near Woodstock in Oxfordshire. The raw product from the underground workings was at once laid out and earthed over, to preserve the 'quarry sap' or original moisture in the stone. Then when a sharp January or February frost was certain, the stone was rapidly uncovered. If frost came unexpectedly in the night, the church bells would be rung to wake the villagers and bring them tumbling out to their chilly labour. After frosting, a few sharp taps were enough to split the stones into roof thicknesses. But once the 'sap' dried out, splitting was impossible. On Dorset roofs one often sees heavier and clumsier limestone roofs quarried in the Isle of Purbeck. In many other counties, south to north (e.g. Surrey, Sussex, Kent, Shropshire, Gwent, Cheshire, Lancashire, North Yorkshire, Derbyshire, Cumbria, Northumberland), various kinds of sandstone have provided roofing tiles, greatly heavy and sombrely black or brown.

*S*TONE ROOFS *at Bradford-on-Avon, Wiltshire. Many of the houses themselves are also built of Bath stone.*

Stoups

To be seen in a few churches, stoups are the small stone basins (the word is properly 'stop', meaning a pail, bucket or basin), without a drain, usually set on the right of the porch or the main door. Like the black marble *benitiers* (often in shell-shape) to be found near the main entrance into every French church, the stoup was the receptacle for holy water, which was mixed with salt, exorcised, and blessed; and frequently renewed. Those who came into the church dipped their fingers into the holy water, and made the sign of the cross on their bodies (a gesture frowned upon after the Reformation), the holy drops recalling the baptismal promises, the shedding of Christ's blood on the cross, and the washing away of sins. Stoups are not to be confused with the PISCINA near the altar.

-stow

In English place-names -stow has two common meanings, one deriving from the other. First, the Old English word *stōw* meant a place where people met together, for one purpose or another. Chepstow was the stow for trading, the *cēap stōw*; Bristol the *bʳycg stōw*, or meeting-place by the bridge. Often the stow was where you met for the assembly of the hundred (*see* HUNDRED MEETING PLACES). But you also met to worship; and with a patron saint's name attached to it, stow came to mean a church. Stow-on-the-Wold (on Cotswold) was once Edwardstowe, with its church dedicated to the martyred St. Edward; Morwenstow on the Cornish cliffs is the stow or church of the Cornish saint Morwenna.

Strat-

Strat-, stret-, streat-, street-, sometimes Street by itself, in place-names generally indicates that the place is on or near a ROMAN ROAD. The Old English word was *strǣt*, *strēt*, borrowed from the Latin *strata* (i.e. *via strata*, paved way), a word the English picked up from their Romanized British neighbours.

Stratus

That type of cloud, low, dark and horizontal, thin and long like a double-ended wedge, which one often sees stretching across the white flanks of a thunder cloud.

Stucco

Stucco became the surface mark of Regency buildings in town and country, partly because its use was a way of giving a building in inexpensive brick or rubble the blandness of a building in expensive freestone. The word, the idea and the substance came from Italian architecture. But English stucco was unsatisfactory until proprietary cements were invented and marketed in the last thirty years of the 18th century. They were popularized by various architects and builders, by the Adam brothers and especially by John Nash in 1812 on his houses in Regent's Park. Regency stucco was scored with joints in imitation of stone, and then painted to produce the effects of the weathering of stone.

Submerged forests

Submerged forests are often visible at low spring tides around the east, south and west coasts (e.g. at Cliff End near Hastings, Leasowe on the Wirral peninsula in Merseyside, Borth Sands and other low-lying fringes of north Dyfed, Marros Sands, south Dyfed). They are remnants of land surfaces flooded by an alteration, in post-glacial times, of the relative levels of land and sea. A shift of sand may reveal for a while the stumps of large oak trees or pines rooted into clay, or untidy stumps of willow, alder, hazel or birch. There may be acorns and hazel nuts and stems of royal fern, in a milieu of slip and slide. Ben Jonson's friend, the verse-making scholar Richard James (1592–1638), noticed the oak stumps in the submerged forest off the Wirral and wrote of them in his travel poem *Iter Lancastre* ('Lancastrian Journey'):

. . . in summe places, when the sea doth bate
Down from the shoare, tis wonder to relate
How many thousands of thies trees now stand
Black broken on their rootes, which once drie land
Did cover.

Observers believed the submerged forests were evidence of the Mosaic deluge and they have often been referred to, in the past, as 'Noah's Woods'.

Sundials

Sundials of the kind known as scratch-dials, mass-clocks or mass-dials, are to be seen on the south side of most old churches, on the jambs of a south door or porch, on a south buttress or wall, usually at eye level. There has been much argument about the exact nature and function of these primitive sundials (see A. R. Green's *Sundials, Incised Dials or Mass-Clocks*, 1926). A number of dials carved with formal skill and precision exist from before the Norman Conquest, usually dividing the day on a four-part system, with radial lines inside a double circle, under a cross-line. Some or all of the principal lines on these Saxon dials end in a cross. Inscriptions were added to several of them, notably the Saxon dials of Kirkdale, Edstone, and Old Byland churches and Aldborough in North Yorkshire. The very common post-Conquest dials are marked according to our duodecimal division of the day with radial lines 15 degrees apart, and as objects are much more sketchy or scratchy. Sometimes the radial line which would have been reached by the shadow of the metal style or gnomon (for which the central hole is usually visible) at

9 a.m. is more deeply and clearly incised: this has been called the 'mass line', marking the common time for mass on Sundays and feast days. But it seems that the basic function of the dials was to show when to ring the bell which announced far and wide the canonical hours – or such of the hours as fell in daylight. As one passed one might also look to see if a prayer hour was coming. Thus the 11th century dial over the south door of Edstone church is inscribed *Orlogi(um) viatorum*, 'hour-teller of wayfarers'. Sometimes there is a multiplicity of dials on one church: each is supposed to have been more or less accurate, for a different time of year.

Church clocks of the 14th and later centuries had the same primary function of showing when to ring a bell for the canonical hours. The face was often visible inside the church to the bell-ringer. In the 17th and 18th centuries more scientifically devised and elaborate sundials were fixed to churches, often, as their inscriptions show, to emphasize to the unwary the moral of the passage of time and of man's mortality.

Sun-suckers

Sun-suckers are the 'Jacob's Ladders' or sunbeams from behind the darkness of heavy clouds, which appear, as they incline away or converge in perspective, to be rising from ground to cloud as if the sun were sucking up the cloud-moisture through them.

Swallows

Swallows or swallow-holes are the apertures which dramatically and mysteriously swallow up streams and rivers in a limestone district, especially when dry weather has lowered the water-table. On the Mendips they are known as swallets or slockers (holes by which the water is 'slocked' or enticed away). The carbon dioxide in the river water dissolves the limestone along its joints and bedding-planes, forming the swallows, which are often like colanders in depth. One may see an old swallow now permanently dry and abandoned, the stream having formed, and gradually enlarged, a new swallow higher up. 'Collapse sinks' are sometimes confused with swallows. In chalk at least they are much larger. They are formed by the collapse of part of a cave roof. Such collapse sinks occur in Surrey between Leatherhead and Mickleham along the Mole (which is not the river burrowing like a mole, but the river flowing to Molesey – to 'Mul's island').

Swans

On the rivers of England (but not of Scotland), swans were royal birds as zealously protected in the past as the red and fallow deer of the FORESTS, and for the same reason – they were a valuable source of fresh meat. Only the Crown could grant the right or privilege of owning and disposing of swans, which often descended as a perquisite of manors. Swan ownership and the population of swans were controlled by swan laws and customs and courts of swan-mote in hundreds (for which, *see* HUNDRED MEETING PLACES) where swans foregathered; and by the Royal Swannerd (Swanherd) or Master of the King's Game of Swans and his deputies, whose especial care was the annual upping on the various rivers and the collection of swannage, i.e. the various fees and fines payable by swan-owners. The swans were 'upped' – picked up – so that they could be marked or have their marks checked. Broods were shared between the owners of the cob and the female – the owner of the cob having first choice – and were marked accordingly, every owner having his registered swan-mark, simple or complex, emblematic or heraldic, which was cut along the edges or on top of the superior mandible. Hatching in May, the cygnets were ready for upping in July, when they were still about in family parties, five to seven to a pair. The swan-upper's special instrument on these occasions was the swan-hook, which caught the unwilling bird by the neck.

Royal ownership of swans throughout England was allowed to lapse in the 18th century, though on the Thames swan-rights are still exercised by the Crown, and by two city livery companies, the Vintners and the Dyers, which acquired their rights from Elizabeth I. Her Majesty's Swan-keeper and the companies' Barge-masters and Swan-markers go upstream from Sunbury to Pangbourne, the Crown claiming all unmarked swans and cygnets on the river. The Vintners' Swan-marker cuts a double nick, the Dyers' Swan-marker a single nick on the fledged progeny of their swans. Today it is reckoned that there are some 18,000 mute swans in Great Britain, almost entirely resident, and descended (though the swan was a native bird) from the semi-domesticated stock.

In the Middle Ages and Tudor times, when London had scarcely broken out of the City bounds, a thousand or two thousand swans could sometimes be seen floating on the clean lake of the Thames above London Bridge, one of the notable attractions of London. Swan-owners in the past maintained swan-pits in which the birds were fattened. The only one remaining belongs to Great Hospital or St. Helen's Hospital, Norwich, and was built, or rebuilt, in 1793, a long tank with two feet of water, one end of which is a sloping swan-walk up to the enclosure. Until the end of the last century, young swans were fattened for Christmas in this swan-pit, taking their food out of floating troughs.

Sweat-houses

Sweat-houses in Ireland (where several are preserved, e.g. one by Killelagh Lough, Tirkane, Co. Derry, another at Cadian near Benburb, Co. Tyrone) were in use up to this century, dry-walled little buildings, often constructed like BEEHIVE HUTS, with a corbelled roof, a chimney hole and a stone lintelled doorway, usually near a stream. Four or five households often shared a sweat-house (Irish *tighthe alluis*). It would be heated for some twenty-four hours with a turf fire, the ashes were then swept out, green rushes were spread on the earth or stone floor to protect the feet of naked people who sat round on turf seats or stools for a good sweat; after which they cooled off in the stream or with water from the stream. A sweat-house is to be found among the Dark Age monastic buildings on Inishmurray off the Sligo coast. There is another inside a cashel or stone fort at Moneygashel in Co. Cavan. But it is impossible to say when the Irish first took to using the sweat-house, as a cure for rheumatic aches and pains. It may have originated in the Greek sweating-chamber or *laconicum*. It may have been a peasant adaptation of the hot room in the private or public baths of Roman Britain (*see* HYPOCAUST). It may have been introduced from Rome by Irish monks and missionaries of St. Patrick's time. It may simply be an Irish country version of the hot-air baths employed through most of Europe in the Middle Ages, England included – a crude version of the English 'hothouse' or 'stew' of the 16th and 17th centuries (both of which words, from the goings-on in the public hothouses and stews of London, became synonyms for brothel).

Sycamore

Sycamore (*Acer pseudoplatanus*) is not a native tree, however well it seems to fit into the British Isles. It began to be planted in England in the last decades of the 16th century (Scotland may have had sycamores in the 15th century), when it was found excellent for the newly fashionable shade walks and AVENUES of the country house. It grew quickly, it tolerated different soils, and though it came from southern Europe it was a mountain tree which could withstand high winds – especially sea winds – and extremes of low temperature. John Evelyn (*Sylva*, 1664) did not care for the sycamore because the fallen leaves turned rotten with the first damp of autumn, 'so as they contaminate and marr our walks'. But it was still much planted, and by this time must already have been naturalizing itself as a Jacobean or Caroline addition to the English landscape. Note how the sycamore will flourish high up round very exposed moorland farmsteads, from Scotland to Wales and Cornwall, and in Ireland.

Talkin TARN, *a small mountain lake at Talkin, near Brampton, Cumbria.*

Tal-

Tal- in Welsh place-names, means 'end': Tal-y-llyn, 'lake end'.

Tarn

For small and especially upland lakes, tarn is a word proper to the small lakes of the Norwegian-settled counties of the Lake District and North Yorkshire, from the Old Norse *tjorn* or *tarnu*.

Wordsworth liked the lakes down below for a sense of joy, purity and fertility, the tarns up above for melancholy and a 'not unpleasing sadness'. The differences are well analysed in his *Guide to the Lakes* – down in the vales, the lakes, with fertile shores, fed not only by brooks and torrents, but by 'internal

springs ... which circulate through them like veins', making them 'truly living lakes, *vivi lacus*'; the tarns above, naked, with water 'black and sullen' except in the sunshine, silent, surrounded by broken rocks, overhung by precipices; and he quotes himself on such a tarn where December's snow persists even into the summer month of June –

> There, sometimes does a leaping fish
> Send through the tarn a lonely cheer,
> The crags repeat the raven's croak
> In sympathy austere.
> Thither the rainbow comes, the cloud,
> And mists that spread the flying shroud,
> And sunbeams, and the sounding blast.
> *Fidelity*

Temple

In the names of villages, farms, etc., temple usually indicates that the land there for a time in the Middle Ages belonged to the Knights Templar, the Poor Knights of Christ and the Temple of Solomon, founded in about 1118 to guard the shrines of the Holy Land and the pilgrims who visited them. The Temple in London, on the river side of Fleet Street, was the chief house of the Templars in England. These Soldiers of God were financed in their work by the ownership of manors and estates throughout Europe, on which they sometimes maintained a preceptory, to give shelter to pilgrims, and look after the farming and the flocks. Twelfth century records of the preceptory of Temple Rockley, in a fold of the

Marlborough Downs, in Wiltshire, speak of employment of women to milk the sheep and make cheese. The order was charged in 1308 with unnatural crimes, blasphemies and heresies, such was its wealth and power, and was suppressed, many of its lands in England, Wales, Scotland and Ireland going to the Knights of the Order of St. John, the Hospitallers.

Ten Commandments

When the old wall-paintings of mediaeval Christianity depicting the legends of the saints were destroyed, or plastered over or whitewashed at the Reformation, the authorities encouraged church decorations which they considered more edifying and less superstitious. Under Edward VI the Ten Commandments were painted on the tympana across the chancel arch – literacy being more common in the new age – and under Elizabeth I it was laid down that the Commandments should be displayed at the east end of the chancel, where they would be read by communicants. Sometimes they were painted direct on to the wall, sometimes on wooden panels, sometimes they were made part of the REREDOS above the altar or communion table. Frequently, as one sees, the Ten Commandments were flanked with the Lord's Prayer and the Creed, so that parishioners had before their eyes 'the essentials of Christian morality, Christian faith, and Christian prayer'.

Terracettes

Terracettes, 'little terraces', give a familiar ridged or scarred effect to a grassy slope, if it is steep enough, an effect very clearly seen when the early morning or evening sun strikes across an escarpment or hillside. Since these long steps run in more or less parallel and horizontal lines, and since they are often used by sheep or cattle, common sense misinterprets them as grazing paths. Sheep or bullocks – or man – may tread the terracettes a bit wider, but in fact they are caused by landslipping in miniature, a downward creeping of the soil due to rain-washing and gravity, the opening and filling up of little cracks, and the hold-up of the descent by tufts of grass. If conditions are right, terracettes form on slopes which are never grazed or trodden.

Tessellated pavements

Tessellated pavements bring us into pleasanter touch with Roman Britain than most other things left from the Roman centuries. As Britain became more Romanized and life more secure, between A.D. 300 and 400, the well-to-do moved from town to country, building more luxurious 'manor-houses' or estate houses (ROMAN VILLAS) and employing mosaic artists to floor them. The artists, some from other parts of the empire (mosaic pavements were a Greek invention), some native, all of them probably itinerant, seem to have used cartoons or specimen books, showing the composition of the Graeco-Roman mythical scenes which they pictured in little *tesserae* of different coloured limestone, sandstone, etc. Orpheus charming the Beasts was a favourite subject. Other pavements picture Venus and her Cupids, Europa and the Bull, Bacchus, Oceanus, Perseus and Andromeda, Ganymede, and Bellerophon on Pegasus. British schoolchildren read the *Aeneid*, and the nearly perfect floor-mosaic uncovered at Low Ham, Somerset, in 1946 (now in Taunton Castle Museum), depicts Virgil's story of Dido and Aeneas. The strangest villa mosaic yet unearthed (now in the Hull Museum) was found at Rudston on the Wolds, in Humberside, where the mosaicist interpreted any copy he may have had very much in his own way, producing a savage cavorting Venus, stag, leopard, vine tendrils, etc., with the formal vitality and individuality of a Sunday painter. Most pavement accessories, the dolphins, leopards, apes, peacocks, etc., owe as little as the myths to anything observed in Britain. Yet these myths on many of the villa floors, interpretable e.g. as the triumph of life over death, the triumph of good over wickedness, or the journey of the soul to bliss, give a sense of Romano-British life not to be had from Roman roads or lumps of Roman masonry.

Thatch

In Old English, *thæc* at first meant a roof and then came to mean the material for the commonest and cheapest (and warmest) kind of roof, a vegetable roofing whether of straw, reeds, sedge or rush, all of which were used for thatching in the Middle Ages, when tiles or stone tiles or shingles made of oak were used only for buildings of considerable importance. Cities were mainly thatched, London (and Venice) included; and in many English country towns whole streets were still thatched until late in Victorian times. The essence of thatch is clean straw (wheat, rye or barley) or reed, unbroken, free of leaf or seed, arranged in bundles (yelms) in which the straws or reeds are all parallel, as water-paths. The first yelms

Roofs may be THATCHED with straw or with reed, like the cottage being re-thatched in this illustration. The roof's structure is formed with rafters and laths, and the thatcher then begins in one corner by tying, and then fixing with hazel sways, bundles of reed. The final layer is dressed into position for aesthetic reasons.

are tied to the laths and purlins (timbers) of the roof, after which the superincumbent yelms are pegged down with twisted staples or hairpins (spars; in Ireland, the Highlands, and Wales, 'scollops' or 'scolps') of hazel or willow. The roped thatch of some parts of Wales, the Atlantic shores of Ireland, the Western Isles, and the Isles of Scilly, crossed or criss-crossed with ropes tied to stone pegs in the walls and gables, or weighted with stones, is a more primitive form of this primitive roofing, chiefly to be found where roof-stripping gales are likely. A still earlier practice (as on some country buildings in Iceland) was to form the roof of overlapping sods. In Ireland, Wales and the Highlands the two practices are often combined: sods are laid first, with thatch on top.

Thorp(e)

Thorp(e) or -thorp(e) in place-names (Old Danish *thorp*) is commonest in areas which were occupied and settled by the Danes. The meaning is a farmstead or a farm hamlet dependent on a larger farmstead, estate, or village. Often the thorpe and its progenitor go in pairs, thorpes inclining to be small, though they may have risen to being parishes with a church. Thus Shouldham in Norfolk has its Shouldham Thorpe alongside, two parishes, two churches. In Leicestershire there are five neighbouring Langtons. The parent is Church Langton with an ancient church; its chief colony, Thorpe Langton, has another ancient church.

Three Living and Three Dead

In a few churches (one of them the delightful little church of Widford, in the Windrush valley, in Oxfordshire) a mediaeval wall-painting shows the encounter of the Three Living and Three Dead. The story was told in a 13th century French poem, Baudoin de Condé's *Dit des trois morts et des trois vifs*. In the paintings three young courtiers or kings, sometimes on foot, sometimes on horseback, are out hunting in the forest, enjoying the pleasures of life, when they meet three skeletons, who warn them that all must die, rich and poor, and become as they are.

Thunder and lightning

Thunder and lightning used to be ascribed to the angry behaviour of gods (the more powerful and important god in a pantheon, Zeus of the Greeks, Thor of the Norsemen, Thunor of the Anglo-Saxons and Germans), who viciously wielded their thunderbolts, i.e. the burning, splitting, stunning and slaying effects of flashes to earth. It was not an unreasonable explanation when no one knew of electricity or could understand that the thundercloud itself is the electric generator. The flash of forked lightning zigzags to earth from a cloud-

*T*HATCH *at its best is displayed at the Royal Oak Inn, at Winsford, Somerset — an Exmoor village on the River Exe.*

base some 3,000 to 5,000 feet up, the cloud carrying a negative charge in its lower parts (and a positive charge in the upper parts). Sheet-lightning is caused differently, by short-circuiting flashes in the cloud itself. Thunder reverberates from the sudden expansion of air heated along the path of the flash. It can seldom be heard for a distance of more than seven miles; and you can tell, if not infallibly, how far you are from the discharges in a storm by timing the interval between flash and crack, the noise taking five seconds to travel a mile.

As for danger, the worst way of attracting this malignancy of Zeus or Thunor (who have a particular enmity towards golfers) is to be isolated out of doors, on bare hills (hollows and valleys are safer), under a tree which stands by itself (better to shelter in a copse), alongside a wire fence, or in an isolated hut, barn or cart-shed. For more than 2,000 years it was believed that you could avert lightning or thunderbolt by planting house-leek on the roof – house-leek having been the sacred plant of the Roman thunder-god Jupiter and of the German Thunor. On English thatched houses the house-leek was grown on a clay ridging. This can still be seen on thatched houses in Normandy.

-thwaite

-thwaite names in the Lake District, the North Riding and especially the West Riding, are from the Old Norse *thveit*, which to the Norwegians meant a clearing, a field or meadow won by cutting down scrub and trees.

Toft

A place-name word found where Danes settled, toft meaning a piece of ground in which a house was built, as in Norfolk's Toft Monks (which became monastic property) or Suffolk's Lowestoft (the house-place or house-ground of the Dane named Hlothvír). The lawyer's term 'toft and croft' meant the house-place and the croft or small field which went with it.

Toll-houses

Toll-houses, by which the Turnpike roads of the 18th and 19th centuries were controlled, can usually be recognized by the way they project slightly, and with a slight threat of 'halt and pay', into the line of the road. As buildings reflecting the taste of local gentry on the Turnpike Trusts, they are often classical or neo-Gothic with castellation and pointed windows, or examples of Regency or Early Vic-

torian picturesque, sometimes octagonal or hexagonal, like the miniature COTTAGES ORNÉS often made in Staffordshire earthenware. A board or a stone may still be lettered with the tolls for beast and vehicle; and there may be a blocked-up ticket hole in the wall.

The idea of the Turnpike Trust was thought up in the last years of the 17th century, when the parish repair of roads was found to be altogether inadequate. Trusts proliferated through the 18th century. Each was established by its own Act of Parliament, which empowered the trustees to repair or rebuild a particular length of highway and finance their work by the tolls taken, at turnpikes or gates across the road, by 'pikemen' who lived in the toll-houses alongside. (The original turnpikes, superseded by gates of an ordinary kind, were tapering bars of iron or wood pivoted and turning on a central pillar.) The moderately irksome tolls, ranging from a farthing for a calf, a pig, or a lamb, to sixpence per carriage horse and sixpence per carriage (at some turn-pikes heavily loaded vehicles were weighed on huge weighing machines), did not apply to pedestrians, to farmers' dung carts, harvest carts or wagons or farmers' cattle between farm and field, or to traffic *en route* for church or funeral. But on Sundays tolls were doubled. A ticket at the gate would give a day's clearance out and back only for so much of the turnpike. Not infrequently the Trustees barred the sideroads leading into the route.

Roads once administered in this way show more evidence than an occasional toll-house. The Trustees widened roads, bridged a good many fords, cut through hilltops to reduce gradients, or sent the road sideways up an escarpment to avoid a narrow and impossible depth of hollow way, which often remains as a half-choked path or lane. They also made a good many roads which were altogether new. Surfacing of turnpikes was another matter, not very successful or durable until the methods of J. L. McAdam, himself a turnpike trustee, began to be adopted after the end of the Napoleonic Wars.

Tomen

Tomen in Welsh place-names is a mound – usually the earthen mound or motte (*see* MOTTE-AND-BAILEY) of one of the many campaign castles of the Norman invaders, as at Tomen y Mur ('mound of the wall'), near the Trawsfynydd lake in Gwynedd, where the green motte of the Middle Ages stands up inside a first century Roman fort,

-ton

-ton, a main ending and a main word of English place-names, which is loaded, though not all of the load is decipherable, with the early history of the English people. It is the Old English *tūn*. To begin with, *tūn* may have meant a fence, and then the place inside a fence. The primary thing you fence in a world of uncertainty is your house; and from your house you went out to farm your share of the common lands. So *tūn* came to mean enclosure, house, and farmstead all in one – a word not of the first settlements in a strange land, the first 'hams' (*see* -HAM), but of the farmsteads gradually established over the centuries as more and more land for a livelihood was won from waste and forest. Many descriptive words go with -ton, but the commonest way of distinguishing a *tūn* was to add the name of its owner: you had better buy a horse from Buppa's *tūn* (Bupton), there are two men to see you from Ordric's *tūn* (Orcheston), etc.

The people of the *tūn* increased, more land was taken in, the *tūn* became a village within a larger estate, or manor; and *tūn* became the word for such a complex. The lord built a church, the priest had his surrounding PARISH, often co-extensive with the bounds of the estate. The *tūn*, still with the name of its long-forgotten owner or founder tagged to it, or distinguished perhaps by royal or monastic or episcopal ownership (Kingston, Monkton, Bishopstone, etc.), may not have stopped at being a village. Geographically well placed, it may have grown out of village size. So in the Middle Ages tun, as a separate word, in ordinary speech, comes to mean the larger agglomeration of houses, the town, as we spell it and pronounce it. But old meanings die hard. In the countryside 'churchtown' is still used in some counties for the village or hamlet round a church, and 'town' for a farmstead, the complex of yard, buildings and dwelling-house – the sense which occurs in the song (at least as old as the 15th century) about the fox and the geese:

> John, John, John, the grey goose is gone
> And the fox has run out of the town O.

One class of *tūn* names has been much argued about, the ones ending -ington. Many, but by no means all of these, are like the -ingham names (*see* -HAM). They were the *tūns* of this or that man's family or followers (Hullavington, the *tūn* of the people of Hūnlāf, the 'Hunlafings'; Luckington, the *tūn* of the 'Lacings', Laca's people). They seem to be

the oldest of the *tūn* names, coming after the -inghams.

Toot-hills

Toot-hills (also, on the map, Tot-hill, Tuttle, Tout, etc.), were hills resorted to regularly in times of danger, from which men tooted or toted or kept watch – look-out hills. The name, and function, of a particular toot-hill may be as old as the 9th and 10th centuries, when one may think of watchers on a toot-hill on the look-out for a column of Danish raiders, or a Danish army. Not infrequently there was some kind of a watch-house (in Old English a *tōtaern* or a *weard-setl*, words which survive in place-names) to shelter watchers on the toot-hill – or even a watch-tower. (Wyclif's 14th century version of Isaiah 21. 8, 'Upon the toothill of the Lord I am stondende', became the more familiar 'Lord, I stand continuously on the watch-tower'.) The watch-tower might be no more than a cairn, giving additional height, as on the ward-hills or wart-hills of Shetland and Orkney. In Dorset, Hounstout, Hambury Tout and Worbarrow Tout are clifftop look-outs. Sometimes toot or tout seems to be a word for barrow, though really in a barrow name it signifies that the top was a tooting point. Some garden mounds were also known as toot-hills.

Tor

Tor, for moorland hills in Devon and Cornwall, may go back anciently to a Cornish word for 'belly', and so a bellying shape. This would certainly fit the way in which weathering has moulded the outcrops of a granite tor. Tor names for Derbyshire hills (Higgar Tor, Chee Tor, Pickering Tor, Mam Tor, etc.) are said to be due to Cornish miners who came to work the lead mines of the Peak during the Middle Ages. Tor can also refer to a high rock, or pile of rocks, on the top of a hill.

Glastonbury TOR, Somerset, is familiar as a landmark from many miles away. It is crowned by a 14th century tower which marks the site of a chapel destroyed by a landslide in 1271.

Tower houses

Tower houses are common in Northumberland and across the border, and in Ireland, an expression of the uncertainties of existence in those parts in and after the late Middle Ages. Scotland and Northumberland know them as peles or peels, because the rectangular thick-walled living tower rose to one side of a courtyard inside a peel or pale, i.e. a stockade of earth and logs which was usually replaced (as at Edlingham in Northumberland or Borthwick in Lothian) with a stone wall. In

the north these castles in miniature began to go up early in the 14th century, in Ireland in the 15th century. If there was trouble, the family stayed snug in the hall or main living-room on the first floor, with a fireproof vault of stone between themselves and the entrance room on the ground floor below, having barred the stone steps inside the wall or round a newel, or drawn up the ladder if no stairs were provided. The entrance room was often a dairy. The room above the first-floor hall was the bedroom of the master and mistress. Some Irish tower houses (e.g. Audley's Castle and Walshestown Castle, near Strangford, Co. Down) have a defensive 'murder hole' or peep hole set in the hall floor just above the entrance. Tower houses were built by squires and lairds and small proprietors including clergymen (e.g. the parson's peles at Embleton, Elsdon and Corbridge in Northumberland) and, in some Irish towns liable to attack, by well-to-do merchants. Five merchants' tower houses of the 15th century still grouped in the little port of Ardglass in Co. Down.

Kinnairdy Castle TOWER HOUSE, *near Aberchirder, Banffshire, Scotland, was built to an L-plan and finely restored by Sir Thomas Innes of Learney, later the Lord Lion King of Arms.*

Tracery

Like eyes in a face, windows in a building catch the first look; and in Gothic architecture window tracery, the way of dividing the pointed window space, or more exactly its upper portion, became a characteristic beauty of the style, and one which was not too costly for the parish church. Like much else in mediaeval architecture (e.g., the development of VAULTING, or the FLYING BUTTRESS), tracery achieved an equation between constructional need and aesthetic need. Glass improved, glazing became more common; but if light was to be admitted at all freely, the glazing needing to cover a considerable area, and so needed support against the push of the wind. Tracery was the answer, aesthetically and practically; and the window developed from two lancets set side by side to the 13th century window with the thin mullions (the uprights) criss-crossing into clear-cut arches and small divisions at the top; which in turn changed to the Decorated window of the first half of the 14th century, proliferating into net-like or sinuous openings at the top. The reaction to this flamboyance, last of all, was the Perpendicular window, more flatly arched, with a more dignified emphasis on width as well as on vertical lines from bottom to top. The addition of transoms, horizontal bars of stone from side to side, made this ultimate kind of tracery the perfect frame for light and for STAINED GLASS.

Traeth

In Cornish and Welsh seaside place-names, traeth is a beach, a strand (as the Irish use the word so evocatively), from the Latin *tractus*, a stretch. In Irish and Highland names the word is *tràigh*. Traeth Mawr in Wales, Tramore in Ireland: 'great beach'. Millendreath, near Looe in Cornwall: 'mill beach'.

Treasure trove

Treasure trove is the name in law for valuables of gold and silver which were hidden by the owner in the ground or in some secret place, and have since been unearthed or discovered (Old French *tresor trové*). The owner hides it, not to abandon ownership, but hoping, when a more propitious time comes, to take it again for his enjoyment. If that time has never come and a stranger to him unearths his treasure, the stranger would not acquire ownership. The legal owner would still be the hider or his representative; and the finder is under a duty to report his find. If he fails to do so, he commits a crime. When the find is reported, the coroner summons a jury to say whether in fact it is treasure trove. If it is and the owner cannot be traced, the treasure trove belongs to the Crown; the finder may expect a money reward – *ex gratia*, however, and not of right. If the jury decides it is not treasure trove, the find comes into the category of chattels which have been either abandoned or lost. You abandon a thing to get rid of it: you relinquish ownership, and the finder acquires ownership. He must, though, be able to satisfy the court that nothing suggested to him that the owner could be traced and still wanted the valuables. To keep to yourself what you find, when you know or could know the owner, is the crime of stealing.

Anyone who finds lost chattels has this to remember, too, that stealing is an offence against possession of property, and that the law, astute in devising convenient fictions, often imputes possession that the possessor may not be aware of. In the case of *Hibbert v. McKiernan*, a trespasser on golf-links had found some golf-balls. They were lost, it was true, at least temporarily: they had escaped from the possession of the unlucky golfers; but, said the law, they had come into the possession of the club that owned the links. So it was adjudged that the trespasser had stolen them. In another case, *South Staffs Water Board v. Sharman* (Queen's Bench 1896) the defendant had been employed to clean out a pool on the company's land, and in doing so he found two gold rings in the mud. The owner of the rings was untraceable and the court said it was the company which was entitled to them. 'If', declared the Lord Chief Justice, 'something is found on land, whether by an employee or the owner or by a stranger, the possession is in the owner of the land.'

Treasure trove in England goes to the British Museum, in Wales to the National Museum at Cardiff, in Northern Ireland to a Northern Irish museum; and it is the British Museum which decides the 'full antiquarian value' granted to the finder. Scottish law is not the same. To be treasure trove in Scotland an object does not have to be gold or silver. It can be of any material. It does not have to have been hidden in the earth; and since anything that is found belongs willy-nilly to the Crown, there is no need for coroner or jury.

Tree of Jesse

From about the 12th century onwards much thought and meditation were devoted to the Radix Jesse or Tree of Jesse, father of King David, which frequently appears in church carvings and windows (and illuminated manuscripts). Combined in the concept of the Tree are a statement from the Old Testament (Isaiah 2. 1), 'And there shall come forth a rod out of the stem of Jesse, and a Branch shall grow out of his roots,' and from the New Testament the long genealogy of Christ which opens St. Matthew's Gospel; and according to the widely popular ideas of the mystical theologian of the 12th century, Joachim of Fiore, the Tree expressed both the harmony between the Old Testament and the New, and the Three Ages of the history of Man – the Age of the Law, the Age of the Gospel, and (if there is a dove) the final Age of the Spirit. The ascending Vine or Tree lent itself especially to the height and intricacy of a window. Rooted in the mid-parts of a sleeping Jesse reclining across the central lights, a coloured vine rises and spreads and climbs to the TRACERY, its branches curling left and right around its genealogical fruits, its images of the kings and the prophets who were ancestral to the Virgin and to Christ, until the Virgin is reached with Christ on her lap as the ultimate fruit – or above the Virgin there may be a Christ crucified, and above Christ again, a Dove. There is a particularly splendid Jesse window in Dorchester Abbey, Oxfordshire.

Tree of Life

Very simply schematized, the Tree of Life was frequently carved on Romanesque fonts or on a TYMPANUM over a church door. The font and the church door were regarded as entrances into life, and the carver, or those who instructed him, would have had in mind not only Christ saying 'I am the door' (John 10. 1), but two sentences from the Revelation, 'To him that overcometh will I give to eat of the tree of life which is in the midst of the paradise of God' (Rev. 2. 7) and 'Blessed are they that do his commandments, that they may have right to the tree of life, and may enter in through the gates into the city'. The evil-doers were outside, the good inside. Sometimes the Tree of Life is displayed with lions on either side eating the fruit.

Tree-rings

Tree-rings are in fact the marks of growth year by year. Count the rings from centre to circumference across a tree-trunk or the stump, and you have the age in years – more or less, since for an exact count the cross-section would have to be exceptionally clear and smooth. The rings arise from the seasonal alteration of growth and rest, mild and frosty. In the spring a new layer of wood forms under the bark around the previous year's growth, consisting of large cells with thin walls; this layer of 'spring-wood' thickens, but as growth tails off in summer the cells become smaller and the walls between them less thin, showing – when the trunk is cut across – as a darker circle of 'autumn-wood' bordering the spring wood. The growing season comes to an end, and the tree rests, until next year's season of new wood and a new dark-edged ring; and so on. The older the tree gets the narrower the rings, which is where one usually trips up in the count; and now and again one year may have a double ring, growth having started, slackened off, stopped, and started again. Counting from outside inwards – if you know when the tree was felled – you can sometimes tell which year was good or bad for growth, and it may be possible to check this against weather records. A ring wider than its neighbours indicates a good growing year – which probably was less good for humans – while a ring narrower than its neighbours indicates that there was drought and starvation that year – an extra 'fine' spring and summer. The ring variations repeat themselves from tree to tree in a climatic area. So archaeologists – or dendrochronologists – can work out a standard growth plot for different periods, historic and up to a point prehistoric, by which timber can be dated.

Tref-

Tref- or Tre- (Welsh), Trev- or Tre- (Cornish), very common at the beginning of place-names in Wales and Cornwall, primarily means a homestead or farmstead. A Welsh *tref* may have grown into a village or even into a town (*tref* is the modern Welsh for a town, though it also keeps the old meaning of home). But in place-names *tref* corresponds, with differences owing to a different way of life, to the English *tūn* (*see* -TON). The *tūn* developed frequently into the village complete with manor-house and church and surrounding parish. The *tref* (in Welsh a village is a *pentref*, or chief *tref*) more often remains, as one can see

from a glance at the map, an isolated farmstead, which is true of the Cornish *trev* or *tre*. The church (or LLAN- of Welsh, and Lan- of Cornish place-names) and the *tref* do not coincide, the *llan* having been founded earlier by the wandering Celtic saint whose name it is likely to bear, as a hermitage or small eremitical monastery. In the Middle Ages the *llan* became a Catholic church for a congregation, but often remained as isolated as ever, altogether separate from the farmsteads and gathering no village around itself.

'Trespassers will be prosecuted'

An idle notice, though a very common one. In the days when unauthorized interference with another's land had a brawl as the usual consequence, a man could be fined or imprisoned for such interference, such 'trespass', which was a crime as well as a civil wrong; the threat to prosecute, i.e. to bring him to trial on a criminal charge, could be fulfilled. But that had gone even before the Limitation Act of 1623, which gave the trespasser a defence against a civil suit – the defence being that 'if the defendant disclaims any title to the land and proves that the trespass was negligent or involuntary and that he had tendered sufficient amends before the action was brought, the plaintiff will be non-suited'. In Shaw's play *Back to Methuselah* the Elderly Gentleman knows his law: when he is challenged he says 'Is this land private property? If so I make no claim. I proffer a shilling in satisfaction of damage (if any), and am ready to withdraw if you will be good enough to show me the nearest way.'

You can be prosecuted for trespass in pursuit of game or trespass on a railway, Parliament for those offences having revived the old penalizing of trespass. But you cannot be prosecuted for trespass to look at the view or to pick primroses or bluebells or blackberries or mushrooms, or for taking a short cut across the field. The farmer or landowner can seek damages. Learning the difference between the words 'sue' and 'prosecute', he could change his notices and make them read 'Trespassers will be sued',

Triforium

In mediaeval churches, triforium is properly a passage in the thickness of a CLERESTORY wall, with openings into the church, provided so that the clerestory windows above could be cleaned. But it is the name commonly given to the more considerable arcaded gallery, lower down, which runs (over the aisles) between the arches of the nave, etc., and the clerestory.

Trigonometrical stations

Marked △ on the 1:25000 and 1:10000 Ordnance Survey maps, trigonometrical stations are the vital survey points from which angles, horizontal and vertical, are determined in the 'triangulation' of the country. Mapping depends on working out a set of triangles, which begin with a base-line. The base-line alone needs to be measured; and from that datum the map-makers can calculate by trigonometry the length of the other two sides of triangle No. 1 established on the base-line – and so on, as they add triangle to triangle. The first triangulation or trigometrical survey, on which our Ordnance Maps are founded, began in 1791 and was finished (England, Wales, Scotland, Ireland) by 1852. Since then many of the carefully determined and marked triangulation points have been lost or obscured. With the new Survey of Britain, i.e. the new primary triangulation, these hilltop points, or trigonometrical stations, are marked and protected and made more permanent by pillars of concrete, with inlays of metal for the surveyor's implements. The sign △ on the map and the concrete pillar on the ground are sure indication of a good view through all points of the compass. Often the trigonometrical station is sited on an ancient BEACON.

Tudor coastal forts

Forerunners of the MARTELLO TOWERS against Napoleon and the concrete pillboxes against Hitler, Henry VIII's castles and blockhouses along the south coast from Kent to Cornwall were the first co-ordinated defence against invasion built since the Romans established the FORTS OF THE SAXON SHORE. Several of them are left: from east to west, Deal Castle (1538–40), the largest and most complex, and Walmer Castle (1538–40), two miles away, now the official residence of the Lord Warden of the Cinque Ports (Sandown Castle, also in Kent, has been reduced to a fragment); Sandgate Castle (1539–41); Camber Castle, between Rye and Winchelsea (building, but not finished, in 1541); West Cowes Castle, on the Isle of Wight, Calshot Castle thrust out into Southampton Water, and Hurst Castle, even more romantically placed on a spit running into the Solent (all building in 1540); ruined Sandsfoot Castle at Weymouth (c. 1541), and Portland Castle (c. 1540), on the Isle of Portland; and in Cornwall, on either side of the Fal estuary, St. Mawes Castle (1540–43) and Pen-

*D*eal Castle, Kent, is the most impressive and best preserved of the chain of TUDOR COASTAL FORTS established by Henry VIII to guard against invasion. The castle is designed in a clover-leaf shape, with a central tower, a water well below and a double set of staircases above. Although the garrison was small it could provide formidable firepower.

233

dennis Castle (*c.* 1541–6). For the royal clerk of the works at St. Mawes, John Leland, the king's antiquary, who was a noted Latin poet, made up lines of Latin verse to be inscribed on the walls – 'Ships, lower your sails to the might of Henry'; 'Henry the Eighth, most invincible king of England, France and Ireland, set me here to watch over the state and bring terror to its enemies'. The enemies were the French, provoked by Henry, who had good reason to fear an attack; and all these fortresses (rather than castles, in the old mediaeval sense) belonged to the gunfire age, each of them, with variations according to position and terrain, a design of low semicircular lunettes, or bastions, round a central tower, with gunports splayed out in the very thick walls to give a wide field of fire. They still had moats and drawbridges, but the squat elevation reduced the target, and the usually circular shape, the rounded lunettes and the rounded battlements were meant to deflect shot. The military significance of these fortresses is explained in B. H. St. J. O'Neil's *Castles and Cannon*, 1960.

Tullagh

Tullagh, tullow, tully, in Irish place-names, tulloch in Highland names, means a hillock (Irish and Gaelic *tulach*).

Turf-dials

Turf-dials were at one time cut in the close grass of sheep-walks and hills in many parts of England, the word dial surviving here and there in such names of fields, hills, etc., as Dialhill (which occurs as far apart as Cumbria and Gloucestershire), Red Dial, Blue Dial (as if the dials were sometimes given coloured divisions), Dial Bank, Dial Mead. The clue comes from Shakespeare, from the king's soliloquy on Towton Field (*3 Henry VI*, Act 2, Scene 5), in which he compares his harassed royal life with the happiness of shepherds –

> O God! methinks it were a happy life
> To be no better than a homely swain;
> To sit upon a hill, as I do now,
> To carve out dials quaintly, point by point,
> Thereby to see the minutes how they run,
> How many makes the hour full complete
> How many hours brings about the day . . .

Perhaps the turf-dial originated as a shepherd's counterpart of the scratch-dial on the mediaeval church (*see* SUNDIALS), telling him out on his distant hills when to observe the canonical hours of prayer. See A. J. L. Gossett's *Shepherds of Britain*, 1911.

Turloughs

In Irish limestone districts, including much of Co. Clare, turloughs are peculiar 'land lakes' (Irish *tur loch*, 'hole lake') – hollows which flood in wet weather into considerable lakes or lakelets, and then dry out as the water-table drops again and the water soaks away through the fissures of the underlying rock. When they have dried out, turloughs, bare of anything like shrubs or trees below a certain level, have several peculiar features: a lining of the vividest green turf, an abundance of wild violets, and often a surrounding zone of dark moss which marks the flood level.

Tympanum

One of the pleasures of the exploration of churches is to find a carved Romanesque tympanum (recessed face of a pediment) over the door. Its symbolism is likely to be fundamental, since the purpose of a carving over the main entrance to the church and the divine presence was to announce forcefully and immediately the ends and objects of Christian observance. Favourite subjects therefore include the formalized TREE OF LIFE; the AGNUS DEI; Christ in Majesty; the Cross; and St. George or St. Michael (*see* ST. MICHAEL'S CHURCHES) slaying the dragon; the DEVIL and death. Among the symbolic animals, as well as the dragon, are LION, GRIFFIN, Wild Boar and Serpent.

Undercliff and overcliff

Along the Devon and Dorset coast and in the Isle of Wight, undercliff and overcliff have been produced by the commonest of landslip mechanisms, a forward movement on wet clay. Bedded on gault clay, the rocks had a dip to the sea. Heavy rain soaked to this impermeable clay and turned it to a slippery inclined plane. The sea having cut into the foot of the cliffs and removed some of the support of the chalk rocks overhead, the rocks broke away, glissaded forward, and then crashed to the sea. Hooken Cliff, between Branscombe Mouth and Beer Head, broke, slid, and fell in this way in 1790, nearly ten acres of land dropping between 200 and 260 feet. Between Seaton and Lyme Regis the same *modus operandi* created the great undercliff region of Dowlands, Whitlands, Pinhay, and Ware, mostly ancient, but much increased by slides and falls in the 18th and 19th centuries, and now forming an exquisite peculiarity of English coast, a broken, low-level tract on its own, floriferous, and with its own micro-

*I*n this external carved TYMPANUM over a doorway to the church of Stretton Sugwas, Hereford and Worcester, Samson is depicted killing a lion.

climate. These are the undercliffs mentioned with delight by Jane Austen in *Persuasion* (finished in 1816, twenty-three years before the great Dowlands slip of 1839) as among the charms of the neighbourhood of Lyme Regis – 'above all, Pinny, with its green chasms between romantic rocks, where the scattered forest trees and orchards of luxuriant growth declare that many a generation must have passed away since the first partial falling of the cliff prepared the ground for such a state, where a scene so wonderful and so lovely is exhibited as may more than equal any of the resembling scenes of the far-famed Isle of Wight'.

Unicorns

In church carving unicorns were Christ-symbols of some complexity. Mediaeval legend said that the powerful, milk-white unicorn was hunted (the hunters were those who did not believe) and could be captured only by a virgin, on whose lap the unicorn laid its head. This scene is sometimes visible on bosses and MISERICORDS, signifying in the incarnation of Christ the Spiritual Unicorn in the Virgin's womb, the unicorn having made himself meek and gentle. Single unicorns occur on bench-ends and fonts; and the horn of Christ the Unicorn was linked to several texts, to the verse in the Psalms (92. 10) speaking of the exaltation of David's horn 'like the horn of an unicorn', and the verse (Luke 1. 69) on the exaltation of the horn of God's salvation in the house of David, i.e. in his descendant, Christ.

Upping-stocks

Upping-stocks or upping-blocks, stone platforms with steps built against farmhouse or farmyard walls, still useful for mounting a horse, speak of the long era of the 'double horse' or riding pillion, before the new macadamized surfaces of the 19th century, the era of horseback rather than horse and trap or dogcart, when the horse alone could manage the deep mud of the winter roads. Behind master or man-servant the women of the house rode pillion for social calls, church-going, visits to shop or market. Notice how often the upping-stock or block (variously known as horse-stone, horse-steps, horse-block, mounting-stone) is so built that the pillion passenger can mount or dismount straight into the garden without stepping into the mud of the road or the muck of the farmyard. For the return journey there would be upping-blocks outside the inns of town or village, such as the ones

Cobbett remarked upon as a symbol of lost prosperity when he came in 1826 to the decayed village of Withington in the Cotswolds.

Vapour trails

One of the notable beauties added in our time to the sky by day (and often by night), vapour trails are a form of cloud or condensation of vaporized water into visibility. They are produced in the same way as the fog of our breath in cold damp air. Like the air we breathe out from our lungs, the warm exhaust from the aeroplane has its content of vaporized water. So has the cold air which it discharges into, and by which it is cooled until between the two there is more water vapour than the air can hold: around the dust particles in the air the vapour then condenses into the trails of 'cloud' we see from the ground, white or pink according to the time of day, against a blue background; or perhaps lit by a full moon, if the planes continue into the night.

Vaulting

Vaulting in stone, tierceron vaults, lierne vaults and fan vaults, will be seen in parish churches usually on a small scale over porch or chantry chapel or under a tower. Vaulting having been introduced in the 12th century, Gothic masons elaborated the division of each vaulted compartment of a roof by introducing 'tiercerons', extra subdividing ribs crossing to the ridge-ribs; and then subdivided the vaulted compartment still more with shorter internal ribs or liernes, which• create overhead an extraordinary intricacy of star-patterns between boss and boss. Fan vaulting, the ultimate form of vaulting a mediaeval roof with stone, is one of the most dramatic distinctions of the English Perpendicular style. The ribs fan up and out in half-trumpets or half-cones from either wall, curving up on each half-trumpet from a single point; and the spaces between rib and rib are filled with blind TRACERY. King's College Chapel in Cambridge is the classic example of fan vaulting on the grand scale; and fan-vaulted chantries and porches in pale freestone were often added to parish churches – especially to churches in the wealthy wool district of the Cotswolds – during the pre-Reformation decades.

Vega

Above all the star of summer, more or less overhead in the zenith during the summer months, Vega is the most conspicuous star in

The Capture of the UNICORN, *on a misericord (1390), Chester Cathedral.*

the not very conspicuous constellation of Lyra (the lyre of Orpheus, the first poet, and proper patron of poets). It is among the minimum number of stars one needs to be able to recognize, and know with affection, long singled out by the various peoples of the world. Despite Orpheus and his Lyre, Vega is a shortening of the star's Arabic name *al nasr al waqis*, the falling vulture (*nasr*, vulture).

Vestry

In the Middle Ages the priest vested himself in the chancel and the sacred vessels for the mass were usually kept in an AUMBRY in the chancel wall, the vestments in an oak chest (such as the one which survives in Old Radnor church in Wales, in which there were chantry altars as well as the high altar). Even the great monastic churches managed as a rule with cupboards and no vestry. But though the vestry, or sacristy, of a parish church is often modern, sometimes built on, sometimes contrived by shutting off part of an aisle or adapting an old chantry, little rooms for the purpose began to be added quite commonly for the priest's convenience when churches were rebuilt or refashioned in the 14th century, usually on the north side of the chancel, with a priest's door between the two. The vestry, though (particularly in town churches), might be ample enough for parish meetings. So 'vestry' became the common word for such a meeting, which decided on parish and church affairs, a function now divided between parish council and parochial church council.

Village greens

Who owns the green? It is often a difficult (and a necessary) point to decide. The look and charm and comfort and convenience of a village may depend on the green open spaces among the houses; and by customary right, if no other, it is used for village games or entertainments, as a site for fairs and fêtes and so on. It may be common land, as part of the enclosed waste of the manor, and villagers may have rights of common on the green, turning sheep or cows or geese out to graze on its turf. Or it may be part of the king's highway, threaded now by a road with permanent boundaries, but in former times allowing plenty of room for a way around ruts and holes and pools. The Royal Commission on Common Land recommended in 1958 that greens should be registered as common, and then maintained by local authorities; and this was the way in which a green was defined:

'Any place which has been allotted for the exercise or recreation of the inhabitants of a parish or defined locality under the terms of any local Act or inclosure award, any place in which such inhabitants have a customary right to indulge in lawful sports and pastimes and in a rural parish' – since there are town as well as rural greens – 'any uninclosed open space which is wholly or mainly surrounded by houses or their curtilages and which has been

continuously and openly used by the inhabitants for all or any such purposes during a period of at least twenty years without protest or permission from the owner of the fee simple or the lord of the manor.'

Villages

However changed, villages retain evidences and relics of the way in which they originated and developed, and the older ways in which they worked. Essentially the village, with church, manor-house and village green, in the middle of parish lands, is an institution deriving from the Anglo-Saxon settlements which began late in the 5th century: it does not belong to the Celtic areas of Great Britain in which life was differently organized.

Village names are likely to end with -ton, from the Old English *tūn*, which, from a farmstead with its small community, came to

The VILLAGE *of Castle Coombe in Wiltshire, as well as being one of the most visited villages in England, is also one of the most characteristic. At the centre of the system is the church (mainly Perpendicular) and the manor house (to its left, but not in the picture). The stone cottages follow the line of the Bye brook, crossed by a romanesque bridge, and lead up to the ancient market cross.*

mean the larger community of several farms, adding up to a village. Often the village name is a combination of *tūn* with the name of a man who may have established and owned the first settlement – Fittleton, Fitela's *tūn*, Orcheston, Ordric's *tūn*, etc. – though of course the particular *tūn* may have been distinguished by name in many other ways, e.g. by its relation to a natural feature, Wotton (wood *tūn*), or its size, Broad Town (large *tūn*), or a peculiarity of its early inhabitants, Fisherton (*tūn* of the fishermen – a Wiltshire village whose people gave time to fishing in the river Wylye). If its name is one foundation relic, or early relic, of a village, another may be some still detectable peculiarity of geology, shelter, soil, dryness in wet surroundings, etc., which determined the site; and particularly the presence of a spring, which may still be the village supply.

The village began as associations of families of peasants, who lived by shares in the great open FIELDS: they were free, but owed various services and dues to their king. By the seventh century many villagers found themselves, under a lord, less free than they had been, the king having granted to the lord the services due to himself. Living on his home farm, the lord came to exact labour service from the peasants in exchange for their houses and lands: they became serfs bound to the lord's estate, subject in daily life to justice in the courts of the estate.

When village estates passed to new Norman and other lords after the Conquest, new French definitions came to be applied. The village estate with its open fields became a manor (Old French *manoir*, a dwelling). The land which the lord kept in his own hands became his demesne (Old French *demeine*, *dominiun*, the land of the *dominus* or lord). The villagers, or serfs, or villeins (Old French *villain*) called the lord's house the 'hall': among homes more in the nature of hovels (*see* FARMHOUSES) it would have been the one substantial dwelling, consisting in the main of a large hall open to the roof. In Elizabethan times the hall in this special sense became known as the manor-house.

The fact that even today the farmsteads, or several of them, may continue to be grouped together in the village is explained by the Anglo-Saxon village of family farmsteads, and family lands made up of holdings in the open fields. The church – or the first church built on the present site – may have been provided by the lord before or after the Conquest, the parish having been determined as the church district (*see* PARISHES, PARISH CHURCHES). Evidence of the ways in which the village estate or manor was organized may remain in the relation of the village to the bounds of the old open fields and pastures, still discernible in spite of the enclosures of the 18th century: in the COMMON; in the VILLAGE GREEN; in the manorial WATER-MILL, or windmill in a streamless district, at which all tenants had to grind; and in the pound, the stone enclosure (sometimes contrived with access to water) in which the pinder shut up the stray animals, which might be redeemed with a fine. Evidence of the lord's position and privileges may show not only in a manor-house, and a farm still known as Home Farm or Manor Farm, but in a CONYGER for his rabbits, a DOVECOTE of stone or brick for the pigeons which only a lord of the manor could possess, a deer PARK for his venison; in ancient effigies in the church; in a special family pew with a fireplace and a separate entrance, perhaps contrived in the 18th century within the limits of a former CHANTRY in which prayers were chanted for the lord's soul.

Contrariwise the nonformist chapel, the school, the village institute, the council houses in place of dilapidated cots, the notice of a meeting of the parish council, bus stops, private garages, and TV aerials, and much else, speak of the emancipation of the village from lordship, paternalism, and cap-touching.

Vine

Vine, with grapes, in church carvings and decoration, is one of the commonest and most ancient symbols of Christ, and his church, deriving from St. John's Gospel (15. 1, 5), in which Christ says 'I am the true vine' and 'I am the vine, ye are the branches: He that abideth in me, and I in him, the same bringeth forth much fruit'. Representations of the vine and grapes go back to Byzantine, Coptic and Syrian art, and will be found on the early 8th century crosses carved by Northumbrian sculptors, e.g. (*see* RUNES) the shafts of the famous Ruthwell and Bewcastle crosses.

Vineyards

Carvings of the grape harvest on MISERICORDS (as in Gloucester Cathedral, or the church at Ripple, near Tewkesbury) are not all of them depicting something which was unfamiliar in mediaeval England. Vineyards were maintained in many counties, especially in the south and south Midlands, from the 11th century at least, and the name Vineyard remains not uncommonly attached to the old sites, e.g. in

Hereford and Worcester, Warwickshire, Somerset, and particularly Gloucestershire, which was celebrated for its wines in the 12th century, and still kept up a tradition of viticulture in the 18th century. William of Malmesbury, in his account of the bishops and monasteries of England written *c.* 1123, stated that no English county had more vineyards and that wines from the Vale of Gloucester were not unpleasantly sharp and fell little short of French wines in sweetness. There were vineyards belonging to the Gloucestershire monks, including the monks of what is now Gloucester Cathedral, up and down the Severn, around Gloucester, and on the well-drained limestone slopes of the Cotswold escarpment, on sites facing south, or south-east, sheltered from northerly winds and the prevailing south-west wind. It is tempting to think that growing vines in Gloucestershire began with the Romans. In 1894–5 a Roman pit with grape skins was excavated in the middle of Gloucester itself. But the floruit of the English vineyard seems to have coincided with an exceptionally warm period from about A.D. 1000 to 1300 (when the Viking colonies in Greenland also flourished), which was followed by a resumed decline in temperature. Somerset vineyards included one of seven acres at Dunster (on the slopes behind the mediaeval Luttrell Arms Hotel), maintained from the 12th to the 15th century by the Mohuns of Dunster Castle, who supplemented the wine from their own press with much wine from France; and a vineyard on the south slope of the famous Wirral Hill at Glastonbury, which was long cultivated for the Benedictines of the abbey. Vineyards were also placed on the sheltered valley slopes leading down to Bath, for instance at Colerne, by what is now the Vineyard Restaurant, and at Claverton. John Aubrey considered that the vineyard at Claverton planted in his day by Sir William Bassett was the best in England. Wine was still being made from the Claverton grapes in 1705. Vines were grown further north, but possibly more for verjuice (the juice of unripe grapes used in sauces, etc.) than wine. If the Welsh 14th century poet Iolo Goch is to be trusted, the Bishop of St. Asaph's, in north Wales, dispensed wine from his own grapes. In one of his poems he writes of taking wine in the Bishop's Palace 'From his vineyard, from his white hand'. In another of his poems (*see* DOVECOTES) he mentions the vineyard at Owen Glendower's mansion of Sycharth in Clwyd.

Virga

The meteorological term for the dark-seeming veils of rain which depend from rain clouds and thunder clouds like wispy twigs (*virga* is Latin for twig) or wispy fingers, but never actually reach the ground.

Voe

In Shetland a voe (Old Norse *vágr*) is a bay, usually a long winding inlet such as Gruting Voe or Ronas Voe on the west coast, a firth or fjord, in contrast to the small WICK or GEO. It is one of the many relics of the Norse spoken by the Shetlanders till the 18th century.

Wall-paintings

Wall-paintings in a church were looked upon as an essential means of instructing the unlettered and rousing their devotion. Words written by St. Gregory the Great in 604 established and justified the principle that pictures were *biblia pauperum*, the bible of the poor – that is to say, books for those who could not read – and an English monk writing about 1200 on the proper subjects for the church wall agreed that paintings suggested to the unlearned that which belonged to God, while exciting in the learned a due love of the scriptures. Paintings, in consequence, were the proper finish to a church, as newly built or transformed, rather than an adornment which might or might not be added subsequently. Painters by profession went from church to church. The newly plastered walls were wetted with lime-water and smoothed with a ground of lime putty (i.e. stiff slaked lime), and then painted with inexpensive earth colours (mostly), ground and tempered with skim-milk or lime or lime-water. Lime was the medium. 'If a particle of pigment is surrounded by lime water, and the water dries away, the particle of pigment gets caught in the net of lime crystals like a fly in a spider's web' (Daniel V. Thompson). Some of the more delicate work was done with pigment and size. The pigments certainly included the iron oxides, the great colourers of the surface of the earth (giving red, brown, purple and yellow); malachite (green carbonate of copper); lampblack (soot from candles) and fine charcoal blacks; and for white, lime putty. Blue effects were achieved by setting charcoal greys alongside warm colours, though azure or azurite (carbonate of copper) was also used. Vermilion (derived from red sulphide of mercury) went into the more garish wall-paintings of the 15th century. Scallop shells came in

239

A modern and productive **VINEYARD** *at Lamberhurst, Kent.*

handy for taking enough pigment to the wall; and the painters' brushes were hair from squirrels' tails for fine work and hogs' hair. Painters, it was complained, often ground their pigments on the stone slab of the altar.

Wall-paintings, the St. Christophers facing the south door, the Christs of the trades, the Seven Works of Mercy, the Seven Deadly Sins, the Dooms, etc., suffered like the rest of church imagery after the Reformation, between the fifteen-forties and the end of the Commonwealth. But though some were hacked away, luckily the cheapest, least messy and most effective way of getting rid of them as Popish idolatry was a coat or two of whitewash. The modern problem when the forgotten paintings are rediscovered under their whitewash, is to preserve them from damp and from the fading which has now made ghost pictures of the many which came back to light in church restorations of the last century. But the chemistry of the paintings is understood; and to see what can be done one should visit the little Gloucestershire church of Kempley, under the Forest of Dean, where restoration and preservation of its hieratic scheme of Romanesque paintings has been completed. English wall-painting is best judged by the solemn Romanesque work and by the more lyrical and tender early Gothic paintings, not by the work of the 15th century which survives in greater quantity, and belongs to a decline due in part to our later mediaeval preference for filling up larger and larger Perpendicular windows (*see* Tracery) with stained glass. Alan Caiger-Smith's *English Mediaeval Mural Paintings* (1963) is the best introduction to this fragmentary and fading wall art, giving, too, a select catalogue of paintings still clear enough to be worth visiting.

Wapentakes

Wapentakes correspond, in the once Danish-speaking Leicestershire, Northamptonshire, Nottinghamshire, Lincolnshire and parts of Yorkshire, to the hundreds elsewhere, the ancient divisions of the shire for the purposes of law and justice. The odd word is from the Old Norse *vápnatak*, which might be translated 'weapon-flourish'. The word first described the way of saying yes at an assembly by a wave of one's weapons, then the assembly itself, then the special assembly of the hundred-like sub-division of the shire, which took place every four weeks; and last of all the sub-division itself.

Waterfalls

Neither very tall, voluminous, or thunderous in Great Britain, waterfalls have certain special areas, including the Lake District and north Wales, Craven and the north-west dales of Yorkshire, and a little-known area in south Wales, near Ystradfellte, which offers some of the most beautiful of 'spouts' – i.e. falls shooting over their inclined cornice in a bow and leaving a space behind them and under them. After the gigantic fosses of Iceland, for example, the falls in all these districts show what poor criteria height and volume are by them-

selves. Analysing waterfalls in his *Guide to the Lakes* (1810), Wordsworth maintained that a fall is often at its best when the flow is moderate, between a flood and a trickle; and he saw the charm of falls partly in 'the contrast between the falling water and that which is apparently at rest, or rather settling gradually into quiet in the pool below'. This expert in the aesthetics of phenomena considered that the beauty of the agitated scene of a fall is heightened 'in a peculiar manner, by the *glimmering*, and towards the verge of the pool, by the *steady* reflection of the surrounding images'. But there is a case for saying that Yorkshire, from Hardrow Force to High Force, and neither the Lake District nor north Wales, has the fosses with the greatest combined charm of water, rock, gorge, and vegetation, falling over their cornices in threads or in curtains. The cornice is the determinate element in falls, preventing the river from cutting down into rapids. It may be a hard stratum of limestone above softer shales (Hardrow Force), a hard stratum of sandstone (the Ystradfellte waterfalls), or a hard vertical upthrust of WHINSILL (High Force, in Teesdale).

A WATERFALL *turned to ice in the Brecon Beacons, Powys.*

Water-meadows

Found in shallow river valleys such as that of the Wylye, water-meadows developed as a farming speciality of the chalk counties of Wiltshire, Hampshire and Dorset. Water was drawn off in a leat from the lucid chalk-streams and allowed to flow into the meadows, which were carefully divided into parallel beds along the downward slope. Old water-meadows can be recognized by these beds, each about 35 feet wide, curved in section, and up to 200 yards long. Flooding or 'drowning' the meadows was an intermittent process very exactly and minutely controlled to produce the highest yield and quality of grass. It went on at proper intervals from November to early spring, when sheep and lambs were folded for a while on the new grass. Drowning then continued till the hay on the meadows was cut, and after the hay harvest it was started again to bring on grass for the autumn grazing of the sheep. Only the light-hoofed sheep were grazed in water-meadows. Cattle were too heavy and clumsy, and would have damaged the carefully managed complex of beds and water-courses. The water flowed on to the beds at the upper end, percolated down their length and into the gullies between them, and flowed back to the river again by drains. It fertilized the soil with mineral salts and kept it warm for the early grass. The great era of this subtle form of cultivation was the 18th and 19th centuries. But there is some evidence that this drowning of meadows goes back to the Middle Ages, and even to Anglo-Saxon farming in the 9th century.

Water-mills and windmills

The water-mill, the primary machine, invented (by the Greeks) in the 1st century B.C., was used in Roman Britain, by the military (e.g. along the Roman Wall) and by civilians; and was certainly used as early as the 8th century by the Anglo-Saxons (a re-introduction?). There is evidence of water-mills at several ROMAN VILLAS, two in Gloucestershire, one in Hampshire; which is in keeping with later history, for the water-mill and in waterless districts the later windmill (an invention of waterless Arabia which reached England by the last decades of the 12th century) became a part of the organization of every mediaeval estate or manor, which was the counterpart of the villa.

For what was probably the earliest kind of water-mill one must go to Orkney to see the Klick Mill near Birsay, now preserved as an ancient monument. In this type, adapted from the QUERN, the grinding stone, or overstone, is revolved direct from a horizontal paddle wheel underneath it on the same spindle; the mills of this kind were tiny, each of them owned by a farmer or by five or six families in concert. They were common in the Norse areas, including the Isle of Man, Shetland, the Faeroes, etc., with a range eastward to China. The mill in which a vertical wheel is geared to drive a horizontal stone was already known by the end of the 1st century B.C., and is the type which spread to England, and has survived to this century, whether overshot from a mill-pond fed from a small stream along a valley-side leat, or undershot, or breast-shot (i.e. with the water striking the 'breast' of the wheel about the level of the axle) by a greater flow of water stored from a slower and larger stream (*see* LASHER) or stored from the tide waters of an estuary. (The Roman water-mill, as described in the 1st century B.C., was undershot.)

Windmills are:

(*a*) Post-mills (the type introduced in the Middle Ages), if the whole 'body' of the mill, with its machinery and its steps down to the ground, revolves, so as to suit itself to the wind, around a 'main-post' of oak. The bottom part of the main-post and its timber supports may be protected, under the revolving body, by a round house.

(*b*) Tower-mills (mid-17th century and later), if the body is built in brick or stone, nothing swivelling around with the sails except the cap on top.

(*c*) Smock-mills (same date), if they are fixed mills built of wood instead of brick or stone, weatherboarded, tapering and usually octagonal. They wear their white weatherboarding like a woman's smock or shift.

Often the miller set his post-mill on an artificial mound (sometimes a barrow). Mill-mounds which long ago lost their mill may still be criss-crossed 'rather like large hot cross buns', because in the earlier mills the housing of the mainpost, consisting of quarter-bars sloping to cross-trees, which rested on stone piers, was set inside the mound.

Millstones often survive all other traces either of windmill of water-mill. Usually four or five feet in diameter (though both larger and smaller stones were employed), they are commonly of two kinds. The stones fashioned of a single block were mostly quarried in Derbyshire of MILLSTONE GRIT (*see also* EDGES) and were transported to market towns as far as

This post WINDMILL represents one of the mediaeval carpenter's greatest achievements of design and construction. Chillenden Mill, Chillenden, Kent, is a small timber-framed building, designed to balance and pivot on a single vertical post. Oak cross-trees provide the base for the structure, while the weight of the body or 'buck' of the mill is borne by a transverse beam, the 'crown tree'. From the back of the buck projects a tail pole that was used like a tiller to orient the mill towards the wind. A wheel on the end of the tail pole (in the foreground) helps support some of the weight of the tail ladder.

*latford Mill, East
Bergholt, Suffolk,
is a large, attractive 18th
century undershot
WATER-MILL complex.
It once belonged to John
Constable's father and
was the subject of some
of Constable's most
famous paintings, such
as 'The Hay Wain'.*

246

possible by water. These stones of 'Derbyshire Peak' were best for grinding barley. For grinding wheat, oats, maize and beans the miller preferred composite stones, which were made up of fourteen or so pieces of 'burr' or 'burrstone', a quartzite imported from France, cemented together and bound with a circumference of iron bands. If a millstone is slightly concave on one side it will have been the runner stone, which revolved on top of the fixed bed-stone. Millstones of a small diameter lying about around a farmyard will have come from a horse-mill or a donkey-mill. The grinding grooves on the surface of the millstone are cut in ten divisions, or 'harps' from their shape, of four grooves apiece, arranged to bring the flour to the edge of the stone. In Scotland mill place-names are likely to begin with Moulin-, in Ireland with Mullin-, in Wales with Melin- or its mutation Felin-, in Cornwall with Mellin- or Millen-, all, like our English word, coming from the Latin *molina*.

Water-wheels and wind-sails were adapted to many more uses. As in Holland, the Fens have their drainage windmills. Water-mills worked the stamps for crushing ore at the tin streaming works of Devon and Cornwall, the hammers and bellows of iron works in Sussex and elsewhere (*see* BLOOMERIES), and from the Middle Ages the hammers of the fulling-mill or tucking-mill (Welsh *pandy*) which compacted the new-woven cloth.

If you find a corn mill, wind or water, still at work, listen to the clack of the stones. When the runner is revolving and working at a steady pace, millers, those once prime figures of envy and blame in English country life, used to say that the stones were calling out *For profit, For prof-it, For prof-it*. When the mill slowed down the message of the stones changed sadly to *No . . . prof-it, No . . . . prof . . it, No . . . prof . . . it*. Of millers it was said that 'hair grows in the palm of an honest miller'.

-wath

In place-names in Cumbria, North Yorkshire, etc., -wath frequently indicates a FORD, from the Old Norse *vath*. It might, for example, be a ford across sand, a Sandwath or Sandwith; a ford like a 'dub' or deep pool, a Dubwath; a darkly flowing ford, a Bleawath; a ford discoloured by dung (Old Norse *skítr*), a Skitwath – all of which are Cumbrian fords.

Weathercocks

Weathercocks, above church tower or spire, are often worth scrutinizing with field-glasses as lively pieces of hollow sculpture in metal, hard to date but frequently looking as if they were mediaeval, or renewed, perhaps time and again, from a mediaeval prototype. An Anglo-Saxon riddle of about 750 in the Exeter Book – answer, a weathercock – speaks of the hollow belly pierced by a rod as if this kind of weathercock was familiar above the English village more than a thousand years ago. A bronze triton on top of the octagonal Horologium of Andronicus at Athens, the 'Tower of the Winds' of the 1st century B.C., is said to have been the first weathervane. In the Middle Ages the standard cock above the church tower would have been understood as the bird whose bright crowing at dawn dispelled evil and the particular bird (on watch in all weathers against sin) which crowed when St. Peter denied Christ. On top of which no other bird – allowing that the airy position demands a bird – has the right shaped tail for catching the wind. The word weathercock is in consequence also used to describe a person of changeable disposition.

Weepers

Small figures placed below the effigy around a mediaeval chest-tomb whose attitude and presence indicate sorrow over death, weepers began to appear on tombs, sometimes with their heads bowed, at the end of the 13th century, and became common throughout the Middle Ages. In general the weepers are the dead man's family, men and women, knights and ladies, perpetuating the funeral procession, sometimes cloaked, sometimes hooded, sometimes with their heads bowed, with hands clasped or together in prayer or poised in a formal attitude of mourning. Or they may carry the flaming torches which were often carried at the grander funerals. On the tomb of Thomas Fitzalan, Earl of Arundel (d. 1415), in Arundel church, each weeper's niche is filled with one of the chaplains or deacons of the secular college his father had founded with the church in 1380. The earl was childless, so perhaps the chaplains were thought of as his family or his children. Weepers, especially on the alabaster tombs, become winged angels holding shields. This long weeper tradition of the mediaeval tomb survived in a very familiar and coarsened shape on Elizabethan and Jacobean tombs, on which the weepers lost their formal and rhythmic dignity and became graduated lines of kneeling sons and kneeling daughters (dead sons and daughters holding a skull).

The WEATHERCOCK *has a dual purpose: its tail is shaped for catching the wind, and it is the Christian symbol for the watch against evil.*

West galleries

West galleries were frequently added to mediaeval churches in the 18th and 19th centuries. for two reasons: to house a larger congregation, the country and town populations having increased; and to provide a loft, corresponding to the old ROOD LOFTS, in so far as the rood lofts had housed singers and musicians or an organ. Sitting or standing along the front of the gallery the village musicians played their viols, hautboys, flutes, bassoons, serpents, etc. Thomas Hardy recalls in one of his poems how about 1836 his mother had caught a first sight of his father, dressed in a blue swallow-tailed coat with gilt buttons, playing a viol in the west gallery (it exists no longer) of Stinsford Church, in Dorset:

> She turned in the high pew, until her sight
> Swept the west gallery, and caught its row
> Of music-men with viol, book, and bow
> Against the sinking, sad tower-window light.

There they were playing 'New Sabbath' and 'Mount Ephraim', with the overflow of the congregation no doubt behind them. Occasionally a late mediaeval rood loft which had not been pulled down was actually transferred to the tower end and refashioned into a gallery. Other west galleries, to the added horror of Victorian restorers, were often built on cast-iron pillars. Galleries across the west end and continuing up the north and south sides of the nave were usual in the Georgian churches of the 18th century.

Wheel-houses

In the northern and western isles of Scotland, wheel-houses belong to the family of round homesteads strongly built in stone, all of them a natural result of having to hand more stone than timber – and slabby stone which lent itself to neat and easy building. The walled circle of a wheel-house, with an inside diameter say of twenty-five feet, was. divided into seven or eight paved divisions by spoke-like lengths of internal wall moving inwards towards a round central space, much of which was taken up by an oblong hearth. Little cupboards like a church AUMBRY were contrived in the inside face of the encircling wall. The wheel-house probably had a corbelled roof. Sometimes wheel-houses are to be found cosily fitted around the ruins of a BROCH, as at Jarlshof on the southern tip of Shetland, where the abandoned broch and the later cluster of wheel-houses have been excavated and preserved. There the broch belongs probably to the 1st century A.D. and the wheel-houses to the 2nd and 3rd centuries. This family of stone homesteads includes also the 'aisled round-house', of rather larger dimensions, in which there is a space forming an aisle between the 'spokes' and the encircling wall. An aisled round-house of this kind was built up against the broch at Jarlshof, and then cut into by one of the wheel-houses. In upland Caithness and Sutherland there are also stone-built 'wags' (Gaelic *vaigh*, a cave), the wag being strictly one part of a composite herdsman's home, a long bean-shaped building with floor below the level of the ground, divided into stalls or aisles, and attached to the circular house or hut which was the living quarters.

Whinsill

'Sills', geologically, are spreads of rock which rose in a molten state from the interior of the earth and squeezed or intruded between the layers of bedded rock. The Great Whin Sill is the wide spread or sheet of the finely crystalline whin, whinstone, or dolerite, in the north-east, which is exposed in many places, and which often cooled into hexagonal columns. It is the rock crossed by much of Hadrian's Wall, the rock of the Farne Islands, of the fort-crowned Beblowe on Holy Island, and of the sturdy sea-platforms which uphold Dunstanburgh and Bamburgh castles. Hard stretches of the whin thrusting through limestone and shale are great WATERFALL makers, as at High Force, in Teesdale.

Wick, -wick

From the Old English *wic*, and very common in English place-names either by itself (Wick, Wike, Wyke, Week) or at the end of a name (-wick or -wich), this word usually meant a building or several buildings where people lived, or to which they went every so often, for a special purpose. Sometimes the name states the purpose, which is likeliest to have been agricultural. Often a wick was a subsidiary farm, an outlier from the main village, where barley was grown, a Berwick or Barwick; and there are even more wicks where they ran sheep or cows or goats and milked them for cheesemaking – Chiswicks and Keswicks, which began perhaps as a collection of sheds. Also there are Butterwicks, Cowicks, Shapwicks ('sheep wick'), Hardwicks ('herd wick' or 'flock wick'). Sometimes the wick is still distinguished by the name of the larger settlement it belonged to. Bath has its Bathwick, of what were once lush, often flooded, meadows across the Avon. Church Lench near Evesham in Hereford and Worcester has its outlying Lenchwick in the bend of another Avon. (For the salt 'wiches' of Cheshire, see SALT WAYS.)

From the Old Norse *vík*, in many far northern names around the coast Wick or -wick means a small bay or creek. Around Iceland *vík* inlets are very common – Sandvík, Grimolfsvík, etc. Orkney and Shetland have them in equal plenty, Lerwick, Harold's Wick, Sandwick, etc. Highland has a few. South of the border they are scarce, including North Yorkshire's Runswick Bay and the 'wykes' inland in the Lake District, round the lakes.

Will-o'-the-Wisp

Will-o'-the-Wisp, the commonest term for the small flames sometimes seen on marshes or in ditches, preserves the belief that they were lights carried by a minuscule demon or goblin to entice night travellers into a quagmire (wisp, i.e. wisp of hay or dry grass used for a light). The flames occur, but they are not exactly explained. They could be flames of hydrogen phosphide which ignites on contact with air, or flames of marsh gas (methane) ignited by hydrogen phosphide, either gas having arisen from vegetable decay. Look for the Will-o'-the-Wisp at ground level or just above, along ditches, in bogs, and especially peat bogs, and in fens, on warm dampish nights of summer or autumn. There may be one, or several, in the shape of candle-flames, up to a middle finger in height, up to two inches broad, blue or yellow, popping into flame, and burning maybe for quite a long time, even hours on end, with next to no heat and little smell. John Aubrey described one he saw from horseback: 'Riding in the north lane of Broad Chalke in the harvest time in the twy-light, or scarce that, a point of light, by the hedge, expanded itselfe into a globe of about three inches diameter, or neer four, as boies blow bubbles with soape. It continued but while one could say one, two, three, or four at the most. It was about a foot from my horse's eie; and it made him turn his head quick aside from it. It was a pale light as that of a glowe-worme' (*Natural History of Wiltshire*). At Syleham in Suffolk, Will-o'-the-Wisps were so frequently seen along the marshes by the Waveney that they were called Syleham Lights or Syleham Lanterns.

Ignis Fatuus, which has become the 'correct' name for Will-o'-the-Wisp, was coined or used to ridicule the supernatural names and explanations ('ignis fatuus, foolish fire, that hurteth not, but only feareth fooles' – William Fulke, 1563). Other names which make the cold flame a goblin's light are Kit with the Candlestick, Jack-a-Lantern, Joan in the Wad (wad = wisp). Also, Pinket, Dick-a-Tuesday, Dank Will, Spunkie (= little flame), Weeze (i.e. wase = wisp); and, in Milton's *L'Allegro*, Friar's Lantern. It seems likely that road and land drainage and reclamation of marshes, and the general lowering of the water-table, have made the Will-o'-the-Wisp much less common than it used to be.

Willow

The tree willows along slow, winding rivers in the British Isles are the Crack Willow (twigs easily and audibly snapping; red water rootlets) and the White Willow (leaves white with soft hairs, thickest underneath; whitish water rootlets) – native trees, but planted to conserve river banks and provide timber and poles for making hurdles and fences and for burning ('far the sweetest of all our English fuel . . . provided it be sound and dry; and emitting little smoak . . . the fittest for Ladies' chambers'). These kinds are pollarded to a height above the reach of cattle, which like willow leaves; and the stave timber is cut every three to five years. John Evelyn (quoted above) gives a delightful account of willows in his *Sylva* (1664), not forgetting to say that choice anemones, ranunculuses and auriculas are best raised in a mixture of soil and the rotten 'loamy earth' out of old hollow willows, and rising to a peroration that the 'fresh boughs, of all the trees in nature, yield the most chaste and coolest shade in the hottest season of the day'. They are trees which also spoke strongly to William Morris in his Thames-edged, willow-surrounded house at Kelmscott. The Weeping Willow of gardens was introduced in 1692, too late for Evelyn's classic book, but in time to mature for 18th century *chinoiserie* (China is its original home) and sentimentalism, the Chinese tree of the early 19th century Willow Pattern designs, and the mourning tree, quickly identified with the willows of sorrow in Babylon on which the captive Israelites hung their harps (Psalm 137. 1, 2), of church monuments and especially the neo-classic BLACK-AND-WHITE TABLETS. 'When any mist or dew falls, a drop of water is seen hanging at their extremities which, together with their hanging branches, cause a most lugubrious appearance' (note added to the 1776 edition of Evelyn's *Sylva*).

Windbreaks

Long screens or belts of sheltering trees (especially pine, beech or larch) across such exposed country as the sandy brecks of Norfolk or the chalk downs of Wiltshire, windbreaks became a noticeable element of the landscape only in the 19th century when parliamentary enclosure was extended from the good arable land to the wide wastes and commons. Humphry Repton, the landscape designer, who disliked any kind of belt which resembled 'a curtain drawn across the most interesting scenes', complained in 1816 that the landed proprietor, new or hereditary, had given up 'beauty for gain, and prospect for the produce of his acres': he procured 'an Act to enclose the commons and doubled his rents' – not unnaturally, since the Napoleonic wars had put up the price of corn, and made it worth enclosing and cultivating marginal land. Hence the 19th century concern with windbreaks, which contradicted the landscape aes-

These crack WILLOWS, of the type that have been used for basket-making since Saxon times, grow near William Morris's Thames-edged home, at Kelmscott, Oxfordshire.

thetic of the 18th century and its demand for 'natural' planting. Repton also complained of another feature which remains with us and was intensified in the Victorian era – the high exclusive fences and gloomy belts which new and old proprietors had begun to set around their estates, mentioning one estate whose newly rich proprietor had fenced it with a high paling, 'not to confine the deer, but to exclude mankind; and to protect a miserable narrow belt of firs and Lombardy poplars'.

Windows and window tax

A blocked window in a house – if it is genuinely blocked, and is not a blank window put there for effect in balancing and completing the window pattern – may be the result of the window tax, levied for more than a hundred and fifty years. The more well-to-do English rehoused themselves between the fifteen-seventies and 1700. By the middle of Elizabeth's reign new country houses spread across lowland England, 'showing to the world ranges of windows much larger than had ever been seen before in any building but a church' (M. W. Barley), and with new windows there were new chimneys, another sign of wealth and status. The rehousing accelerated under James I, slackened before and during the Civil War, and picked up again after the Restoration. This allowed first for a chimney tax, then for a window tax. The hated chimney-money, a tax of two shillings on every fire-hearth, was extracted from 1674 to 1689. In 1696 Parliament imposed a graded tax on windows (windows outnumber chimneys). The tax at two shillings for a house with more than six but less than ten windows, and was doubled for ten windows to nineteen, and so on. The blocking of a single window could thus reduce one's tax class. The tax endured with changes and increments. Pitt doubled it in 1784. In 1850 Harriet Martineau in a book surveying the years of peace since Waterloo wrote of the tax as a duty 'on fresh air, sunshine and health'; and in that year the tax produced £1,856,000 from about 6,000 houses with more than fifty windows, about £270,000 from houses with over ten windows, and about £725,000 from houses with seven windows or less. In 1851 the tax was abolished, and replaced by an 'inhabited house duty'.

Winterbournes

Bournes or streams in chalk country in the south which do not flow except in winter or very wet seasons, when the saturation-level of the porous chalk rises to the surface. Many villages in Wiltshire and Dorset are named after winterbournes. The upper run of the Kennet above Avebury in Wiltshire is a winterbourne which has given its name to Winterbourne Bassett and Winterbourne Monkton. In summer the course of a winterbourne is often no more than a dry grassy fold winding through the meadows, though a line of willows may indicate the underlying damp. On the Wolds of the East Riding they are 'gipseys'; in Kent 'nailbournes' (eylebourns – 'spring streams', from the Old English $\bar{æ}well$, a spring or source). John Warkworth's 15th century chronicle records of a Hertfordshire eylebourne that its sudden flowing tokened famine, pestilence, or a great battle, a belief which seems to have attached to the sudden activity of many winterbournes and gipseys. In fact a heightening of the water-table can cause a polluting inflow of cesspit water into wells.

Woad

As the chief dye of the pre-chemical age, 'the best and most necessary Drug in the Art of Dying' (1705), woad has left only a slight mark on the countryside. There are minor names and village names derived from woad (in Old English $w\bar{a}d$), including various Woodfields and Woodhills, Waddon (i.e. 'woad hill') in Somerset and Dorset, and Watton ('woad farm') in Hertfordshire. Glastonbury, named from the British for blue (dye) or woad, recalls Caesar's statement that the British wore a blue battle-paint of woad, and Pliny's sequel that British women appeared naked and blue with woad in religious ceremonies. Woad was still grown around Glastonbury in the Middle Ages, by the Benedictines of the great abbey.

Every woad name conceals a stench, which occurred in one stage of the complex process of preparing and oxidizing the dye, and made the woadmen or wadmen unpopular. After harvesting, the plants were dried and ground to powder in a mill. The powder was wetted and dried into loaves, which were pulverized again with wooden clubs, mixed with water, and 'couched', or fermented, for several stinking months, the smell filling the air and spreading into neighbouring houses. Then the liquor was dried out and the woad fashioned into the balls which the wadmen sold to the dyers by the sackful (see *The Woad Plant and Its Dye*, by J. B. Hurry, 1930). As a Mediterranean or southern species (actually a tall, skimpy crucifer clouded with honey-scented yellow flowers and showing scarcely a hint of blue in its leaves), the woad plant has not naturalized itself securely. After 2,000 and more years of cultivation, which came to an end in Lincolnshire in the nineteen-thirties, woad survives only on some of the red sandstone cliffs along the Severn (e.g. the Mythe, outside Tewkesbury) in exceptional conditions of sun and open habitat.

Wodewoses

Wodewoses, being wild men with long beards, armed often with a club and in company with lions, appear frequently – and one would think incongruously – on 15th century fonts, misericords, etc. It is true that the Wodewose began as a demon who guarded European woods and forests, and that he was blended later on with the hairy satyr of Greek myth. But in time, living in the woods, away from civilization and wickedness, he became a symbol of the pure life. Legend had made him strong and fierce, and given to the catching and control of such savage beasts as the lion; but it also declared him susceptible to love, and to being captured on that account by courtly damsels. On fonts (especially in Suffolk, e.g. at Orford, Barking, Chediston, Framlingham, Saxmundham), the wodewoses, standing around the stem between lions, seem to have imaged the soul of man, master of all the beasts, yielding itself in baptism to divine love.

Wold, weald

At Stow-on-the-Wold
The wind blows cold

– this wold being Cotswold. Wold derives – a little surprisingly, since what we call the Wolds, in various counties, are bare and windswept – from the Old English *wald*, woodland. But the word gained a new significance. The old woodland sense survives in various wald and wold and weald names (the West Saxons spoke of *weald* instead of *wald*) in districts which were once heavily wooded. One sees it especially (the old spelling having been revived in the 16th century) in the Weald of Sussex, Kent, and Surrey, all that is left of *Andredes Weald*, the forest of the place called Andred (i.e. Pevensey). When an old woodland area was cleared, it did not always lose its name with its trees: it was still referred to as *wald* or *weald*; and in the Middle Ages the word came to be used of open tablelands. The Weald is most of it on heavy clay, which tends to oak forest. The Wolds are on porous limestone,

making for dry open sheepwalks. Cotswold, 'that great king of shepheards' that 'hath pure wholesome ayre and daintie crystall springs' (Drayton in *Poly-Olbion*), is an upland of oolitic limestone; the Leicestershire Wolds and the Nottinghamshire Wolds are on the lias; the Lincolnshire Wolds and the Yorkshire Wolds are on the chalk. Michael Drayton had more to say of the Yorkshire Wolds, or Yorkswold (as it was called by analogy with Cotswold) –

> . . . that large and spacious Ould
> Of York that takes the name, that with delighted eyes,
> When he beholds the sun out of the seas to rise,
> With pleasure feeds his flocks, for which he scarce gives place
> To Cotswold, and for what becomes a pastoral grace
> Doth go beyond him quite.

Publishing the last of his *Poly-Olbion* in 1622, Drayton was the first poet to express a modern feeling about the wolds as tracts of a delightful airy difference, a feeling subtilized and extended two centuries later by Tennyson, whose childhood environment was the wolden country of Lincolnshire. He was in love with the place and the word – 'Calm and deep peace on this high wold'.

Wolf place-names

Wolf place-names occur in fair number in England, chiefly in old woodland country (including names which indicate trapping in a fall-pit – Wolfpit, Woolpit), and there must have been a considerable population of wolves in the centuries of Anglo-Saxon settlement and the early Middle Ages. In England the last wolf is said to have been killed in Cheshire in the last years of the 15th century; in Scotland, on the Findhorn river, in Grampian, in 1743; in Ireland, on the Knockmealdown Mountains in 1770 (other accounts say in Co. Carlow in 1786). Wolves in church carving betray more attention to improving legend than to knowledge gained in the woods. The wolf was evil and may be seen with paw to mouth, according to the tale that it lubricated its paws with spit to make its approach inaudible or actually bit a paw if it was clumsy enough to break a twig. A good wolf is occasionally to be seen in churches, especially in East Anglia, its forelegs astride the head of St. Edmund, King of the East Angles, who was captured in 870 by the heathen Danes, bound to an oak tree, pierced with arrows like St. Sebastian, and then beheaded. Pious legend said that when the

East Anglians searched for his head, they found it guarded by a grey wolf who had neither eaten it himself nor allowed other beasts to eat it. The carving (Pulham St. Mary and Walpole St. Peter, Norfolk; Hadleigh, Suffolk) often suggests that the 15th century carver had never seen a live wolf.

Workhouse

On the outskirts of a country town the workhouse or union workhouse, now transferred to kindlier use as hospital, convalescent home, etc., can usually be identified at once by its characteristic plan. Most of these houses of separation and sorrow for the village poor were built immediately after the Poor Law Amendment Act of 1834. They are classical in a meagre way, since the classical style was still the proper thing for official buildings, whether National Gallery, prison or workhouse. And the classical look fitted a cold and lofty attitude to poverty as something brought upon the village poor by themselves, and not by enclosures. Charity without warmth is reinforced in these workhouses by a greyish-yellow stock brick. Authority and control are suggested by a high central feature, with pediment and portico, or a domed turret ('this appendage, trifling as it is, gives to the whole that characteristic feature which distinguishes it as a public building' – Humphry Repton in a note on workhouse design, reprinted in 1839). A courtyard and radiating or extending wings recall the distribution of the poor through the wards by sex, age, infirmity, and illness; and this wide spread of the workhouse indicates what a multitude of poor might be admitted from each group of parishes which the Act had combined into a workhouse union. Frequently the workhouses were designed by able local architects, but without grace or ornament, to which (Humphry Repton again) 'the answer is obvious, – the first consideration in a poorhouse is economy'. Under the Act, the poor, removed from their parish, came to these workhouses to work, if they were able-bodied; or to die. The word for them was pauper, and the typical workhouse was, and looks as if it was, a receptacle for paupers; of which verbal stigma they were not to be relieved until the old age pension, health and unemployment reforms of 1908–11.

-worth

-worth, -worthy, -wardine, in place-names, mean an enclosure, and so an enclosed homestead (Old English *worth*, *worthig*, *worthign*), which may afterwards have grown into a village, and a parish. -worthy names, from *worthig*, abound in Somerset and Devon (e.g. Woolfardisworthy, 'Wulfheard's enclosure'), and -wardine names, from *worthign*, in Hereford and Worcester and Shropshire (e.g. Bredwardine, 'hillside enclosure').

Yew

Long-lived, evergreen, producing hard timber, evidently a powerful tree, the yew was important in ancient practice and belief. Yews are not among the commoner wild trees, since they prefer a well-drained limestone soil (particularly escarpments of chalk or hard limestones), but they were more abundant in the drier climate of the Bronze Age, by which time they had long provided the material for weapons. Two spears of Upper Palaeolithic date, the oldest wooden weapons yet discovered, were made of yew. For its power, the yew came to be regarded as both holy and wicked – if a right wood for weapons, or weapon shafts, equally (in Ireland) a wood for croziers and for shrines to enclose relics. Yew was also used to make magic wands inscribed with ogham (*see* OGHAM STONES) in Ireland, and with runic letters (*see* RUNES) in England; and the Old English word for yew was itself the name given to one of the letters in the runic alphabet.

Evidence for yews close to churches goes back in Ireland to the end of the 8th century; and the churchyard yew probably stems from a pre-Christian belief in a protective deity which inhabited the yew, and in a sense *was* the yew, green and hale when everything else seemed dead in winter. That would explain why, at any rate in some parts of England, yews were also so commonly planted near houses. There seems evidence that Norman clergy planted churchyard yews (having adopted the tree from their Celtic neighbours in Brittany?). They grow in churchyards in Normandy and may have been more commonly planted in England and some parts of Wales and Ireland after the Conquest. Sprigs of churchyard yew have been employed as 'palm' on Palm Sunday, and have been put with corpses into the grave. It is true that in the fervour for home defence and archery in Henry VIII's time (*see* BEACONS, BUTTS) churchyard yews were lopped for bowmaking. But yew bows were normally made from the trunk-timber, a fair-sized tree cutting only into four or five bows; and bowyers preferred the less knotty yew imported from

Spain – facts which rule out a hackneyed explanation of the presence of yews in churchyards. Yew woods, once commoner than they are now, to judge from yew-wood place-names (Euridge, Ewhurst, Uley, Iwode, etc.), were possibly maintained as a source of bowyers' timber. Some of the best of these dark, scratchy, eerie woods are, in Wiltshire, Great Yews, Homington; in Surrey, the Cherkeley yews near Mickleham; in Dorset, Hambledon Hill and Iwerne Courtenay (Iwerne is a yew name). The eeriness of yew woods is greatly increased by the under-presence of dead junipers, as around Box Hill, in Surrey. The dead junipers never rot and they raise their dead branches in a shrieking attitude.

Ynys

Ynys in Welsh place-names; innis in Cornish names; inch, innis, ennis in Irish names (Irish *inis*); inch, innis in Scottish names (Gaelic *innis*) – means island, or an island-like place, such as a riverside meadow. Some examples: Ynys Enlli (Bardsey Island), 'island of the race or current'; Yeats's lake isle of Inisfree, 'heather island'; Inchcolm, in the Firth of Forth, St. Colum Cille's island.

Ystrad

Ystrad in Welsh place-names (and strath, from Gaelic *srath*, in Scottish names) means a vale or flat valley. The vale of the Cistercian monastery in Dyfed is Ystrad-fflur, Vale of Flowers, or Strata Florida.

Zodiacal light

Not one of the most spectacular or frequently looked-for of the phenomena of the night sky, zodiacal light is worth noting all the same. Look for it after sunset on dark moonless nights rising along the zodiac from the western horizon, a tall cone of pearly light, rather soft and faint – nights of January, February and March, when it is best seen and when the Zodiac and the Ecliptic rise at a steep angle from west to south-west. The light is caused by a zone of cosmic dust around the sun which 'scatters' the sunlight. In September, October and November it is well seen once more – or as well as it can be – in a reverse direction, before dawn, rising from the eastern horizon to the south, again along the zodiac, at its then reversed angle. Zodiacal light is recognizable by its fairly wide, blunt-ended cone or triangle shape.

Index

Acknowledgements

Illustrations

All the illustrations in this book were drawn by
Robert Micklewright

Photography

Ace Photo Agency (Graeme Spink): *54/55*

Adams Picture Library (Mike Sirett): *230*

Aerofilms: *96, 116*

Airviews (Manchester) Ltd: *82, 196/197*

Nigel Cassidy: *160, 245*

England Scene: *20, 109, 114/115, 202/203, 220/221*

Jorge Lewinski: *Endpapers, 2/3, 5, 6, 9, 26/27, 34/35, 41, 42, 46, 51, 62/63, 66/67, 72/73, 104/105, 128, 132/133, 136/137, 141, 150, 152/153, 154/155, 159, 165, 167, 168/169, 179, 180/181, 182/183, 189, 198, 208/209, 211, 214, 216/217, 233, 240/241*

West Air Photography: *14/15, 21, 68, 156/157, 228229*

Andy Williams: *Front cover, 18, 92/93, 119, 185, 224/225, 236/237, 246/247*

Trevor Wood: *10, 33, 57, 58, 70/71, 88, 100, 123, 147, 190, 191, 242/243*

George Wright: *78/79, 81, 86, 98/99, 110, 126/127, 171, 172/173, 176, 204/205, 212 and back cover*